Transconstitutionalism

Transconstitutionalism is a concept used to describe what happens to constitutional law when it is emancipated from the state, in which can be found the origins of constitutional law. Transconstitutionalism does not exist because a multitude of new constitutions have appeared, but because other legal orders are now implicated in resolving basic constitutional problems. A transconstitutional problem entails a constitutional issue whose solution may involve national, international, supranational and transnational courts or arbitral tribunals, as well as native local legal institutions. Transconstitutionalism does not take any single legal order or type of order as a starting point or *ultima ratio*. It rejects both nation-statism and internationalism, supranationalism, transnationalism and localism as privileged spaces for solving constitutional problems. The transconstitutional model avoids the dilemma of 'monism versus pluralism'. From the standpoint of transconstitutionalism, a plurality of legal orders entails a complementary and conflicting relationship between identity and alterity: constitutional identity is rearticulated on the basis of alterity. Rather than seeking a 'Herculean Constitution', transconstitutionalism tackles the many-headed Hydra of constitutionalism, always looking for the blind spot in one legal system and reflecting it back against the many others found in the world's legal orders.

Volume 10 in the series Hart Monographs in Transnational and International Law

Hart Monographs in Transnational and International Law

Series Editor: Craig Scott, Professor of Law, Osgoode Hall Law School of York University, Toronto

The objective of this series is to publish high-quality scholarship in public international law and private international law, as well as work that adopts 'transnational law' as its thematic, theoretical or doctrinal focus. The series strives to be a leading venue for work of the following sort:

* critical reappraisals of foundational concepts and core doctrinal principles of both public and private international law, and their operation in practice, including insights drawn from general legal theory;
* analysis and development of conceptions of 'transnational law', including in relation to the role of unofficial law and informal processes in transnational regulation and in relation to theories and studies of 'governance' in transnational spheres; and
* empirical studies of the emergence, evolution and transformation of international and/or transnational legal orders, including accounts and explanations of how law is constructed within different communities of interpretation and practice.

The series will also be home to monographs that explore the interactions between the ever-integrating fields of public and private international law. Of special interest are explorations of the extent to which these interactions are structured by higher-order principles and policies, on the one hand, and by politics and the exercise of various forms of power, on the other hand.

The series is open to work not only by law scholars but also by scholars from cognate disciplines.

Recent titles in this series

Volume 5: Rough Consensus and Running Code: A Theory of Transnational Private Law

Gralf-Peter Calliess and Peer Zumbansen

Volume 6: The Payment Order of Antiquity and the Middle Ages: A Legal History

Benjamin Geva

Volume 7: The Concept of Unity in Public International Law

Mario Prost

Volume 8: Interlocking Constitutions: Towards an Interordinal Theory of National, European and UN Law

Luis I Gordillo

Volume 9: Transnational Terrorism and State Accountability: A New Theory of Prevention

Vincent-Joël Proulx

Transconstitutionalism

Marcelo Neves

translated by

Kevin Mundy

to Jack,
with best wishes,
[illegible]
New Haven, July 16, 2015

·HART·
PUBLISHING

OXFORD AND PORTLAND OREGON

2013

Published in the United Kingdom by Hart Publishing Ltd
16C Worcester Place, Oxford, OX1 2JW
Telephone: +44 (0)1865 517530
Fax: +44 (0)1865 510710
E-mail: mail@hartpub.co.uk
Website: http://www.hartpub.co.uk

Published in North America (US and Canada) by
Hart Publishing
c/o International Specialized Book Services
920 NE 58th Avenue, Suite 300
Portland, OR 97213-3786
USA
Tel: +1 503 287 3093 or toll-free: (1) 800 944 6190
Fax: +1 503 280 8832
E-mail: orders@isbs.com
Website: http://www.isbs.com

This book was originally published in Portuguese as *Transconstitucionalismo*
(São Paulo, WMF Martins Fontes, 2009).

This English edition has been revised and enlarged by the author.

British Library Cataloguing in Publication Data
Data Available

ISBN: 978-1-84946-418-5

Typeset by Hope Services, Abingdon
Printed by CPI Group (UK) Ltd, CR0 4YY

To my friends Hauke Brunkhorst
and Franz von Weber, with gratitude

Preface

I first thought of writing this book during my stay as Jean Monnet Fellow at the European University Institute (EUI) in Florence, Italy, in the autumn and winter of 1999–2000. Discussions with colleagues and students in highly productive seminars and conferences led me to think differently about state constitutionalism, and although I later wrote several essays on related subjects,[1] my involvement with other projects prevented me from starting on this larger study, in which I planned to develop a more comprehensive outline of transconstitutionalism.

Later, while teaching and researching at the Universities of Frankfurt am Main, Hamburg, Flensburg, and Humboldt (Berlin) in Germany, and the University of Fribourg in Switzerland, I studied the subject in greater depth. In this context, conversations with colleagues Hauke Brunkhorst, Gunther Teubner, Karl-Heinz Ladeur, Ingeborg Maus, Andreas Fischer-Lescano, Dieter Grimm, Christian Joerges and Rüdiger Voigt, among others, were vitally important to clarify and contribute to my understanding of issues relevant to constitutionalism in contemporary world society.

After returning home to Brazil in 2008, I began writing the first draft of this book in Portuguese. In this phase I had invaluable discussions with Deisy Ventura, Thales Morais da Costa, Virgílio Afonso da Silva, José Afonso da Silva, Régis Dudena, and Rodrigo Mendes. Deisy, Thales, and Régis contributed highly clarifying comments on various points, particularly with regard to European law. With regard to transnational law in the strict sense (legal orders constructed primarily by private or quasi-public actors), Régis and Rodrigo made important contributions. Virgílio and José Afonso were of precious assistance, supplying bibliographical references on the contemporary constitutional debate both in Brazil and elsewhere.

In December 2008 and January 2009, I completed the Portuguese version of the book while in Heidelberg as Visiting Fellow at the Max Planck Institute for Comparative Law and International Law at the invitation of Armin von Bogdandy, the Institute's director. While there I was offered exceptional conditions for study and research, and this was decisive in enabling me to finish the book. Intense discussions with colleagues at the Institute helped me avoid certain excessively peremptory formulations. The Institute's excellent library provided invaluable support and its outstanding librarians tirelessly assisted me in my efforts.

After revision and proofreading by Aline Nunes and Pedro Souza, the Portuguese edition was published by Editora WMF Martins Fontes in November 2009.

[1] Neves, 2002; 2006a, pp 259–83; 2007a, pp 191–200; 2007b; 2007c; 2009a; 2009b; 2009c.

I am immensely grateful to the institutions and individuals mentioned for their help and companionship during this journey. I also want to thank the German Academic Exchange Service (DAAD) and the Alexander von Humboldt Foundation for enabling me to spend valuable periods researching in Germany. Heartfelt thanks, also, to my friend Franz von Weber, with whom I enjoyed highly instructive conversations on the subject addressed by this book over many years in Switzerland, Brazil and Germany.

Pedro Henrique Ribeiro and George Galindo, to whom I am very grateful, gave me important technical help with the English translation.

While overseeing the English translation I found it best to translate a number of extracts from foreign theoretical and doctrinal works myself, as well as passages from foreign case law and legislation. In the bibliographical references, I have mentioned any acceptable English translations located. The footnotes to many citations also include references to the corresponding pages in the English translations available to me. In some cases, I have adapted these translations where appropriate. My main purpose in doing so is to help readers without access to the originals, especially if they are conducting their own research on the subjects discussed.

Original publication dates are frequently shown in square brackets following the date of the edition used. This is intended to offer readers an indication of the historical context for the theory, argument or thesis concerned, or the chronology of the author's theoretical or doctrinal development and the respective paradigm.

For this English edition, while it has unfortunately not been possible to undertake an exhaustive review to include new cases and the institutional changes that have taken place since I finished writing the book (such as the changes deriving from the Lisbon Treaty on the European Union), I have nevertheless amended and updated the text to a certain extent. In this phase, I was again fortunate to receive the inestimable encouragement of Elvira and Bernardo, for which I am enormously grateful.

Marcelo Neves
São Paulo, August 2012

Contents

Abbreviations

AB	Appellate Body (WTO)
ACHR	American Convention on Human Rights
ACO-AgrR	Agravo Regimental na Ação Cível Originária [Internal Interlocutory Appeal in an Ordinary Civil Suit] (Brazil)
ADPF	Ação de Descumprimento de Preceito Fundamental [Claim of Non-Compliance with a Fundamental Precept] (Brazil)
ADI	Ação Direta de Inconstitucionalidade [Application for Constitutional Review] (Brazil)
All ER	The All England Law Reports [the number placed before the abbreviation refers to the volume for the respective year; the number that follows the abbreviation refers to the first page of the judgment]
BGE	Entscheidungen des Bundesgerichts [Decisions of the Federal Supreme Court; official compilation of this Swiss Court; the numbers placed after the abbreviation refer to the volume, tome, and first page of the judgment respectively]
BGH	Bundesgerichtshof [Federal Court of Justice] (Germany)
BGHZ	Entscheidungen des Bundesgerichtshofs in Zivilsachen [Decisions of the Federal Court of Justice in Civil Matters; official compilation of this German Court; the numbers placed before the abbreviation refer to the volume; the number that follows the abbreviation refers to the first page of the judgment]
BVerfGE	Entscheidungen des Bundesverfassungsgerichts [Decisions of the Federal Constitutional Court; official compilation of this German Court; the numbers placed after the abbreviation refer to the volume and first page of the judgment respectively]
CA	Court of Appeal (United Kingdom)
CAAD	Comisión de Apelación y Arbitraje del Deporte [Commission of Appeal and Arbitration for Sport] (Mexico)
CAS	Court of Arbitration for Sport
CCSA	Competition Commission of South Africa
coord(s)	coordinator(s)
DJ	Diário da Justiça [Law Reports; official compilation of judgments handed down by Brazil's higher federal courts]
DJe	Diário da Justiça eletrônico [electronic version of Law Reports; official compilation of judgments handed down by Brazil's higher federal courts]
ECtHR	European Court of Human Rights
ECJ	European Court of Justice
EFTA	European Free Trade Association
EU	European Union
Ext	Extradição [Extradition] (Brazil)
FIFA	Fédération Internationale de Football Association

FMF	Federación Mexicana de Fútbol
HL	House of Lords
HC	Habeas Corpus (Brazil)
IACHR	Inter-American Court of Human Rights
ICANN	Internet Corporation of Assigned Names and Numbers
ICAS	International Council of Arbitration for Sport
ICJ	International Court of Justice
IGF	Internet Governance Forum
IGPA	International General Produce Association
ILO	International Labour Organization
IP	Interpretación Prejudicial [Prejudgment Interpretation] (Court of Justice of the Andean Community)
JCC	Constitutional Court Judgment (Spain)
Mercosur	Mercado Común del Sur [Southern Common Market]
NTIA	National Telecommunications and Information Administration
QO	Questão de Ordem [Point of Order] (Brazil)
RE	Recurso Extraordinário [Extraordinary Appeal] (Brazil)
RFEC	Real Federación Española de Ciclismo [Royal Spanish Cycling Federation]
SALR	The South African Law Reports [official compilation of judgments handed down by South Africa's Constitution Court and Supreme Court, and by the supreme and higher courts of Namibia and Zimbabwe; the number in round brackets placed before the abbreviation refers to the volume for the respective year; the number that follows the abbreviation refers to the first page of the judgment]
SCR	Canada Supreme Court Reports [official compilation of the judgments handed down by the Supreme Court of Canada; the number placed before the abbreviation refers to the volume for the respective year; the number that follows the abbreviation refers to the first page of the judgment]
STF	Supremo Tribunal Federal [Federal Supreme Court] (Brazil)
T	Turma [Division of the Brazilian Federal Supreme Court]
t	tome
TP	Tribunal Pleno [Plenary; Brazilian Federal Supreme Court]
TRIPS	Agreement on Trade-Related Aspects of Intellectual Property Rights
UCI	Union Cycliste Internationale [International Cycling Union]
UN	United Nations
US	US Reports (the number placed before the abbreviation refers to the volume; the number that follows the abbreviation refers to the first page of the judgment)
VfSlg	Erkenntnisse und Beschlüsse des Verfassungsgerichtshofes [Judgments and Decisions of the Constitutional Court; official compilation of this Austrian Court; the numbers placed after the abbreviation refer to the volume, judgment number, and the first page of the judgment]
WADA	World Anti-Doping Agency
WTO	World Trade Organization
WT/DS	World Trade/Dispute (WTO)

Table of Cases

Austria

Brazil

Canada

Court of Arbitration for Sport (CAS)

Court of Justice of the Andean Community

European Court of Human Rights

European Court of Justice/Court of Justice of the European Union

Alphabetical

Chronological

France

Germany

Inter–American Court of Human Rights (IACHR)

International Court of Justice

Mercosur Permanent Review Court

Portugal

South Africa

Spain

Switzerland

United Kingdom ....

United States of America

WTO

Table of Legislation

Austria

Bolivia

Brazil

Canada

Colombia

European Union

France

Germany

Nicaragua

Peru

Portugal

South Africa

Spain

Switzerland

United Kingdom

United States of America

Table of Conventions, Treaties etc

There is an Inviolate level – let's call it the I-level *– on which the interpretation conventions reside; there is also a Tangled level – the* T-level *– on which the Tangled Hierarchy resides. So these two levels are still hierarchical: the I-level governs what happens on the T-level, but the T-level does not and cannot affect the I-level. No matter that the T-level itself is a Tangled Hierarchy – it is still governed by a set of conventions outside of itself. And that is the important point.*

As you have no doubt imagined, there is nothing to stop us from doing the 'impossible – namely, tangling the I-level and the T-level by making the interpretation conventions themselves subject to revision, according to the position on the chess board. But in order to carry out such a 'supertangling', you'd have to agree with your opponent on some further conventions connecting the two levels – and the act of doing so would create a new level, a new sort of inviolate level on top of the 'supertangled' level (or underneath it, if you prefer). And this could continue going on and on. In fact, the 'jumps' which are being made are very similar to those charted in the Birthday Cantatatata, *and in the repeated Gödelization applied to various improvements on TNT. Each time you think you have reached the end, there is some new variation on the theme of jumping out of the system which requires a kind of creativity to spot.*

(Douglas R Hofstadter)

Introduction

TOWARDS THE END of the last century, scholars of constitutional law from different theoretical traditions and a wide array of different countries, but all strongly linked to the study of state constitutions, began to concern themselves with the new challenges of cross-border constitutional law relevant to other legal orders, including non-state orders. In the United States, for example, Bruce Ackerman acknowledged that 'American practice and theory have moved in the direction of emphatic provincialism', and stressed that 'we should resist the temptations of a provincial particularism'.[1] Later, in a paper delivered to the Hague Institute for the Internationalisation of Law, Mark Tushnet spoke of 'the inevitable globalisation of constitutional law',[2] clarifying that he was concerned with domestic constitutional law and not with the 'separate question of . . . whether there is something fairly called a constitution of the international order or a global constitution'.[3] On the other side of the Atlantic, JJ Gomes Canotilho, basing his argument on Lucas Pires, referred to 'interconstitutionality', albeit restricted to the relationship between the legal order of the European Union and the constitutional orders of EU Member States.[4] Meanwhile, in Germany, Ingolf Pernice has also developed a model of 'multilevel constitutionalism', mainly taking into account the European experience.[5]

Outside the circle of constitutional lawyers working in the tradition of national law, it has become commonplace to use the term 'constitution' in other disciplines to refer to widely differing situations: the Constitution of Europe,[6] the Constitution of the International Community,[7] 'global civil constitutions',[8] and so on. This inflation in the use of the term has led to considerable vagueness, and 'constitution' has begun to lose much of its historical, normative, and functional meaning. In this context, 'the importance of being called a Constitution'[9] has taken the spotlight, resulting in persistence of the mistake of nominalism to which Ackerman refers in his analysis of comparative constitutional law: 'Important differences are frequently obliterated by loose talk invoking a common label'.[10]

[1] Ackerman, 1997, 773 and 794.
[2] Tushnet, 2008.
[3] Tushnet, 2008, 2, note 7.
[4] Canotilho, 2006, 265 *ff*; Lucas Pires, 1997, 101 *ff*.
[5] Pernice, 1999; 2002.
[6] Weiler, 1999, among many.
[7] *See*, eg, Fassbender, 1998; Tomuschat, 1995, 7.
[8] Teubner, 2003a [Engl trans 2004b].
[9] Maduro, 2006, 335 *ff*.
[10] Ackerman, 1997, 794.

This book aims to avoid the tendency to invoke the creation of a new constitution whenever a legal order, institution, or organisation emerges in contemporary society. Starting from the solid notion that the meaning of 'constitution' in the strictly modern sense is linked to the constitutionalism that resulted from the liberal revolutions of the eighteenth century in France and the United States, as well as from British political and legal history, albeit atypically so in the latter case, I set out to identify the problems that presented themselves as a condition for the historical possibility of the emergence of the constitutional state. Having determined the problems, it is relevant to ask what functional and normative answers were intended to be embodied in the constitutions of modern states. It is precisely this relationship between problems and solutions that enables the concept of constitution resulting from constitutionalism to be fixed.

As we will see, two problems were of vital importance to the appearance of constitutions in the modern sense: on one hand, the emergence of demands for fundamental or human rights in a society of increasing systemic complexity and social heterogeneity; on the other, and associated with this, the organisational question of the limitation and internal and external control of power (including participation by the governed in procedures, especially those involved in determining the composition of government bodies), which also related to the question of the growing specialisation of functions, a condition for greater efficiency of state power. As world society has become more integrated these problems have recently become untreatable by any single national legal order within its territory alone. Problems of human or fundamental rights and power limitation or control are increasingly becoming relevant to more than one legal order at the same time; many of these are non-state orders but they, too, are called upon to offer solutions to such problems. This entails permanent cross-cutting relationships among legal orders revolving around shared constitutional problems. Thus, constitutional law emancipates itself from the state, in which its foundations were originally located, not exactly because a multitude of new constitutions have appeared, but rather because other legal orders are directly involved in resolving basic constitutional problems, frequently prevailing over the orientation of the legal orders of the respective nation states. Furthermore, permanent direct relations are formed between states to deal with the constitutional problems they have in common. The exception has become the rule in both cases.

To address this situation I introduce the concept of transconstitutionalism.[11] Thus, what I am not discussing is international, transnational, supranational, national, or local constitutionalism. The concept of transconstitutionalism points precisely to the development of legal problems that cut across the various

[11] Transconstitutionalism is not to be confused with mere transjuridicism, such as, for example, in relations between legal orders in mediaeval pluralism, especially between canon law (including Roman law), urban law, royal law and feudal law (*cf* Berman, HJ, 1983, Fig 2, 522–6), since mediaeval experience did not involve constitutional problems in the modern sense. Thus it was not a matter of fundamental rights, or of the legal limitation and control of power, much less of various claims for the self-referentiality of the foundations of law (ultimately the law had sacred foundations – *see* below, pp 9–11 and 14, note 63).

different types of legal order. A transconstitutional problem entails an issue that may involve national, international, supranational and transnational courts or arbitration tribunals, as well as native local legal institutions, in the search for a solution. In discussing transconstitutionalism I refer to Wolfgang Welsch's concept of 'transversal reason',[12] although I keep my distance somewhat from this ambitious concept, to analyse the limits and possibilities of the existence of 'transversal rationalities' (or 'bridges of transition'), both between the legal system and other social systems (transversal constitutions) and among legal orders within the law as a functional system of world society. Moreover, in discussing transconstitutionalism I do not consider it merely as a functional requirement and normative claim for transversal rationality among legal orders, but also take into consideration empirically the negative aspects of transconstitutional entanglements, such as cases where the problem involves situations of anti-constitutional orders or practices, that is, those which counteract the protection of human and fundamental rights, or which counteract the control and limitation of power.[13] Similarly, I address the question of anti-constitutional practices found within the orders of typically constitutional states.[14]

Chapter 1 sets out the theoretical presuppositions, starting with a critique of the metaphorically arbitrary use of the term 'constitution' and emphasising the need for a precise historical location and semantic delimitation of the concept. It goes on to consider pre-modern hierarchical social formations in which the notion of a constitution in the modern sense is inconceivable. A brief reference is made to the transition period to explain why the charters of fundamental freedoms and political settlements at the threshold of the modern era did not correspond to a constitution in the modern sense. Next, the multicentric nature of modern society is considered as a condition for the emergence of constitutionalism. The Chapter concludes with a proposal to supersede the concept of structural coupling between functional systems of modern society (Niklas Luhmann) by using the concept of transversal rationality, which entails reciprocal learning between spheres of society.

Chapter 2 deals with the modern constitution as an institution of transversal rationality linking law to other social systems. The concept of constitution that arose historically in the context of the constitutionalist movement is presented first. Next, the nation state's constitution is considered not only as an example of structural coupling between the legal and political systems, but also as a mechanism for transversal rationality between politics and law. Lastly, the limits and possibilities of applying the concept of a transversal constitution beyond the state are discussed, in regard to both international, global and supranational constitutions and the question of transnational constitutions, properly speaking.

[12] Welsch, 1996; 2002, 295–318.

[13] It is worth distinguishing transconstitutionalism (genus), which includes relations between constitutional and anti-constitutional orders, from interconstitutionalism (species), which comprises only relations between legal orders to fulfil constitutionalist requirements.

[14] *See*, eg, Scheppele, 2006; Roach, 2006; Gross, 2006.

In Chapter 3 the central topic is addressed more directly with a discussion of transconstitutionalism between legal orders. The limits and possibilities of developing transversal rationality within the legal system and on the specific plane of constitutional law are considered. To what extent can legal orders deal jointly with constitutional issues in a transversely rational manner, that is, without acting destructively or as a hindrance towards other legal orders involved or towards themselves? Concrete cases involving both conflict and cooperation are analysed to highlight the entanglements that have developed among legal orders in resolving concrete constitutional problems.

Chapter 4 looks at transconstitutionalism not just between two legal orders (of the same or different types), but also among several legal orders in a 'multilevel' or multicentric world system characterised by entangled hierarchies. Again, actual cases involving constitutional issues are discussed to examine how situations can simultaneously involve various orders in the search for a solution. In this context, the multidimensional transconstitutionalism of human rights has particular relevance, involving as it does a multiplicity of legal orders. The Chapter concludes by presenting a methodological outline of transconstitutionalism.

The prospects for transconstitutionalism are the focus of a brief excursus in Chapter 5. Its limits and possibilities are examined, taking into account both the empirical conditions for its materialisation and development, and the fact that it appears to be a functional requirement and normative claim of today's world society. With regard to the empirical conditions, the key concern is the problem of asymmetrical forms of law as a negative condition for transconstitutionalism. As for the functional requirement, transconstitutionalism is shown to be a factor in the system integration of today's hypercomplex society, not least in promoting a 'differentiated order of communication'. In respect of the normative claim, transconstitutionalism is seen as fundamental to social integration today, especially for addressing the problem of inclusion/exclusion concerning persons and groups.

Transconstitutionalism does not take any single legal order or type of order as a starting point or *ultima ratio*. It rejects nation-statism, internationalism, supranationalism, transnationalism, and localism as privileged spaces for solving constitutional problems. Instead, it points to the need to build 'bridges of transition', promote 'constitutional conversations' and strengthen constitutional entanglements among the various legal orders, be they national, international, transnational, supranational or local. The transconstitutional model avoids the dilemma of 'monism versus pluralism'. From the standpoint of transconstitutionalism, a plurality of legal orders entails a complementary relationship between identity and alterity. The orders involved in solving a specific constitutional problem continuously reconstruct their identity at the level of their self-referential foundations by means of transconstitutional entanglement with another order or with other orders: identity is rearticulated on the basis of alterity. Thus rather than seeking a 'Herculean Constitution', transconstitutionalism points to the need to tackle the many-headed Hydra of constitutional problems by articulating reciprocal observations among the various legal orders of world society.

1

Theoretical Background

I. CONSTITUTION AS METAPHOR?

A DISCUSSION OF transconstitutionalism presupposes semantic delimitation of the concept of constitution with which notions of constitutionalism and constitutionalisation are associated. Because this involves terms that are intensely ambiguous (on the connotative level) and extensively vague (on the denotative level), there is a risk of committing 'fallacies of ambiguity',[1] as well as the 'danger of inflationary use and lack of distinctness'.[2] A related idea – which recently became more widespread – claims that constitution is a metaphor of discourse or political rhetoric,[3] available for use discursively in a wide array of structural contexts. This approach, which to some extent is linked to postmodernism and desconstructionism,[4] does not seem productive in the discussion of the legal and political problems of modern world society, in which constitutionalist semantics relates to changes in social structure.

It must be admitted that if metaphor is taken to mean not simply a 'displacement of words' but 'a transaction between contexts', that is 'an interaction . . . between two kinds of semantic content, that of the expression in its metaphorical use and that of the surrounding literal context',[5] all uses of natural language are metaphorical to a greater or lesser extent. In this sense there can be no question that 'constitution' is one of the metaphors of contemporary social semantics. However, this does not necessarily result in a lack of meaning, a 'floating signifier' or 'zero symbolic value',[6] or an 'empty signifier'.[7] Constitutionalism as a construct of modern society involves certain contours of meaning that prevent an absolute disconnection between constitutional semantics and structural change, and enable crises in semantics to be related to emerging problems in the sphere of structure. True, there are tensions between the semantics developed at the level of society's self-description or reflection and the structural sphere of

[1] Copi, 1961, 73 *ff*.

[2] Wahl, 2002, 191. *Cf* Biaginni, 2000, 452, referring to Europe.

[3] Wahl, 2002, 200 *f*.

[4] Derrida himself, however, while stressing that 'language is originarily metaphorical' (1967, 382), acknowledges that 'a precise and exact language should be absolutely univocal and literal [*propre*]: non-metaphorical'.

[5] Ducrot and Schaeffer, 1995, 488, referring to 'contemporary theories of metaphor' (pp 488–91).

[6] Lévi-Strauss, 1973 [1950], xlix *f*, note 1.

[7] Laclau, 1994.

the selective delimitation of possible operations, but structural change evidently influences changes in semantic artefacts and vice versa.[8] It is worth noting not only that semantic innovations are related to structural changes,[9] but also that obsolescence of specific semantic artefacts may be associated with depletion of the respective structures, since 'if the level of complexity of society changes, the semantics that orients experience and action must adapt to that change, otherwise it loses the connection with reality'.[10]

Thus, 'constitution' cannot be considered a 'mere metaphor' with no link to certain structural implications. What is meant by 'mere' in this context is a metaphor lacking in any function or descriptive value because it can be infinitely, arbitrarily, or randomly displaced. A serviceable synonym for such metaphors would be 'arbitrary'. This type of metaphor should be distinguished not only from a concept in the strict sense,[11] but also from a 'conceptual metaphor'[12] or a metaphor linked to the history of concepts.[13] This means it is not possible to use the concept of constitution indiscriminately in any social context. To do so would be to convert it into a component of an 'odd process' in the Wittgensteinian sense, belonging to a 'language game' that is foreign to the concerned form of life[14], that is, without structural support.[15] Without denying the existence or social relevance of metaphorical language games, I nevertheless suspect they may have an inadequate relation to structural contexts, insofar as they do not assist either in understanding or resolving properly the social problems that emerge from the deficiency of structures. Constitution in the modern sense depends at the structural level on broad presuppositions and at the semantic level requires conceptual clarity so that it is capable as a category of serving to clarify decisive problems of contemporary world society.

Not just because of the semantic problem of vagueness and ambiguity, but above all owing to the pragmatic dimension of its use, 'constitution' is a term that has lent itself to arbitrarily metaphorical uses. In the sphere of liberal revolutionary constitutionalism, moreover, the term 'constitution' was linked to a

[8] *See* Luhmann, 1980, especially 17, 22 and 34.

[9] Luhmann, 1990a, 177, invoking Skinner, 1989.

[10] Luhmann, 1980, 22.

[11] On the distinction between *metaphor*, which leaves open 'fundamental elements' of the description, and *concept*, which is associated with 'precise' description, *see* Möllers, 2005a, 286 *f*.

[12] Alt, 2002.

[13] In a different context and based on other presuppositions, Blumenberg (1998, 10 and 13) refers to 'absolute metaphors': 'determination and analysis of their conceptually inseparable propositional function' constitute 'an essential element of the history of concepts (in this broader sense)' and are 'useful' to the 'history of concepts (in the terminologically strict sense)'.

[14] Averring that 'to imagine a language means to imagine a form of life', Wittgenstein says, 'in misunderstanding the use of the word, one takes it to signify an odd *process*', earlier adding that a 'sentence seems odd only when one imagines it to belong to a different language game from the one in which we actually use it' (Wittgenstein, 1997 [1945–1949], 246 and 380, §§ 19, 195 and 196).

[15] Of course, there are language games that have no direct relation to social structure, as in literary fiction, where they can therefore freely use 'arbitrary metaphors'. But the social sciences and law cannot be reduced to mere literary fiction unless by doing so it is intended to deny the importance of studying the relations between law and literature (*see*, eg, Posner, 1988).

very diverse range of desires and interests.[16] The weekly paper *Révolutions de Paris* (no 20, dated 21–28 November 1789) contained the following assertion: 'A Constitution is desired by all: every citizen sacrifices his fortune, personal affairs and leisure to this goal'.[17] Associated with this desire for a constitution, Societies of Friends of the Constitution, better known as Jacobin Clubs, sprang up all over France,[18] and the Constitution was called the 'catechism of the human race'.[19] In the US the Constitution was called 'marvellous' and a 'magic parchment'.[20] It was 'the political bible of the State. Scarcely a family was without it,' said Paine.[21] This original constitutionalist enthusiasm lasted a long time, eventually paving the way for a certain tendency for the concept of constitution or constitutionalism to lose its distinctness and cease to be a 'guiding concept', becoming instead a 'panacea concept'.[22]

This problem relates to the fact that the constitution has become a 'support for hope';[23] indeed, the concepts of both constitution and constitutionalisation have become part of a 'victorious offensive',[24] and are being used as a 'fighting political concept'.[25] Thus, they match what Reinhart Koselleck calls 'asymmetric counterconcepts', which morally disqualify those who oppose them by introducing 'a depreciative meaning' that functions for their adversaries 'as a linguistic deprivation, in actuality verging on theft'.[26] Inasmuch as 'constitution' in the modern sense originally invokes 'the opposite of a political order of oppression',[27]that is, suggests emancipation, it has become usual to use the term rhetorically as a label for the righteousness and correctness of those who defend it and of what it designates. This situation leads to a tendency to apply the term 'constitution' to quite distinct institutions and legal and political situations, in highly different contexts. Thus in actuality the constitution has become a contextually unlimited metaphor. The notion has become decoupled from the history of the concept and from its structural foundations. It has become unrecognisable as a semantic artefact and no longer refers reflexively to a specific social structure.

[16] This use is associated with a certain 'constitutional fetishism' (Walker, 2002, 324–7), currently revived as 'global' (Fischer-Lescano, 2005, 208). In this context, Maduro (2006, 335 *ff*) refers to the 'importance of being called a Constitution'.

[17] Quoted by Schmale, 1988, 13. *Cf* Preuss, 1990, 12; Biaggini, 2000, 445.

[18] Schmale, 1988, 64–6.

[19] Schmale, 1988, 13. *Cf* Biaggini, 2000, 445 *f*.

[20] In a 1913 speech by New York lawyer Henry R Estabrook, quoted by Gabriel, 1940, 402; Bickel, 1978, 15; Preuss, 1990, 11; Biaggini, 2000, 446. Bickel (1978, 14 *f*) refers to a comment made in 1936 by Supreme Court Justice George Sutherland, recalling how he had been taught in his youth that the US Constitution was a 'divinely inspired instrument – as I truly think it is'.

[21] Paine, 1992 [1791–1792], 149. *Cf* Preuss, 1990, 17; Vorländer, 1999, 9; Biaggini, 2000, 446.

[22] Wahl, 2002, 191.

[23] Biaggini, 2000, 465.

[24] Biaggini, 2000, 447 *ff*; Wahl, 2002, 191.

[25] Biaggini, 2000, 464.

[26] Koselleck, 1989, 211 and 213 [Engl trans 2004, 155 *f*]. *Cf* Preuss, 1990, 73; Biaggini, 2000, 464.

[27] Preuss, 1990, 74.

It is vitally important to avoid this temptation. In this book, it is not a matter of discussing simply whether there is such a thing as a 'constitution without a state'[28] or whether 'the constitution in the process of denationalisation' is transferable to the international level,[29] a debate that contributes greatly to the arbitrary use of constitutional metaphors. What is necessary instead is to examine the meaning and function of the constitution in the modern sense to address questions referring to the new challenges of constitutional development as well as its limits and possibilities in the modern societies of the present day. To do this, it is fundamental to seek the precise historical location and rigorous semantic delimitation of the conceptual contours of 'constitution' and 'constitutionalism', as we will see in the rest of this Chapter.

II. THE PREMODERN HIERARCHICAL SOCIAL FORMATION

The concept of constitution in the modern sense relates to the structural changes that lead to the functional differentiation of society, which is inconceivable in the premodern social formation. In this formation the hierarchical structure manifested itself in two fundamental aspects of the integration of society: systemic integration, which refers to the relation of dependence between spheres of communication; and social integration, which refers to the relations between people and communication systems.

As far as system integration is concerned, the summit of society comprised an amalgam between the political structure of domination, reproduced on the basis of the difference between higher and lower power levels,[30] and moral-religious semantics built on the foundation of the (moral) distinction between good and evil,[31] which was inseparable from the (religious) difference between the transcendent and the immanent. This amalgam prevailed over all other spheres of communication, which therefore remained undifferentiated and were heteronymously determined. The semantics of good related above all to the upper portion of the structure of social (political) domination, residing in the 'nobility' or a functionally equivalent layer; the semantics of evil related above all to the lower pole of the structure of domination and was expressed in the 'plebs' or a functional equivalent. The 'lower orders' only practised good when acting in accordance with behavioural models determined by the 'higher orders'. The latter only practised evil when acting in accordance with the former's standards. The other spheres and respective codes of communication were subordinated to this supreme framework, comprising morality impregnated with religion and political domination. The arts, knowledge, law and the economy were semantically subordinated to the difference between good and evil, and

[28] Biaggini, 2000, 457.
[29] Grimm, 2004a, 13.
[30] Luhmann, 1986a, 199.
[31] Luhmann, 1997, vol 2, 939 *f* and 1036.

oriented by the criteria of the higher or lower levels of power. Thus the difference between lawfulness and unlawfulness was not clearly distinguished from the difference between good and evil, but on the contrary practically merged with it. Its positive side was associated with superiority in domination and its negative side with inferiority. The same was true of the differences 'having/not having' (economics), 'true/untrue' (knowledge) and 'beautiful/ugly' (art).

As for social integration, the distinction between upper and lower estate entailed different ways of considering men by society, conceived as a broader social system. On one hand, it entailed a model in which men belonging to the higher estates or levels were socially *included* as full members of society, thus enjoying ample access to society's benefits and amenities. On the other hand, men who belonged to the lower estates or levels were socially *excluded* as non-members of society, thus lacking access to its benefits. There could be intermediate situations, of course, but this was the basic structure of social integration. Because society and territorial political organisation were seen as one and the same, the distinction between inclusion and exclusion was identical to the distinction between members and non-members.[32] The concept of a person, associated with the modern semantics of individuality, was not present since there was no clear distinction between man and society-organisation: man was conceived as member or non-member depending on the social stratum to which he belonged.[33] Because the concept of a person in the modern sense did not exist, social integration related not to the institution of rights but to the attribution of status privileges.

Power was legitimated by sacred law, which was indisponible (*unverfügbar*) – not at the disposal of the ruler.[34] Strictly speaking this indisponibility did not signify any legal constraint on power. Sacred law justified the sovereign's investiture, titular rulership, and exercise of power, individually or collectively. The maxim *princeps legibus solutus est* prevailed, however. This did not mean the sovereign was not subject to certain legal restrictions when acting as a private person (and hence precisely not as sovereign)[35] or that his actions were not

[32] On the differentiation of system levels between interaction (grounded in the difference between presence and absence), organisation (based on the difference between members and non-members), and society as a broad social system (constructed in accordance with the difference between communication and non-communication), *see* Luhmann, 1986b; 1997, vol 2, 813–47; Luhmann and De Giorgi, 1992, 316–34. It can be said that whereas archaic societies (segmentary differentiation) are anchored in interaction, societies in premodern high cultures (hierarchical differentiation) are grounded in territorially centralised political *organisation*; only with modern society (functional differentiation) can interaction, organisation and society be distinguished (*see* Luhmann, 1997, vol 2, 634 *ff*; Luhmann and De Giorgi, 1992, 260 *ff*; Neves, 2006a, 6 *ff* and 18 *ff*).

[33] *Cf* Luhmann, 1997, vol 2, 688; 1989, 156 *f*.

[34] Habermas, 1992, 582 *f* or 1986, 261 *f*.

[35] *See*, eg, Grotius, 1950 [1625], 90, 171 and 270. Solon (1997, 31) argues that 'even in Bodin, the concept of sovereignty is not given an absolutist expression, as princes must submit to divine and natural law, with the latter category including private-law contracts'. On this subject *see* Bodin, 1986 [1576], especially 190 and 192 *f*. However, it should be noted that for Bodin the sovereign was unlimited with regard to the norms of positive law (*cf* 1986 [1576], especially 191 *f* and 306 *ff*), and that with regard to contracts and conventions (not only of the private-law kind) with his subjects,

limited to some extent by legal and de facto conditions.[36] Fundamentally, it meant that there were no relevant positive legal constraints on the sovereign in exercising *jus imperium*, that is, normative restrictions established and imposed by other men on his coercive action.

In this context it is possible to speak of the subordination of law to power. So-called 'sacred law' is best thought of as an epiphenomenon of power legitimated by religion-based morality. Subordination of law to political power in a social formation where power is at the centre of society leads to an asymmetrical relationship between higher and lower power, or between the sovereign and his subjects. In the strata at the top of the social pyramid were located status privileges or sovereign prerogatives to be enjoyed or exercised at the expense of the lower strata. For these, lacking in privileges or prerogatives, there remained the duties of subjecthood or obedience. The result was a structure of domination grounded in the religious semantics of sacred law, which was 'indisponible', thus maintaining these structural traits of the hierarchical social formation.

This 'indisponibility', in the context of a society primarily oriented by what has crystallised in the past,[37] implies the idea of true and immutable law on the plane of general and abstract norms.[38] This order itself differs from archaic law, which was entirely undifferentiated and lacked both law-making procedures and law enforcement procedures: the law was applied by the community collectively or by its members in a diffuse manner, via concrete forms such as retaliation and reciprocity, with no distinctions between norm and action, between the normative and the cognitive.[39] The differentiation of enforcement procedures entails an evolutionary step in the transition to law as it is found in the premodern hierarchical social formation.[40] In Roman law, above all, complex procedures developed for the solution of legal cases but the 'law remains embedded in general social arrangements, remains dependent on structures that also serve other functions (for instance, the family or a morality founded on religion)'.[41] However, the structural conditions were missing for the differentiation of legislative procedures which

the person of the 'prince' did not enjoy the condition of a sovereign in principle (*cf* 1986 [1576], 195 and 217 *ff*). According to Esmein (1913, 205 *f*), there were spheres of private law in which, in Bodin, *princeps legibus solutus est* prevailed without these restrictions; he alludes, for example, to Bodin, 1986 [1576], 219: testaments and a donation celebrated by King Philip VI (Philippe de Valois). Before alluding to these and similar cases, however, Bodin refers to a 1531 court ruling according to which the prince could ignore civil laws 'provided the rights of private persons were not impaired' (*ibid*).

[36] *See* Esmein, 1913, accompanied in this specific case by Luhmann, 1993a, 271, note 69 [Engl trans 2004, 254, note 69].

[37] In this sense, *see* Tönnies, 1979, especially 73, opposing (the old) community to (the new) society.

[38] *See* Luhmann, 1987a, 183 and 185.

[39] *See* Weber, 1985, 445 *f*; Schluchter, 1979, 146; Luhmann, 1987a, 150 and 154–7; 1993a, 257 [Engl trans 2004, 243 *f*]; Habermas, 1982a, vol 1, 349 and 351; vol 2, 261 *f* [Engl trans 1984 (vol 1), 257 *f*; 1987 (vol 2), 175 *f*]; 1982b, 135; Neves, 1992, 25; 2006a, 20 *f* and 54.

[40] *See* Luhmann, 1987a, 171 *ff*; Habermas, 1982a, vol II, 264 *f* [Engl trans 1987, vol 2, 177 *f*]; Neves, 2006a, 21 *f*; 1992, 26.

[41] Luhmann, 1993a, 58 [Engl trans 2004, 92].

would entail laws that could be changed on the plane of general and abstract norms. The immutability or structural 'indisponibility' of law related directly to the maintenance of a hierarchical social order and the dogmatic unquestionability of the dominant political status quo.[42] Sacred law, immutable and indisponible, and actual power, unquestionable and uncontrollable, supported each other.[43]

The typical model of the premodern hierarchical social formation is most evident in the ancient oriental state, also known as 'theocratic', as it was immediately founded on divinity. Georg Jellinek distinguished between two basic species of this territorial political organisation. In the first, 'the sovereign is considered a representative of divine power, and his will is therefore considered similar to the divine will'. In this type, 'the state itself takes on the character of an object submitted to an alien and superior power', so that 'a peculiar dualism is imposed' insofar as 'the state requires a transcendent, i.e. superhuman, complement through which it genuinely acquires the ability to be alive'.[44] In the second species of ancient oriental state, the sovereign (human power) 'is limited by divine power, which manifests its supra-state will through other organs', affirming an internal dualism in which the power seen as arising from a divine origin and administered by the priesthood not only limits human power but is capable of dominating it.[45] In both cases all social life was submitted immediately to the difference between power at the top and bottom of the hierarchy, which difference in turn was grounded directly in the religious worldview that oriented the difference between good and evil.

In the case of ancient Greece it is possible to observe a greater degree of differentiation of the social formation. However, given that the model of hierarchical differentiation was incompatible with the constitution in the modern sense, it is not appropriate to associate it with the Greek concept of *politeia*. Although the notion of *politeia* varied a great deal in Greek thought, so that for example in the entire writings of Aristotle and within the *Politics* itself there are 'contradictions the author did not try to eliminate',[46] the received definition in the modern constitutional debate is above all that found in Book IV of the *Politics*, referring to the basic order of the *polis*: 'a constitution (πολιτεία) is the regulation (τάξις) of the offices of the state in regard to the mode of their distribution and to the question what is the sovereign power in the state and what is the object (τελος) of each community'.[47]This definition referred both descriptively to elements of the real power structure[48] and to the teleological dimension[49] of the organisation of the *polis*. However, until the end of the eighteenth century

[42] *Cf* Luhmann, 1997, vol 1, 553; Luhmann and De Giorgi, 1992, 238.
[43] *Cf* Habermas, 1992, 177–9 [Engl trans 1996, 142–4].
[44] Jellinek, 1966, 289 *f*.
[45] *Ibid*. Jellinek points to the ancient state of Israel as the most important example of the second type, affirming the existence of 'democratic tendencies in the laws of Israel': *ibid*, 290 *f*.
[46] Bordes, 1967, 436.
[47] Aristotle, 1944, 281 (IV, 1, 1289a); *see also* 173 (III, 1, 1274b) and 201 (III, 6, 1278b).
[48] McIlwain, 1940, 28; Maddox, 1989, 51.
[49] Mohnhaupt, 1995, 9.

the term *politeia* was translated into English more approximately as 'government'.[50] It is odd that the Greek word should have been first translated as 'constitution' precisely in the revolutionary period, when structural changes made such a translation entirely inadequate. The semantics of constitutionalism was a conquest, construction, or invention of modern society that was incompatible with the notion of *politeia* in ancient Greece, which pointed to a hierarchical and exclusionary model of non-differentiation between politics and law.

For the ancient Greeks, *politeia* was not a holistic concept that encompassed everything social, since it presupposed a distinction between *polis* and *oikia* or *oikos*. In the modern sense, *polis* cannot be understood to mean all of society. It was a space for citizens who were equal under one and the same law of equality, and comprised only male heads of households (*oikoi* or *oikiai*). As a parenthesis, it is worth noting that *oikos* (pl. *oikoi*) had a broader meaning than *oikia* (pl. *oikiai*), in that it included the property owned by the head of household outside the home as a physical domestic space.[51] The *oikos* as a space dominated by the head of household was not part of the *polis*. This was the *excluding* 'public' space in which heads of *oikoi* or *oikia* related with each other. There was no *polis* in a mere 'village' conceived as an agglomeration of *oikiai*.[52] The *oikos* was the domestic (private) social space in which the head of household exercised complete dominion over his family, servants and property (including slaves) – a sphere of *dominium* over things and *potestas* over dependants. Just as the Greek *oikos* or *oikia* (the domestic social space of family relations or the extended family, grounded in the arbitrary power of the head of household) corresponds neither to the domestic space of the 'nuclear' modern family (the 'private' in the familiar sense), nor to the space of the world market (the 'private' in the economic sense), so the exclusive *polis* (a dimension of the 'public' in the Greek sense) should not be confused with the political system of modern society, much less with the pluralistic inclusive public sphere in the contemporary sense.[53]

The Aristotelian conception of *politeia* referred strictly to the basic order of the *polis* as a political community, as the space of rational citizens. It excluded all those who were subordinated to the master of the *oikos* as domestic space of 'family' relations – family members, slaves, bondmen, servants. To a certain extent these were base or vile beings, that is individuals of an inferior nature to any member of the *polis* as a 'political animal' (*zoon politikon*).[54] Thus the

[50] Stourzh, 1975, 99 *ff*; Mohnhaupt, 1995, 8. A widely read twentieth-century translation of the *Politics* contains the following sentence: 'the constitution is the government' (Aristotle, 1944, 201 [III, 6, 1278b]).

[51] *Cf* MacDowell, 1989, 10.

[52] *Cf* Luhmann, 2000a, 7.

[53] The tendency to relate and even confuse the difference in Greek between *polis* and *oikos* with the simplified distinction between public and private in modern society is associated with the work of Hannah Arendt (*see* 1989 [1958], 28 *ff*).

[54] Aristotle, 1944, 9–11 (I, 1, 1253 a).

politeia entailed a structure that distinguished between two strata or types of men: those included in the *polis*, that is, the heads of *oikoi* or *oikiai*, who were citizens (*zoa politika*); and those excluded from the *polis*, that is, the dependants or objects of the heads of household in the domestic family space. This difference entailed a hierarchical distinction in social integration between rational (superior) beings and base (inferior) beings.

Such structure was justified by the strong semantics of a morality grounded in religion. Fustel de Coulanges notes in this regard: 'As soon as the families, the phratries, and the tribes had agreed to unite and have the same worship, they immediately founded the city as a sanctuary for this common worship, and thus the foundation of a city was always a religious act.'[55] But the hierarchical exclusionary structure of domination was not propped up only by sacred law. The dominant philosophy of ancient Greece itself served as a semantic bulwark for the structural model of the *polis*, reflecting back to itself the worldview (identity) of the Greek city-state.

The Roman state, by contrast, emerged with *civitas* (the community of citizens), comprising patrician families, and also developed in the form of *res publica* (community of the people), simultaneously constituting a community of worship.[56] Jellinek goes as far as stating that everything he says about the Greek state is valid in principle for the Roman state, 'which also develops out of a city-state and maintains the marks of its origins until the very end'.[57] One difference, he notes, resides in the absolute *potestas* of the *pater familias* over his family for life. This included his children, whereas in the Greek world, for example, children were subordinated to the head of household only until they came of age.[58] Among the Romans, the basic hierarchical distinction consisted of the difference between patricians and plebeians, leaving aside the slaves. There were of course intermediate categories, such as clients.[59] Nevertheless, despite all the development from Monarchy to Republic and Empire, the difference between patricians and plebeians remained dominant. Although Roman law attributed *majestas*, *imperium*, and *potestas* to the *populus*,[60] strictly speaking, the latter's power was predominantly wielded by the limited community of patricians, with rare exceptions. Moreover, there was a legal distinction between Roman citizens and *peregrini*,

[55] Fustel de Coulanges, 1908 [1864], 151 [Engl trans 2001, 110]; specifically on the Greek city, *cf* 1908 [1864], 157 *ff* [Engl trans 2001, 114 *ff*]. As Fustel de Coulanges explains: 'Civitas, and Urbs, either of which we translate by the word city, were not synonymous words among the ancients. Civitas was the religious and political association of families and tribes; Urbs was the place of assembly, the dwelling-place, and, above all, the sanctuary of this association' (1908 [1864], 151 [Engl trans 2001, 110]).

[56] Jellinek, 1966, 312.

[57] *Ibid*. On community of worship, *see also* Fustel de Coulanges, 1908 [1864], 151 *ff* [Engl trans 2001, 110 *ff*].

[58] Jellinek, 1966, 313.

[59] *See* Mommsen, 1982, 10–16; De Ulhoa Cintra, 1963, 18 *ff*. More complex than the distinction between patricians and plebeians, Mommsen (1982 [1907], 29 *ff*) distinguishes between 'privileged' and 'non-privileged' classes of citizens, with the patricians constituting the basis of the former (*ibid*) and the plebeians the latter (pp 40 *ff*).

[60] Solon, 1997, 21.

foreigners and free persons who were not citizens of Rome. The *peregrini* were excluded from Roman law under the Empire.[61] Thus the hierarchically differentiated power anchored in the community of worship was the basis for reproduction of the state.

It is relevant to recall that in Rome there was already a certain differentiation between law and politics. As noted above, however, differentiation of complex Roman law referred to the dimension of law application procedures. The law itself remained grounded in tradition and principles of a religious nature. It was not permanently changeable by decision, as law was to become only with the differentiation of law-making procedures in the modern state associated with the appearance of the constitution as a reflexive instance of the legal system.

In the mediaeval period, the territorial political organisation faced two distinct tendencies: on one hand, the internal force of feudal disintegration; on the other, external pressure from the papal power. Although the latter did not become significant until the late eleventh century as a result of the 'Papal Revolution',[62] since before that 'the clergy of Western Christendom – bishops, priests, and monks – were, as a rule, much more under the authority of emperors, kings, and leading feudal lords than of popes',[63] the traditional character of law persisted throughout the Middle Ages: 'All law derived its validity from its divine origin in Christian natural law . . . As supreme judicial authority, the sovereign stood under sacred law. Only in this manner could the legitimacy of the latter carry over into his worldly power.'[64] Thus in the mediaeval social formation as well, religious semantics serve to justify the hierarchical structure of domination grounded in the primary difference between higher and lower power, as expressed in distinctions such as suzerain and vassal, sovereign and subject, and divine power and secular power.

In sum, a constitution in the modern sense cannot be present in any type of premodern hierarchical social formation, with an apex in which are interwoven a structure of domination grounded in the distinction 'higher power/lower power', and religious moral semantics based on the difference 'good/evil'. The term 'constitution' used to refer to one of these experiences points descriptively

[61] De Ulhoa Cintra, 1963, 35 *ff*. This situation changed formally in 212 AD with the Edict of Caracalla, which offered citizenship to the peregrini, albeit keeping some categories out of *status civitatis* (*ibid*, 53 *f*).

[62] Berman, HJ, 1983, 85 *ff*.

[63] Berman, HJ, 1983, 88. In my view, however, it does not appear correct to say that owing to changes occurring in Western Europe between the eleventh and thirteenth centuries 'law became *disembedded*', 'both as a political institution and as an intellectual concept', or that 'Western Europe experienced . . . the development of the concept of law as an autonomous . . . body of legal principles and procedures' (*ibid*, 86). Only with constitutionalism does it become possible to speak of law as an autonomous system, without grounding in natural law. The autonomy to which Berman refers was partial: it applied to the legal professions, on a *semantic* plane of reflection, without any corresponding *structural* autonomy. On this subject Luhmann is ambiguous: in one place he appears to agree with Berman (Luhmann, 1993a, 62 [Engl trans 2004, 94), while elsewhere he says 'the constitution closes the legal system' (1990a, 187). *See* pp 41*f* below.

[64] Habermas, 1992, 582 or 1986, 261.

to the social or political structure that characterises a given society, serving merely as an empirical concept valid for each and every social formation.[65]

III. THE TRANSITION PERIOD: CHARTERS OF FREEDOM OR POLITICAL SETTLEMENTS

The appearance of the modern state does not yet signify the advent of constitutionalism. Absolute monarchy as the emerging state order of the early modern era does not yet entail functional differentiation between politics and law. In terms of philosophical semantics, this lack of differentiation continued to be seen in part as related to the sacred or divine inspiration for the power of princes,[66] associated as it was with the revived formula *princeps legibus solutus est*, which meant that the sovereign was not subordinated to laws made by others. Nevertheless, what was new was the tendency to transcend the sacred foundation of power, that is, to desacralise law.[67] Thus the tension between the instrumentality and the 'indisposability' of law becomes evident.[68]

In absolutism this pendular tension swings sharply toward the political instrumentalisation of law, which is not hindered by the semantics of the new natural law that has no link to the transcendent: instead, the metajuridical principles of jusnaturalism (considered immutable) are invoked to legitimate a juridically free space for the sovereign, within which he had the power to establish and enforce the law. On this point Habermas offers the following clarification, albeit from a different perspective regarding the consequences of this change on the threshold of modern society:

> To the extent that religious worldviews gave way to a pluralism of privatised gods and demons, and common-law traditions were more and more penetrated, via the *usus modernus*, by scholarly law, the tripartite structure of the legal system had to collapse. Law shrank to just one of the three dimensions; it hence occupied only the place that bureaucratic royal law had previously filled. The political power of the ruler was emancipated from its tie to sacred law and became independent. It was, accordingly, burdened with the task of filling the gap that the theologically administrated natural law had left behind and of achieving this on its own, through political legislation. In the end all law was supposed to flow from the sovereign will of the political legislator. Making, executing and applying laws became three moments within a single, politically controlled feedback process.[69]

Absolutism marks the passage from sacredly founded indifferentiation of power and law to instrumental subordination of law to politics. In this context

[65] See, eg, Grimm, 2004a, 2; Biaggini, 2000, 461.

[66] *See* Bodin, 1986 [1576], especially 295 *ff*.

[67] In accordance with this tendency, for example, Hobbes says: 'And first it is manifest, that Law in generall, is not Counsell, but Command; nor a Command of any man to any man; but only of him, whose Command is addressed to one formerly obliged to obey him' (1992, 183 [1651, 137]).

[68] Habermas, 1992, 582 *f* or 1986, 262.

[69] Habermas, 1992, 583 or 1986, 262.

the hierarchical structure of the traditional order remains in the relations between sovereign and subjects. In ideal-typical terms, the former holds powers, prerogatives and privileges with regard to the latter but no duties or responsibilities legally enforceable by them. Thus the subjects enjoy no rights against the sovereign but only duties and responsibilities toward him. Clearly the absolutist period already entails a significant degree of juridification (by positive norms, that is, norms imposed and changeable by decision) of the horizontal relations between private persons. This first wave of juridification, however, did not entail actionable subjective public rights against the sovereign.[70]

Moreover, an aspect related to this juridical dimension was that the upper pole of power was not divisible: the idea of an institutionalised political opposition was intolerable.[71] Contesting the identity of the nucleus of power violated 'reason of state' and constituted the felony of high treason (*lèse-majesté*). The institutional intolerability of opposition, in a society that had already reached a high degree of complexity, and thus already involved a variety of worldviews, necessarily led to the idea of revolution and to revolutionary movements. In this sense, constitutionalism itself presupposed revolution.[72]

Even with regard to the absolutist period, however, it would be mistaken to overlook the positive legal constraints on the holders of power. Charters of liberties or fundamental freedoms, and similar political settlements,[73] the first of which emerge during the Middle Ages, with the Magna Carta of 1215 as an outstanding example, develop under the aegis of conflicts of interest that pit feudal barons and the emerging bourgeoisie against the monarch in the absolutist state. But these late mediaeval and absolutist settlements should not be confused with constitutions in the modern sense, either from the sociological standpoint of the social dimension (the people involved), the material dimension (the topics regulated) and the temporal dimension, or in the legal language of the personal, material, and temporal spheres of validity.[74] In this regard it is

[70] Habermas, 1982a, vol 2, 525–7 [Engl trans 1987, vol 2, 358 *f*]. In respect of an entirely different context, the ancient oriental state, Jellinek (1966, 289) analogously remarks that 'an individual's rights cannot be upheld against the sovereign but only against one who is at the same level' [as the individual concerned]. However, it does appear proper to speak of a subject's having actionable individual rights against another subject in an autonomous manner in the social formation of the ancient state. The exercise of a right depended in this case too on a grant from the sovereign.

[71] *See* Luhmann, 1987b, especially 127, nevertheless adverting to the fact that the theory of the absolutist state was already concerned with the paradoxical problem of 'a singular lack of power on the part of those in power and, on the other side, power on the part of the powerless' – a problem which democratic differentiation between government and opposition was to deparadoxise: 'The opposition does not have the power to govern; precisely for this reason, it can make use of the power of its lack of power.'

[72] Grimm, 1987, 45 *f* and 56 *f*; 1989, 633 *f*.

[73] On this subject *See* Böckenförde, 1983, 7 *ff*.

[74] In this context I relate the Luhmannian sociological or theoretical-social concepts of the social, material and temporal dimensions (Luhmann, 1987a, 94 *ff*) to the juridical concepts of the personal, material and temporal spheres of validity (Kelsen, 1960, 12 *ff* and 291 *f*), although of course I am well aware that the assumptions and implications of the respective categories are quite distinct. In my view, nevertheless, it is possible to find a certain analogy between the two conceptual models.

appropriate to invoke Dieter Grimm's analysis of the differences between the two models of political regulation.[75]

In the social dimension or personal sphere of validity, political settlements were 'particular' and referred to certain agreements between the monarch and the nobility or part of the bourgeoisie. Modern constitutions, in contrast, claim to be 'universal' and refer inclusively to all members of the respective juridico-political organisation, attributing fundamental rights to each person. In other words, political settlements can be said to entail a particularistic and exclusionary language at the pragmatic level of those who are empowered to employ it and those to whom it is addressed, whereas the modern constitution claims to be a pragmatically universalistic language, despite the difference between nationals and aliens.

In the material validity sphere or dimension, political settlements were 'restricted' in the sense of referring to specific issues in politics and state law. Constitutions in the modern sense are 'comprehensive' in their content, since they refer to the various branches of law and different processes of political decision making. In the terminology of linguistic theory, while political settlements dispose semantically of a sphere of strict denotation and connotation, constitutions carry a breadth of signifieds and referents, making much more complex the task of interpreting their text and concretising their norms.

Grimm also argues that political settlements were 'empirical'. This evidently cannot be understood as meaning that they did not contain legal norms, but rather as expressing that they did not involve a functional distinction between politics and law. Instead, they constituted a simple legal manifestation of the real relations of domination. In connection with this, in the temporal validity sphere or dimension, political settlements were merely 'rule-modifying', expressing changes that occurred in the structure of domination. Constitutions in the modern sense, however, are 'normative', not simply because they are made up of legal norms, but specifically because they point to a functional distinction between law and politics, meaning that power is bound by law and can thus be limited and controlled by it. In this sense, constitutions in the modern sense are 'rule-constituting' in the temporal validity sphere or dimension, inasmuch as they institute a new political structure and renew its normative foundation by giving it a positive legal existence.

In this regard it is important to make another fundamental distinction clear. The political settlements of the period still coexisted with the idea of natural law, which, albeit considered immutable and thus primarily subordinated to the structure of cognitive expectations, served as a justification for the ample mutability of law by the sovereign. They were therefore seen as mutable law subordinated to the immutable and true natural law of princes. This means the distinction between normative and cognitive expectations was not yet clearly

[75] The discussion in what follows of the differences between constitutions in the modern sense and political settlements, *leges fundamentales* or charters of liberties is based on Grimm, 1987, especially 48 *ff*; 1989, col 633 *f*; 1995a, 100 *ff*; 2004a, 4 and 7.

affirmed in the social formation at the threshold of modern western society in the sphere of the absolutist state. The constitution in the modern sense presupposes precisely a clear distinction between the normative and cognitive in the context of positivation of law,[76] that is, law that changes to become permanently changeable by decision.[77] The problem that arises is this: Once the fundamentals of institutional natural law have been superseded, what foundations can be laid for law itself so as to prevent it from becoming a mere instrument of whoever happens to be in power? This question brings us face to face with that of the emergence of constitutionalism itself. Before dealing with this topic, however, it is worth making some preliminary observations about the structural type of modern society.

IV. MULTICENTRIC MODERN SOCIETY

Functional differentiation in face of the premodern amalgam of politics and religious morality at the top of the social pyramid occurs initially in the spheres of the economy (profit-making efficiency distinguished from the good and the politically dominant), of science (truth independent of religious morality and power), and of art (the 'beautiful' or aesthetically appropriate becoming autonomous from religiously grounded moral goodness). These are traumatic social processes with destructive consequences for the biological and mental environment of social systems, for 'body' and 'soul' alike. Suffice it to recall Galileo in the sphere of science (although, to take a quite different sphere, we should not forget *Romeo and Juliet*, a tragic allegory of the modern claim to the autonomy of love from politics and family, a claim that will not be fully realised until much later, thanks also to the novel).[78] These processes of struggle for the autonomy of social spheres at the start of the modern era evidently do not yet imply the operational autonomy of law from power as domination. Only with the advent of revolutionary constitutionalism at the end of the eighteenth century did the modern process of differentiation between politics and law begin. Indeed, as discussed in the previous section, political settlements and fundamental laws in England (Magna Carta, the Habeas Corpus Act, the Bill of Rights) pointed to a development that was functionally equivalent to that which led to the revolutionary Constitutions of the United States and France, but in isolation were not semantic expressions of constitutionalism. Rather, they were elements of an evolutionary process of differentiation between law and politics, which resulted in an atypical constitutionalism in the nineteenth and twentieth centuries.

Constitutionalism relates to structural changes that engendered the foundations for the emergence of modern society. Growing social complexity led to an

[76] Luhmann, 1983b, 138 *ff*. On this distinction, *see* Luhmann, 1987c, 436–43 [Engl trans 1995, 319–25]; 1987a, 40–53; Neves, 1992, 22 *f*.

[77] Luhmann, 1981a, 113–53; 1987a, 190 *ff*; 1983a [1969], 141–50; Neves, 1992, especially 27–30.

[78] *Cf* Luhmann, 1990b [1982], especially 11 *f*; 1997, vol 2, 731.

impasse in the hierarchically differentiated social formation of premodernity and to the emergence of an increasingly insistent claim to autonomy for the spheres of communication, in terms of functionally differentiated systems in modern society. There was not merely a 'disentangling' of law, power and knowledge,[79] nor merely the conquest of religious and economic freedom by human beings,[80] but a broad process of systemic functional differentiation.

Through this process society becomes 'multicentric' or 'polycontextural'.[81] This means, first, that the difference between system and environment develops in various spheres of communication, so that several counterposed claims of systemic autonomy are affirmed; and second, insofar as every difference becomes a 'centre of the world', that polycontexturality entails a plurality of self-descriptions of society, leading to the formation of several conflicting partial rationalities. What is missing, therefore, is the one last difference that is supreme in that it can impose itself on all the other differences. In other words, society lacks a single centre in a privileged position from which it can be observed and described; there is no system or social mechanism from which all others can be comprehended.

This leads to a plurality of difference codes that orient communication in the various social fields. The difference 'having/not having' prevails in the economic system,[82] the code 'power/not power' has primacy in the political system,[83] and the distinction 'legal/illegal' predominates in the legal system.[84] In science, art, education, religion and love, the following codes prevail respectively: 'true/untrue',[85] 'beautiful/ugly' ('aesthetically apt versus aesthetically inapt'),[86] 'pass/fail' (as a code that demarcates the limit of the gradual difference 'learning/not learning' expressed in grades and predicates),[87] 'transcendent/immanent',[88] and the love code ('pleasure/love' or 'love/lovelessness'),[89] which serves as a basis for the formation of the modern nuclear family.[90] This evidently leads to tensions, since the various rationalities confront other rationalities in this manner, each with a claim to universality.[91] Thus any form of 'autism' that develops in one sphere may have destructive effects in other social spheres, and eventually also on the social and system integration of a complex society. Differentiation does not mean isolation, but rather an intense cognitive capacity with regard to the environment.

[79] Lefort, 1981, 64.
[80] Marx, 1988a [1844], 369.
[81] Luhmann, 1987c, 284 [Engl trans 1995, 208]; 1997, vol 1, 36 *f*.
[82] Luhmann, 1988a, 181 *f*, 184 and 187 *ff*.
[83] Luhmann, 1988b [1975], 56; 1990a, 193.
[84] Luhmann, 1986a; 1993a, 165 *ff* [Engl trans 2004, 173 *ff*].
[85] Luhmann, 1990c, 194 *ff*.
[86] Luhmann, 1996, 309 *ff*; 1997, vol 1, 562.
[87] *See* Luhmann, 2002a, 64 *ff*; 1997, vol 2, 750; 2004 [1986], 27 *ff*.
[88] Luhmann, 2000b, 77 *ff*.
[89] Luhmann, 1990b, 107 *ff*; 1997, vol 2, 750.
[90] *Cf* Luhmann, 1997, vol 2, 730 *f*; 1990b, 183 *f*.
[91] *See* Teubner, 1996a; Fischer-Lescano and Teubner, 2006.

Given the impossibility of having a single or privileged point from which to observe society, it is therefore necessary from the standpoint of systems theory to insist that not even politics is a centre of privileged place in society, but rather a system in competition with the others.[92] The opposite view, which puts politics at the centre as a supersystem of modern society, has led only to disillusionment. Moreover, the theory of society itself is only a partial observation or description of society, and counts as its most comprehensive observation only from the standpoint of the scientific system. Religion, politics, economics, the family, art, education, and so on also make their observations of society as a whole and compete with the observation of social theory. The latter is all the more socially adequate insofar as it describes this multicentricity of the social in modernity.

But modern society is born as world society,[93]as a social formation detached from territorial political organisations, although the latter in the form of states constitute one of the fundamental dimensions for its reproduction. In principle it implies that the horizon of communication transcends the territorial frontiers of the state. To use a more extensive formula, the confluence of communication and the stabilisation of expectations become increasingly regular and intense, extending beyond national or cultural identities and politico-juridical borders.[94]

[92] Lyotard, 1983, 200 [Engl trans 1988, 138] takes a different view: 'Were politics a genre [of language] and were that genre to pretend to that supreme status, its vanity would be quickly revealed. Politics, however, is the threat of the differend. It is not a genre, it is the multiplicity of genres, the diversity of ends, and par excellence the question of linkage . . . It is, if you will, the state of language, but it is not *a* language. Politics consists in the fact that language is not a language, but phrases.' Based on this affirmation, Nassehi proposes an extension of the functional concept of politics, going so far as to sustain – also supported by the concept of 'political society' proposed by Greven (1999) – that ' indeed, there are almost no limits to the political' (Nassehi, 2002, 43 *f*). In the context of this discussion in search of a more comprehensive functional concept, it is worth recalling the Schmittian conception of politics as the 'domain of all domains', as formulated by Göbel (1995, 282) with reference to Schmitt, 1996 [1932], especially 24, and based on Meier, 1994, 59 and 62. *See* Nassehi, 2002, 39 *ff*.

[93] Luhmann, 1975; 1987a, 333 *ff*; 1993a, 571 *ff* [Engl trans 2004, 479 *ff*]; 1997, vol 1, 145–71; Luhmann and De Giorgi, 1992, 45–54; Heintz, 1982; Stichweh, 2000. On the various facets of world society, *see* Heintz, Münch and Tyrell (eds), 2005. In respect of systems theory, Willke (1997, 9 *f*) does not admit the concept of world society, arguing that the concept of society entails 'a territorially and normatively delimited unit' with the conditions to establish the 'deep-seated structures of its (self-) regulation', adding: 'As long as there is no instance, no procedure and no rules that can establish binding norms of self-regulation for the world, the discourse of world society makes no sense.' For Willke, the 'totality of reciprocally accessible communication should therefore be the "world", not society'. He then refers to 'lateral world systems' (Willke 1992, especially 356; 2001, 131 *ff*; 2002, especially 190). But the specificity of world society is that it still reproduces itself primarily on the basis of globally stabilised cognitive expectations, as will be shown below. Moreover, to say that a link with delimited territoriality is a key feature of a society is to ignore even the existence of nomadic societies in the past, especially in the case of archaic societies. Although Willke acknowledges the existence of supranational societies, such as the European Union (1992, 366), it seems to me that his critique would be more fittingly addressed to the notion of a 'world statehood [*Weltstaatlichkeit*]' proposed by Albert and Schmalz-Bruns (2009; Albert, 2007; 2005). Willke himself uses the concept of 'world society' at various points in his work (*cf* Willke, 2001, 17 *et passim*; 2002, 84, 119 and 207).

[94] Neves, 2006a, 217.

A world society is constituted as a *unitary* connection of a *plurality* of spheres of communication in competitive and simultaneously complementary relations. Thus it is *unitas multiplex*.[95] It cannot be confused with the international order, which refers fundamentally to relations among states.[96] The international order is just one of the dimensions of world society.

Nor can the concept of world society be confused with the controversial notion of 'globalisation', not least because of the strongly prescriptive connotation with which the notion is frequently used, in the context of an ideologically loaded discussion, and because when used descriptively it often refers to a system of relations among different regional societies and is based on a concept of society centred on the nation-state.[97] On the contrary, globalisation should be seen as the result of an intensification of world society. This society began in the sixteenth century and became structurally consolidated when 'a single world time' emerged in the second half of the nineteenth century in a process of gradual change that eventually became irreversible,[98] reaching a degree of development so pronounced at the end of the twentieth century that what was already grounded in the plane of social *structures* became dominant in that of *semantics*: society began to observe itself and describe itself as global.[99] This situation relates to the growing intensification of 'social relations' and worldwide supra-regional communications, with profound effects on the reproduction of politico-juridical systems territorially segmented in the form of states.[100] Thus 'resistance against the concept of world society loses persuasive force to the extent that typical characteristics of modernity increasingly have to be incorporated into the concept of "globalising tendencies"'.[101] In other words, 'globalisation' presents itself in the plane of semantics as a reflection or self-description of (the structure of) world society.

Although world society cannot be identified economically with the global capitalist system in the sense of the term used by Immanuel Wallerstein,[102] since it is multicentric, it can appropriately be defined as a society that develops *primarily* on the basis of cognitive expectations (economics, science, and

[95] On the discussion about the use of 'singular' or 'plural' in connection with 'globalisation and world society', *see* Tyrell, 2005. Eisenstadt seeks a common denominator with the expression 'multiplicity of modernity' in the singular (2000a), but also uses the plural in speaking of 'multiple modernities' (2000b), as noted by Tyrell, 2005, 13 *f*.

[96] Luhmann, 1975, 57 *f*; 1997, vol 1, 159 *f*; 1998, 375 *f*; 2000a, 221 *f*.

[97] *See* Luhmann, 1997, vol 1, 159 *f*; 1998, 374 *f*; 2000a, 220 *f*; 1995a, 117, note 30; Teubner, 1996b, 258, note 1 or 1997b, 22 *f*, note 6.

[98] Luhmann, 1997, vol 1, 148; Luhmann and De Giorgi, 1992, 47.

[99] In this sense, Brunkhorst (1999, 374) acknowledges on one hand that it is possible to define 'modern society from the beginning as a *world society*', stressing on the other hand: 'Only at the end of our century has *globalisation* . . . become so evident that society can recognise itself as a world society in its description'.

[100] 'Globalisation can thus be defined as the intensification of worldwide social relations', argues Giddens (1991, 64), although he starts from a concept of modern society centred on the nation-state (1991, especially 13).

[101] Luhmann, 1998, 374; 2000a, 221; *see* 1994, 4.

[102] Wallerstein, 2006, especially23 *ff*; 1979; Hopkins and Wallerstein, 1979.

technics).[103] To use a more specific formula, it can be characterised as displaying the 'social primacy of the economy' or as an 'economic society'.[104] It is not a matter of a primacy that is 'ontically essential'[105] or necessarily of a loss of autonomy by other social systems. However, it is important to bear in mind that, in the context of the various partial systems of (modern) world society, the economy (associated with technics and the dimension of science linked therewith) constitutes the most relevant factor and the one to be observed primarily. In other words, the economy is equipped with the strongest binary code between a 'yes' and a 'no', that is, the difference between 'having' and 'not having'. In some cases, especially in situations where there are enormous inequalities and widespread exclusion with regard to the economic system, this primacy may lead to experiences of economically conditioned de-differentiation in the sphere of the world economy, a problem that is persistent in the social constellation of peripheral modernity.[106]

If the primacy of economics can be affirmed on the structural plane, it should be noted that at the level of semantics, i.e. self-description of society, the mass media system assumes primacy in world society. The reason is that this system, which reproduces itself on the basis of the difference 'information/not information', operates selectively in response to the various possible self-descriptions of society.[107] On this topic Luhmann says: 'The messages that the mass media broadcast from day to day and from fact to fact crystallise what is treated in societal communication as "knowledge".'[108] Thus religious, pedagogic, legal and political 'knowledge', as well as scientific, technical and economic 'knowledge', acquire meaning for 'public opinion' only after passing through the selective filter of the media.[109] It can be said that the scientific knowledge that predominates for 'public opinion' is that determined by the media. However, this does not mean that knowledge selected by the media is immediately valid for all social spheres, as having primacy does not mean being the centre of the society's semantics. Science, education, economics etc are not necessarily reproduced via construction by the media; there may be 'critical' reactions within a given social sphere against the 'absurdity' or 'simplification' produced by the media. But these reactions will be treated as an expression of 'knowledge' on the plane of overall societal communication only if they are again selected and

[103] Luhmann, 1975, especially 55 and 57 *f*; 1981a, 32 and 149 *ff*; 1973a, 5; Neves, 1992, 75 *f*. Luhmann later moves away from this position to emphasise the horizontality of autopoietic systems, thus proposing a radicalisation of the thesis of autopoiesis (*see*, eg, 1988a, especially 27; 1997, vol 2, especially 747 *f* and 762 *f*). In respect of systems theory, Fischer-Lescano and Teubner (2006, 7) have recently returned to the former position.

[104] Luhmann 1981a, 150.

[105] Luhmann, 1975, 63 *f*.

[106] Neves, 1992, especially 72 *ff*.

[107] *See* Luhmann, 1997, vol 2, 1096 *ff*.

[108] Luhmann, 1997, vol 2, 1106. Based on different theoretical assumptions (such as the notion of 'hybrids'), Latour (1997, 9) argues that 'reading the daily paper is modern man's form of prayer'.

[109] Public opinion is understood here as the 'medium' produced and reproduced by the system of mass communications, ie the media (*cf* Luhmann, 1997, vol 2, 1098).

transmitted by the media. Thus scientific, educational, medical, economic, and technical 'knowledge' with validity for 'public opinion' as produced and reproduced by the media are not identical to (and indeed often diverge radically from) the 'knowledge' internally constructed by science, education, medicine, and economics, although the former predominate over the latter, constituting society's 'knowledge' as opposed to the specialised 'knowledge' of experts.

An important point to consider about world society is that the systems that have primacy on the structural and semantic planes, that is economics (associated with technics and science) and the media respectively, do not depend on territorial segmentation for self-reproduction. In the case of politics, the situation is different. Although politics is a world society system, its reproduction still depends closely on territorial segmentation into states. Politics differentiated itself first and foremost as a functional system of world society, since it differs from other spheres of communication. This primary form of differentiation of the world political system – the functional – is associated with a secondary one, that is, its segmentary differentiation into 'political systems' which are territorial. These, in turn, are differentiated at a tertiary level in terms of the distinction between the state and other political organisations of each territorial system, in accordance with the schema 'centre/periphery'.[110] Strictly speaking, states are the organisations that enable the political system of world society, differentiated primarily according to the functional model, to be differentiated internally in segmentary fashion into various territorially delimited subsystems. According to Luhmann, this second differentiation of the political system conditioned by statehood persists today because the premises for political legitimation are still linked to regional contexts, and there are no prospects of a comprehensive world politics that could dispense with the formation of states – because the chances of collectively binding decision making still remain strongly dependent on political processes that develop first and foremost on the respective territorial plane.[111] These observations on politics can be applied by analogy to law, insofar as 'the structural coupling of the political system and the legal system through constitutions does not have an equivalent at the level of global society'.[112] To a certain extent, this persistent dependence of territorial segmentation on states, especially with regard to the problem of legitimation, makes politics and law relatively weak compared with the systems that are reproducing themselves with increasing intensity on the global plane and developing primarily on the basis of cognitive expectations, either on the structural plane (economics, technics, and science) or at the semantic level (mass media), without depending on territorial segmentation.

But the growing strength of the systems based primarily on cognitive expectations, either on the structural plane (economics, technics, and science) or at the semantic level (mass media) of world society, have made practically inevitable

[110] Luhmann, 2000a, 244.
[111] *See* Luhmann, 1998, 375 *f*; 2000a, 222 *f*; 2005, 72.
[112] Luhmann, 1993a, 582 [Engl trans 2004, 487 *f*].

the emergence of a 'new world order' concerning not only collectively binding decision-making processes, but also mechanisms for stabilising normative expectations and legally controlling behaviour. This entails a transformation in the sense of a normative counterpart to the dynamic expansion of the cognitive momentum of world society.

This new world order can be understood in two basic ways depending on the dimension foregrounded. One is as 'an order based on an intricate three-dimensional web of links between disaggregated state institutions'. Anne-Marie Slaughter explains:

> A disaggregated world order would be a world latticed by countless government networks. These would include horizontal networks and vertical networks; networks for collecting and sharing information of all kinds, for policy coordination, for enforcement cooperation, for technical assistance and training, perhaps ultimately for rule making. They would be bilateral, plurilateral, regional, or global. Taken together, they would provide the skeleton or infrastructure for global governance.[113]

On one hand, according to Slaughter, these government networks would be clearly distinct from networks of global non-governmental organisations: although government actors might interact with a wide array of non-governmental actors, be they representatives of large corporations or civic movements, the dividing lines between the two would not disappear because government actors 'must represent all their different constituencies', whereas 'corporate and civic actors may be driven by profits and passions, respectively'.[114] On the other hand, government networks are not to be confused with the classic international system, which is located above the states, because they do not constitute an order designed to regulate states: 'In a world of government networks, by contrast, the same officials who are judging, regulating, and legislating domestically are also reaching out to their foreign counterparts to help address the governance problems that arise when national actors and issues spill beyond their borders.'[115] In sum, according to this model the new world order relates specifically to the work done in cooperation and conflict management networks linking various state actors, given the emergence of problems that go beyond the borders of the respective states.

A different school of thought emphasises networks of private and quasi-public actors in the global plane. Although the model of analysis relating to collisions between autonomous regulatory regimes points to large-scale networks that include a confluence of actors, organisations, and private and public regimes in the context of fragmentation of global law,[116] to some extent this perspective has underestimated the state dimension of the new world normative orders. In this regard, the following statement by Gunther Teubner stands out:

[113] Slaughter, 2004, 15 *f.*
[114] Slaughter, 2004, 10.
[115] Slaughter, 2004, 16.
[116] Fischer-Lescano and Teubner, 2006.

'Globalisation cuts the bonds that closely tie law to the democratically legitimated political discourse of the nation-state.'[117] While also stating that despite 'the importance of international relations and international private and public law, politics and law still have their centre of gravity in the nation-state',[118] he adds that the 'other social sectors have clearly overtaken politics and law on the road to globalisation' and stresses that in this process politics not only 'has lost its leading role'[119] 'but has clearly regressed compared with other partial spheres of society'.[120] Hence the demand for law to decouple from democratic politics in the state sphere and for emphasis on the 'civil constitutions' of world society.[121]

It seems to me that this diagnosis has not been confirmed empirically. The decline in the regulatory capacity of the state with the emergence of new global problems relates paradoxically to the increase in the duties the state is required to perform in order to address the new challenges of world society. In this sense it would seem more fruitful to adopt an approach which, without overlooking the emergence of new actors, systems, 'regimes', or global 'networks' with a claim to make collectively binding decisions and produce legal norms, can take into account the fact that the state is still a key focus for the reproduction of the new world normative order. As for Slaughter's model, however, it also seems problematic in propounding the idea of clear-cut boundaries between government networks and private or quasi-public networks of global actors.[122] What has actually occurred, in fact, is an entanglement or interweaving of state, international, supranational, transnational, and local orders under the umbrella of a 'multilevel' world legal system, and this is the foundation on which the transconstitutionalism of world society has developed.

V. FROM STRUCTURAL COUPLINGS TO TRANSVERSAL RATIONALITY

Modern multicentric society comprising a plurality of communication spheres in conflict with each other, and each with its own claim to autonomy, would be condemned to self-destruction if it did not develop mechanisms to enable the various social spheres to build links, and learn from and influence each other.

[117] Teubner, 1996c, 248.
[118] Teubner, 1997b, 5.
[119] *Ibid*.
[120] Teubner, 1996b, 259.
[121] Teubner, 2003a [Engl trans 2004b]. *See* below ch 2, at III.A. Teubner has recently relativised his thesis on societal constitutions by considering the constitution of the nation-state in connection with them (2012, especially 33 *ff* [Engl trans 2012, 15 *ff*]).
[122] Analogously to the distinction between a model that emphasises state actors (Slaughter) and a model that emphasises non-state actors (Teubner) in the new world order, Tushnet (2008, 4 *ff*) distinguishes between a perspective that privileges 'top-down processes' (Slaughter) and another that highlights 'bottom-up processes [by means of market processes] of the globalisation of constitutional law' (Tushnet, 7 *ff*, referring to Law, 2008), but this hierarchical image of processes does not appear to be well suited to an effort to understand emerging phenomena in a heterarchical world society.

But means that enable only event-related and instantaneous relations at the level of system operations, so-called 'operative couplings', are not enough. There must be structural links that enable the various autonomous spheres of communication to influence each other.

On this subject, Niklas Luhmann used the biological theory of Humberto Maturana and Francisco Varela[123] to develop the sociological concept of structural coupling.[124] The purpose of structural couplings is to promote and filter reciprocal influences and instigations between various autonomous systems in a lasting, stable and concentrated manner, linking them on the plane of the respective structures but without a loss of autonomy for any of these systems. Structural couplings are filters that exclude certain influences and facilitate others. There is a simultaneous relationship of independence and dependence between structurally coupled systems. Through structural couplings the structures of a system become relevant and even indispensable to the reproduction of the structures of another system and viceversa.

In the external relations between society and consciousness, Luhmann defines language as a structural coupling.[125] He argues that language enables instigation and reciprocal influence between communication and mental representations, mutually and selectively excluding some flows of meaning and admitting incorporation of others into each of the coupled systems. Language makes it possible for the content of communication, as elementary units formed by a synthesis of information, utterance, and comprehension, to be perceived within consciousness, albeit while internally switching meanings. In the relations between subsystems of a society, Luhmann elects various different forms of structural coupling that assure stable links between social processes in autonomous systems.

Thus, in the relations between economics and law, property and contract are presented as structural couplings between the economic and legal systems.[126] In the sphere of law, contract and property serve as orienting criteria for defining what is legal or illegal; in that of economics, instruments, criteria and programs orient profit according to the binary difference 'having/not having'. The economic and legal meanings of 'contract' remain specific to each of the systems, one primarily normative and the other primarily cognitive. However, no modern economy can do without the legal instruments for development, and modern law presupposes a fast dynamics of exchange, circulation and economic appropriation of goods and assets to maintain and permanently renovate the institutes of contract and property transfers.

[123] *See* Maturana and Varela, 1980, xx *f*; 2006 [1984], 49 *ff*; Maturana, 1982, 143 *ff*, 150 *ff*, 251 *ff* and 287 *ff*.

[124] *See in general* Luhmann, 1990c, 38 *ff* and 163 *ff*; 1993a, 400 *ff* [Engl trans 2004, 381 *ff*]; 1997, vol 1, 100 *ff*; vol 2, 778 *ff*; 2002b, 118 *ff*; Luhmann, 2000a, 372 *ff*; 2000c, 397 *ff*; Luhmann and De Giorgi, 1992, 33 *ff*.

[125] Luhmann, 1997, vol 1, 108 *ff*; 2005, 106 *ff*; Luhmann and De Giorgi, 1992, 36 *ff*.

[126] Luhmann, 1993a, 452 *ff* [Engl trans 2004, 390 *ff*]; 1997, vol 2, 783 *f*.

In the relations between economic and political systems, above all the fiscal regime of revenue and expenditure presents itself as a structural coupling.[127] It is indispensable for economic actors that fiscal policy, tax collection, and public spending are present so the economy and business can develop. At the same time, the regular functioning of the economy is indispensable for there to be a balanced system of revenue and expenditure that sustains the state. However, whereas for the political system the key point is that there should be conditions to prepare and make collectively binding decisions, for the economy the fiscal regime matters primarily from the standpoint of profit.

In addition to the aforementioned, Luhmann considers the following structural couplings between partial systems: assistance from experts in the relations between politics and science; universities in the links between education and science; degrees and certificates in the relations between economics and education; art galleries in the link between economics and art; medical certificates in the relations between medicine and economics; public opinion in the connections between politics and the mass media system.[128] Finally, he points to the constitution as a structural coupling between politics and law,[129] a question to which I will return in the next section.

Structural couplings are fundamentally mechanisms of concentrated and lasting *interpenetration* between social systems. In the context of Luhmannian theory, interpenetrations merely enable each system to place disordered complexity reciprocally at the disposal of the other's self-construction. In other words, 'the complexity each system makes available is an incomprehensible complexity – that is, disorder – for the receiving system'.[130] Thus, there is no possibility that, reciprocally, the 'preordered complexity'[131] and the very rationality processed by one of the systems can be placed at the disposal of the other, which would make them accessible to it as the receiving system. This is what permits the construction of a transversal rationality between autonomous spheres of communication in world society. Here we are not dealing with mere *operative* 'interferences' as defined by Teubner,[132] but rather with *structural* mechanisms that enable experiences to be constructively exchanged by various partial rationalities. The exchange will vary intensely in form and content in accordance with the type and singularity of the respective systems or discourses and their specific relations. Thus, in the sense used here, the concepts of transversal rationality and structural coupling are

[127] Luhmann, 1997, vol 2, 781; 2000a, 383 *f*. Structural coupling between politics and economics can also be seen in the reserve bank and the link between political success (election) and economic conditions (1993a, 451 [Engl trans 2004, 390]; 1997, vol 2, 781 *f*; 2000a, 385 *f*).

[128] Luhmann, 1997, vol 2, 784 *ff*; Luhmann, 2000a, 382 and 393 *ff*. However, according to Luhmann (1997, vol 2, 787), 'there are functional systems, such as religion, that form almost no structural couplings'.

[129] Luhmann, 1990a, 193 *ff*; 1993a, especially 470 *ff* [Engl trans 2004, 404 *ff*]; 2000a, 389–92; 1997, vol 2, 782 *f*.

[130] Luhmann, 1987c, 291 [Engl trans 1995, 214].

[131] Teubner, 1989, especially 110; 1988, 55 *ff*.

[132] *Ibid*.

closely related, since affirmation of the former supposes the existence of the latter. However, the notion of transversal rationality entails a plus with regard to that of structural coupling.

The concept of transversal rationality I am using derives from that of the transversal reason proposed by Wolfgang Welsch,[133] but here it is reconstructed in light of other theoretical presuppositions. According to Lyotard, Welsch considers multicentric society from the standpoint of the heterogeneity of 'language games'.[134] This means there is no supraordered discourse imposed on the others as regulator. Imposition of one of the fields of language on the others would mean destruction of the heterogeneity of the discursive spheres and the respective communication systems. However, he does not accept the postmodern idea that there is no metadiscourse or metanarrative which serves as a yardstick for particular discourses, especially in relations among them.

From this perspective, Welsch proposes the concept of 'transversal reason', which 'does not have the status of a hyperintellect, but precisely the status of reason – of an ability not to impose decrees but to make transitions'.[135] In other words, it is a reason that is not embodied in particular language games but, on the contrary, is involved with entanglements that serve as 'bridges of transition' between heterogeneous genres of language.[136] Welsch thus speaks of a 'postmodern metanarrative'. Unlike the 'old' metanarrative, which imposes itself via oppression on particular discourses, its effect on the latter is not 'voluntarily or involuntarily oppressive, but consciously liberating'.[137] He adds: 'It might be said directly that it is the only true *meta* narrative – the others were actually mere particular narratives functionally converted into metanarratives'.[138]

For Welsch, this metanarrative is 'entirely empty of content', expressing itself both in the descriptive and normative perspective. From the descriptive standpoint it can be represented by the following utterance: 'There are distinct forms of life, systems of orientation, types of discourse, and so on, with basic differences'. And normatively as follows: 'The various different concepts should not be measured, discredited or coactively united in the name of a supermodel – which in reality could only be a partial model (corresponding to a particular narrative).'[139] The normative dimension points to a link between transversal reason and justice, with the latter conceived as a 'new guiding idea' for the

[133] Welsch, 1996; 2002, 295 *ff*.

[134] Welsch, 1991; 1996, 401 *ff* Lyotard (1979, 20 *ff*) refers to types of language game grouped according to the dominant utterance, eg denotative, performative and prescriptive, alongside question, promise, literary description and narration, noting that they are determined by a 'complex of rules' (p 22). The conceptual framework for Lyotard's discussion of language games derives in turn from Wittgenstein (1997 [1945–1949], 250, § 23), who stresses that there are countless types of language game. *See* Teubner, 1996a, especially 218; Ladeur, 1992, especially 41–5.

[135] Welsch, 1996, 759; *see* 2002, 296.

[136] Welsch, 1996, 754.

[137] Welsch, 1991, 178.

[138] *Ibid*.

[139] Welsch, 1991, 178 *f*; *see* 2002, 227 *ff*.

former.[140] It is a 'justice without consensus',[141] or more precisely, as 'justice faced by the heterogeneous',[142] it is grounded in 'a primary consensus on the fact that at the second level, that of content, profound dissensions are legitimate', or to use a more radical formulation, in a 'consensus precisely on the fact that what is at stake is a basic dissensus according to which it is no longer possible to *agree on the content*'.[143] He clarifies:

> For under contemporary conditions it is necessary precisely to reckon with the possibility that the activity of reason does not ultimately lead to consensus, but rather to the articulation of basic dissensus. Without doubt, in this case, too, the intent to reach an understanding continues to orient the discussion – but it ends with an understanding on the impossibility of agreement about the content.[144]

First of all, justice plays the role of acting correctively on particular forms of rationality, while intervening in the relations among them to prevent exclusions, 'accretions', and totalisations, and assuring rational interchange and rationality itself in conflicts among them.[145] Ultimately, it serves to maintain the 'plurality of the whole',[146] that is, the differences between the various levels of a discursive world that is heterogeneous in complex ways.

In this regard, the model of justice proposed by Welsch resembles the concepts of justice propounded by two authors with sharply differing theoretical assumptions: on one hand, the understanding of justice in terms of 'deconstruction', as formulated theoretically by Derrida, who influenced Welsch.[147] According to this understanding, justice, unlike law, cannot be 'deconstructed' because it is itself 'deconstruction'.[148] As in the idea of justice as metanarrative, justice as deconstruction enjoys a privileged position. On the other hand, the idea of spheres of justice put forward by Michael Walzer[149] resembles Welsch's formulation to some extent. This is especially clear in Walzer's definition of complex equality: 'What the equality norm demands is a society in which those men who have more money, power or technical knowledge – and such men will always exist – are prevented from taking possession of any other social good just because they have more money, power or knowledge.'[150] But Welsch's formulation is more comprehensive and ambitious because it claims that justice serves transversal reason as enunciated in an all-encompassing metanarrative.

Welsch does not deny that the 'postmodern metadiscourse' occupies a supraordered position in relation to the corresponding particular narratives:

[140] Welsch, 1996, 698 *ff*.
[141] Welsch, 1996, 323, note 37, invoking Lyotard, 1979, 106.
[142] Welsch, 1991, 176, based on Lyotard, 1983, 256.
[143] Welsch, 1991, 179 and 181.
[144] Welsch, 1996, 937.
[145] Welsch, 1996, 702 *ff*.
[146] Welsch, 1996, 707–15.
[147] *See* Welsch, 1996, 245–302.
[148] Derrida, 1994, 35 [Engl trans 1990, 945].
[149] Walzer, 1983.
[150] Walzer, 1998, 12.

'A metanarrative is by definition a narrative that is structurally superior to particular narratives while also referring to them, implicitly or explicitly, with consequences for its feature and proportion.'[151] In this respect his formulation differs from the postmodern paradigm, according to which a discourse unrelated to the heterogeneity of language games, as in the case of politics for Lyotard (see note 92 above), is considered a 'non-discourse' that threatens the multiplicity of discursive genres and the contest between them. On the contrary, according to Welsch the supraordered metadiscourse acts as guarantor and promoter of the heterogeneity of language games.

Although Welsch refers to a metanarrative that is 'highly formal, not linked to content such as particular narratives',[152] his concepts of an all-encompassing transversal reason and a supraordered postmodern metanarrative seem debatable under the conditions of reproduction of a multicentric, polycontextural world society. Given that various differences, claims to autonomy, and self-descriptions of society are found in very distinct reciprocal relationships, the idea of an all-encompassing reason and a related metadiscourse becomes meaningless for the differentiated domains of communication. Every sphere of communication, when connected to another, can develop its own stable mechanisms of mutual learning and influence. It is appropriate therefore to speak of partial transversal rationalities capable of serving the constructive relations among the particular rationalities of the systems of language games that are in confrontation. Each partial transversal rationality is structurally coupled with the corresponding particular rationalities and acts as a specific 'bridge of transition' between them.

Transversal rationality, like structural coupling, is a two-sided form. The negative side of structural coupling is the reciprocal blocking of systemic autonomy via corruption of the systems involved. Here the code of one of the systems is sabotaged by the code of another system, so that the former loses its ability to reproduce consistently. Thus, if the code 'having/not having' (economics) corrupts the rules of the democratic game, via the electoral process or taxation, directly sabotaging the code of politics (the democratically constructed difference between government and opposition), systemic corruption will follow if the political system proves unable to react to negative superimposition by the economy, in accordance with its own criteria and programmes. Conversely, however, subsidies politically granted to inefficient economic groups who support the government may be seen as political corruption of the economy, amounting to political sabotage of the economic code. Analogous problems occur in the relations between law and economics. Bribing a judge to 'buy' a favourable verdict, or a policeman to obtain an indictment or a public prosecutor to win favours in an investigation (or have charges dismissed), constitutes corruption of law by the economy, imposing the code 'having/not having'

[151] Welsch, 1991, 177.
[152] Welsch, 1991, 178.

directly on the difference 'legal/illegal' in the solution of primarily legal problems. If the law is unable to react to this intrusion, the result is an episode of systemic corruption. It also necessary to treat political corruption of the law, for example in those cases where power succeeds in obtaining legally inconsistent decisions from the courts, police, or public prosecutors by using illicit pressure, and where the law is unable to fight back using its own codes and criteria. There are innumerable cases of systemic corruption, the negative side of structural coupling, including the systematic corruption of law and also of politics by the family code 'kin/not kin', the amorous code 'love/lovelessness', and the diffuse difference between friend and enemy.

On this topic, Luhmann[153] – albeit affirming the fragmentation of morality as a special form of communication because in his view the binary code of morality, that is, the difference between esteeming and disesteeming people, is not compatible with generalised criteria or programmes – refers to systemic corruption as the moral problem of contemporary world society:

> In sum, the autonomy of functional systems, guaranteed by specific binary codes, excludes metaregulation by a moral supercode *and morality itself accepts, and indeed remoralises, this condition*. Thus, code sabotage now becomes the moral problem, such as corruption in politics and law, doping in sport, the purchase of love, or fraud in empirical research data.[154]

With the 'supercode' and the 'moral integration of society' ruled out, and the 'polycontextural form of societal self-observation' thus affirmed, morality 'concentrates its attention on pathologies'[155] and acts diffusely in the context of social systems via a binary code that helps assure their autonomy by raising the alarm and 'denouncing' sabotage of the respective codes and corresponding systemic corruption.

Systemic corruption may remain in the operative plane, in which case it is momentary and only event-related. It becomes problematic when it reaches the structural level, in which case it acts on the plane of stabilisation of expectations. If so, there is a certain guarantee that the corrupted system will be unable to react to episodes of corruption. The problem becomes serious in social contexts of hypercomplex contemporary society, when structural corruption of one system by another tends to become generalised. In this case there is not only a danger of de-differentiation but a concrete episode of systemic de-differentiation. In the sphere of systems theory, I have referred elsewhere to this situation as a case of the allopoiesis of law, meaning that the system in question is directly determined (not merely conditioned) by another or by others and incapable of consistent self-production or operative closure.[156] In a sense, although he insists on the primacy of functional differentiation in modern society,[157] Luhmann

[153] Luhmann, 1990d; 1993b.
[154] Luhmann, 1997, vol 2, 1043. *Cf* Teubner, 1998a, 21 *f*.
[155] Luhmann, 1997, vol 2, 1043.
[156] Neves, 1995; 2007a, 140 *ff*.
[157] *See*, eg, Luhmann, 1997, vol 2, 743 *ff*; 1994, 4 *f*; 1993a, 572 [Engl trans 2004, 480].

admits this link between extreme systemic corruption and lack of autopoiesis: 'In the most extreme cases, there is no autopoietic closure to be found.'[158] Thus, in the absence of operative autonomy for one of the systems involved, extreme systemic corruption prevents construction of the respective structural coupling. In this case, for broad social contexts and regions of the planet, we are dealing with a 'pathology of normalcy', to quote Erich Fromm with respectful irony,[159] although not with traditional hierarchically differentiated societies in which the notion of systemic corruption is not present and the corresponding moral problem therefore does not exist.[160] In contemporary world society, even where systemic corruption occurs as a 'pathology of normalcy', the problem of code sabotage reappears, close up or from afar, as a moral problem.

To take a step forward and reflect a little more upon transversal rationality, it is worth noting that its negative side is not exhausted by systemic corruption. Systemic corruption refers to a breakdown in the capacity for consistent reproduction (self-reference) due to external blockages that undermine the selective function of structural couplings. At the level of the entanglements that act as 'bridges of transition' constituting transversal rationalities between heterogeneous social spheres (learning and reciprocal exchange between partial rationalities via structural interferences), the negative side resides specifically in autism and in expansion of one sphere of rationality without recognition of the other. Alterity is denied, given that one sphere of rationality loses the capacity to learn from the other or has a negative impact on its development.

In the former case, the problem is associated with the 'danger of atomisation'.[161] Excessive focus on a specialty leads to lethargy with regard to the other forms of rationality present in society. The 'antidote' to atomisation, that is the construction of 'entanglements',[162] is not imposed in these cases; instead, there is indifference and apathy toward them on the part of the 'autistic' system. To some extent, it is appropriate to associate this situation with the stabilisation of '*Fachidiotismus*' ('craft idiocy') on the systemic plane of communication and expectations. Two consequences flow from this problem. On one hand, internal consistency becomes something absolute, neglecting the need for the system to match its environment. In other words, there is excessive redundancy and a low degree of variety.[163] The system or discourse tends to become insular and crystallised. Related to this on the other hand, there is a negative or inadequate effect on the other social spheres. A system has a certain inability to offer its structures, through entanglement, as criteria to be incorporated constructively by another. Evidently this calls for

[158] Luhmann, 1993a, 82 [Engl trans 2004, 110]. In the sphere of law, this also entails the impossibility of 'any cognitive learning in relation to norms' (*ibid*).

[159] Fromm, 1956, 12 *ff*.

[160] *Cf* Luhmann, 1983a, 64 *f*, note 10.

[161] *See* Welsch, 1996, 433–5.

[162] Welsch, 1996, 434 *f*.

[163] On the balanced combination of redundancy and variety as a condition for autonomy, *see* Atlan, 1979. *Cf* Neves, 1992, 80 *f*.

so-called re-entry,[164] provided incorporation entails a discursive exchange of information in the receiving system. However, the key trait is a degree of external inadequacy in the response to the other because of a limit to heteroreference. Both aspects of 'atomisation', acting as the negative side of a specific transversal rationality, impair the respective particular rationalities of the systems involved, since the concept of rationality refers basically to the internally consistent and externally adequate reproductive capacity of any system or language game. Excessive consistency to the detriment of adequacy entails irrationality.[165]

In addition to 'atomisation', there is a danger of 'imperialist expansion' by one rationality against the rest. To use a metaphor *à la française*, it might be said that one tree tends to grow in a garden in such a way that its roots and branches may prevent or jeopardise the survival of the others.[166] This is not necessarily a matter of systemic corruption by means of code sabotage. As the negative side of transversal rationality, this situation may merely mean that communication codes have been weakened by the excessive force of another, without a breakdown of internal communication in a given system via external blockages. In the case of contemporary society, as noted above, this tendency contrary to transversal rationality is found above all in the economy and the media, which have primacy in the structural and semantic planes, respectively.

However, primacy of one sphere is not sufficient to characterise the 'expansion' of a field without recognition of the relevance of another's unique rationality. The 'hegemony' of one field does not imply its 'imperial expansion'.[167] There may be primacy without neglecting the importance of another communicative or discursive sphere, that is, without consequently underestimating its significance to heterogeneous society. 'Imperial expansion' as the negative side of transversal rationality occurs when a system with a strong code relegates another to insignificance and in doing so not only impairs the 'bridges of transition', but also prevents the respective systems from acting adequately toward society: in one case because of a hypertrophic tendency, in the other because of an atrophic propensity. In this respect, discussing the question of justice in a recent paper, Teubner also points to 'justicialisation', or 'the imperialism of legal rationality, parallel to economic, political and scientific expansionism' (and one might add 'mediatisation'), as one of the disastrous imperialisms of a partial rationality that lead to 'unidirectional' processes of self-regulation oriented by a specific formula of contingency (justice, scarcity, legitimacy, limitationality, and so forth) and thus incompatible with the heterogeneity of society: 'All these contingency formulas promise to produce the good society, although in fact they can give only partial answers for their limited sector.'[168] Thus the

[164] Spencer Brown, 1971, 56 *f* and 69 *ff*.

[165] The irrationality that results from systemic corruption can be defined conversely, as excessive external adequacy to the detriment of consistency (subjection to another).

[166] *See* Deleuze and Guattari, 1976, 12 *ff*; Welsch, 1996, 356 *ff*.

[167] In a different argumentative context, *see* Buckel, 2007, 221 *ff*.

[168] Teubner, 2008, 32 *f* [Engl trans 2009, 23].

expansionary partial rationality does not recognise its own limits and is therefore unwilling to integrate constructively with the entanglements that promote transversal rationalities, preventing the other spheres from contributing adequately to heterogeneous society.

Just as systemic corruption – the downside of structural couplings – constitutes a moral problem of contemporary world society, 'atomisation' and the 'imperial expansion' of a particular rationality – the downside of transversal rationalities – can also lead to moral issues. This is a matter of the morality of structural dissensus, reproduced diffusely and requiring an exchange and respect for the plurality of perspectives of observation and description of society. It implies the presence of a certain 'moral reason' which does not constitute a 'supercode', yet runs transversally and fragmentarily through the various particular rationalities, and 'orders one to look ahead, to include alternatives and dissension, and reflect on their relations'.[169] Thus, as already noted above, 'only a consensus about the dissensus [between different types of rationality] can present itself *legitimately*'.[170] This fragmentary morality of dissensus acts as a condition of the possibility of autonomy and rationality of particular systems and discourses – both on the inside and on the outside – insofar as it is a condition of the possibility of the emergence, maintenance, and development of transversal rationalities in multicentric society. The 'self-sufficiency' or 'imperialism' of a given partial and particular rationality tends to lead, in any part of the planet, close up or from far away, to reactions of contempt but also of shock and indignation. In this case, too, it is possible to speak of a 'pathology of normalcy', especially in the form of continuous episodes of 'imperialism' of economic, political, or media rationality at the expense of other rationalities,[171] but this does not exclude the persistent moral reactions of contempt in the various contexts of world society. Without doubt, transversal rationality is a 'scarce product' of the contemporary social world, but this does not exclude its being both a functional requirement and a normative claim characteristic of today's world society.

It is appropriate to note that, like structural couplings, the entanglements that serve as 'bridges of transition' for transversal rationalities vary intensely in their characteristics, proportions, and meanings, according to the type of system involved. But the existence of a structural coupling, albeit a necessary condition, is not a sufficient condition for transversal rationality to be present. The structural couplings serve rather to guarantee reciprocal autonomies via the selection of influences, relating disordered complexities in reciprocal observa-

[169] Welsch, 1996, 941 *f*.

[170] Welsch, 1996, 322 (my emphasis). *See* Neves, 2006a, 136 *ff*.

[171] There are also strong tendencies for religion to expand destructively in the form of 'fundamentalism' (Ladeur and Augsberg, 2008), but these already imply internal de-differentiation of the religious system itself, since their goal is to eliminate 'segmentary differentiation' in various religions (Luhmann, 2000b, 272; *cf* Tyrell, 2005, 43 *f*, with arguments against the adequacy of the concept of segmentary differentiation in the case of a plurality of religions) and hence they are necessarily also irrational from the internal standpoint of religion.

tion (stable and concentrated interpenetration). The entanglements that promote transversal rationality contribute above all to exchange and reciprocal learning between experiences with different rationalities, entailing the mutual sharing of complexity pre-ordered by the systems involved and thus comprehensible to the receiver (stable and concentrated interference in the plane of structures). For example, a transversal rationality does not necessarily emerge from contract and property, structural couplings that permit irritation and reciprocal influence between economics and law. Transversal rationality will be present only if contract and property are structured so as to contribute positively to the development of both systems: economically inadequate legal regulation of contracts and property does not imply transversal rationality; conversely, a well-structured contract and property regime from the economic standpoint may act negatively against juridical rationality with regard to the legal rights of those involved or of third parties. Similarly, the fiscal regime of revenue and expenditure, a structural coupling between politics and economics, will not lead to transversal rationality if fiscal policy is detrimental to the economy; or, even if it is economically superadequate, it acts negatively on the democratic legitimacy of political decisions. The same can be said of the constitution as a structural coupling between politics and law: it may or may not contribute to the construction of a transversal rationality between the two systems, with the negative contribution hypothesis being likely where there is a tendency to judicialise politics and politicise law.

Lastly, it is relevant to note that in Luhmann's systems theory, structural coupling is presented bilaterally as a mechanism between two autonomous systems. With regard to transversal rationality, it can be suggested that the entanglement of more than two systems is involved in certain cases. To take the fiscal regime as an example, it can be seen to contain a trilateral entanglement of politics, economics, and law. Taxation is an economic, legal and political fact, just as the budget is an institution directly involved with the economy, the law and politics. Transversal rationality therefore entails a degree of learning and constructive exchange between these three systems. The same goes for the central bank, which is entangled with politics, economics and law. Analogously, it is clear that just as the results of an election both depend on and influence economic conditions (cf. note 127 above), under the constitutional state elections are directly linked to their legal regulation, and this also entails the requirement of a transversal rationality that can enable a constructive exchange between politics, law and economics. In some cases, however, it is not a matter of trilaterality, but rather of organisations that make several structural couplings possible. Thus, for example, universities not only require a transversal rationality between the scientific and educational systems, but depending on the school, institute, department, or laboratory also develop bilateral entanglements that serve distinct transversal rationalities: between education and medicine in medical schools (or more broadly between the healthcare system and education system in health centres); between law and education in law schools; between education and art in arts centres; between the economy and education in schools of economics; between education and technics in the strict sense in polytechnics, and so on.

An understanding of these theoretical presuppositions is essential to the argumentation developed below, based on the concepts of transversal constitution and transconstitutionalism, assuming not only structural couplings but also entanglements as 'bridges of transition'. Without these, even if systemic corruptions on the structural plane are overcome, we will remain stuck in an autistic constitutionalism that will be provincial[172] and self-sufficient (endangering atomisation), or slide toward imperial constitutionalism as *ultima ratio* of the social world.

[172] Indeed, as asserted by a renowned American constitutionalist, 'we should resist the temptations of a provincial particularism' (Ackerman, 1997, 794).

2

From Transversal Constitution . . .

I. THE CONSTITUTION OF CONSTITUTIONALISM

THE CONCEPT OF constitution in the modern sense dates from the historical experience of constitutionalism associated with the revolutionary movements of the late eighteenth century. Constitutionalism initially presented itself as politico-juridical *semantics* that reflected structural pressure for differentiation between politics and law in the context of the emergence of the multicentric society of the modern era. Constitutionalist semantics reacted constructively at the level of *structures*, serving as a revolutionary 'ideology' for the appearance of constitutions as artefacts that made possible and guaranteed the difference between the political and legal systems. Although constitutionalist semantics arose at the centre of emerging bourgeois society, especially in Britain and France, the constitution was first affirmed at the structural level 'in 1776 on the periphery of what was then the western world, in North America', only reaching Europe 'thirteen years later, in 1789'.[1] As already noted (see p 18), in Britain the process of constitutionalisation was evolutionary: despite its name, the 1688 Glorious Revolution cannot be considered to have founded a constitution in the modern sense, since it was 'a revolution in defence of the old order, namely the rights of parliament, against the crown's transformative designs'.[2] This is associated with the fact that the practical conversion of constitutionalist semantics into constitutional structures presupposed the occurrence of a revolution in the sense of a clean break with the old political order.[3]

Thus, the concept of constitution discussed here is not a historical or universal one.[4] Normally this concept presents itself at the empirical level, showing

[1] Grimm, 2004a, 1. *Cf* Luhmann, 1993a, 470 [Engl trans 2004, 404].

[2] Grimm, 2004a, 4.

[3] *See* Grimm, 1987, 45 *f* and 56 *f*; 1989, 633 *f*.

[4] Canotilho, 1991, 59. According to this historical–universal concept, the formula 'no state without a constitution' is valid (Biaggini, 2000, 447). Writing from the perspective of a history of the constitution, Koselleck (2006) extends the concept to include 'all legally regulated institutions and their forms of organisation, without which a social community of action is not politically capable of acting'. And he clarifies this as follows: 'My proposal that the history of the constitution should encompass all domains characterised by repeatability by virtue of legal rules is therefore designed to bridge the gap between premodern histories of law and modern histories of the constitution so as to include not just interstate but also post-state and to some extent suprastate phenomena of our times' (2006, 370 *f*).

that every society or state has basic structural power relations that also determine juridical forms. According to this conception, which is to be found in authors as disparate as Engels, Lassalle and Weber,[5] the presence of a constitution cannot be excluded from any social order, including archaic societies, since basic structures of 'diffuse power'[6] exist there too. But the historical-universal concept also presents itself in the idea of a constitution in the material sense as a set of supreme positive legal norms,[7] since a supreme normative nucleus can be detected in any legal order. A concept of this type could exclude primitive legal orders, insofar as they lack the secondary rules of organisation, especially the ultimate rule of recognition, considered as a constitution in the material sense; nevertheless, for each and every state there must be a constitution (ultimate rules of recognition).[8] Lastly, the culturalist concept may also be historical-universal, when it defines a state constitution either as the 'dialectics' of political normality and juridical normativity[9] or as a 'process of integration',[10] since 'dialectics' and 'processes' of this kind can be found in any type of state including premodern, absolutist and authoritarian states. It is very hard to analyse the specificity of the meaning and function of a constitution as one of the few 'achievements of modern civilisation' that are 'the result of intentional planning',[11] when the analytical tools to be used are these historical-universal concepts.[12]

The decisionist concept is equally unsuited to an analysis of the constitution in the modern sense. In defining the 'constitution in a positive sense' as 'the complete decision over the type and form of the political unity',[13] Schmitt subordinates law immediately to politics, especially because constitutional laws ('the relative concept of the Constitution')[14] are subordinated to the fundamental political decision.[15] From the point of view of constitutionalism, this concept is strictly speaking not historical-universal, since it applies only to states that lack the functional differentiation between law and politics, with the former being an epiphenomenon of the latter. It is not a concept that can be used to analyse and understand the constitution of constitutionalism, since this constitution presupposes differentiation between the political and legal systems, so that law is operationally autonomous with regard to politics.

As part of the broad process of change in the primary form of social differentiation in certain spatial spheres of modern society from the hierarchical to the

[5] Engels, 1988 [1844], especially 572 *ff*; Lassalle, 1987 [1862], 130; Weber, 1985 [1922], 27.

[6] Burdeau, 1949, 249–51.

[7] Kelsen, 1960, 228–30; 1946, 124 *f*; 1925, 251–3.

[8] *Cf* Hart, 1994, 91–123 *ff*, especially 107. Hart also speaks of 'constitutional matters' in respect of the secondary rules for alteration (1994, 60).

[9] Heller, 1934, 249 *ff*.

[10] Smend, 1968 [1928], especially 136 *ff* and 189–91.

[11] Luhmann, 1990a, 176.

[12] *Cf* Luhmann, 1990a, 212.

[13] Schmitt, 1993 [1928], 20–36 [Engl trans 2008, 75–88].

[14] Schmitt, 1993 [1928], 11–20 [Engl trans 2008, 67–74] .

[15] *See* Schmitt, 1993 [1928], especially 22 [Engl trans 2008, 76].

functional type, the idea of a supreme political power above the law, orienting the absolutist notion of sovereignty, lost its meaning owing to pressure from movements for the differentiation of law with regard to politics. This development was not linear: it entailed reactions and was fully accomplished only in very limited portions of the planet. It was associated with the appearance of the constitution as a social construction of modernity. The constitution is the mechanism that makes differentiation between politics and law possible in the sphere of states. However, it is a mechanism whose development depends on substantial social presuppositions. Without a certain social context of functional differentiation and social inclusion, there is no place for a constitution as a mechanism of reciprocal autonomy between law and politics. Without functional differentiation of the various social spheres, and without a clear and radical distinction between society and the individual as person, it is impossible to conceive of fundamental rights as a response of the legal system to these social processes of differentiation.[16] Similarly, if politics is not autonomous with regard to the particular values of family, ethnic and religious groups, and with regard to concrete economic interests, it is impossible to construct democracy as the generalised support that enables operative closure of the political system.

At the same time as it makes possible the differentiation between politics and law, the constitution acts as a structural coupling between these two functional systems of modern society.[17] On one hand, the constitution makes the difference code 'legal/illegal' relevant to the political system; this means the requirements of the rule of law and fundamental rights become structural contours for the reproduction of the political processes involved in the pursuit of power and the making of collectively binding decisions, not least because democratically deliberated majority decisions can be declared unconstitutional. On the other hand, it makes the difference code 'power/not power' or, in contemporary terms, 'government/opposition', relevant to the legal system. This means the democratic process of political decision making, in terms of the formation of a majority, becomes a structural variable in the reproduction of the legal procedures for conflict resolution and absorption, not least because the production of legal norms by the legislature is dependent on political decisions that are democratically deliberated and made by a majority.

This structural coupling is concretised and realised by means of constitutionally instituted procedures – judicial, administrative, legislative-parliamentary, electoral, and directly democratic – on a scale that runs from emphasis on legal rationality in the first (judicial) to prevalence of political rationality in the last (parliamentary, electoral, and directly democratic). Thus there is a political legitimation of law (democracy) and a legal legitimation of politics (rule of law). Evidently, the relationship established by the constitution as a structural coupling is not one of harmony, but a paradoxical one of reciprocal complementation and

16 Luhmann, 1965.

17 Luhmann, 1990a, 193 *ff*; 1993a, especially 470 *ff* [Engl trans 2004, 404 *ff*]; 1997, vol 2, 782 *f*; 2000a, 389–92. On this topic *see* Neves, 2006a, 95 *ff*.

tension. The rule of law and fundamental rights without democracy find no guarantee of realisation, since any model of political exclusion stymies the legal principles of legality and equality which are inherent in the rule of law and fundamental rights, respectively.[18] Democracy without the rule of law or fundamental rights, in turn, degrades into a dictatorship of the majority. These are the dimensions of complementarity. On the other hand, the fact that democratically deliberated laws passed by a majority can be declared unconstitutional because they violate the rule of law and the fundamental rights guaranteed by the constitution points to the permanent tension between democratic politics and positive law in the constitutional state. In the limiting case this same tension also manifests itself when the democratic constituent power arises as the political impetus toward general reconstruction and refoundation of the state legal system. Thus, the constitution as structural coupling involves permanent complementarity and tension, as well as ruptures, between politics and law. However, this means it excludes the structural subordination of one system to another, especially of law to politics, developing instead a horizontal or orthogonal relationship between the two.

This ambivalence of the constitution enables it to be seen as both an instance of the political system and an institution of the legal system.[19] In the former case, it encompasses basic processes for decision making with regard to state building and rebuilding: that is, constituent, parliamentary, administrative-governmental, and electoral or direct democratic processes. Thus the constitution entails *basic structural circulation and contracirculation between administration* (in the broad sense of the procedures used by authorities for political decision making and execution), *politics* (in the narrow sense of the processes of party programme formation and choosing among people and programmes), the *public* as recipient of decisions, and the *people* as the public responding actively to the administration's decisions.[20] According to this concept of constitution, *'the people' closes the political system.* On this topic, invoking a classic formula from Rousseau,[21] Luhmann says: 'Closure of the system occurs at the point where the public, made up of individuals, groups and organisations, recipient of orders, administratively importuned, becomes the people; at the point where *la volonté de tous* becomes *lavolonté générale*'.[22] This means that aside from a *constitutional people*, a procedural construction of the constitution, there is no political legitimation as generalised support for the circulation of power, but only particularisms and personalisms that negate or corrupt democracy. From this perspective it can be said that the circular process of democracy is the constitution in the political sense, that is, the political dimension of the constitution as structural coupling.

[18] *Cf* Luhmann, 1965, 136 *f*.

[19] 'A certain synthesis of political and legal functions is indispensable – but on the particular basis of their different functions' (Luhmann, 1993a, 153 [Engl trans 2004, 165]).

[20] Luhmann, 2000a, 253 *ff*; *see*, albeit without referring to the 'people', 1981b, 42–9; 1981c, 164.

[21] Rousseau, 1922 [1762], Book II, ch III, especially 162.

[22] Luhmann, 2000a, 265.

From the standpoint of law, the constitution is the most comprehensive reflexive instance of the legal system, permeating all its spheres of validity – material, temporal, personal and territorial. As the norm of norms, it cuts transversally across the entire legal system, giving it consistency. The constitution entails a reflexive level of the code 'legal/illegal' within the system: the code 'constitutional/unconstitutional'. Constitutionality caps legality.[23] Thus, the constitution in the modern sense overcomes the jusnaturalist, external foundations of the law. Law is self-grounded constitutionally. Thus, 'the Constitution closes the legal system',[24] establishing normatively the basic procedures for recourse to the law. It allows the re-entry of politics into law via constitutional procedures, especially the legislative kind. On the other side of the coin, this means that the constitution structures the cognitive openness of the legal system by delimiting its capacity for learning and recycling, above all via the establishment of procedures for constitutional reform. However, the core of constitutional identity (the so-called 'entrenchment clauses') is the unsurpassable limit of the capacity for learning of the respective legal order, requiring a political rupture in the limiting case of comprehensive negation, in the form of a constituent power that reconstructs the structural coupling of the rule of law with democracy, in a new constitutional model. This establishes a new relationship between closure of the legal system by constitutional law and closure of the political system by a constitutional people.

The constitution as structural coupling and, at the same time, a mechanism of functional differentiation between politics and law that emerged in the wake of radical transformations of social structure in modernity, was – as already stressed – both factor and product of a new semantics, constitutionalism. This constitutionalist semantics is expressed paradigmatically in Article 16 of the Declaration of the Rights of Man & the Citizen, passed by the National Constituent Assembly of France in August 1789: 'Any society in which no provision is made for guaranteeing rights or for the separation of powers has no constitution.' In the American experience, the semantic formula presents itself analogously in affirmation of the Constitution as the 'grammar of liberty'.[25] In the widest sense, the constitutionalist semantics was manifested in the conception of popular sovereignty, the rule of law, and the rights of man and the citizen. While this semantics served to consolidate and fortify the new political and legal structures, it also played a relevant symbolic role, often of an ideological nature.

The existence of census suffrage in practically all countries called constitutional during the nineteenth century, excluding the masses from the political process, unquestionably proves that there was a mismatch between the semantics of

[23] In this sense, it can be said that the constitution has normative primacy and is self-enforcing in the legal order of the constitutional state (*see* Wahl, 2002, 198).

[24] Luhmann, 1990a, 187.

[25] 'The *American Constitutions* were to Liberty what a *grammar* is to language' (Paine, 1992 [1791–1792], 64). *Cf* Vorländer, 1999, 7; Biaggini, 2000, 458.

popular sovereignty and the structural limits of political democracy. The persistence of legal slavery until the second half of the nineteenth century and of institutionalised racial segregation until *Brown v Board of Education* (1954)[26] – officially, and in actuality until the advent of affirmative action in the 1960s[27] – is unquestionable proof of the chasm between constitutionalist semantics and the structural limits to fundamental rights in the United States.[28] Finally, it is worth recalling the Restoration in France, the British Crown's governmental powers until the early twentieth century and colonialism as structural limits to the rule of law in contrast with constitutionalist semantics. However, the gap between constitutional structures and constitutionalist semantics should not obscure the fact that in the states of central modernity this semantics led to the gradual consolidation of those structures. Thus despite all the structural limitations, the following self-description of constitutional states remains valid: *'the constitution closes the legal system'* and *'the people' closes the political system*, self-legitimating them.

II. THE TRANSVERSAL CONSTITUTION OF THE CONSTITUTIONAL STATE

Moving beyond the pure structural coupling concept, it is possible to understand the constitution of the constitutional state not merely as a filter for irritations and reciprocal influences between autonomous systems of communication, but also as an instance of the reciprocal and lasting relationship of learning and exchange of experiences with the particular rationalities already processed in politics and law, respectively. This involves entanglements between both systems in the form of 'bridges of transition', so a specific transversal rationality can develop. In terms of language games, it can be said a synthesis occurs here concurrently with a meaning commutation. The re-entry of politics entails a shared 'imaginary space' that makes a discursive commutation possible.[29] What is politically predefined is legally comprehensible via the constitution. Several constitutional procedures serve this exchange and mutual learning, enabling legal consistency and the political adequacy of law to contribute to political consistency and the legal adequacy of politics.

[26] *Brown et al v Board of Education of Topeka et al*, 347 US 483 (1954). For a brief commentary on this decision as an 'act of constitutional politics', *see* Ackerman, 1991, 133 *ff*. On the legacy for American constitutionalism, *see* Tushnet, 2004. On the international context, *see* Ginsburg, 2005a.

[27] *See* Kaufmann, 2007, 129 *ff*.

[28] Referring to the 'founding failures' of the US constitutional system, Ackerman (1998, 88) says: 'The most obvious is the Founders' politics of exclusion. To win the right to speak for the People, the Federalists did not suppose they needed to appeal to women or slaves or Native Americans.' And he warns: 'But the Founding project in dualist democracy would have lost all credibility if Americans had not moved far beyond the narrow Founding conception of We the People' (1998, 88 *f*). By 'dualist democracy' ('dualist constitution'), Ackerman means that feature of the US constitutional system that seeks 'to distinguish between two different decisions that may be made in a democracy. The first is a decision by the American people; the second, by their government' (1991, 6).

[29] Teubner (2008, 10 *f*) ([Engl trans 2009, 3]) stresses the connection between 're-entry' and 'imaginary space' in the work of Spencer Brown (1971, 69 *ff*).

It should be noted that the transversal constitution is not restricted to a structural connection at the level of first-order observation between systems. It presupposes that politics and law are constructively linked at the reflexive level, entailing second-order reciprocal observations. There are structural forms of transversality in the plane of specific ordinary legislation, concrete regulations, and so forth. However, in this case there is no claim to comprehensive reflexiveness in either of the two systems. In the case of the transversal constitution, the link occurs between two structural reflexive mechanisms: on one hand, the legal constitution as a set of norms of norms, or rather a process or structure of normatisation of normatisation processes; and on the other hand, the political constitution as decisions on decisions, or rather a decision-making process and structure governing collective binding decision-making processes.[30] This reflexive transversality enables learning to be intensified but may ultimately be parasitic upon one or both systems.

But how are the particular rationalities that are transversally linked via the state constitution constructed? On the side of law, it is appropriate to define its specific rationality as 'justice'.[31] This entails, in respect of the legal system, 'juridical consistency' in the plane of self-reference (normative closure) and 'adequacy' or 'complexity' adequate to society (cognitive openness), especially in processes of deciding court cases,[32] and is characterised as a 'formula for contingency' because it motivates action and communication in the legal sphere.[33]

If it cannot count on a legally consistent solution, the system loses its rationality. This means that in a legal system oriented primarily by constitutionality (and correspondingly by the constitutional principle of legality) – that is, without 'internal constitutional justice' – it is not possible to speak of legal rationality in a complex society. Decisions will therefore be subordinated to particularistic factors of all kinds, without a specific legal significance for the orientation of behaviour and the stabilisation of normative expectations. Thus, the rationality of law requires constitutional consistency in the legal system.

Furthermore, justice as legal rationality involves the social adequacy of law. Evidently this is a difficult question, since in the environment of law there are various claims to systemic autonomy in conflict. The economic adequacy of law, for example, may have negative impacts on education, the environment, the arts and science, and viceversa. Moreover, there are all kinds of different moral values and perspectives in today's complex and fragmented world society. Something that appears adequate to one group may appear inadequate to another. There is no single hegemonic project either in the plane of functional systems or that of the lifeworld, as noted by Sonja Buckel: 'There is not only one

[30] On reflexive mechanisms or reflexivity (processual self-reference), *see* respectively Luhmann, 1984a; 1987c, 601 and 610–16 [Engl trans 1995, 443 and 450–5]. *Cf* Neves, 2007a, 131 *f*.

[31] The concept of 'justice' evidently has a broader meaning, as a normative reference relating to the various different social spheres (*see* above pp 28 *f*; *cf* also Teubner, 2008 [Engl trans 2009]), but there is also a legal-systemic specificity in the problem of justice.

[32] Luhmann, 1993a, 225 *f*; 1988c, 26 *f*; 1981a, 374–418.

[33] Luhmann, 1993a, 214 *ff*. [Engl trans 2004, 211 *ff*].

project of this kind that could dominate the social context, but competing projects in correspondence with the multiplicity of antagonistic differences.'[34] Thus, the constitutionally grounded social adequacy of law may not signify an adequate response to specific claims of particular content, but instead the capacity to enable a range of different projects and perspectives to coexist non-destructively, leading to the legitimation of constitutionally established procedures, inasmuch as these procedures serve to reorient expectations toward the law, especially of those that have their claims rejected by legal decisions. In general, the constitutionally grounded social adequacy of law, that is, external constitutional justice based on procedures, requires from the legal system a highly developed cognitive capacity, considering the complexity and even the fragmentation of its environment. In respect of politics, this entails a constitutional model that supports pluralism with regard to parties, pressure groups, public opinion, and so on.

However, it is not possible to imagine a perfect balance between legal consistency and the social adequacy of law, that is, between internal and external constitutional justice. The justice of the legal system as a formula for contingency always entails an orientation that motivates behaviour and expectations that seek this balance, which is always imperfect and is defined in each concrete case. On one hand, a model of mere constitutional consistency leads to socially inadequate formalism. Excessive emphasis on juridico-constitutional consistency may lead to serious problems of social inadequacy of law, which thus loses its capacity to reorient normative expectations and hence to legitimate itself socially. On the other hand, a model of mere social adequacy leads to legally inconsistent realism. In the absence of congruently shared values, morals, and interests in the supercomplex modern society, an excessive emphasis on social adequacy tends to lead to the subordination of law to particular projects with a claim to absolute hegemony. In this sense, albeit always defective because it is never fully achieved and depends on experience in each case,[35] a balance between internal and external constitutional justice serves as an orientation for those involved in the network of communications of the state legal system. This is a functional paradox of law, since as a rule an increase in legal consistency entails a reduction in the social adequacy of law and viceversa. This paradox can be processed and resolved in concrete cases, but it will never be completely transcended because it is a condition for the very existence of functionally differentiated law: as a formula for contingency, transcending the paradox of justice would mean the end of law as an autonomous social system, leading to involutionary de-differentiation or a 'moral paradise' in which justice is fully realised, just as the end of scarcity as a formula for contingency in the economy[36] would lead to a 'paradise of abundance', that is the end of the economy.

[34] Buckel, 2007, 223.

[35] Here it is worth recalling Derrida: 'Justice is an experience of the impossible' (1994, 38 [Engl trans 1990, 947]).

[36] Luhmann, 1988a, 64 *f*, 70 and 191 *f*.

Legal consistency and the social adequacy of law, that is, internal and external constitutional justice, depend on the principle of equality.[37] Law itself is understood as a 'mechanism for equal/unequal treatment'.[38] It is clear that this is not a matter of textualisations or of equality as a mere form of observation of the difference between equal and unequal, but rather of concretised and realised normative structures[39] in which the preference for the positive side of the form, equality, prevails. As a norm, equality serves to immunise law against irrelevant legal differences that are relevant in other spheres of society. This does not mean that law does not construct its own asymmetrical differences, such as plaintiff and defendant in litigation, credit and debtor in the law of obligations, employer and employee in labour law, or convict and acquittee in criminal law. Using the concept of complex equality put forward by Walzer (see p 29 above) with specific regard to law, it can be said that the juridico-constitutional principle of equality means that economic, educational, religious, political, cultural or knowledge-related differences, even if legitimate in the respective fields of the social context of law, *should not* transit immediately to law, especially if they are asymmetrical (inequalities). This is the dimension of equality that relates to legal consistency. However, by the same token the criteria for legal equality *should not* transit immediately to other social fields, preventing or hindering the legitimate construction and development of differences in them, even if such differences are asymmetrical. In this sense, it is necessary for juridico-constitutional equality to be adequately complex, in accordance with the social sphere to which it relates – family, economics, politics, sport, education, and so on. Thus, for example, it would be complexly inadequate if the principle of equality entailed negation of the norms of parental rights, jeopardising the asymmetry between parents and children in family relations; if it negated the efficiency or inefficiency of sectors and companies by imposing equality contrary to legitimate differences in the economic field; if it ignored the distinction between majority and minority in democratic politics; if it denied the sportingly relevant asymmetries between athletes, destroying competition in sport; if it absolutely ignored asymmetries in learning ability among students and teaching ability among teachers, impairing legitimate selection in the sphere of education. In the dimension of adequacy, complex equality always requires constructive openness with variations and permanent adaptations so that it does not lead to 'imperial' legal equality, pseudo-equality.

Although the legal principle of equality neither entails nor is designed to lead to de facto equality, or even strictly speaking to equality of concrete rights (there are always asymmetries between the active and passive poles in legal relationships), but rather to the counterfactual imposition of egalitarian access to legal rights and remedies,[40] it cannot be denied that strong asymmetries in other

[37] *See* Luhmann, 1993a, 110 *ff* and 223 *ff* [Engl trans 2004, 131 *ff* and 217 *ff*].
[38] Teubner, 1996a, 211.
[39] *Cf* Luhmann, 1991; 1993a, 111 *f* [Engl trans 2004, 132 f]; Neves, 2006a, 168 *f*.
[40] Neves, 2006a, 166 *f*.

social fields may undermine legal equality. In this case, vast inequalities transit immediately to the detriment of the principle of complex legal equality. Law loses its capacity to immunise differences deriving from other social spheres, which entails juridically illegitimate privileges and discrimination. Particularly in the case of major economic inequalities and inequality in political power, as well as in the educational field, abyssal asymmetries erode concretisation of the principle of legal equality, so that some people (who lack money, power, education) have limited access to rights while others have excellent access to rights but often refuse to submit to the duties imposed by the legal system. This question referring to the plane of legal consistency therefore requires that legal equality be adequately complex in order to allow equitable access to rights. In this sense, the legal principle of equality becomes ineffectual if it does not offer rights that allow for equality of opportunity in other spheres of society.

According to Niklas Luhmann's conception of systems theory, the principle of equality varies in its political and legal use: 'Politics requires people to be treated as equals. The law requires cases to be treated as equal.'[41] Thus, Luhmann would reduce the legal norm of equality to the requirement of regularity in legal application, which with the positivation of law constitutes the principle of legality. But this does not correspond to the understanding of the principle of equality at the reflexive level of the constitution. As a norm of norms, both in the dynamic plane of the reproduction of the legal system (constitution/law) and at the level of legal statics, that is, the normative content of the system (principle/rule), the constitutional principle of equality supposes equal treatment of cases, but is not limited to this. From this vantagepoint, Luhmann's formulation should be reconstructed in light of the following assertion: 'The principle of equality in a constitution, seen as a legal norm, may lead to situations in which political equality is interpreted legally as equality/inequality [of cases].'[42] If we use Kelsen's language in this context, we can state that the principle of equality in its strictly juridico-legal dimension entails equality *before* the law, whereas the so-called 'principle of political equality' as the content of constitutional provisions signifies equality *in* law.[43] When the topic is the constitutional principle of equal treatment as the expression of rationality in the sphere of law, what comes to the fore is equality in law. The issue in debate is primarily egalitarian inclusion of human beings as persons in the legal order, and only secondarily equal treatment of legal cases.

The constitutional principle of equal treatment as the expression of legal rationality in the plane of the law's internal coherence and external adequacy entails a passage from equality as logical form to equality as norm. This means that as a two-sided form embodying the difference 'equal/unequal', equality as norm entails a preference for equal treatment, requiring an argumentative over-

[41] Luhmann, 1993a, 113 [Engl trans 2004, 133].
[42] *Ibid*.
[43] *Cf* Kelsen, 1960, 146 and 396.

load from unequal treatment.[44] In this case it is necessary to prove that equal treatment in a given context promotes, leads to, or maintains illegitimate unequal treatment in other broader contexts, as occurs particularly in the justification for so-called 'affirmative action': sedimentation and crystallisation of the *negative social discrimination* that prevents or hinders access to fundamental rights requires *positive legal discrimination* in order to affirm the principle of equality.[45]

On the side of politics, democracy can be characterised as its particular rationality both in the plane of self-reference (political consistency) and in the dimension of heteroreference (adequacy to society). With regard to self-reference, the question is located at the reflexive level of the orientation of decision-making processes grounded in a constitutional people. Despite all the symbolism that can be lent them, formulas such as 'we the people'[46] or 'all power comes from the people and is exercised on its behalf' have a relevant practical significance for the construction of political rationality in complex modern societies. In this regard it is again worth invoking the process of circulation and contracirculation between administration, politics, the public, and the people (see above p 40), which enables decisions to be selected within the political system. This process closes at the point where the public as plurality changes into the people as a constitutionally constructed procedural unit: the 'will of all becomes the general will'. Political decisions reach a limit of justification in the procedural people. It is impossible to legitimate *internally* within the democratic political system a decision grounded in the assertion or argument that the people is wrong or is incapable of making decisions. Unless the rules of the game are broken, the constitutional 'people' is the limit of democracy, despite its involvement in the circulation and contracirculation of power. If the people as procedural instance is questioned or the corresponding procedures are perverted, democracy as the rationality of the political system is abolished, or at the very least thrown into crisis. Manipulation of the political system by particularistic interest will prevail, to the detriment of 'generalised political support', above all the kind embodied by democratic elections.[47] For this support to be established, however, it is indispensable that there be a split in the upper pole via institutionalisation of the difference 'government/opposition' as a broad two-sided form of the existing political forces (see above p 16). Only then can there be a minimum of neutralisation of the political particularisms that persist at the expense of generalised support. Thus democracy as the rationality of the

[44] Luhmann, 1993a, 111 *f* [Engl trans 2004, 132].

[45] Neves, 2006a, 168–75. For different assumptions but similar results, *see* Bandeira de Mello, 1993; Dworkin, 1991, 223–39.

[46] Referring to Ackerman (1991, 1998), Grimm (2004b, 455 *f*) notes the symbolic significance of the 'constitutional momentum' expressed in this formula for the normative strength of the US Constitution. Ackerman (1991, 34 *ff*) refers earlier to the 'bicentennial myth', which in his view should not be confused with 'mystification', since as a 'myth', 'the narrative we tell ourselves about our Constitution's roots is a deeply significant act of collective self-definition' (1991, 36).

[47] *Cf* Luhmann, 1983a, 164 *f*.

political system entails input legitimation, a chain or network of procedures connected in a circular manner, linking political decisions to the support and control of a constitutional people as the procedural instance that closes the political system. This is the dimension of internal rationality as the democratic consistency of the political system.

In democracy, however, input legitimation is related to output legitimation.[48] This points to the social adequacy dimension of democratic politics. It is not a matter of corresponding to the various particular interests present in the sphere of the political system, but of enabling antagonistic forces to coexist in an all-encompassing political public sphere. In this sense, it can be said that while *a constitutional people closes the political system, thepublic sphere opens it up.*[49] The public sphere is the instance of the political system's heterolegitimation, since it presupposes political procedures that are susceptible and open to its instigations and influences. It should not be confused with the 'public' as a dimension of the political system, nor is it made up of functional systems that are part of the environment of politics and law as the social systems structurally coupled by the constitution. The political public sphere is made up of all the *values*, *interests*, *expectations*, and *discourses* that emerge from the various functional systems and from the so-called 'lifeworld' (operationalised via the countless day-to-day interactions not structured systemico-functionally or systemico-organisationally, and reproduced via non-specialised natural language)[50] and lose their specific pertinence to the respective systemic communication links and concrete references to the lifeworld with the claim and requirement to influence the procedures for the making and execution of political decisions in the constitutional state. Thus, in the public sphere, intersystemic conflicts of rationality become structural dissension *around* the making and execution of collectively binding decisions in the political system.

Nevertheless, the heterolegitimising force of the public sphere with regard to the political procedures of the constitutional state cannot be thought of unilaterally, that is, based on the external conditioning factors of the legal and political systems. It is indispensable that political procedures be structured so as to absorb dissension in the public sphere without eliminating it, but on the contrary making it possible and promoting its emergence. This means that although a constitutional people as the procedural instance of closure has a strong selective function toward the complex plurality of values, interests, expectations and discourses that relate to each other dissensually in the public sphere, politico-constitutional procedures are heterolegitimised only if they remain open to the dissension present in the public sphere.

[48] Brunkhorst, 2002, 187 [Engl trans 2005, 139], referring to the distinction proposed by Scharpf (1999, 6 *ff*) between 'input-oriented legitimization' ('government by the people') and 'output-oriented legitimization' ('government for the people').

[49] Neves, 2008, 488 *ff*; *cf* 2006a, 131 *ff*.

[50] *See* Neves, 2006a, 125 *ff*.

However, here, too, there is not a perfect balance between the consistency of self-legitimation by a constitutional people as procedural instance and complex adequacy to society via heterolegitimation deriving from the pluralistic public sphere. Analogous to what happens in the legal system, a functional paradox occurs in politics: if there is an excess of input legitimation by the political system, its output legitimation is weakened, and vice versa. This relates to the fact that *legitimacy* as a formula for contingency which motivates action and communication in the political system[51] constitutes a paradox that cannot be definitively transcended, but only controlled and resolved in concrete procedural cases. On this subject, Luhmann says: 'So this means politics becomes active under conditions of legitimacy, just like economics with regard to the problem of scarcity.' Pointing to the 'limited function of such formulas', given the 'system's differentiation, operative closure and structurally instituted contingency', he adds: 'And while politics must see this in the sense that unless there is a need for legitimation, politics becomes unnecessary, external description sees the situation the other way around: without a differentiated political system, there are no legitimacy problems.'[52] This is why eliminating the paradox of legitimacy as a formula for contingency would mean the end of a differentiated political system, by virtue either of regressive dedifferentiation toward traditional politics (still present at the start of the modern era in the absolutist state) oriented to the 'common good'[53] or of the construction of a 'paradise' of the unnecessariness of legitimacy deriving from a communitarian moral consensus, models incompatible with the complex politics of today's world society.

The question that arises with regard to the constitutional link between law and politics is this: How are the particular rationalities of the respective systems connected via the transversal constitution? In other words, how do the principle of equality and democracy relate constructively at the constitutional level?

On one hand, it should be noted that the constitutions of modern states establish the relevance of the principle of equality to democracy. Primary legal equality is built into the democratic system via the procedural commutations established in the constitution as a 'bridge of transition' permitting constructive 're-entries' between legal and political rationalities in the structural plane. Without citizens who have equal political rights, democracy has no meaning. Without equal votes, disconnected from the voter's other positions and social roles, democracy lacks political rationality. Thus, other politically illegitimate differences impose themselves in the sphere of politics, leading to the dominance of particularisms which are incompatible with generalised support. Such disconnection between political process and universal suffrage persisted widely until the late nineteenth century, especially in the case of census suffrage, and even into the twentieth, as in the case of the ban on voting by women and the

[51] *See* Luhmann, 2000a, 122 *ff*.

[52] Luhmann, 2000a, 126.

[53] Luhmann, 2000a, 120–2.

illiterate.[54] Overcoming these problems in Western democracy does not mean real political equality in terms of influence or participation. This is an illusion. Here, too, it is crucial to bear in mind that equality of citizenship rights acts to immunise or neutralise the democratic system against politically illegitimate differences, especially asymmetrical ones, within politico-constitutional procedures. The immunising force of the institutionalisation of equality of political rights depends on external social factors, as comprehensive social inclusion, that is, effective access to the benefits and service provision of the various functional systems. In the presence of significant social exclusion of people and groups, or very substantial inequality, especially in the economic and educational spheres, the immunising and neutralising force of equality in political rights is greatly weakened. Procedures are practically taken over by intrusions of differences that are not democratically legitimated. Under such conditions it is difficult or impossible for the transversal constitution to be concretised, in the sense of enabling democratic politics to appropriate legal rationality.

On the other hand, normative concretisation of the juridico-constitutional principle of equality cannot be guaranteed without the democratic procedures of lawmaking, voting in elections, and direct participation (via plebiscites and referenda), or without the difference between politics and administration in the plane of the political system. As far as democratic procedures are concerned, this means no democratic majority can suspend or destroy the constitutional principle of equality on pain of not only destroying justice itself as a formula for contingency in the legal system, but also preventing the emergence of generalised support in a complex heterogeneous society, by denying equal political rights. Under the transversal constitution, the legal equality presupposed by democratic politics requires the procedural majority to act as a support for its maintenance, assuring equal rights for minorities and neutralising the difference 'government/opposition' with regard to the legal system. If this difference is suspended in politics or if it becomes decisive to resolve legal disputes, equality before the law loses its practical meaning. The difference between politics and administration, in turn, 'enables the principle of equality to be applied in practice' in the sphere of state bureaucracy.[55] Civil servants are thus in a position to apply the law in an egalitarian manner regardless of the concrete interests of those who wield most power in the political game or who enjoy more political influence by virtue of other social variables (economic, familial, scientific, and so forth). If the difference between politics and administration does not materialise satisfactorily or lacks political relevance, the immunising force of legal equality is evidently negligible and the transversal constitution is therefore absent.

The modern state constitution emerges as an institutional 'bridge of transition' between politics and law, thus contributing to the development of a specific transversal rationality that prevents the destructive effects of each of these systems on

[54] In the same sense, *see* Zolo, 2007, 46 *f.*

[55] Luhmann, 1965, 155.

the other, while promoting learning and a reciprocal exchange of experiences with a different form of rationality. However, just as the constitution as structural coupling has systemic corruption as its negative side, so constitutional transversality between politics and law is a two-sided form that involves irrationalities which feed into each other. Examples include the politicisation of law (to the latter's detriment) and the juridification of politics.[56] These are two models of systemic expansion at the expense of the relevance of a different rationality. This is not necessarily a matter of systemic corruption referring to consistency, since it also includes reciprocal difficulties with the provision of adequate responses to the other system: an excess of democracy weakens the rule of law, oriented by the legal principle of equality; an overzealous rule of law undermines democracy. Constitutional procedures may not be capable of immunising law against the parasitic action of politics;[57] law, in turn, may act as a parasite against another parasite.[58] Under these hypotheses, constitutional practice becomes inadequate for the other sphere and for society in general: the judiciary with claims to occupy the space of political legitimation, parliament and government with aspirations to be the instance that settles legal disputes – two subcomplex alternatives that lead both to disrespect for justice as equality assured by the rule of law and to contempt for political legitimacy grounded in democracy.

This is the paradox of the transversality between the rule of law and democracy, which cannot be definitively transcended but can be controlled and resolved in concrete cases of conflicts between legal and political rationality. In this respect, constitutional courts play a key role. Although they constitute the summit of one of the coupled functional systems, law, they are 'extravagant organisations in which the problem of structural coupling manifests itself in a concentrated manner'.[59] Besides their function as a selective filter for influences and irritations, they help assure the proper functioning of the constitution as a 'bridge of transition' between different rationalities. To a certain extent, constitutional courts can be said to act as guardians of the legitimacy of whatever crosses this 'bridge' in either direction, thereby contributing to the realisation of transversal rationality in constitutional cases.[60] While contributing casuistically to control and solution of the paradox resulting from the constitutional entanglement of politics and law, they cannot abolish the paradox definitively, since that would mean abolishing the constitution. And they can often irrationally intensify the paradox, through judicialising or politicising attitudes.

[56] This problem should not be confused with the reference by Möllers (2003, 3–18) to two partial dimensions of the constitution ('types'), one relating to 'the constitution as politicisation of law' and the other to 'the constitution as juridification of politics', but both entailing 'the constitution as coupling between politics and law'. *See* above pp 39 *f*.

[57] *Cf* Luhmann, 2000d, 45 *ff* Luhmann refers here to Serres, 1997 [1980].

[58] Luhmann, 2000d, 47.

[59] Luhmann, 2000c, 398.

[60] Considering the propensity of constitutional courts to expand their controlling function, especially in the German experience, Maus (1989) refers critically to the 'Judiciary', in a comprehensive and peremptory manner, as 'society's superego'.

As noted earlier with regard specifically to legal equality and democratic politics (p 45 *ff*), the formation of state constitutions as institutions of transversal rationality depends on broad social presuppositions. There is no room for constitutions as 'bridges of transition' between law and politics when there is no social context of functional differentiation and broad social inclusion.

From the perspective of law, if mechanisms of functional dedifferentiation of the various social spheres predominate and if primary comprehensive exclusion is present[61] in the sphere of reproduction of society within the respective state territory, it is not possible to immunise the legal systems against inequalities not constructed juridically, that is, the normative force of the constitutional principle of equality is not structurally affirmed. Textualisation in constitutional provisions is not sufficient for something so full of presuppositions to become a legal norm.[62] Generalised normative concretisation in settling legal cases is necessary for a principle as norm of norms to have practical significance for the legal order. If the difference 'inclusion/exclusion' systematically cancels out the validity of the legal code 'legal/illegal', the equality principle becomes a textual illusion. Related to this problem, the systemic presence of (immediate) blockages to the autonomy of law, a system grounded primarily in the code 'legal/illegal', by other systemic differences, such as 'having/not having' or 'government/opposition', means the equality norm loses its functional significance, since to a certain extent it presupposes and guarantees the legal system's operational autonomy.[63]

In turn, if politics should lack autonomy from the particular values of familial, ethnic, or religious groups and concrete economic interests, it will not be possible to build democracy as generalised support for the political system, which is a precondition for the possibility of closure of this system. Moreover, linked to this issue, the prevalence of the code 'inclusion/exclusion' may erode equality of political rights to such an extent that it leads to situations in which democracy is reduced to a political formula or is strongly defective. Clearly this does not exclude the presence of so-called 'polyarchy'.[64] However, this by no

[61] Müller (1997, 50 *ff*) distinguishes between 'primary exclusion', which has destructive effects on the validity of the legal code, and 'secondary exclusion', which 'restricts 'only' the actual extent of its efficacy' (p 51).

[62] On the distinction between normative text and norm, *see* among many Müller, 1994, especially 147–67 and 234–40; Grau, 2002, especially 71–3; De Barros Carvalho, 2008, 126–31. Alexy (1986, 42 *ff*) distinguishes analogously between normative statement and norm.

[63] According to Luhmann (1993a, 112 [Engl trans 2004, 133]), the functional differentiation of society relates to the practical ability 'to interpret the form as a norm' of equality.

[64] But my intent in using this term should not be confused with full acceptance of the distinction between the empirical or real concept of 'polyarchy' and the normative or ideal concept of democracy proposed by Dahl (1972, especially 8). Instead, I believe it is more productive to link the concept of 'polyarchy' to the functioning of 'governmental techniques' open to the different political forces, even if the direct influence of particularisms and privileged interests systematically perverts the rules of the game, so that systemic corruption prevails in the plane of political procedures. The concept of democracy requires many more presuppositions, but at the very least it requires regularity of respect for the procedural rules of the democratic game established or grounded in the constitution.

means guarantees the presence of democracy as a functional requirement and normative claim of the modern state. Moreover, even if we were to use a realistic procedural concept of democracy,[65] the existence of constitutional texts, elections, pressure groups and so on would not be sufficient to characterise the existence of a democratic regime: if the rules of the game are not regularly respected (for example, if there is systematic fraud and illegal campaign funding), procedures will become rituals,[66] and the democratic 'method' will cease being a guide to the 'polyarchic' struggle for power.

In this context, the structural subordination of one system to another, especially of law to politics, prevents the construction and development of a transversal constitution capable of promoting learning or the productive and lasting exchange of experiences with the rationalities proper to each of these systems. In the absence of structural coupling with its presupposition, the respective transversal rationality cannot develop. The emergence, formation, and development of a state transversal constitution can be blocked at various levels.

In the case of so-called 'failed states',[67] the problem lies precisely in the state-centred nature of politics. In the absence of a centralised territorial political organisation, there is no state as an address for communications, for either domestic or international politics.[68] Fragmentation of political disputes between dispersed groups – as the experiences of African countries have been typically presented – does not enable state power to emerge as a 'political unit of action and decision', that is, it prevents the existence of the state as the 'organising unit of decision and action' in Heller's words,[69] so that it is impossible even to imagine a transversal constitution in this context. The destructive reciprocal blockages between law and politics relating to the 'tribal' struggles entailed by territorial dispersal of power prevent formation of the state as a territorial political organisation and hence the emergence of a corresponding state constitution.

Similarly, a transversal constitution cannot be developed under autocratic regimes, either in the radical form of totalitarianism or in authoritarian variants. In such cases there are mere 'semantic constitutions', in Loewenstein's terminology, as instruments of those who happen to be in power.[70] In other words, these are 'instrumentalist constitutions'.[71] In typical situations, heteronomising subordination of the legal system to politics occurs directly via the issuance of constitutional texts or 'supraconstitutional' laws of exception. In limiting cases, this means the supreme authorities are not linked to the juridico-constitutional mechanisms that control power, either because the (supra)constitutional provisions themselves keep the supreme political bodies outside any

[65] Schumpeter, 1942, 269 *ff*.

[66] *Cf* Luhmann, 1983a, especially 51 *f* and 172 *f*.

[67] On this topic, *see* Thürer, 1996; Herdegen, 1996; Geiss, 2004; 2005, especially 42–6; Brooks, 2005; and Gordon, 1997, who criticises the 'neocolonial' implications of the concept.

[68] *Cf* Luhmann, 2000a, 194, 196 *f*, 225 *f*, 241 *ff*, and 244.

[69] Heller, 1934, 228 *ff*.

[70] Loewenstein, 1965, 149 *f*.

[71] Neves, 1992, 69–71.

legal limit or control, or because constitutional changes are imposed 'casuistically' to prevent invocation of the instruments of control, if any exist. Thus the development of a transversal constitution is already blocked at the level of the issuance of (supra)constitutional laws. The destructive effect of politics on law not only affects legal rationality, but also has self-destructive consequences for democratic political rationality. To the extent that the difference 'legal/illegal' does not function as a second code of power,[72] politics becomes blocked by intrusions from all kinds of particularisms and by immediate pressure from other social spheres, especially the economic. Under these circumstances, the conditions for learning from the other's rationality are missing; on the contrary, the oppression of law by political power not subject to juridico-constitutional limits is affirmed.

In the case of symbolic constitutionalisation,[73] there is also an expansion of the political sphere at the expense of autonomous development by legal rationality. In this case, however, dedifferentiating politicisation of the legal system does not inherently flow from the content of constitutional provisions. On the contrary, the constitutional text proclaims a political-legal model according to which legal rationality is allegedly guaranteed. Nevertheless, while the constitutional text is being concretised, autonomous reproduction of the legal system is blocked. On one hand, the catalogue of fundamental rights contained in the constitutional text, a catalogue founded on the principle of legal equality, does not meet with generalised support in the everyday life of the respective state and does not even contribute to generalised stabilisation of the normative expectations of state agents. On the other, the democratic procedures for which the textual model of the constitution provides are blocked so frequently by other social variables that legal rationality itself is also affected. Thus, the constitution remains an artefact or symbolic façade of politics referring to law, insofar as the 'bridges of transition' that can serve transversal constitutional rationality are blocked.

In light of the above, it can be said that the constitution of the modern state as promoter of the specific transversal rationality between the particular rationality of law and that of politics has developed to a significant extent only in very limited regions of the globe. As can be said in general of transversal rationalities, so, too, it can be said that transversal state constitutions are 'scarce products' in contemporary society (*see* p 34 above). Moreover, it is also necessary to ask whether the trend toward a paradoxical 'peripherising of the centre' in today's world society may lead to a situation in which the transversal constitutions of the developed western democratic constitutional state are transformed or deformed into symbolic constitutions.[74] In this context, practical and theoretical efforts become

[72] On the difference between legal and illegal as a second code of power, *see* Luhmann, 1986a, 199; 1988b [1975], 34, 48 *ff* and 56.

[73] For a comprehensive discussion of this topic, *see* Neves, 2007a.

[74] Neves, 2007a, 191 *ff*. On peripheralisation ('Brazilianisation') trends in the developed West, *see* Beck, 1997, 266–8; 1999, 7 *ff* and 94 *ff*. *Cf* Zolo, 2007, 47 *f*.

increasingly intense with regard to the emergence of constitutions beyond the state, to which is attributed the function of developing new forms of transversal rationality.

III. TRANSVERSAL CONSTITUTIONS BEYOND THE STATE?

The emergence of international, transnational and supranational legal orders, in distinct forms of classic international public law, is an unquestionable fact that has drawn attention and increasingly become a focus of interest for studies not just by jurists but also by economists and social scientists in general. What intrigues traditional legal 'science' is the claim of these new legal orders to affirm themselves categorically either as legal orders that dispense with the state[75] or as legal orders that prevail against states, calling into question the very principle of state sovereignty, the cornerstone of classic international public law. This is the context for the debate about transversal constitutions beyond the state, where neither reference to the notion of juridification[76] nor recourse to the historical-universal concept of constitution are sufficient, since what is involved is the controversy about the emergence of institutions that configure functional equivalents to the transversal constitution of the constitutional state.

Although modern state constitutions were *structural* mechanisms of the transversal rationality between law and politics at birth, the semantics of transversal constitutionalism became significant only as a result of the new problems with which today's international order and emerging supranational and transnational orders are faced with increasing intensity. In this regard, the spheres of security policy, world trade, environmental law, and human rights can be designated as exemplary. Here the state constitution is initially pushed into the background, but later it once again becomes entangled with international, supranational, and transnational constellations.[77]

The word 'transnationality' is semantically ambiguous. It is often used to refer broadly not only to orders, institutions, and problems that are transnational in the strict sense but also to international and supranational orders, institutions, and problems.[78] The core of this generic concept resides in the notion of dimensions that transcend the frontiers of the state. In the stricter sense to which I give preference in this study (albeit not denying there are intermediate uses), the same word refers to the *trans*national in the sense proposed by Teubner, which points to private or quasi-public normative orders that emerge and develop at the global level independently of both the state and its

[75] Teubner (ed), 1997a.

[76] Grimm, 2004a, 14-6; Wahl, 2002, 201 and 205.

[77] *See*, eg, Walter, 2000, 2–4.

[78] Thus Jessup uses 'the term "transnational law" to include all law which regulates actions or events that transcend national frontiers. Both public and private international law are included, as are other rules which do not wholly fit into such standard categories' (1956, 2). *See* in this same sense Friedman, 2004; Zumbansen, 2006.

frontiers and of orders built on state foundations, that is, supranational and international orders.[79] As for 'supranational', I shall restrict its use to broad orders in the temporal, material, and social dimension in which all norms and decisions relating to the founding treaty (but not the treaty itself or its amendments) directly link the citizens and bodies of Member States, the European Union being paradigmatic. As for the new international institutions that have also given rise to a debate regarding constitutions beyond the state, the question relates to the presence of forms of more intense bindingness than the eminently dispositive model of classic international public law, such as *jus cogens*, the *erga omnes* principle, and the new regulatory framework for international trade embodied by the World Trade Organization (WTO).

In this section, I consider first the topic of the emergence of new norms, institutions, and organisations that lead to the debate about the constitutionalisation of international law, also bearing in mind the proposals for the creation of a supranational constitution in the global plane (A). Next, I analyse the question of supranational constitutionalism in the regional plane, considering above all the experience of the European Union (B). Last, I examine the possibilities and limits of the so-called transnational 'civil constitutions' studied by Teubner (C).

A. Models of a Global Supranational Constitution and Constitutionalisation in the Plane of the International Order

A paradigmatic theoretical tendency points to the emergence of an international or supranational constitutionalism in the global plane. In this regard, the focus varies a great deal and the theoretical foundations are also highly diverse, ranging from models of a world state and conceptions of 'global domestic politics' to characterising the United Nations Charter as a constitution for the international community.

One model is normatively oriented in favour of the idea of a 'federal and subsidiary world republic'[80] or, similarly, a world statehood as a supreme level with regard to continental and national statehood.[81] The central concern is maintaining and guaranteeing peace, which recalls the Kantian notion of a 'federation of free states',[82] but goes beyond it by affirming a hierarchical model in the relationship between the mooted state or world republic and continental or national territorial political units. This model clearly raises the question of a corresponding world constitution, but to some extent the debate remains on the

[79] *See* Teubner, 1996b or 1997b; 1998b [Engl trans 2000]; 2000 [Engl trans 2004a]; 2003a [Engl. 2004b]; 2006 [Engl trans 2006]; 2012 [Engl trans 2012]; Fischer-Lescano and Teubner, 2006; Calliess, 2002, especially 186–9; Fischer-Lescano, 2003; 2005; Ladeur, 1997; 2004a.

[80] Höffe, 2002a, 225 *ff*; 2002b; 2008.

[81] Lutz-Bachmann, 2002, especially 43 *ff*.

[82] Kant, 1993 [1795], 208–13.

level of philosophical idealisation. The empirical elements that could show how a unitary political order might be realised in accordance with this model are missing, given that world society is immensely asymmetrical and fragmented at the political level.

Also, the project of a 'world domestic politics without a world government' proposed by Habermas[83] involves a discussion about the 'constitutionalisation of international public law', a 'constitution for the pluralist world society' or a 'cosmopolitan constitution without a world republic'.[84] Even while moving beyond Kant's 'international' model of a 'federation of free states', Habermas, unlike Höffe and Lutz-Bachmann, argues on the basis of existing international institutions and organisations, proposing that they be comprehensively reformed, especially the UNsystem, with a view to building a 'world domestic politics' capable of exploring procedures and institutions that promote 'world citizenship' grounded in 'consciousness of an obligatory/compulsory cosmopolitan solidarity'.[85] This would entail representation of citizenship movements in a sort of lower chamber of the UN General Assembly, as well as a model for the separation of powers based on a reform of the Security Council and on strengthening the international courts and the General Assembly.[86] This project could lead to a 'global welfare regime', driven by the transfer to supranational spheres of functions hitherto performed by the welfare state in limited parts of the world,[87] and to normative regulation of so-called 'humanitarian intervention'.[88] As I have noted elsewhere,[89] the Habermasian model of a constitution for world domestic politics seems to me to be excessively informed by an idealised vision, based above all on Western Europe's positive experience with supranationality.[90] In particular, the notions of a 'global welfare regime' and 'consciousness of a compulsory cosmopolitan solidarity' in a world society impregnated with geopolitical conflicts, huge asymmetries of power, acute economic inequality, and dispersive cultural fragmentation are indications that the idea of a 'cosmopolitan constitution without a world republic', in Habermas's words, might rather serve to conceal serious problems that depend on far more complex variables to be adequately addressed in the political and legal arenas.

[83] Habermas, 1998a, 156 and 165 [Engl trans 2001, 104 and 110 – such translation makes use of the word 'policy' instead of 'politics', which does not make any sense in this context]; 2004, 133 *f*; 2007, 452; *see also* 1996; 2000. For an analogous formulation, *see* Ferrajoli, 1997, 51–2.

[84] Habermas, 2004; 2005; 2007, especially 447 *ff*.

[85] Habermas, 1998a, 88 *f* and 168 [Engl trans 2001, 55 *f* and 112]; 1998b, 77 *f*.

[86] *See* Habermas, 2000, 60; 2005, 352 *ff*; 2007, 450 *ff*.

[87] Habermas, 1998b, 75 and 80; 1998a, 86 [Engl trans 2001, 54].

[88] Habermas, 1996, 225 *f*; 2000.

[89] Neves, 2006a, 269 *ff*.

[90] It should be noted that although Habermas stresses supranationality, he admits that in a world system with multiple 'levels' the transnational dimension must also be considered (*cf* 2004, 134 *f*; 2005, 346; 2007, 452–5). The recent economic crisis in the eurozone, however, points to a negative experience that may have repercussions for the European Union in the political and legal spheres (in this respect, *see also* Habermas, 2011, especially 97 *ff*).

With a descriptive claim in respect of world society, the model of an *inclusive* world statehood (which 'does not imply the disappearance of other forms of statehood')[91] refers to the 'simultaneity of processes of constitutionalisation and processes of fragmentation in the political system, as well as in the legal system of world society'.[92] Indeed, this is not a case of a finalistically oriented process, but rather an evolutionary process; yet it can also be described as a 'project for a politics *in world society*, surrounded by a breath of utopia'.[93] In this context, it is argued that typical functions of the modern state are being or are in a position to be taken over by political instances at the level of world society.[94] It is undeniable that functions until recently performed by territorially delimited state entities have been opened up to international and supranational instances. It is even possible to speak of a sharing of tasks in a 'multilevel' system. However, it does not seem to me that the emergence of statehood can be inferred. The concept of a state implies the notion of a central organisation of the territorially segmented political system, so that its functions are performed under these conditions. Thus it is neither theoretically advisable nor productive to apply the concepts of statehood or state to a strongly decentralised and even fragmented order such as that of world politics, in which several organisations are in conflict and permanent competition. If this is conceded, it also is not clear what processes of constitutionalisation would be involved in the plane of this global statehood. If a world state is the answer, it would be more appropriate to speak of a single global constitution structured in analogous or functionally equivalent terms to state constitutions. In this case, however, we would reduce our perspective to an ideal project, which would also be highly controversial from the standpoint of adequacy to the requirements of world society.

In the plane of international public law, the debate takes on a different perspective since it is a matter of attributing a constitutional character to the existing order or an emerging one. As long ago as 1926, Alfred Verdross referred to the 'Constitution of the international legal community', based on the experience of the League of Nations.[95] Later, with the founding of the UN, the notion of a constitution for the international community was disseminated. This was to be achieved either by attributing such a function to the UN Charter itself,[96] or by giving the institutions of international public law and international politics a

[91] Albert, 2007, 11.

[92] Albert and Schmalz-Bruns, 2009, 57.

[93] Albert, 2005, 236.

[94] Albert, 2007, 9; 2005, 229.

[95] Verdross, 1926. A little later, in the 1930s, the expression 'international constitutional law' makes a few scattered appearances (*cf* Mello, 2000, 3 *ff*, noting the ambiguity of the phrase).

[96] Fassbender, 1998; 2007, 281 *ff*; Dupuy, 1997. On this topic, Giegerich (2003, 11) says 'the UN Charter is currently the only world constitution capable of consensus'. Much earlier, Alf Ross (1950) already referred to the 'Constitution of the United Nations'. Verdross and Simma (1984, 69 *ff*) also use this expression.

broader remit.[97] Without neglecting the fact that it is not a matter of a 'closed' constitution like a state constitution, the proponents of this approach point to the juridico-constitutional content of international public law in the dimensions of organisational structure and material elements, as well as to constitutional law in the formal sense.[98] As for the organisational level, they note the presence of multiple bodies with authority in the spheres of legislative, judicial, and executive functions.[99] As for material elements, those most emphasised are the human rights treaties and conventions, especially the European Convention on Human Rights, and international economic law, with the WTO on point.[100] As regards constitutional law in the formal sense, stress is laid on the *jus cogens* principle, as formulated in Article 53 of the Vienna Convention on the Law of Treaties (1969),[101] and on the decision that defined obligations *erga omnes* in the 1970 *Barcelona Traction* case brought before the International Court of Justice,[102] both of which add partial verticality to the horizontal system of inter-

[97] *See*, eg, Tomuschat, 1995, 7, who also refers to 'international law as the Constitution of mankind' (1997). With certain restrictions, Kadelbach and Kleinlein (2008) propose a model based on constitutional principles from international law. Verdross and Simma (1984, 59 *ff*) refer to the 'Constitution of the non-organised community of states' and 'constitutional principles of the community of states'. Others prefer to speak of 'international constitutional law' (Uerpmann, 2001; Mello, 2000; Piovesan, 2008a), although use of the expression is highly ambiguous. Some more cautiously treat the constitutionalisation of international public law as a process (Wahl, 2002, 192 and 199 *ff*; Biaggini, 2000, 470 *ff*; Frowein, 2000; Giegerich, 2003, 2 *f*). Von Bogdandy (2004a, 242) acknowledges the fragility of 'international constitutionalism', but stresses its potential compared with other options. Peters (2006) rejects a model based on affirmation of a constitutionalisation of international law, preferring 'international constitutionalism' to compensate for deconstitutionalisation in the domestic sphere, but strictly speaking her thesis points to the development of 'multilevel' global constitutionalism (p 610). Koskenniemi (2004, 206), discussing the problem of hegemony in international law, argues that something like the constitutionalisation of international law could not resemble the formation of a constitution in the domestic space, not only for lack of a constituent power in the international sphere, but also because 'the constitution it would enact would not be one of an international but an imperial realm'. Tushnet (2008) keeps his distance from the debate about the existence of a global or international constitution (p 2, note 7) and avers that 'the globalisation of domestic constitutional law is inevitable' (pp 4 and 22) given the 'convergence and (sometimes) harmonisation, but not uniformity' 'among national constitutional systems in their structures and in their protection of fundamental human rights' (p 3), not only by virtue of 'top-down processes' (pp 4 *ff*) or even merely 'bottom-up processes' (pp 7 *ff*), but in a broader, more complex context of pressure and counterpressure (pp 11 *ff*), in which there are 'races to the top and bottom, and elsewhere' (pp 19 *f*); and he concludes by linking the globalisation of domestic constitutional law with the problem of the separation of powers (pp 20 *ff*).

[98] Uerpmann, 2001, 565.

[99] Uerpmann, 2001, 566–9.

[100] Uerpmann, 2001, 569–71.

[101] The title of Article 53 of the Vienna Convention, which was adopted on 26 May 1969, and came into force internationally on 27 January 1980, is 'Treaties conflicting with a peremptory norm of general international law ("jus cogens")'. The text of the article states that: 'A treaty is void if, at the time of its conclusion, it conflicts with a peremptory norm of general international law. For the purposes of the present Convention, a peremptory norm of general international law is a norm accepted and recognised by the international community of states as a whole as a norm from which no derogation is permitted and which can be modified only by a subsequent norm of general international law having the same character.'

[102] *Barcelona Traction, Light and Power Company, Limited (New Application: 1962) (Belgium v Spain), Second Phase*, Judgment, ICJ Reports, 1970, 3, §§ 33 and 34 (p 32) (judgment of 5 Feb 1970).

national public law.[103] Cogency is attributed above all to prohibition of the use of force, prohibition of genocide, and a human rights core. In the case of obligations *erga omnes*, the signatories to treaties and conventions assume binding undertakings not only towards each other but also towards any person or organisation covered by the norm of protection concerned.[104] This is a complex structure in which it is possible to observe the presence of problems to face which the modern state emerged: control of power and affirmation of human rights.

Nevertheless, this raises the question of whether the structural changes at the international level are really suited to the formation of a functional equivalent of a constitution in the modern sense, and to serving the transversal rationality between law and politics. All societies (and their partial systems), organisations and interactions have a constitution in the broadest meaning of the word.[105] The legal concept of constitution, as a supreme normative and legal framework, is also universal and can be transported to any legal order. However, when the constitution is said to be 'an evolutionary achievement of modern society',[106] the concept of constitution is invoked in the strictest sense of the word, as stressed in Section I of this Chapter. If it is admitted that 'the structural coupling of the political system and the legal system through constitutions does not have an equivalent at the level of global society',[107] the identification of constitutions in the plane of international public law or a global juridico-political supranationality becomes controversial. Which institutions could make possible this horizontal relationship involving the structural selection of reciprocal influences between the political and legal systems? The situation is more problematic when a transversal constitution is regarded as a structure for reciprocal learning and a constructive exchange between both systems in the plane of interstate law and relations.[108] At least until now, despite strong juridification at the international level, it does not appear so straightforward to transfer the con-

[103] Fischer-Lescano, 2003, 718. *See ibid*, 743 *ff*; 2005, especially 20 *f*, 185 *f*, 220 and 230; Uerpmann, 2001, 571 *f*; Giegerich, 2003, 2; Fassbender, 2007, 276 *ff*; Dupuy, 1997, 4 *ff*; Ragazzi, 1997, especially 1 *ff*, 43 *ff* and 189 *ff*; Frowein, 1994, especially 363–5; 1983, especially 257 *ff*; Münch, 1983; Kadelbach, 1992, especially 23–35; Hannikainen, 1988, especially 1–16 and 269–77; Oeter, 2007, associating *jus cogens* directly with protection of human rights.

[104] In connection with the norms affected, Uerpmann (2001, 572), using dubious concepts from Alexy (1999, 252 *f*), speaks of a 'weak priority' for obligations *erga omnes* and a 'strong priority' for the *jus cogens* principle, to argue that in the former case the norm is null and void whereas in the latter only a deviant legal act is characterised as illegal.

[105] As noted by Mosler (1980, 16): 'Any society, however unorganised it might be, must have one essential constitutional rule in the absence of which it would not be a community but simply a collection of individuals.' *Cf* Fischer-Lescano, 2003, 718, note 10. Similarly, Uerpmann (2001, 566) remarks: 'Not all communities have a written constitution but all communities have constitutional law.'

[106] Luhmann, 1990a.

[107] Luhmann, 1993a, 582 [Engl trans 2004, 487 *f*] (*see* 23 above).

[108] 'Interstate' can be used provided it is borne in mind that although states are not the only subjects of international public law (as stressed long ago by Verdross, 1926, 83 *f*), they are its primary or fundamental subjects, as stressed respectively by Cassese (2005a, 71 *ff*) and Mosler (1976, 15 *f* and 26). *Cf* Uerpmann, 2001, 566, note 13.

cept of a constitution in the modern sense, dependent on broad presuppositions, to global instances of an international or supranational nature. The conceptual transfer would entail recognition of certain constraints at the very least. What would be the obstacles to the affirmation of one or more transversal constitutions in the international sphere?

First, the problem presents itself in the subordination of international public law to the politics determined by the major world powers. At the international level, a practice of asymmetrical relations between law and power develops, pointing simultaneously to characteristics of 'semantic' or instrumental constitutions and 'nominalist' or symbolic constitutions in the state sphere.[109] The application of normative models is defined via a strongly discriminatory selective process in which the distinction between powerful and weak states in the international constellation is decisive. Normative texts have a low density of normative concretisation compared with the concrete and particular variables of power. On one hand, there is the predominantly symbolic function of the Universal Declaration of Human Rights (1948)[110] and the provisions guaranteeing respect for them in the UN Charter (1945), as well as the various charters and conventions proclaiming human rights in specific areas or regions.[111] In this context, the increasing textualisation is out of step with the normative force of human rights in the plane of international law. On the other hand, the lack of a model for the 'separation of powers' due to the effective supremacy of the Security Council over the International Court of Justice and the UN General Assembly leads to instrumentalisation of normative texts via this executive body, which also performs functions of a 'quasi-legislative'[112] and jurisdictional nature (for example, decisions on cases of human rights violation). Thus, international public law is left aside, to the extent that it does not correspond to the expectations of those of the great powers that show interest in the respective case or are involved in it.[113] In sum, either in the sphere of the core material elements (human rights) or at the organisational level (the 'separation of powers'), there are severe constraints on satisfactory development of a transversal rationality between international law and international politics, so that caution is required before affirming a constitution as a self-binding order with normative primacy.

[109] *Cf* Fischer-Lescano, 2005, 275 *f*; 2003, 757 *f*; Peters, 2006, 608. *See* pp 53 *f* above.

[110] *See* von Bernstorff, 2008a, 905 *ff*, referring to (p 906) the sceptical position taken by Lauterpacht (1950, 416 *f*) at the time of the Declaration:'Given that it was not a legal instrument, the Declaration appeared to be outside international law . . . [T]he determination to refrain from captious criticisms should not interfere with the duty that falls to the science of international law to refrain from lending an artificial legal existence to a document that was never intended to have one.'

[111] On the development of international protection for human rights in conventions, treaties and charters, *see*, eg, Comparato, 1999; Trindade, 2000 (emphasising Brazil's position); Piovesan, 2008a (highlighting the instruments ratified by Brazil: 367 *ff*). On its significance for the world today, *see* among many Tomuschat, 2008; Cassese, 2005b.

[112] Wagner, 2003.

[113] In this sense, Ferrajoli (1997, 43) argues that the problem is not one of an 'absent third' (Bobbio, 1989), but of an 'impotent third'. *Cf* Zolo, 2007, 49.

On one level, this question relates to the difficulty of determining organic competence, material domain, and capacity for generalised protection of human rights in accordance with pre-established rules and procedures (rule of law and due process of law). Who is competent to decide on and implement protection for human rights against states or organisations that systematically violate them? In what cases are control and sanctions required or justified? Are there presuppositions and instruments to make such generalised protection possible? On another level, the problem is associated with the political use of human rights rhetoric to impose the interests of certain powers.

In the plane of normative articulation, determination of the competent body or bodies to define cases that entail human rights violations and implement generalised protection of human rights involves problems of legal doctrine, legitimacy, and practical conditions, all mutually entangled. An example is the question of military intervention to protect human rights. From the standpoint of legal doctrine, several difficulties arise. In particular, there is the vagueness of the notion of a threat to 'international peace and security' to be maintained in accordance with decisions by the UN Security Council (Article 39 of the UN Charter). This notion has served to justify interventionist practices. There is also a conflict-ridden relationship between the human rights guarantees proclaimed in Articles 1.3 and 55–56 of the UN Charter and the principle of non-intervention enshrined in Article 2.7, which becomes more even problematic in light of the principle of 'self-determination of peoples', mentioned in Article 1.2. The extremely vague concept of threats to international peace and security has come in practice to constitute a 'carte blanche declaration' for interventionism by the Security Council.[114] Similarly, the relationship between human rights guarantees and the principle of non-intervention 'can only be determined by successive acts of application by UN political organs in accordance with the political logic of the moment'.[115] This situation leads to the problem of the legitimacy of the Security Council – for whose functioning the principle of the right of veto for all five permanent members (Article 27.3) plays a key role – in claiming to provide generalised protection for human rights. It is as if international protection was hyper-politicised and, being arbitrary, did not correspond to the requirements of a generalised legal model in terms of the rule of law. In this context, law is subordinated directly to power. Even competences of the International Court of Justice have been ignored by the Security Council without incurring any sanctions.[116] Thus the Council stands for 'arbitrary interventionism' with regard to human rights,[117] which involves 'paternalistic intentions' inherent in interventionist proposals and 'selective' classification of human rights violations to justify intervention.[118]

[114] Koskenniemi, 1995, 326.
[115] Koskenniemi, 1995, 327.
[116] Koskenniemi, 1995, 325 *f.*
[117] Brunkhorst, 1999, 382.
[118] Maus, 1997, 168 and 190.

In the plane of concretisation and realisation, it can be observed that the Security Council and great powers resort to the rhetoric of human rights mainly to justify intervention in weaker states. This use of symbolic force is evidently manipulative and has a negative effect on any tendency for human rights to gain normative strength. In this regard, it is worth raising 'the suspicion that human rights also serve as a pretext for intervening in political relations that can only be resolved responsibly in the national sphere, whether democratically or not'.[119] Referring to the interventionist model, Koskenniemi says: 'Rational imperialism turned out to be a façade for cynical imperialism.'[120] In this connection it is appropriate, albeit somewhat paradoxical, to speak of 'human rights imperialism'.[121]

While it can be said that the 'public sphere and world public sphere are phenomena that emerge simultaneously',[122] this problem of globally defective international or supranational constitutionalisation is associated with the fact that a *strong* worldwide public sphere has not developed, that is, one capable of influencing the respective legal and political procedures to a significant extent.[123] If the public sphere is defined as a systemically unstructured dimension of the environment of a given system,[124] oriented both broadly and diffusely to influence the latter, there are a great many relevant world public spheres, in sport, economics, science, and so on. The political public sphere, or more specifically the juridico-political (that is, constitutional) public sphere, is strong in the constitutional state because it effectively and significantly influences the articulation of democratic procedures and of those referring to the rule of law and due process of law. Politics and law are conditioned by the constitutional public sphere. In contrast, the world or international politico-juridical public sphere acts in a localised and intermittent manner, that is, it is incapable of influencing the respective political and legal procedures in a generalised and permanent manner. The decisions made and norms established via these procedures are usually insensitive to the weak and marginal public spheres that operate at the international level of world society.

[119] Luhmann, 1999, 253.

[120] Koskenniemi, 2002, 500.

[121] Neves, 2005, 27 [Engl trans 2007, 436].

[122] Stichweh, 2002, 57; *cf* 2007, 31 *f*.

[123] In distinguishing between 'strong' and 'weak' public spheres, Brunkhorst (2002, 184 *ff* [Engl trans 2005, 137 *ff*]; 2007, 233 *f*) refers to Fraser (1992, 132 *ff*) and Habermas (1992, 373 *f* [Engl trans 307 *f*]), but disagrees with their focus on the difference between organised (strong) and non-organised (weak) public spheres in the constitutional state, instead proposing inclusion in the strong public sphere only of the dimension legally constituted as the 'people' via procedures ('elections and voting') and that wields state or transnational power via the resonance of public opinion in 'its' bodies (Brunkhorst, 2002, 185, note 98 [Engl trans 2005, 215, note 98]). My own use of the term is limited to the so-called 'informal' or 'non-organised' public sphere around the legal and political systems (Neves, 2006a, 131 *ff*), reducing the concept of a constitutional people to a procedural dimension internal to the legal system (*see* p 40 above). The public sphere is strong when it influences constitutional procedures in a broad and relevant manner, and weak when it influences those procedures only occasionally and with scant relevance, thus not contributing satisfactorily to their heterolegitimation (Neves, 2008, 508 *f*).

[124] In the field of systems theory, Stichweh (2002, 60 *f*) diverges by defining the public sphere as the 'internal environment' of a system and, correspondingly, defining the world public sphere as the 'internal environment' of world politics.

Lastly, it should be noted that the problem also relates to the non-existence of a constitutional people or functional equivalent at the level of world society, that is, the absence of an instance that can assure operative closure of the political system, making generalised support possible in the context of a hypercomplex society. For a wide array of reasons – mainly geopolitical conflicts, hugely asymmetrical levels of development, and the various perspectives regarding decision-making agendas – the capacity for generalised political support, in the sense of neutralising particularisms and persistent pressure from concrete relations of domination, remains basically restricted to the constitutional state and is not transported to the global plane.[125]

The above problems result in the oppression of legal rationality (the principle of equality) by a 'superior/inferior' code of power that reproduces itself within the sphere of asymmetrical global geopolitics and thus is not grounded in political rationality (democracy). This in turn means that, without global institutionalisation of a horizontal difference between government and opposition (or a functional equivalent), the *hierarchical* structure of domination present in international relations, albeit not an expression of the hierarchical model of premodern societies, has an element of 'tribalism'[126] and even a certain presence of the 'law of the strongest' in terms of the Hobbesian state of nature,[127] so that it is incompatible with a constitution in the modern sense. In this context, the transversal constitution between law and politics remains a rhetorical artefact insofar as the heteronomous and destructive reproduction of politics over law is incompatible with rational entanglement of both spheres via reciprocal learning and a constructive exchange of their respective experiences with democracy and equality.

Evidently, when a regional order is involved, such as that constructed by the European Convention on Human Rights and concretised in the European Court of Human Rights, its normative force in the sphere of the states involved is undeniable, especially owing to the presence of obligations *erga omnes* and application of the general principle of *jus cogens*.[128] Also in the case of the WTO, albeit based on a decision-making model to which highly unstable negotiations are central and which is easily blocked (the intergovernmental model),[129] the binding normative strength of decisions with regard to the states, organisations, and corporations affected is undeniable. Nevertheless, I do not believe that it is opportune to apply the concept of constitution to these partial international orders without broad

[125] *See* Luhmann, 2000a, 222 *f*.

[126] '[T]he world legal order instead resembles the forms of the order of tribal societies' (Luhmann, 1993c, 544). On this topic, with restrictions, Fischer-Lescano, 2003, 719 *f* Kelsen (1960, 323 *f*; 1946, 339–41) refers to international public law as a 'primitive legal order'.

[127] According to Hobbes (1992, 149 [1651, 110]), relations between states occur in a 'state of nature', in which the law of the strongest prevails (1992, 118 [1651, 85 *f*]). *Cf* Locke, 1980 [1690], 13, §14, although Locke's conception of the state of nature is different.

[128] *Cf* Uerpmann, 2001, 571 *f*.

[129] Nettesheim, 2001, 402, referring however to a 'need for constitutionalisation'.

restrictions.[130] Instead, they should be considered in light of an analysis of trans-constitutionalism between legal orders, since they face significant constitutional problems that are intrinsic to world society and transcend the limits of statehood.

B. Supranational Constitutionalism in the Regional Plane

The issue presents itself differently when the question asked addresses the possibilities of a supranational constitutionalism that develops in a given region of the world. However, in this case it is also indispensable to fulfil certain presuppositions for the formation and development of a transversal constitution as the functional equivalent of that which characterises the constitutional state. What are those presuppositions?

It seems plausible that a certain symmetry at the level of the development of the respective Member States is a key condition for the construction of a supranationality, which entails broad norms and decisions in the social, material and temporal dimensions, directly binding the citizens and organs of the state. In cases of highly disparate budget conditions, educational levels, health systems, employment and work situations, and so on, the immediate normative incorporation (without ratification) that characterises a supranational order is impossible or at least hindered. The European Union's efforts to assure a certain minimum level of budget balance on the part of states that apply for membership and the corresponding controls after admission (this is at least a formal requirement for joining the euro) are a sign that, in contrast with internationality, stable supranationality cannot bear acute disparities of development.[131]

Furthermore, the emergence and realisation of a supranational constitution as an institution capable of serving the transversal rationality between politics and law in the regional plane presuppose that the territorially differentiated political and legal systems of the Member States are constructively linked via transversal constitutions. It is inconceivable that a transversal supranational constitution, through which legal equality and political democracy are entwined, could develop on the basis of autocratic states with instrumental constitutions or in apparently democratic states with symbolic constitutions.[132] This is one of the obstacles, for example, that Mercosur would have to overcome to make the transition from being an interstate organisation to becoming a suprastate organisation that could

[130] For a different view of the WTO, *see* Krajewski, 2001, especially 131. On the European Convention on Human Rights, Walter (1999) is more cautious, describing it as a 'constitutionalisation process'.

[131] Evidently, this situation can be interpreted differently: supranational integration can be understood as an opportunity to reach a higher level of economic and social development, especially for the less developed states in the region involved (in this regard I am grateful to Deisy Ventura and Armin von Bogdandy for their comments and criticisms). However, there are plenty of indications that acute disparities between states in terms of development create decisive difficulties for constructing and maintaining a stable supranational order.

[132] *See* Neves, 2009a.

at last begin to draw up a transversal supranational constitution. It is noteworthy that, while in the European Union the problem does not directly relate to the rule of law, that is, the formation of a *domestic European law*, but rather to democracy (a democratic deficit?), that is, the legitimation of a European *domestic politics*, the case of Mercosur is more serious. Although these two dimensions are interdependent in the plane of the rule of law, the deficiencies present in the Member States jeopardise the formation of a South American *domestic law* in Mercosur, quite apart from the fact that its structure is incompatible not only with democratic legitimation but also with the construction of a South American *domestic politics*. Thus there is not only a *double democratic deficit* in Mercosur, given the presence of the problem both in most of the Member States and in the regional organisation itself.[133] It is also appropriate to speak of a *double deficit of the rule of law* (oriented to the principle of equality), which hinders the legal limitation and control of public and private agents both in the sphere of Member States and in that of intergovernmental organs. In this respect, Mercosur is still far behind the European Union, where the limitations on the rule of law have been transcended in both spheres, despite all the normative and jurisdiction-related conflicts.[134] Thus, whereas the presuppositions for the formation of an organisation grounded in transversal constitutionalism are present in the European Union, at least in the sphere of the Member States, as regards both democracy and the rule of law, Mercosur does not yet meet even these minimum conditions.[135]

In addition to the presuppositions at the level of states, the formation of a supranational transversal constitution depends on the construction of a constitutional people to *determine procedures* at the suprastate level. However, this is not a matter of a people characterised by a collective cultural identity or by a community of values, which indeed does not exist in the constitutional state either;[136] but rather of a people that can be distinguished, first and foremost, by strong cultural heterogeneity. A supranational constitutional people is necessary to the extent that it enters into political procedures and can thereby lead to closure of the political system (*see* p 40 above). Thus, the generalisation of political support and democratic rationality are assured.

[133] Ventura, 2003, 590, also distinguishing Mercosur and the European Union in this respect, since in her view in the European Union the problem of the 'democratic deficit' relates only to the Union and not to the Member States. This remark should not lead us to overlook the anti-democratic tendencies in the experience of EU Member States, but the point is precisely that such tendencies are a problem for European supranational integration.

[134] *See*, eg, Weiler, 1999, especially 28.

[135] Neves, 2009a, 76.

[136] *Cf* Heller, 1934, 241. On this topic, the formulation put forward by da Silva, JA (2000, 123 *f*) is precise: 'All forms of *ethical state* produce their own ethical conception in light of the values they defend and the ends they set out to achieve, which leads to totalitarianism because it means the state is built on moral foundations comprising certain omnipotent and ubiquitous ethical criteria according to which no behaviour that is not rigorously in conformity with official morals is allowed.' To support his assertion, da Silva invokes the following statement by Dallari (1991, 89): 'What happens in practice is that the predominance of this orientation leads to exaggerated moralism, which provides a basis for the absolute supremacy of the will of the rulers, since they are the ones who dictate the moral rules on behalf of the state.'

The so-called 'democratic deficit' in the European Union relates to the hypothesis that, owing to the deficient development of a people capable of determining procedures, pressure from particularist interest constellations is not neutralised and therefore the generalisation of political support remains blocked.[137] Nevertheless, there are strong indications that increasingly strong supranational integration in the European Union may lead to consolidation of a European constitutional people, which, if so, would be highly heterogeneous and fit to determine political decision-making procedures in the broadest array of forms. A supranational democratic rationality appears to be emerging through the circulation and contracirculation of administration, government, public and people in the European Union, and should eventually be in a position to link up with the already consolidated legal rationality via a transversal constitution between European domestic politics and European domestic law.[138]

This situation can be observed in the circular relationship between legislative, executive, and jurisdictional procedures analogous to the model of state constitutionalism. Stefan Oeter points to three 'fundamental legislative organs' in the European Union – the Council of Ministers, the Commission and the Parliament – whereby its functioning resembles federalist bicameral parliamentary systems of the German type, with a governing body (the Commission, which has an administrative bureaucracy), and a supreme decision-making jurisdictional body, the European Court of Justice (ECJ).[139] He adds that 'even the phenomenon of comitology, which significantly limits the Commission's legislative scope in the sphere of pure executive lawmaking, has obvious parallels in the praxis of the German cooperative federal state'.[140] Analogous to the establishment of general norms by the European Commission, the regulatory activity of the German federal government, subject to agreement by the Federal Council (Bundesrat), is impregnated with the 'coordination of countless professional associations', entailing a system with multiple 'levels'.[141] Considering these similar characteristics and comparing the thenEuropean Community with international organisations that operate in the plane of intergovernmental cooperation, Oeter says: 'What distinguishes the Community from any other international organisation, however, is the combination of immediate applicability with the

[137] *See* Grimm, 1995b, 14 *f*. Problematising this hypothesis, *see* Weiler, 1999, especially 77 *ff* and 264 *ff*. Against the hypothesis, della Cananea (2003, 107 *ff*) argues for a 'double electoral legitimation of European institutions' (pp 109–12). Maduro (2006, 225 *ff*), however, refers to a 'European democratic surplus' (on this, *see* the critique by Hespanha, 2007, 280, note 363).

[138] I restrict myself here to the supranational experience of constitutionalisation in the European Union, leaving aside the wide-ranging debate on the so-called 'European Constitution' (of which the European Union's constitution is said to be a 'partial constitution' – von Bogdandy, 2003, 157, note 1), which entails dimensions of regional international law, such as the European Convention on Human Rights.

[139] Oeter, 1999, 906 *ff*.

[140] Oeter, 1999, 909. On the initial discussion of 'comitology', *see* Pedler and Schaefer (eds), 1996; Vos, 1997; Bradley, 1997; Joerges and Neyer, 1997. For a consideration of recent changes, *see* Almer, 2008, Joerges, 2007. For a comprehensive overview, *see* Bergström, 2005.

[141] Oeter, 1999, 909.

primacy of community law.'[142] This means, if we share Oeter's viewpoint, that it is imbued with a constitutional circulation of a plurality of legal and political procedures.

While acknowledging the relevance of these painstaking reflections, I venture to take the view that 'comitology' in the European Union is different in nature from what happens via the presence of the technical agencies and professional associations that provide assistance with the drafting of bills in the German parliament and federal executive. First, the fact that the European Commission not only has legislative powers but constitutes the governing body of the European Union makes its relationship to technical agencies and professional agencies hard to control. The weak European Parliament does not yet have sufficient powers to enable it to appraise and select legitimately, via transparent discussion, normative content produced by processes of deliberation in professional associations and technical committees. With regard to the latter, there is no guarantee that the particularism of interest groups will be neutralised. It is true that the presence of *arcana imperii* has also been noted as a factor that erodes democracy in the constitutional state.[143] In this case, however, there persists the possibility that the debate on this form of particularist and privileged power may be rearticulated in the sphere of the Parliament and lawmaking procedures, with repercussions for a broad public sphere. The question that arises in respect of the European Union is precisely that of the limits to the circulation of power, which in each case is open to inflows from a pluralist public sphere. From this is derived a polycentric process of legislation characterised by 'ample exclusion of the public sphere'.[144]

It is therefore pertinent to conclude by noting that, alongside a constitutional people which *determines* procedures, the emergence and stability of a supranational transversal constitution in the regional sphere requires the formation of a public sphere that is strong, that is, *relevant* to procedures, and can help open up the political system and thus serve as an instance of its heterolegitimation. This depends on political procedures that remain open and sensitive to the instigations and influences of the respective public sphere. Once again, this is not a matter of homogeneous cultural unity or collective identity,[145] although the discussion is developing in this direction, for example, with regard to the search for a European identity as the basis for a supranational constitution.[146] What is missing from this perspective is precisely that structural dissension is indispensable to the public sphere. If we wish to insist on the term, 'identity' can be presented only as the 'identity of difference', that is, can be present only insofar as it supports dissension regarding content, admitting and promoting procedures and institutions that enable non-identical

[142] Oeter, 1999, 910.
[143] Bobbio, 1984, 17 *f* and 22.
[144] Oeter, 1999, 908.
[145] In a different sense, *see* Grimm, 1995b, 46 *ff*.
[146] *See* among others von Bogdandy, 2003; 2004b.

perspectives to coexist. The key is the relevance of public debate to supranational constitutional procedures.

To some extent Joseph Weiler is right to argue that the Treaty of Maastricht (1992) was the threshold of constitutionalism in the European Union ('the most important constitutional "moment"'), given its public impact on a population that had hitherto been 'conveniently indifferent', that is, given the public reaction or the public debate that followed its entry into force.[147] Nevertheless, it is important to consider the argument that 'national' public spheres articulated around state political procedures continue to enjoy primacy over the developing European public sphere and are still occupied to a limited extent with the respective supranational procedures. Political procedures that are alien to the public sphere are incompatible with transversal constitutions, but there are strong signs that the increasingly intense condensation of common themes at the European level makes the formation of a procedurally relevant supranational public sphere highly probable, potentially leading to the stability of a European transversal constitution.

A strategy to fortify a European public sphere and build a European constitutional people needs to focus on a comprehensive reform of the European Parliament in order to strengthen its representative and decision-making role in the context of a rearticulation of the division of powers within the European Union.[148] In this perspective, the presence of a relevant legislative and parliamentary body would instigate the articulation of a public sphere around its procedures. To a certain extent, this model was designed into the Constitutional Treaty ('Treaty Establishing a Constitution for Europe'), agreed by the European Council on 18 June 2004, and signed on 29 June 2004, but rejected in referenda by the French and Dutch (2005).[149] Following this rejection, a lengthy process led to the Treaty of Lisbon, which 'Amends the Treaty on European Union and the Treaty Establishing the European Community' (the latter was renamed the Treaty on the Functioning of the European Union) and entered into force on 1 December 2009. This document also strengthens European integration in the direction of constitutionalisation.[150] With respect to this model, there is widespread suspicion that attributing more competencies to a parliamentary body that lacks a relevant public sphere around it, instead of strengthening democracy at the European level, will weaken democracy in the Member States.[151] While this suspicion deserves to be pondered, it seems to me that a reform of

[147] Weiler, 1999, 3 *f*.

[148] *See* in this sense Habermas, 2001; more carefully, 2008.

[149] On the implications of these referenda, *see* Brunkhorst, 2008b.

[150] This Treaty was signed in Lisbon on 13 December 2007, but its approval was provisionally blocked because of rejection by Ireland in a referendum held on 12 June 2008. In a second referendum, after concessions made by the European Union, the Irish finally approved it on 3 October 2009. The Czech Republic was the last Member State to ratify the Treaty, in November 2009, also after EU concessions. As regards the insufficiency of this Treaty to solve the problems of European integration, *see* Habermas, 2008, 97 *ff*.

[151] *See* Grimm, 1995b, especially 47; 2004b.

the model for the distribution of powers to include stronger democratic representativeness and decision-making power for the European Parliament could stimulate the development of a procedurally relevant public sphere that would have a complementary and competitive relationship with 'national' public spheres throughout the European Union in the context of a system with multiple entangled 'levels'.

Lastly, it should also be noted that the constitutionalisation of the European Union is driven mainly by developments that take place at the centre of the legal system, comprising national and European judges and courts, and with the European Court of Justice (ECJ) as its supreme body. It is therefore appropriate to speak of an incomplete supranational constitution, not strictly because 'you could create rights and afford judicial remedies to slaves',[152] since conceptually slaves are chattels, but because the principle of equality linked to the rule of law suffers restrictions when the respective legal and political order lacks the support of democracy.

In sum, juridification is in a strongly asymmetrical relationship with democratisation at the European level. A balanced and constructive entanglement between legal rationality (the equality principle) and political rationality (democratic legitimacy), in the context of a European Constitution as a 'bridge of transition' to transversal rationality between politics and law at the supranational level, has not been fully consolidated in a manner functionally equivalent to the experience of the successful constitutional states (although even in the latter it is not a perfect or finished product). Rather, if we do not limit ourselves to a historical-universal concept of constitution, the constitutionalisation of the European Union is still a developing process that is open to reversal but will probably tend to consolidate a transversal constitution in the plane of supranational federalism.

C. Transnational 'Civil Constitutions'

A very different perspective from transversal constitutionalism in world society is the idea of transnational constitutions which develop primarily through private and quasi-public actors without the state. This is the direction taken above all by Gunther Teubner.

As I have stressed in previous writings,[153] the concept of 'global civil constitutions' proposed by Teubner[154] is part of a theoretical project in which, in a later development of systems theory, the accent of the operative self-production of law is shifted to global legal orders, characterised by heterarchy and pluralism.[155] According to this project, world society, in the context of globalisation,

[152] Weiler, 1999, 336, accompanied by Brunkhorst, 2002, 232.
[153] Neves, 2006a, 260 *ff*; 2007a, 194 *ff*; 2007b, 385 *ff*.
[154] Teubner, 2003a [Engl trans 2004b]; 2000 [Engl trans 2004a].
[155] Teubner, 1996b or 1997b; 1996c; 1998a; 1998b [Engl trans 2000].

is seen as leading to the development of rule of law and due process of law in various differentiated domains of communication. Thus, it is argued that rule-of-law procedures have lost their specific relationship of belonging to a nation-state and have been given new momentum in the sphere of 'global villages' as autonomous systems, such as economics, science, technics, healthcare, social security, transport, the media and tourism as world systems.[156] In this process the significance of the constitution as a structural coupling between politics and law has become negligible. Teubner starts from Luhmann's diagnosis, according to which there is no correspondence in the structural coupling between politics and law via the constitution at the level of world society,[157] but develops his argument in a different direction, considering the loss of importance of politics on the global plane. On one hand, the weakening of politics and law structurally coupled via the constitution is attributed to the strong link between both systems and the nation state; on the other, law has become decoupled from democratic politics in the process of globalisation (see pp 24 *f* above). This emancipation of law from the nationstate has occurred, according to Teubner, with the emergence of plural legal orders that developed through structural couplings with the respective autonomous world systems. Associated with this process, the 'spontaneous sectors' of world society have gained prominence compared with the 'organised sectors'.[158] In this context, there has been a fragmentation into 'law's global village[s]',[159] requiring emphasis by the theory of law and legal doctrine on the 'heterarchical plurality of legal orders',[160] in contrast with the conception of the hierarchy and unity of law in the constitutional state. In the model proposed by Teubner, this process is summed up as a pluralisation of the operative self-production or autopoiesis of law.

In the terms posed by this pluralist theory of world law without the state, the concept of constitution is semantically broadened to a significant extent, since it extends to links between rationality oriented by the principle of equality and the rationalities of world systems that *do not depend on democracy* for their reproduction – differently from Luhmann, who restricts the concept of constitution to a specific type of link between two specific systems, politics and law. Whereas Luhmann argues, for example, that the structural coupling between law and economics resides in contract and property, Teubner also refers to the civil constitution that structurally couples *lex mercatoria* and the world economic system, as well as various other global civil constitutions. It is a moot point whether this involves an inflationary or arbitrarily metaphorical use of the term 'constitution', pointing to an object 'desired by all' (see Chapter 1, Section I). Teubner, however, seeks to delimit the concept of constitution seman-

[156] Teubner, 1996b, especially 259 or 1997b, 5 *f*.
[157] Teubner, 1996b, 260 or 1997b, 6; 1996c, 248. *See* pp 23 and 60 *f* above.
[158] Teubner, 2000 [Engl trans 2004a]; 2003a, 25 *f* [Engl trans 2004b, 27 *f*]. *Cf* Fischer-Lescano, 2005, 254 *ff*.
[159] Teubner, 1996b, 261; *cf* 1997b, 5–7.
[160] Teubner, 1996c, 245.

tically, indicating only the links between law and another social system at the *reflexive* level.[161] In the case of civil constitutions, two reflexive processes, one in law and the other in one of the global social spheres (economics, sport, the internet, science, and so on – except politics, which relates to state constitutions), are seen as structurally coupled, assuming the autonomy of the respective systems.

If this conceptual reconstruction is allowed, the civil constitutions identified by Teubner present themselves equally as 'bridges of transition' between social subsystems and plural legal orders in the global plane. Civil constitutions can therefore be said to serve transversal rationality between global social spheres and world legal orders as and when, at the respective reflexive levels, they entangle the self-production of law with that of the corresponding subsystem of society. In this theoretical constellation, the concept of civil constitutions is associated with the problem of regime collision, as formulated here: 'The characteristics of self-constitutional regimes is their linkage of legal reflexive processes with reflexive processes of other societal spheres, and precisely not only with those of politics; in other words, self-constitutional regimes as inter-systemic coupling institutions relate law with fundamental principles of rationality in autonomous social domains, through secondary rule-making in law.'[162] The indication is that maximisation of the rationality of the various functional systems can have destructive effects even on polycentric world society. The result is the requirement, both legally and constitutionally, of autonomous regimes that can confront the expansionary tendencies of some global functional systems at the expense of the autonomy of other subsystems.[163] From this perspective, concern with the destructive effects of partial spheres of fragmented world society on man and nature is equally foregrounded, highlighting the question of determining how plural legal orders and the corresponding civil constitutions of world society can respond to this problem. It should be noted that Teubner's argument about regime collision and civil constitutions is ultimately oriented towards a search for transversal rationalities between law and the respective social subsystems of world society.

The emphasis Teubner places on plural global legal orders ('law's global villages'), structurally coupled with one of the world systems (economics, science, sport, the internet, etc) through civil constitutions, is undoubtedly very significant to clarify the relationship between law and society at the global level. It is a key contribution to comprehension of the transversal entanglement between spheres of communication oriented primarily in accordance with normative expectations, and domains of communication structured primarily in accordance with cognitive expectations in world society. However, there are also certain specific empirical conditions that limit the development of civil constitutions

[161] Fischer-Lescano and Teubner, 2006, 53 *ff*; Teubner, 2003a, especially 17–25 [Engl trans 2004b, 18–27].

[162] Fischer-Lescano and Teubner, 2006, 54.

[163] Fischer-Lescano and Teubner, 2006, 25–33.

in world society. As expounded by Teubner, symptoms of the limits to global civil constitutions can be identified. With regard to *lex mercatoria*, for example,[164] it is important to note its deficient autonomy from global economic processes, and in particular that it is extremely weak with regard to both the attacks of economic actors and political pressure: in this sense it is, and for the foreseeable future will remain, a 'corrupt law'.[165] Thus, it is possible to posit the thesis that this legal order is rather an instrument of the world economy and must first and foremost serve the efficiency of this system. In other words, *lex mercatoria* places law at the service of money or makes law a medium for money. Strictly speaking, it is not an operatively autonomous form of law with respect to the economic system. As long as *lex mercatoria* as global economic law is subordinated to the world economy or remains economically trivialised, it cannot be suitable as a legal order to the promotion of equal/unequal treatment that is not only economically adequate but also legally consistent. It is opportune to favour the legal stability of the economic game, but it is not in a position to guarantee legal equality. In light of the highly dynamic reflexive processes of the monetary mechanisms that operate in the world economy, the reflexivity of *lex mercatoria* is still very weak. For this reason, the process of formation of a constitution or a functional equivalent that can serve the transversal rationality between law and the world economy is significantly defective. Indeed, what is at stake is a relationship between the weak reflexivity of law due to insufficient development of a corresponding constitutional law, and the strength of the world economic code, which invades the 'legal field' of *lex mercatoria* in a heteronomising, instrumental, or destructive manner. This also applies to other 'global legal villages' in their relations with the respective global social systems, highlighting the instrumentalisation of world legal orders by other partial spheres of communication in world society (*lex mercatoria* for the economy, *lex digitalis* for the internet, *lex sportiva* for sport, and so on). As a result, the formation of transversal constitutions in the transnational plane has hitherto remained merely a prospective project and, in part, constitutes a normative claim of world society that should be taken seriously, as shown by the question of human rights.[166]

It seems to me, however, that it is not entirely appropriate to define the forms of relationship existing between transnational legal orders and the corresponding global functional systems in terms of 'civil constitutions'. It appears more fruitful and appropriate to the treatment of the constitutional problems of world society today to incorporate these orders into the network of entanglements between legal orders (state, supranational, international and local) in the sphere of the affluent transconstitutionalism.

[164] Teubner, 1996b, 264 *ff* or 1997b, 8 *ff*.
[165] Teubner, 1996b, 279 or 1997b, 19.
[166] Teubner, 2006 [Engl trans 2006].

3

. . . *to Transconstitutionalism between Legal Orders*

I. TRANSCONSTITUTIONALISM BETWEEN LEGAL ORDERS AS A MODEL FOR TREATING CONSTITUTIONAL PROBLEMS

THE CONCEPT OF transversal constitutions refers to the entanglement of law and politics or, in the case of the 'civil constitutions' of world society, another social system. The question resides in the relations between functional systems, focusing on the limits and possibilities of constructing a transversal rationality via reciprocal learning and creative exchange. This entails externalising and internalising information between social spheres that perform different functions and reproduce primarily through different binary codes of communication.

The question changes when transconstitutionalism is at stake. In this case, the problem consists of delineating the forms of relationship between different legal orders. In other words, the distinct legal orders that proliferate within one and the same functional system of modern world society, law, are all subordinated to the same binary code ('legal/illegal') but with different programmes and criteria.[1] Hence, the plurality of legal orders, each with its own elements or operations (legal acts), structures (legal norms), processes (legal procedures) and reflection of identity (legal doctrine).[2] This leads to differentiation within the legal system. This differentiation between orders, however, is not limited to segmentary differentiation between state legal orders with delimited territorial spheres of validity. Moreover, there is not only a differentiation of 'levels' between state, supranational and international legal orders, but also the functional differentiation of transnational legal orders decoupled from state law by their transterritoriality.

This multiplicity of differentiated orders inside the legal system does not entail reciprocal isolation. The relations of input/output and interpenetration

[1] On the difference between code (binary form difference) and criteria (for problem solving) or programmes (for decision making), *cf* Luhmann, 1986c, 82 *f* and 89 *ff*, considering that the autonomous reproduction of a system presupposes a combination of 'coding' and 'programming', since codes would become empty forms if they were not combined with programmes and criteria. On the legal system specifically, 1986a, 194 *ff*; 1993a, 165 *ff* [Engl trans 2004, 173 *ff*].

[2] *See* Teubner, 1989, 49 *ff*; 1987a, 106 *ff*; 1987b, 432 *ff*.

between them are not something new. As far as the connection between classical international law and state law is concerned, under the Treaty of Westphalia (1648) the incorporation of international norms into internal law is effected by means of ratification, just as reproduction of the international legal order depends on the presence of state representatives legitimated by this same order. Also, in the relationship between state legal orders, complex re-entry mechanisms were developed in the classical terms of international private law. What is new in the entanglements among a plurality of legal orders in the world society of the present is their relative independence from the forms of political intermediation via international treaties and state legislation. The forms taken by formal and informal relations between governmental and non-governmental actors multiply in the sphere of law. This situation becomes all the more significant in light of the fact that to a large extent the 'bridges of transition' between legal orders develop directly from their respective centres, that is, their judges and courts.[3]

This is to say that not only world society but also its legal system is multicentric, so that from the perspective of one legal order's centre (judges and courts) another legal order's centre is a periphery. Thus for the Brazilian judiciary, for example, both judges in other countries and courts in international, supranational and transnational legal orders, when their decisions are taken into account by it, present themselves as periphery and viceversa. The same can be said of any type of legal order with a claim to autonomy. This situation entails relations of mutual observation, in the context of which there develop forms of learning and exchange without any possibility of supremacy for one of the orders as a legal *ultima ratio*.

In this sense, there is said to be a 'conversation' or 'dialogue' between courts, which can take place on various 'levels': for example, between the European Court of Justice (supranational) and the courts of the Member States, between the European Court of Human Rights (international) and national courts or the ECJ, between national courts and so on.[4] This 'conversation' (which strictly speaking consists of transversal communications across frontiers between legal orders) should not lead to an idea of permanent cooperation between legal orders, since conflicts between different legal perspectives are frequent.[5] In the last instance, any 'conversation' between courts can potentially lead to a dispute. The problem is how to settle such disputes without top-down imposition in the relations between orders.

[3] *See* Luhmann, 1993a, 321 *ff* [Engl trans 2004, 293 *ff*]; 1990 *f*, 466 *ff*.

[4] Baudenbacher, 2003, 507 *ff*. 'The result, paradoxically, is more dialogue and less deference' (Slaughter, 2003, 194). I use 'dialogue' and 'conversation' not in the sense of understanding- or consensus-oriented discourse but rather to refer to forms of communication designed to absorb dissent, assuming double contingency (*see* note 130, this Chapter, and Section III of Chapter 4), although I am well aware that these words are not usually deployed with such meanings. Between different legal orders, especially on the plane of constitutional problems, these terms point to transversal communications.

[5] *See* Slaughter, 2003, 204 *ff*; 2004, 85 *ff*.

However, not all entanglements of legal orders occur between courts. There is often an incorporation of norms from another order without the intermediation of 'dialogue' between courts. A reinterpretation of the order to which a court belongs may occur in response to the incorporation of normative meanings extracted from other legal orders. Moreover, other 'levels' of the legal system undergo permanent learning and exchange, as is the case in relations among the legislatures, governments, and administrations of several countries.[6] Without doubt, however, the most relevant form of transversality between legal orders is that which involves judges and courts, whether or not it occurs interjudicially.

What is peculiar to transconstitutionalism is not the existence of these entanglements between legal orders, or so-called 'legal transnationalism'. In the case of transconstitutionalism, orders interrelate at the reflexive level of their normative structures, which are self-binding and enjoy primacy. This 'constitutional conversation' is incompatible with a 'constitutional diktat' imposed by one order on another.[7] Thus, it is not appropriate to speak of a hierarchical structure between orders: reciprocal incorporation of content entails a re-reading of meaning in light of the receiving order.[8] There is a reconstruction of meaning which involves a certain deconstruction of the other as well as self-deconstruction: at one and the same time, the 'other's' meaning content is decomposed (falsified!) and recomposed internally, while meaning content originating within the same order is decomposed (falsified!) and recomposed in response to introduction of the 'other'.

On one hand, transconstitutionalism brings out 'constitutional cross-fertilisation'.[9] Constitutional courts 'cite each other not as precedent, but as persuasive authority'.[10] In terms of transversal rationality, courts are willing to engage in constructive learning with other courts and to be bound by their decisions.[11] On the other hand, there is a 'combination of both active cooperation and vigorous conflict among national courts involved in transnational litigation between private parties across borders'.[12] 'Global litigation' leads to the emergence of 'judicial comity', which 'provides the framework and the groundrules for a global dialogue among judges in the context of specific cases',[13] to 'judges

[6] *See* Slaughter, 2004, 104 *ff*; Möllers, 2005b.

[7] Weiler, 1999, 322.

[8] In this sense, Berman, PS (2005, 551 *ff*) refers to 'the multidirectional interaction of local, national, and international norms'.

[9] Slaughter, 2000, 1116 *ff*; 2003, 194 *ff*; 2004, 69 *ff*.

[10] Slaughter, 2003, 193.

[11] Slaughter, 2003, 199 *ff*; 2004, 75 *ff*.

[12] Slaughter, 2003, 193.

[13] Slaughter, 2004, 87; 2003, 206. Slaughter refers to the 'comity of nations' as 'a venerable concept with a long legal and political pedigree', asserting that 'it means the respect owed to the laws and acts of other nations by virtue of common membership in the international system – a presumption of recognition that is something more than courtesy but less than obligation' (2004, 86; 2003, 205); in this passage she invokes a definition contained in *Hilton v Guyot*, 159 US 113 (1895), 163 *f*. However, the concept of 'judicial comity' should be extended to include the various judges and courts, not just national, but also international, supranational, transnational and local extra-state, decoupling it from the idea of membership. On arbitration tribunals and *lex mercatoria*, *see* Mendes, R, 2010, 107.

judging judges', and to 'judicial negotiation'.[14] With regard to these new phenomena, the constitutional dimension is more clearly expressed when constitutional courts are involved in the broad sense, that is, courts whose remit is exclusively or mainly to judge juridico-constitutional questions.

But how to define the constitutional issues that give rise to transconstitutionalism? Here it is appropriate to decouple the notion of constitutional law from classical constitutionalism, that is, from a concept of constitution associated exclusively with a particular state, without the need to refer to other 'constitutions'. Constitutionalism, originally linked to the nation-state as a territorial organisation, arose to answer two questions: (1) How to determine coercively the rights and fundamental guarantees of individuals? (2) How to limit and control expansionary state power, while at the same time assuring its organisational efficiency?[15] The answer came with state constitutions, since these normative problems still had a territorially delimited dimension. Over time, growth in transterritorial relations with fundamental normative implications led to a need to open up constitutionalism beyond the state. Problems of fundamental rights or human rights transcend borders, so that state constitutional law became too limited an institution to address those problems. The same happened with the organisation of power, with the question of how to combine limitation and control of power with its organisational efficiency. Treatment of these problems ceased to be a privilege of state constitutional law and could be legitimately addressed by other legal orders, since they had proved relevant to the latter.[16] Thus, the question of transconstitutionalism does not arise from inflationary references to the existence of a constitution in practically every new legal order that emerges with a claim to autonomy. Neither identifying the order to which a constitution belongs, nor defining it as a state privilege, is of primary importance to the concept of transconstitutionality. The crucial point is that constitutional problems arise in various different legal orders and require solutions grounded in the entanglements between them.

Thus, a given fundamental rights issue can be presented to a state, local, international or supranational order, or a transnational order in the strict sense – or more than one of these orders, as frequently happens, entailing cooperation and conflict and requiring reciprocal learning. With regard to transnational

[14] Slaughter, 2003, 204 *ff*; 2004, 85 *ff*; *cf* 2000, 1112 *ff*.

[15] Evidently the idea of legal-constitutional limitation and control of power entails the notion of 'participation' by citizens in procedures for normative production ('legitimating function'). However, in my view it is not advisable, especially in the present context, to extend constitutional problems and their respective functions to include not just the functions of 'organisation and legitimation' as well as that of 'limitation (protection of fundamental rights)', but also the 'integration function', as proposed by Walter (2000, 5 and 7–11), based on Smend (1968 [1928]). This is because the holistic conception of the constitution (in the modern sense) as the 'fundamental order of the collectivity' (*see*, eg, Hesse, 1980, 11; Hollerbach, 1969, 46; Böckenförde, 1983, 16 *ff*) is excluded by the theoretical perspective within which this text has been produced (*see* Luhmann, 1973a, 2; Neves, 2007a, 67 *f*; 1992, 50).

[16] In this direction, Cassese, S (2007) refers to the 'constitutional function of non-state judges'. Meanwhile, Delmas-Marty (2007, 42 *ff*) notes the 'internationalisation of national judges'.

legal orders in the strict sense, which involve above all private and quasi-public actors, it is undeniable that fundamental or human rights issues come before them. It is less clear that they are related to problems of limitation and control of power. If it is a matter of political power in the systemic sense, which is primarily oriented to collectively binding decisions, these orders are undeniably distant from the problem. However, the *influence* exerted by private actors in the sphere of these orders, without direct control by a political authority (state, international or supranational), makes them into wielders of power with relevant political repercussions.[17] Thus, juridico-constitutional problems also reappear in transnational orders wearing new clothes.

Given this emergence of constitutional problems to be faced by the widest variety of legal orders, reappearing at each moment like a Hydra, no Hercules-like constitution can solve them. The fragmentation of constitutional problems would remain unstructured if every legal order tried to address them alone in every case. Hence, the need for a transconstitutional 'dialogue' or 'conversation'. It is evident that transconstitutionalism is incapable of leading to constitutional unity of the world legal system, but it appears to have been the only effective way of providing and structuring adequate answers to the constitutional problems that emerge fragmentarily in the context of today's world society.

The problem of the legal system's constitutional self-foundation is displaced in this context. As *unitas multiplex*, the legal system finds several centres of self-foundation depending on the legal order it takes as a startingpoint. In the context of a reconstruction of the pure theory of law based on a 'theory of the normative coupling between systems', Jestaedt defends the thesis of 'competition among interpretations of law instead of coexistence among legal orders'[18] and argues that the validity of a norm can be considered only with reference to a given legal order, taking into account the respective basic norm.[19] From this argument he derives the conception according to which 'a legal order can enter into a normative relationship with ought-statements initially belonging to another legal order only if through reception, delegation, transformation, or in any other way it raises them to normative statements of the legal order itself'.[20] In this sense, he maintains that a legal order's monist interpretation of the relations between normative layers is inevitable,[21] and asserts the inevitability and openness, from the standpoint of the theory of law, of the 'choice' of monism, that is of the order or basic norm that is taken as startingpoint: 'The fact that a monist interpretation of the legal order is inevitable says nothing about how a

[17] On the distinction between influence in general and differentiated power as communication medium, *see* Luhmann, 1988b [1975], 74 *ff*, especially 78; 2000a, 39 *ff*.

[18] Jestaedt, 2008, especially 234.

[19] 'The validity of a norm can be affirmed only relatively to or immanently in a legal order' (Jestaedt, 2008, 234–6).

[20] Jestaedt, 2008, 234 and 236 *f*. It does not seem to me that this assertion necessarily entails the thesis that there are 'relations between norms only in the same sphere of validity', that is, the same legal order (Jestaedt, 2008, 236). I return to this topic later.

[21] Jestaedt, 2008, 234 and 239 *f*.

choice must be made among possible monist interpretations.'[22] And strictly following the Kelsenian model, he supplements this assertion with an affirmation of the neutrality of the choice of monist construction with regard to the content of law,[23] as well as the political nature of this decision.[24] Coherently with these presuppositions, Jestaedt asserts that the 'correlate of monism of the legal order is pluralism of legal interpretation',[25] stressing that 'the hypothesis of the monist choice can be characterised as a theory of legal relativity', since legal construction will vary in accordance with the order taken as startingpoint.[26] However, going beyond these plausible arguments based on a reconstruction of Kelsen, Jestaedt defends the thesis that normative relations exist only in one and the same sphere of validity (that is, within the same legal order), that '(solutions) of collisions' can emerge only when they are 'immanent in the legal order' and hence that 'communication' occurs 'exclusively' in 'monologic' form at the 'intra(legal)-systemic' level.[27]

This reconstruction of Kelsenian monism taken to a constructivist extreme is open to objections, in my view. Strictly speaking, in methodological monism the choice of one of the basic norms is a 'political-ideological' question. Whether from the 'imperialist' standpoint of the monism that starts from a basic norm of a given national order, the pacifist standpoint of a monism that starts from a basic norm of international public law, or that of a supranationalist or transnationalist type of monism, the 'political-ideological' choice of a given legal order is irrelevant to the 'science of law' or theory of law.[28] Once a choice has been by made by one of the orders, the normative contents of the various 'other orders' (a notion that is not compatible with the monist conception) are considered merely lower normative layers of the order whose 'basic norm' is the starting point.

In this sense, from the standpoint of the theory of law it is also inappropriate to speak of competition among 'interpretations of law'. This would only make sense, starting from the Kelsenian monist model, in a 'political-ideological' perspective on law. If a basic norm is chosen using political criteria, the order in question would be 'blind' to competition from other orders because they would be merely lower layers of a single order.

In this monist hierarchical model there is no place for a 'theory of the coupling between normative systems', as per Jestaedt. If one's startingpoint is a basic norm as *ultima ratio* of the legal system, the basis for all arguments must be a single legal order, in accordance with a model comprising higher and lower norms but never a plurality of systemic interpretations of law: the single order

[22] Jestaedt, 2008, 235 and 240 *f.*

[23] 'The 'choice' of one of the monist constructions, regardless of which of the monist constructions it relates to, has no influence on the content of the law considered' (Jestaedt, 2008, 235 and 241–3).

[24] Jestaedt, 2008, 246.

[25] Jestaedt, 2008, 235 and 244 *f.*

[26] Jestaedt, 2008, 235 and 245 *ff.*

[27] Jestaedt, 2008, 234 and 237–9.

[28] *See* Kelsen, 1960, 333–45; 1946, 376–88; 1925, 128–32.

that serves as starting point for this construction sees even an ought-statement not as belonging to another order but as an internal dimension of itself (for example, anyone who starts with the Brazilian legal order must recognise international public law as a layer inferior to the Constitution). Jestaedt's reconstruction is not consistent either with the Kelsenian model or with the idea of couplings between normative systems: all monisms lead to extreme, autistic constructivism that cannot offer useful elements for a theory of the multicentric legal system of world society, within which several legal orders relate orthogonally and horizontally with a plurality of self-founding cores, facing the same constitutional problems.

Transconstitutional relations between legal orders result not only from reciprocal input/output, interpenetration, and interference between systems in general,[29] but above all from the fact that the different legal orders belong to the same functional system of world society, a system which claims to reproduce itself primarily on the basis of the same binary code, that is, the difference between legal and illegal or lawful and unlawful.[30] But because this unity of a difference is radically distinct from a hierarchical unity grounded in a single basic norm, plural legal codes and criteria can proliferate in a multiplicity of legal orders, each of which claims to affirm its identity in the internal handling of the binary preference-code of law. Not only does this problem lead to the possibility, already emphasised by Luhmann, of normative closure of the legal system combined with cognitive openness,[31] but also, because normative orders in the same functional system of world society (law) are involved, there occurs what can be called normative learning between them, given that they are subordinated to the same binary code. This code's lack of content enables *normative* closure in the determination of norms according to criteria immanent in the order itself (whether it be national, local, supranational, international, or transnational) to combine with *normative* openness in the reciprocal learning that can occur through the settlement of legal cases in which two (or more) orders are involved.

[29] Luhmann distinguishes between mere 'performances' ('input/output relations' – 1987c, 275 *ff* [Engl trans 1995, 201 *ff*] and interpenetration (1987c, 289 *ff* [Engl trans 1995, 213 *ff*]). Interpenetration exists when each of the systems reciprocally makes its own complexity available for the process of constructing another system (Luhmann, 1987c, 290 [Engl trans 1995, 213]). It differs from 'interference' as defined by Teubner (1989, especially 110; 1988, 55 *ff*), since whereas in the case of interference each of the systems places pre-ordered complexity at the other's disposal, in interpenetration the receiving system has at its disposal 'an incomprehensible complexity – that is, disorder' (Luhmann, 1987c, 291 [Engl trans 1995, 214]). *See* pp 27 *f* above.

[30] Günther and Randeria (2001, 94 *ff*) refer to the 'emergence of a universal code of legality', but despite an eclectic theoretical perspective they overload this code with programmatic content from a specific liberal tradition: 'In addition to constant reference to the key difference – in the language of systems theory the 'binary code' between 'lawful and unlawful' – the universal code of legality includes other concepts, principles, rules and legal institutions: the concept of rights attributed individually and exercisable individually . . . the concept of strict responsibility dependent on guilt . . . the presumption of innocence, institutionalisation of the role of an impartial third party including the right of appeal, the principle of *adiatur et altera pars* etc' (p 94). *Cf* Günther, 2001.

[31] Luhmann, 1983b, especially 139; 1984b, 110 *ff*; 1993a, 393 *ff* [Engl trans 2004, 346 *ff*].

The relevance of the problem case for both orders means not negation of the internal criteria of normative validity for one of the orders or both, but transformation of normative content in light of the problem in the concretising process, enabling orders to coexist constructively. In the construction of the legal norm and the decision-making norm, each of the orders involved may consider as a dimension of its own 'field of normative operation' elements of the 'area of subject-matter' originally relevant to another order, as well as incorporating as a dimension of its own normative programme parts of the normative programmes of other orders.[32] In other words, starting simultaneously from normative texts and common cases[33] it is possible to construct different norms considering the possible processes of concretisation that will develop in the colliding or partner order.

Thus, closure of the internal chain of validation must be made compatible with the capacity for reciprocal learning in the network of legal concretisation for the construction of the norm of each legal order to deal with the various cases that emerge with simultaneous relevance for the different entangled orders. Normative openness, therefore, does not break the internal consistency of the chain of validation; instead, it serves a process of legal concretisation that is normatively adequate to the plurality of orders involved. Normative closure refers originally to attribution of the norm to normative texts or statements of the order itself. Normative openness refers originally to the community of the problem case to be resolved in a polycentric world society. Unresolvable conflicts or collisions between legal orders cannot be avoided, nor is it possible to eliminate definitively the 'imperial' claim of one of the orders involved with regard to the others: nationalism, internationalism, supranationalism, transnationalism, and localism are averse to reciprocal normative learning, especially in the broad reflexive terms of transconstitutionalism. In the context of a legal system constructed heterarchically via the relations among a plurality of normative orders, this entails a hetero-blocking irrationality that has self-blocking implications for the solution of cases.

The existence of problems common to more than one legal order, requiring different normative models, is nothing new, as demonstrated above all by the above-mentioned experience with re-entries in the sphere of classical international private law. At one time, cases arose sporadically and were resolved in accordance with norms of domestic ordinary law and treaties ratified by states, and included the expectation that legal acts initially practised in light of a

[32] I allude here to the distinction between a 'legal norm' (a criterion for settling a concrete case) and a 'decision-making norm' (which effectively settles the concrete case), and the difference between the 'field of normative operation' [*Normbereich*] (primarily 'real' data) and the 'normative program' [*Normprogramm*] (primarily linguistic data), as well as the notions of 'area of subject-matter' [*Sachbereich*] and the 'area of the case' [*Fallbereich*], in accordance with the conceptual model proposed by Müller (1994, 232–4, 253–6 and 264 *ff*; for an explanation, *see* Canotilho, 1991, 208 *ff* and 221 *ff*), although I recognise that this model has certain limits (*cf* Neves, 2006a, 200–3).

[33] According to Müller (1990, 20), a *normative text* constitutes, 'alongside the *case* to be decided in court, the most important input datum in the individual concretisation process'.

different order would be homologated. This situation has been profoundly transformed by the proliferation of legal orders and the emergence of transterritorialised legal cases relevant to various legal orders. The attention these orders simultaneously pay to environmental damage, violations of human or fundamental rights, the effects of international trade and finance, and transnational or cross-border crime, among other things, makes the emergence of common cases a daily problem which affects the reflexive level and the very identity of the orders involved. The problem resides in the fact that a response must be given in the centre of the respective legal orders in accordance with the same binary code ('legal/illegal') but originally different normative criteria. The question about compliance or non-compliance with the law ('lawfulness/unlawfulness') in the same case is brought before a plurality of legal orders.

This empty question may be supplemented with regard to content: what criteria or conditional programmes[34] can help define whether something is properly defined as lawful or unlawful? The various orders will of course begin by invoking their models for constructing criteria and programmes for the settlement of cases. Without doubt, there will tend to be collisions, at least in principle. The problem lies precisely in the incompatibility of the possible solutions presented. Hence, the fundamental importance of seeking 'bridges of transition'. These 'bridges', as models of entanglement that serve as transversal rationality between legal orders, are evidently not constructed permanently and statically in the dynamic sphere of transconstitutionalism.

Case processing requires an inductive approach entailing the construction and reconstruction of coupling structures in the plane of new operations of the system. The dynamics of the relations between structure (normative criteria) and operations (legal acts) for reciprocal learning is intensely circular in the context of transconstitutionalism in contemporary world society. With every unexpected new case, the reflexive structures of the respective orders have to rearticulate themselves consistently in order to allow a solution complexly adequate to society to be reached without undermining, blocking or destroying the competing or cooperating order, but rather helping to encourage it to be disposed to an exchange in future 'meetings' to deal with common cases.

What characterises transconstitutionalism between legal orders, therefore, is that it is a constitutionalism related to (solutions to) juridico-constitutional problems that are presented simultaneously to different orders. When issues of fundamental or human rights are submitted to concrete legal treatment across different legal orders, a constitutional 'conversation' is indispensable. Similarly, when basic organisational issues arise relating to the limitation and control of a power that criss-crosses legal orders, affecting the rights of the respective addressees, 'bridges of transition' must be built between the reflexive structures of the respective orders. Thus, for transconstitutionalism to develop fully, it is

[34] On conditional programming (if–then) as a peculiarity of the legal system, *see* Luhmann, 1993a, 195 *ff* [Engl trans 2004, 196 *ff*]; 1987a, 227–34; 1981a, 140–3 and 275 *ff*; 1973b, 88 *ff* (especially 99).

vitally important that the orders involved have principles and rules of organisation in which the basic problems of constitutionalism are taken seriously.[35]

Undoubtedly there are legal orders, especially state legal orders, which are not willing to collaborate with transconstitutionalism, because they ignore fundamental rights and reject legal limitation and control of those in power. Internally, they do not acknowledge the constitution in the modern sense, that is a constitution at the service of transversal rationality between law and politics. When faced with such orders, transconstitutionalism functions to a very limited extent: transconstitutional irritations, influences and pressure can lead to the transformation of anti-constitutional orders. The alternative to transconstitutionalism in this case is to take a bellicose attitude against orders that are hostile to transconstitutionalism, but this option produces side-effects that make it normatively inadvisable.

In the case of archaic orders the situation is entirely different, since they do not have principles and secondary rules of organisation, and therefore they are not able to deal with constitutional legal problems. Orders of this kind increasingly require a unilateral transconstitutionalism of tolerance and, to some extent, learning: although they are averse to the model of human rights and juridical limitation of power as per the legal system of world society, transconstitutionalism is not compatible with unilateral heteronomous imposition of 'human rights' on members of the respective community, since such imposition might have destructive effects on their minds and bodies and is contrary to the very idea of human rights.[36] Thus, although there are legal orders that are outside transconstitutionalism, the latter cannot exclude the development of institutions capable of leading to a constructive learning- and exchange-based relationship with those orders. This situation evidently entails limits for transconstitutionalism in asymmetrical world society (*see* Chapter 5, Section I below), but does not exclude its significance for the development of the normative dimension of world society.

In this respect it is worth stressing that although world society has hitherto been oriented primarily by cognitive expectations (*see* pp 21 *f* above), transconstitutionalism appears to be the most promising alternative for the strengthening of its normative dimension. State, international, supranational, transnational and local orders, considered as specific types, are incapable on their own of offering complexly adequate answers to the normative problems of world society. The models of international, supranational or transnational constitutionalism, as alternatives to the fragility of state constitutionalism to tackle the serious problems of world society, lead to partial and unilateral perspectives, and when considered in isolation do not offer adequate solutions to the constitutional problems

35 From a different perspective, Fischer-Lescano (2003, 720 *ff*), based on Luhmann and Teubner, refers to 'reflexive transnational law', rejecting the idea of the 'primitive' or 'tribal' nature of 'world law'. *See* p 64 above.

36 Understood as 'intended guarantees of the integrity of mind and body' (Teubner, 2006, 175 [Engl trans 2006, 338]). *See* p 160 below.

of the present. Transconstitutionalism, as a model of entanglement that serves transversal rationality between different legal orders, is open to a plurality of perspectives for the solution of constitutional problems, and as such is more adequate to the relations between legal orders in the heterarchical legal system of world society.

Lastly, it should be noted that transconstitutionalism has developed intensely and rapidly at the structural level of the legal system, but is still very limited in the sphere of the constitutional semantics of world society. In part, this is due to the persistence of constitutional provincialism, especially in the sphere of state law. It is clear that transconstitutionalism cannot eliminate classical constitutional doctrine in the interior of a state legal order: such orders still constitute an important dimension of the legal system of world society and there are interstate constitutional problems of supreme importance. But the openness of constitutional law beyond the state, in view of the transterritorialisation of juridico-constitutional problems and the various different orders to which they are relevant, makes the development of a theory and doctrine of transconstitutional law a necessity. Thus, new methodological approaches are required to provide responses to complex legal cases. This is the great challenge of transconstitutionalism for jurists, especially constitutionalists. Doctrinal analysis and theoretical debate remain very fragmented and sporadic. In the methodological sphere, the state of play remains embryonic.[37] The missing elements are a comprehensive theory of transconstitutionalism and a comprehensive doctrine that serves to stabilise transconstitutional law, both reciprocally presupposing methodological contributions. In the following sections I outline some suggestions for developments in this direction.

II. TRANSCONSTITUTIONALISM BETWEEN PUBLIC INTERNATIONAL LAW AND STATE LAW

In the relations between international legal orders and state legal orders, juridico-constitutional problem cases arise with increasing frequency, and the various orders involved all have a concurrent interest in their solution. These are situations in which more than one court is invoked to settle the case without their necessarily being norms for resolving conflicts of jurisdiction, or, when such norms exist, without there being a convergence on them among the courts involved. Strictly speaking, it is not appropriate to speak of vertical networks,[38] which would entail admitting a hierarchical relationship between orders. Instead, it is appropriate to speak of the entanglement of orders of different types.

[37] *See*, eg, Baudenbacher, 2003, 523, referring to the 'methodological and practical problems of judicial globalisation'; Uerpmann, 2001, 572, alluding to the 'methods of international constitutional law'. *See* Chapter 4, Section III.

[38] In a different sense, Slaughter (2004, 19 *ff*) distinguishes between vertical and horizontal networks.

In this sense, the direction to take in order to solve the problem may look entirely different from different vantagepoints. From that of the state order, the increasing involvement of constitutional courts in these issues, where the classical ratification model has gradually lost ground, heightens the tendency for them to be considered constitutional problems relating to human or fundamental rights or to the limitation and control of power, involving claims that transcend the specific sphere of validity of the domestic order. From the vantagepoint of the international order, this entails the incorporation of constitutional issues into the sphere of competence of its courts, which are beginning to claim the jurisdiction to make decisions that are immediately binding on agents and citizens of states.

This situation requires the development of forms of 're-entry' in the perspectives of reciprocal observation. To the extent that international courts start primarily from the interstate order, they are faced with the corresponding state order's particular understanding of institutions and problems. On one hand, unilateral internationalist imposition is problematic, not because of the possibility of turning to the traditional principles of self-determination or sovereign equality,[39] but because, without self-institutionalisation of constitutionalism in the state sphere, one of the specific legal rationalities needed to affirm transconstitutionalism is missing. The intervention model has shown its precariousness or insignificance for the construction of internal constitutional orders.[40] On the other hand, when national courts try to start exclusively from the juridico-constitutional order, they find it increasingly difficult to ignore the institutions and norms of international public law in the name of sovereignty, especially in the extreme case of *jus cogens*, since sovereignty can no longer be legitimated simply as a concept of territorial autonomy, but must increasingly be considered a notion relating to 'a regional political responsibility under the structural conditions of world society'.[41] Taking 'internal sovereignty' as the state's responsibility towards its social context and 'external sovereignty' as its responsibility towards the interstate context, and assuming that the 'society of states' constitutes a 'system of divergent worldviews' and that 'sovereign equality' represents a 'structure of reciprocal orientation of behaviour',[42] a model that starts from a single perspective seems irrational, whether that perspective be a state or international one. The 'opening up of statehood', on the contrary, has led to 'interpenetration between the state and international order',[43] which increasingly requires reciprocal learning and exchange of experiences with specific rationalities in both perspectives (state and international).

When the claim is to speak of 'international constitutional law', the only possible sense is to link it to the zone of tension between state and international

[39] United Nations Charter, Art 1, § 2, and Art 78 respectively.
[40] *Cf* Koskenniemi, 2002, 514 *f*; 2004, 202 *ff*.
[41] Luhmann, 1995a, 118.
[42] Langer, 1995, 18–34.
[43] Langer, 1995, 18 and 35 *ff*.

law, in the confrontation with and response to basic constitutional problems of world society. In this regard, a leading representative of international public law has this to say:

> The constitution is the manifestation of state sovereignty and public international law is its negation, or at least its growing limitation. International constitutional law does not exist, in my view, for lack of a defined object and specific method. Rather, there are constitutional norms with international scope, which should be analysed case by case in an effort to make the two branches of legal science compatible.[44]

To be more precise on this subject, it can be added that just as state constitutional norms have international scope, international norms have constitutional scope.[45] Thus, it is not accurate to speak of two manifestations of 'sovereignty', with affirmation and negation on opposite sides. Moreover, not only problems relating to the limitation and affirmation of 'sovereign' power but also issues relating to basic (fundamental or human) rights are considered simultaneously from different perspectives. In this sense, the specific transconstitutionalism between the international order and a state order takes the form of a 'constitution' in which the state's responsibility towards its internal social context 'engages' with its 'interstate responsibility',[46] but also encompasses the entanglement of these state responsibilities with the 'interstate responsibility' of the international organisation, which in turn serves the 'intermediation between state social orders'.[47] In other words, from one perspective or the other, constitutional problems take on simultaneous relevance and require new models of analysis: not only statist provincialism must be rejected here; internationalist pseudo-universalism is really just another provincial way of seeing constitutional problems and hence is also an impediment to a rationally adequate approach to conflict resolution.

Transconstitutionalism between a state order and the international order develops on the basis of the following paradox: 'States constitute international public law. International public law constitutes states.'[48] This paradox means that although state sovereignty derives from the status of the state as a subject of international public law (and not the other way round),[49] the latter is instituted only through states as subjects of international law.[50] With the transterritorialisation of constitutional problems in the context of the growing '"entanglement" of inter-

[44] Mello, 2000, 36.

[45] This other side relates to an aspect stressed by Cassese, A (1985, 341), albeit somewhat peremptorily: 'It is common knowledge that international law can only be implemented by State bodies. To be more specific: the majority of international rules are directed to the protagonists of the international community, ie, States, and can only be put into operation if the domestic legal systems of states are ready to implement them.' Slaughter and Burke-White (2007), taking the European experience as their parameter, predict that 'the future of international law is domestic'.

[46] *See* Langer, 1995, 35 *ff*.

[47] Langer, 1995, 43 *ff*.

[48] Fischer-Lescano, 2003, 722.

[49] '[A] state is not a subject of international law because it is sovereign; it is sovereign because it is a subject of international public law' (Radbruch, 2003 [1932], 185).

[50] Fischer-Lescano, 2003, 728.

national relations',[51] this situation entails reactions in both directions. On one side, the constitutional state reacts so that demands for fundamental rights, democracy and social justice are not cast into the common denominator of globalisation, by paying more attention to the international dimensions in their constitutions.[52] On the other, the response to the growing internationalisation of politics and law resides in the 'ascent of the constitution in suprastate spheres', so that 'international law becomes fruitful for constitutional purposes'.[53] In many cases, even constitutional states react to this trend, as manifested, for example, in the position taken by the United States and the United Kingdom in response to the establishment of the Human Rights Committee,[54] or non-ratification of the American Convention on Human Rights by the United States. In other cases, reservations expressed by certain states are declared null and void, as exemplified by Italy's and France's objections to the United States' reservation to the International Covenant on Civil and Political Rights (1966) with regard to the ban on the death penalty for persons under 18 years of age.[55] There are also reactions in the name of the international community to the development of constitutional experiences that do not correspond to the strict model of the developed West.[56] These situations point to an ambiguity in the development of transconstitutionalism. But this does not mean there is not a proliferation of constitutional problems at the interface between international and state law. Such problems still frequently clash with unilateralism and lack of capacity for 'constitutional conversations', yet in some institutional experiences they have met with satisfactory responses. A few examples will serve to illustrate this new juridico-constitutional constellation.

First, it is important to stress the relationship between the European Court of Human Rights (ECtHR)[57] and the legal cultures consolidated in the constitutional orders of the respective European states linked to the Court.[58] Although Article 46.1 of the European Convention on Human Rights states that the 'High Contracting Parties undertake to abide by the final judgment of the Court in any case to which they are parties', the Convention is not enforced equally and harmoniously, and sheer imposition of the Court's decisions against the constitutional orders of the states is neither evident nor plausible. Reactions to the Convention and the decisions of the ECtHR vary considerably from one state to

[51] Langer, 1995, 26 *ff*.

[52] Biaggini, 2000, 454, referring to the experience of the new Swiss Constitution.

[53] *Ibid*.

[54] *Cf* Frowein, 2000, 437.

[55] *Ibid*.

[56] On this subject, Koskenniemi (2002, 515) states: 'Universality still seems an essential part of progressive thought – but it also implies an imperial logic of identity: I will accept you, but only on condition that I may think of you as I think of myself.'

[57] This Court was created by Section II (Arts 19–51) of the European Convention on Human Rights (Convention for the Protection of Human Rights and Fundamental Freedoms), which was adopted at Rome on 4 November 1950, and entered into force on 3 September 1953. The Council of Europe website has more information: http://conventions.coe.int/Treaty/Commun/QueVoulezVous.asp?NT=005&CL=ENG (last visited on 15 December 2008).

[58] *See*, eg, Wildhaber, 2005.

another. Furthermore, the ECtHR must be capable of learning and adaptation in response to the development of particular understandings of fundamental rights in the various national legal orders.

In Germany, even if it is admitted that a development has occurred in the direction of placing the treaty hierarchically above ordinary law,[59] the European Convention on Human Rights is nevertheless said to be grounded in the Constitution.[60] This implies that human rights in the Convention, even when grounded in Article 24.1 of the Basic Law, are segregated from German fundamental rights and thus cannot be invoked immediately in a constitutional complaint.[61] Moreover, the German Federal Constitutional Court – whose ruling in *Caroline von Monaco II* (15 December 1999) emphasising freedom of the press at the expense of privacy (in an application for an injunction to prevent publication of photographs)[62] was overruled by the ECtHR in *Caroline von Hannover v Germany* (24 June 2004), which found that the right to privacy outweighed the public's right to information in this case[63] – consolidated in *Görgülü* (14 October 2004)[64] its position with regard to the establishment of limits to the internal application of ECtHR decisions, considering the hypothesis that they may be contrary to fundamental rights and the principle of the rule of law established in the German Constitution: the German Federal Constitutional Court must take ECtHR decisions into account but is not bound by them.[65] In German constitutional law, the text of the European Convention on Human Rights and ECtHR jurisprudence are considered auxiliary means of interpretation to

[59] In a contrary sense, Kempen (2005, 1511) puts the European Convention on Human Rights at the same level as ordinary law, pointing to the 26 March 1987 decision of the German Federal Constitutional Court (BVerfGE 74, 358), which states (p 370): 'in interpreting the Basic Law, the content and state of development of the Convention are also to be taken into consideration, insofar as this does not lead to a restriction or derogation of basic-rights protection under the Basic Law . . . For this reason, the case law of the European Court of Human Rights also serves in this regard as an interpretational aid in defining the content and reach of the Basic Law's basic rights and principles of rule by law. Even laws . . . are to be interpreted and applied in harmony with the Federal Republic of Germany's commitments under international law, even when such laws have been enacted prior to an applicable international treaty; it cannot be assumed that the legislature, insofar as it has not clearly declared otherwise, wishes todeviate from the Federal Republic of Germany's international treaty commitments or to facilitate violation of such commitments'(http://www.utexas.edu/law/academics/centers/transnational/work_new/german/case.php?id=571 – last visited 2 December 2010). From this same passage, Frowein (2003, 209 *ff*) claims to extract consequences more favourable to the meaning of the incorporation of the European Convention on Human Rights into German law.

[60] *Cf* Walter, 1999, 971.

[61] Walter, 1999, 974, proposing an advance towards primacy of the Convention.

[62] BVerfGE 101, 361 (1999). For a critical discussion of this ruling, *see* Ladeur, 2007a, who argues that 'the right to prominence should fundamentally be considered property law' (p 146).

[63] *Caroline von Hannover v Germany* (Application no 59320/00). On this subject, *see* Rudof, 2006; Hedigan, 2007.

[64] BVerfGE 111, 307 (2004). The case related to application by a German court of the ECtHR ruling against Germany based on Art 8 of the European Convention on Human Rights: *Görgülü v Germany* (Application no 74969/01), 26 February 2004. *Cf* Hartwig, 2005, 870–3.

[65] *Cf* da Silva, VA, 2010; Hoffmeister, 2006; Hartwig, 2005, 874 *ff*; Hofmann, 2004, 30 *ff*; Wahl, 2007, 880–3.

determine the content and scope of fundamental rights and rule-of-law principles, providing they do not lead to a reduction or limitation of the protection for fundamental rights laid down in the Basic Law.

However, narcissistic denial of the norms of ECtHR decisions by state courts does not seem acceptable in the context of European integration. Hence the indispensability, also for national courts involved in the solution of human rights cases, of developing a transversal rationality with regard to the legal order of the European Convention on Human Rights. Any unilaterality may have destructive or irrational effects on European integration in the sphere of human and fundamental rights. German constitutional jurisprudence therefore seeks to invoke Article 53 of the European Convention on Human Rights: 'Nothing in this convention shall be construed as limiting or derogating from any of the human rights and fundamental freedoms which may be ensured under the laws of any High Contracting Party or under any other agreement to which it is a Party.' But this provision should be understood in light of the ECtHR's own competence to interpret the Convention in the last instance. The problem is not simply whether a provision of the Convention is interpreted so as to limit the fundamental rights of a state, but which court has the competence to decide whether this limitation has occurred through interpretation. In this regard, the German Constitutional Court has proved unwilling to submit without restrictions to the ECtHR's decisions in every single case brought before it.[66]

Taking a very different position, the Constitutional Court of Austria opted for immediate internal application of the norms of the European Convention on Human Rights,[67] ruling that the Convention is an integral part of Austrian constitutional law in accordance with the 1964 constitutional reform.[68] This position expressed the Court's comparative openness to international public law in general and can be traced back to the 1920 Constitution, which was strongly influenced by the internationalism of Hans Kelsen.[69] Austria's constitutional

[66] Da Silva, VA (2010, 110), analysing the case under the influence of Alexy, proposes a model of association between 'competing constitutional rights, balancing, rationality, and burden of argumentation'. On this *see* Chapter 4, Section III.

[67] Decision of 14 October 1987: VfSlg 52, No 11500, 347. A similar ruling by the Swiss Supreme Court (15 November 1991) qualified the European Convention on Human Rights as a special treaty whose norms have constitutional law content and are guaranteed by the same procedures as those stipulated to protect fundamental rights by the Swiss Constitution (BGE 117 Ib 367, 370 *f*). On the Swiss position, *see* Wahl, 2007, especially 886 *ff*, stressing a development more favourable to international law in Switzerland than Germany (pp 888 *f*). The Portuguese Constitutional Court has taken an intermediate position: while asserting that constitutional issues should be settled in light of constitutional norms and principles, on 12 October 1999, it ruled that ECtHR jurisprudence 'contributes directly to determining juridical conviction' on the fundamental rights enshrined in the Portuguese Constitution (Judgment [*Acórdão*] no 533/99), and it has striven to adapt to that jurisprudence (*cf* Barreto, 2007, 83 *ff*).

[68] This constitutional reform included, among other things, the attribution of constitutional hierarchy to the European Convention on Human Rights and its first Additional Protocol. All other additional protocols were classed as constitutional amendments (Mayer, 2007, 644).

[69] On Kelsen's internationalism, *see* Brunkhorst, 2008a; von Bernstorff, 2008b; Fassbender, 2008. On Kelsen's contribution to the Austrian Constitution and his influence on its judicial interpretation and on Austrian constitutional doctrine and theory, *see* Öhlinger, 2008, who, however, relativises

self-comprehension points to a more pronounced disposition to hold a transconstitutional 'dialogue' with the ECtHR. Despite the similarity of Austria's and Germany's cultural and social traditions in general, the position taken by the Austrian Constitutional Court on the internal validity of the norms of the European Convention on Human Rights differs significantly from the model adopted by the German Court, pointing to a pronounced diversity of constitutional cultures. It is important to note, nonetheless, that the Austrian Court displays reticence regarding the bindingness of the ECtHR's decisions. With respect to the constitutional principles of the state organisation, the Austrian Court takes the view that a ruling by the ECtHR interpreting an Austrian constitutional norm as contrary to the Convention cannot be the basis for a decision of its own: in this case the breach can be healed only by the 'constitutional lawmaker'. Moreover, the Austrian Court argued that transferring the open development of constitutional interpretation to an international body would exclude the 'constitutional lawmaker' and thus require a 'total reform' of the Austrian Constitution in accordance with Article 44.3, which, in turn, would require ratification by the people of Austria.[70] Thus, the Austrian Court has also determined internal legal conditions for the internal applicability of ECtHR rulings, pointing to the existence of 'tangled hierarchies' as defined by Hofstadter.[71]

The position taken by the French Constitutional Council with respect to the ECtHR points to a certain openness towards a constructive 'conversation'. In the argument on which it based Decision no 2004-505 DC, dated 19 November 2004, the Constitutional Council referred to the ECtHR's ruling in *Leyla Sahin v Turkey* (29 June 2004),[72] stating that the Court's application of Article 9 of the European Convention on Human Rights 'leaves states considerable leeway' ('*une large marge d'appréciation*')[73] in disciplining freedom of religion. Based on this interpretation, the Council ruled that Member States generally, and French courts in particular, are 'free' to allow or prohibit use of the veil by Muslim students.[74]

Given the plurality of European constitutionalisms, the ECtHR must be flexible in making decisions it intends to be binding in cases that affect several countries, which means taking into account specific constitutional self-understandings and metamorphoses thereof. Thus, the ECtHR itself tends over time to change its orientation on admitting cases relating to the protection of

Kelsen's influence in light of recent changes in doctrinal and jurisprudential methods (pp 422 *ff*), not because he considers Kelsen's theory 'false', but because in his view it is insufficient to address the new challenges of Austrian constitutional law (p 424).

70 Decision of 14 October 1987: *VfSlg* 52, no 11500, 347, 365 *f*.

71 Hofstadter, 1979, 10 and 684 *ff*.

72 Case of *Leyla Sahin v Turkey* (Application no 44774/98).

73 Delmas-Marty (2006, 82 *ff*), also referring to *Leyla Sahin v Turkey* (87 and 90), alludes to the 'need for national courts to have leeway' and at the same time considers the difficulties of implementation ['*difficultés de mise en ordre*' – 88 *ff*].

74 Conseil Constitutionnel, Decision no 2004-505 DC, dated 19 November 2004. Because this decision also involves European supranational law I return to it in Chapter 4.

human rights with identical content to applications it has previously rejected and with respect to the same country. For example, the decision of 11 July 2002, in the case of *Christine Goodwin v United Kingdom*, can be said to embody a volte-face in ECtHR jurisprudence inspired by the evolution of internal law in the signatories to the Convention. Until then, the Court had ruled that states were free to discipline the status of transsexuals, that is, to say whether they would continue to be classified as men or women and to establish all the consequences of this recognition (whether they could marry, be eligible for a pension, and so on). In the case in question, however, the ECtHR ruled that the United Kingdom had failed to take the sex change into account and had therefore infringed the European Convention on Human Rights.[75] Another example is the decision in *EB v France*, dated 22 January 2008, where once again the evolution of domestic law in the signatory states served as a basis for the ECtHR to restrict the 'margin of appreciation' for states to regulate the right to non-discrimination.[76] Careful observation of the various constitutional self-understandings is therefore fundamental if the ECtHR is not to lose its capacity to rule legitimately on cases of significance to courts in signatories to the Convention.

One of the interesting points about the ECtHR is the influence of its decisions outside Europe, that is in countries that are not parties to the European Convention on Human Rights. An outstanding example is the US Supreme Court, where Justice Anthony Kennedy's opinion for the majority in *Lawrence v Texas*, argued on 26 March 2003, was that the ECtHR and other nations 'have taken action consistent with an affirmation of the protected right of homosexual adults to engage in intimate, consensual conduct'.[77] Mainly on the basis of this decision affirming the rights of the homosexual minority, a debate developed between Justices Antonin Scalia and Stephen Breyer on the use of ECtHR jurisprudence (and that of other nations) in interpreting US constitutional law, with Scalia arguing against and Breyer in favour.[78] This debate is an indication that even in the context of a constitutional tradition of self-sufficiency, recourse to a constitutional 'dialogue' with other courts, foreign or international, regarding internal constitutional issues has become one of the key points on the new agenda of American constitutionalism.

Another relevant case of transconstitutionalism between international and state orders is developing in the relations between the 'inter-American Human Rights System', introduced by the American Convention on Human Rights, and

[75] *Christine Goodwin v United Kingdom* (Application no 28957/95). On this and other ECtHR cases regarding freedom of sexual orientation and change of civil status following a sex-change operation, *See* Rudolf, 2003; Piovesan, 2008a, 66 *ff*.

[76] *EB v France* (Application no 43546/02).

[77] *Lawrence et al v Texas*, 539 US 558 (2003), 576. On this decision, *see* the brief exposition by Eskridge, 2004.

[78] *See* the debate between Scalia and Breyer moderated by Dorsen, 2005. On the context for this debate, *see* Ginsburg, 2005b. *See also* pp 161 *ff* above.

the constitutional orders of the signatories that have ratified it.[79] In this context, it is not simply a matter of imposing the decisions of the Inter-American Court of Human Rights (IACHR), created and structured by Chapter VIII (Articles 52–69) of the Convention, on national courts with constitutional competence. The national courts are also reviewing their jurisprudence in light of the Court's decisions. Both the IACHR and state courts have displayed a willingness to enter into a 'dialogue' on common constitutional issues relating to the protection of human rights, so that the application of conventional law by domestic courts is being extended.[80]

An interesting case deals with the collision between Article 7.7 of the American Convention on Human Rights and Article 5.LXVII of the Brazilian Constitution. While the latter provision allows civil imprisonment for indebtedness in the case of an unfaithful trustee, the above-mentioned provision of the American Convention prohibits it. In judging three cases on 3 December 2008 (RE 466.343/SP, RE 349.703/RS and HC 87.585/TO), a majority of the Brazilian Supreme Court ruled that treaties and conventions on human rights, when not approved in accordance with the procedure stipulated in Article 5 § 3 of the Brazilian Constitution (identical to the procedure for passing a constitutional amendment),[81] have supralegal but infraconstitutional standing.

These cases sparked a broad debate about the incorporation of human rights treaties by the Brazilian legal order.[82] One tendency in analysis of the case has been to advocate a solution based on the idea of unlimited internal validity for the above-mentioned provision of the American Convention on Human Rights, given that this norm would lead to an extension of the rights established in the Brazilian Constitution and that the law contained in it would therefore be in harmony with Article 5 § 2 of that Constitution.[83] However, even the restrictive interpretation of the provision's internal validity does not exclude a positive solution that extends fundamental rights in practice: the argument in favour of the ratified Convention's supralegal and infraconstitutional validity served as a basis for a decision that because the Constitution only allows unfaithful trustees

[79] This Convention was adopted on 22 November 1969, at San Jose, Costa Rica, and entered into force on 18 July 1978, in accordance with Art 74, no 2. On this subject, *see* Burgorgue-Larsen, 2009; Ortiz, 2009; on the discussion in Brazil, *see* de Oliveira (ed), 2007, highlighting the preface by Trindade, 2007. For an analysis of the jurisdiction of the Inter-American Court of Human Rights (IACHR), *see* Ramírez, 2008.

[80] *See* Ortiz, 2009, 273 *ff*; Burgorgue-Larsen, 2009, 309 *ff*.

[81] Art 5 § 3 of the Brazilian Constitution reads as follows: 'The international treaties and conventions on human rights approved by each house of Congress in two rounds by three-fifths of all members shall be equivalent to constitutional amendments.'

[82] RE 466.343/SP, RE 349.703/RS, HC 87.585/TO, 03/12/2008, TP, DJe 5 and 26 June 2009.

[83] Position defended by Justice Celso de Mello, leading the dissent, with support from Trindade, 2003, 513; Piovesan, 2008a, 51–77; Mazzuoli, 2001, 147–50; 2007, 682–702. Mello (2001, 25 *f*) goes further to argue that treaties and conventions on human rights are supraconstitutional. Art 5 § 2 of the Brazilian Constitution reads as follows: 'The rights and guarantees expressed in this Constitution do not exclude others deriving from the regime and from the principles adopted by it, or from the international treaties to which the Federative Republic of Brazil is a party.'

to be imprisoned for debt,[84] infraconstitutional law could therefore decide freely on permission or prohibition, and if so the Convention had primacy over the Brazilian Civil Code.[85] Only maintenance of the orientation that had predominated previously in Brazilian legal tradition, that is, the principle that ratified international acts have the same level of validity as ordinary law, could lead to an insuperable conflict between the Supreme Court of Brazil and the IACHR, since the Brazilian Civil Code came into force after ratification of the treaty, and the maxim *lex posterior derogat priori* would therefore apply.[86] If it had maintained that position, the Supreme Court would have broken off the constitutional 'dialogue' with the IACHR on their respective understandings of human and fundamental rights. The discussion that did take place, however, appears to have foregrounded an effort to form a transversal rationality that can prove acceptable to both the legal orders involved.

On the side of the IACHR, it is important to note the decision in *YATAMA v Nicaragua*, a case which dealt with the right to democratic participation by members of the indigenous community belonging to YATAMA, a political party, who were forbidden to stand in the municipal elections of 5 November 2000, by a ruling of Nicaragua's Supreme Electoral Council.[87] The IACHR not only ordered the State of Nicaragua to pay compensation for pecuniary and non-pecuniary damages, but also ordered Nicaragua to reform the electoral law in question, concluding:

> The State shall reform the regulation of the requirements established in Electoral Act No 331 of 2000 that, it has been declared, violate the American Convention on Human Rights and adopt, within a reasonable time, the necessary measures to ensure that the members of the indigenous and ethnic communities may participate in the electoral processes effectively and according to their traditions, practices and customs, in the terms of paragraph 259 of this judgment.[88]

This is a clear example in which a norm of the international order is invoked to settle a dispute and support the extension of constitutionally ordained fundamental rights: the application of internal law regarding active citizenship, an

[84] Art 5.LXVII of the Brazilian Constitution reads as follows: 'There shall be no civil imprisonment for indebtedness except in the case of a person responsible for voluntary and inexcusable default on an alimony obligation and in the case of an unfaithful trustee.'

[85] Position defended by Justice Gilmar Mendes, in an opinion leading the majority. In this sense, *see* Mendes, Coelho and Branco, 2007, 665 *ff*.

[86] Jurisprudence consolidated by the Brazilian Supreme Court (STF) in the decision of RE 80.004/SE, Judgment of 1 June 1977, DJ 29 December 1977. On this jurisprudence, *see* Mendes, Coelho and Branco, 2007, 659 *ff*. This is also the position taken by Dimoulis and Martins (2007, 50) for treaties not approved in accordance with Art 5, § 3, of the Brazilian Constitution. Pontes de Miranda (1960, 225), while arguing that treaties are hierarchically equivalent to ordinary law, states that 'the Constitution cannot affect a prior treaty unless said treaty is valid in international law and contains provision for its denunciation or abrogation of its rules. Thus the primacy of international law is unquestionable . . . In this regard, the framers committed grave errors due to careless assimilation of treaties prior to and subsequent to the Constitution.'

[87] *YATAMA v Nicaragua* – Series C No 127 [2005] IACHR 9 (23 June 2005).

[88] *Ibid*, § 275.1 (Judge Montiel-Arguello dissented from this item). On this decision, *see* Volio, 2005.

intrinsically constitutional matter, is linked to international norms and becomes dependent on the interpretation of an international court.

However, there are experiences in the opposite direction, where the international norm of human rights protection to be invoked can be presented as a restriction to fundamental rights as covered by a state constitution. Examples include the collision between the Brazilian Constitution and the Rome Statute of the International Criminal Court, which was adopted on 17 July 1998, and entered into force in the international order on 1 July 2002. Brazil ratified it via Legislative Decree 112 (2002). Whereas under Article 77 § 1 (b) of the Rome Statute, the International Criminal Court may impose a 'term of life imprisonment, when justified by the extreme gravity of the crime and the individual circumstances of the convicted person', this penalty is prohibited under Article 5. XLVII (b) of the Brazilian Constitution. Although Article 5 § 4 of the Brazilian Constitution, introduced by Constitutional Amendment no 45 in 2004, establishes that 'Brazil shall be submitted to the jurisdiction of the International Criminal Court, to whose creation it has expressed agreement', the matter remains problematic because according to Article 60 § 4.IV of the same Constitution, the ban on life imprisonment included in the catalogue of individual rights and guarantees cannot be abolished because it is an 'entrenched clause'.[89]

On one hand, the international public law understanding of human rights focuses on concern with scandalous and shocking crimes against humanity. On the other, the startingpoint for the Brazilian constitutional understanding of fundamental rights is that life imprisonment infringes human rights. A unilateral solution is not adequate in this case.

Precedent suggests a tendency in the Brazilian constitutional jurisdiction to require a specific condition for extradition of an alleged criminal for trial or a convicted criminal by the International Criminal Court: he or she will be handed over only if life is commuted to a maximum of 30 years.[90] Although in the hypothesis of an international court it is not strictly speaking a matter of extradition, since the concept of extradition refers to relations between states, this solution could be adopted for applications to Brazil to *hand over* criminals, defendants or indicted persons to the International Criminal Court.[91] This is an

[89] Art 60, § 4.IV, of the Federal Constitution of Brazil reads as follows: '§ 4 – No proposal of amendment shall be considered if it aims to abolish: [. . .] IV – individual rights and guarantees.'

[90] Confirming precedents in more recent jurisprudence, *cf* the following extradition applications, all decided unanimously by the Plenum of the Supreme Court STF: Ext. 1.104/UK – Reino Unido da Grã-Bretanha e da Irlanda do Norte (United Kingdom of Great Britain & Northern Ireland), 14 April 2008, DJe 23 May 2008); Ext 1.103 – Estados Unidos da América (United States of America), 13 March 2008, DJe 7 November 2008; Ext 1.060/PU – Peru, 15 October 2007, DJe 31 October 2007; Ext 1.069/EU – Estados Unidos da América (United States of America), 9 August 2007, DJe 14 Sep 2007.

[91] *See* Maliska, 2006, 188 *f*, also admitting the hypothesis of handover to the ICC without these conditions (p 189), which to me seems incompatible with Brazilian jurisprudence and precedent, not to mention the fact that it would infringe an entrenched clause. On this, *see* Sabadell and Dimoulis, 2010.

intermediate solution, which, while not entirely compatible with the Rome Statute, might be supported by the International Criminal Court in a constructive, learning-disposed position.

The issue could become more problematic if the Supreme Court considers the hypothesis equivalent to 'extradition' and affirms its jurisprudence contrary to extraditing Brazilians in accordance with Article 5.LI of the Brazilian Constitution. In this case, resolving the normative conflict would not be so straightforward. However, as already mentioned, it does not seem correct to extend this principle semantically so that the prohibition would also apply to handing over a criminal, defendant, or indicted person to the International Criminal Court, since extradition refers to relations between states. Undoubtedly, even if this interpretation of the concept of extradition were accepted, there would be other problems due to invocation of Article 60 § 4.IV of the Brazilian Constitution, which prohibits abolition of guarantees for fundamental rights ('entrenched clauses' – see note 91 to this Chapter). Developments in this normative context appear to be moving in an open direction. Nevertheless, a willingness to learn on both sides through the formation of a constructive transversal network, that is, transconstitutionalism, is the key to success in this area of collision. Internationalism and nationalism, according to this hypothesis, could lead to destructive attitudes for human or fundamental rights.

Lastly, in the plane of economic constitutional law, the approach taken by the World Trade Organization (WTO)[92] to settle disputes relating to the legitimacy of state norms that involve protectionism or limitations to cross-border economic freedom has had a strong impact on the liberal economic model in the constitutional orders of its members, which in most instances merely react to WTO decisions.[93] Grimm himself stresses that 'since 1995 its dispute settlement mechanism has made treaty-based laws independent of the contracting parties and submitted them to the decisions of the WTO authority'.[94] Hence, the frequency with which the WTO's creation is said to have consolidated a shift from the 'diplomacy of negotiation to an international constitutional order' in the sphere of international economic law[95] and the widespread references to the 'juridico-constitutional dimensions' of the WTO.[96]

[92] The treaty establishing the WTO was adopted on 15 April 1994. On this, *see* Petersmann, 1995. Koskenniemi (2004, 206 *f*), in eminently critical mode, has this to say on the basis of empirical data and arguments that to me seem convincing: 'The establishment of the WTO in 1995 was a significant victory for preferences of free trade over the nationally focused regulatory objectives. The domination of Western interests was nowhere more visible than in the conclusion of the Agreement on Trade-Related Intellectual Properties (TRIPS), designed to protect copyrights, patents and trademarks overwhelmingly owned by Western companies . . . The polarisation of the opposition between the North and the South (especially evident in the property intellectual realm) may have diminished possibilities for judicial innovation by the panels or the Appeals Body. Indeed, little has dispelled the concern that the Dispute Settlement Body is a Rich Man's Club: by far most of the cases are still being brought to it by the United States or the European Union.'

[93] *Cf* Nettesheim, 2001, 403 *f*.

[94] Grimm, 2004a, 12.

[95] Nettesheim, 2001.

[96] Von Bogdandy, 2001.

Instead of affirming WTO constitutionalisation or a WTO Constitution, it would seem more fruitful to enquire into the juridico-constitutional problems originally faced by individual states or in the form of bilateral treaties and diplomacy but now largely submitted to the WTO, an institution grounded in multilaterality. Thus, it is of course possible to discuss the WTO's juridico-constitutional problems and functions,[97] given that issues relating to economic constitutional law fall within its remit, especially for dispute settlement, but this should be seen as part of transconstitutionalism between legal orders, especially because the WTO's success in regulating economic relations and settling trade disputes depends substantially on the reactions of the states involved, including the constitutional courts. Forms of protectionism that infringe WTO rules are frequently implemented, above all during 'hard times'.[98] Outside such periods, too, the Organisation's rules and decisions are infringed, even by countries that claim to be in favour of free trade, as exemplified by US non-compliance with the WTO's 26 September 2000 decision that the US Anti-Dumping Act of 1916 infringed WTO rules and must be changed in 10 months.[99]

Moreover, even if effective means are defined to impose WTO decisions,[100] it becomes inadequate in the sphere of transconstitutionalism to adopt a model whereby WTO decisions are simply handed down to states involved in disputes. The development of the WTO in the plane of competences relating to economic constitutional law issues depends on the construction of flexible models capable of being incorporated as widely as possible into the various state legal orders, characterised by a huge diversity of conceptions of economic freedom.

These examples of transconstitutionalism between international and state orders point to the need to transcend provincial treatment of constitutional problems by states, without this leading to a belief in the *ultima ratio* of international public law: not only the former but also the latter may make mistakes when faced with constitutional issues, including human rights problems.

III. TRANSCONSTITUTIONALISM BETWEEN SUPRANATIONAL LAW AND STATE LAW

If the legal concept of supranationality is restricted to an organisation grounded in a treaty that attributes to its own bodies broad legislative, administrative and jurisdictional competences in the personal, material, territorial and temporal spheres of validity, with direct binding force for the citizens and bodies of the Member States, the European Union can be considered the only experience of

[97] Even before the WTO was created, Petersmann (1991) discussed the 'constitutional functions and constitutional problems of international economic law'.

[98] Nettesheim, 2001, 403 *f*.

[99] WT/DS136/AB/R, WT/DS162/AB/R. On this, *see* De Keyser, 2001.

[100] *Cf* Nettesheim, 2001, 404 *f*.

supranationality.[101] Although the founding treaty ('constitutional treaty') and amendments depend on ratification by Member States, ordinary norms and administrative and jurisdictional decisions are immediately binding on citizens and state agents. For this reason, it is possible to speak of 'shared sovereignty' or 'divided sovereignty', pointing to transfer from the sphere of sovereignty ('competence competence') to a broader legal sphere.[102] This becomes evident when it is recalled that not only all individual European Union Member States are WTO members in their own right, but so is the European Union as such (known officially as the European Communities for legal reasons until the end of 2009). The question that arises in the sphere of transconstitutionalism is how the legal order of the Community relates to the legal orders of its Member States, and above all the connection between the European Court of Justice (ECJ) and the state constitutional courts or supreme courts with constitutional functions, linked to strongly consolidated legal traditions that differ among themselves.

While it is possible to affirm the primacy of Community law over national legal orders, the issue becomes far too simple when considered only on the basis of this general assertion: first, because we are dealing here with 'tangled hierarchies' (*see* p 90 above) between normative orders that observe each other;[103] second, because there are constitutional problems relevant to both the constitutional courts of Member States and the European Court of Justice, giving rise to different selections and interpretations of the normative texts to be applied and different understandings (constructions) of the legal cases submitted to judgment. This situation implies a 'complementary' relationship between European Union law and state

[101] In this sense, Langer (1995, 50) states that 'practically speaking, it is correct only in the case of the European Union to speak of a "supranational organisation"'. Similarly, Grimm (2004a, 12): 'So far there has been no supranational arrangement of the same density [as the European Union] either outside of Europe or on a global scale.' However, it is possible to see supranationality developing in the sphere of the Andean Community, albeit limited in practice to the dimension of judicial competence. On the affirmation of the Andean Community's legal supremacy or primacy over national law, see the following judgments, among many, of the Court of Justice of the Andean Community: Case 1-IP-87; Case 50-IP-2008; Case 67-IP-2008. On the significance of this court, *see* Perotti, 1998; Toledo, 2009. Another example is the *Central American Court of Justice*, which is competent among other things to settle internal disputes among the powers of any of the states under its jurisdiction (*See* Perotti, 2002).

[102] Pernice, 1995, 259 (no 44) and 275 (no 66), with comprehensive bibliographical references; Lewandowski, 2004, 253 *ff*. De Witte (1998, especially 302 *f*) questions the expression 'divided sovereignty', arguing that 'sovereignty' ('competence-competence') cannot be transferred, although the exercise of 'sovereignty rights' can. *See* Mendes, G, 2010, 283–4. Questioning the adequacy of these concepts and distinguishing Community law primacy from the issue of the sovereignty of Member States, *see* de Búrca, 2003, 456 *ff*. Maduro (2003, 505 *f*) refers to 'competing sovereignties'. This discussion derives from the ECJ's rulings in *Van Gend en Loos* (1963) and *Costa* (1964), which include the assertions that 'the [European Economic] Community constitutes a new legal order of international law for the benefit of which the States have limited their sovereign rights' (26/62, judgment of 5 February 1963, *NV Algemene Transport en Expeditie Onderneming van Gend & Loos v Netherlands Inland Revenue Administration*) and that 'the transfer by the States from their domestic legal system to the Community legal system of the rights and obligations arising under the treaty carries with it a permanent limitation of their sovereign rights' (6/64, judgment of 15 July 1964, *Flaminio Costa v ENEL*).

[103] On this *see* Dudena, 2008.

law in a 'network of constitutional elements'[104] or, to put it differently, the 'intersection of national and European constitutional law' on behalf of the citizens.[105]

In this sense, it is appropriate to speak of a constitutional 'conversation' based on reciprocal learning rather than on a monolithic hierarchical form. On this topic Weiler is forthright: 'The constitutional discourse in Europe must be conceived as a conversation of many actors in a constitutional interpretative community, rather than a hierarchical structure with the ECJ at the top.'[106] However, this model does not exclude tension between legal orders and the respective courts in the sphere of constitutional law. Poiares Maduro uses the term 'contrapunctual law', referring to the various different understandings at which an extraterrestrial observer of European law would arrive according to whether his startingpoint was the ECJ or the constitutional court of a Member State.[107] The primacy of Community law over national law, espoused by the ECJ according to the interpretation that there is a direct link between the Community treaty and the people of Europe, is not negated by constitutional courts but rather relativised: that is, this primacy can be set aside in exceptional cases, such as when it does not meet certain conditions determined by the constitutional law of a given state.[108] This variance by a Member State from Community law may influence the position taken by other Member States on the same point of law, however, not least because of the equal treatment principle. Hence, the necessity of observing 'the principles of contrapunctual law'[109] to preserve the autonomy of the national 'melodies' that combine with those of the community via non-hierarchical participation to assure the success of supranational entanglement.[110]

The question becomes more complicated when it is considered that not only are the European Court of Justice and the state constitutional courts charged with applying Community law, but the ECJ is also charged with interpreting domestic law to define its compatibility with the common law of the European Union. Thus we arrive at a model with four angles of normative understanding: ECJ facing EU normative texts and state normative texts, and state constitutional courts facing EU normative texts and state normative texts.[111] All these perspectives on normative construction may converge in a given case, whose normative framing may vary significantly depending on whether it is jurisdictionally constructed by the ECJ or by the constitutional court involved in the jurisprudential dispute. Of course, the constitutional 'conversation' may lead to a posture of cooperation, reducing or even resolving conflicts, so that it becomes

[104] Walter, 2000, 12.

[105] Krajewski, 2001, 126 *f*, accompanying Pernice (1995, 275, no 67) in this formulation.

[106] Weiler, 1999, 322.

[107] Maduro, 2003, 502. *Cf* similarly Mendes, R, 2006, 95 *f*.

[108] *See* Maduro, 2003, 508 *ff*.

[109] Maduro, 2003, 524 *ff*.

[110] 'Counterpoint is the musical method of harmonising different melodies that are not in a hierarchical relationship *inter se*' (Maduro, 2003, 523).

[111] In this sense it is appropriate to speak of 'intertextuality' (Christensen and Fischer-Lescano, 2007, 78 *ff*) and 'de facto internormativity' (Delmas-Marty, 2006, 41 *ff*) in European transconstitutionalism.

consistent and adequate to the colliding orders. However, if unity exists in European constitutional law, it can only be the unity of a legal and judicial space for cooperation and conflict among legal orders with different perspectives on juridico-constitutional cases.[112] Rather than speaking of a European Union Constitution, it is appropriate to speak of European transconstitutionalism as the transversality of legal orders in dealing with common juridico-constitutional problems.

The fact that this is not a hierarchy pure and simple, in which a supreme court could decide in the last instance any conflict of a constitutional nature, is evidenced in practical terms by the conditions imposed by the German Federal Constitutional Court in response to rulings by the European Court of Justice. Its decisions in the cases *Solange I* (BVerfGE 37, 271) and *Solange II* (BVerfGE 73, 339) are emblematic in this regard. In the former (dated 29 May 1974), the Second Senate of the German Court decided it was necessary to wait for the integration process to develop further with regard to guarantees of fundamental rights, in the following terms:

> As long as the integration process has not progressed so far that Community law receives a catalogue of fundamental rights decided on by a parliament and of settled validity, which is adequate in comparison with the catalogue of fundamental rights contained in the Basic Law,

a review of constitutionality

> is admissible and necessary if the German court regards the rule of Community law which is relevant to its decision as inapplicable in the interpretation given by the European Court, because and insofar as it conflicts with one of the fundamental rights of the Basic Law.[113]

Thus, the decision affirmed not the supremacy of Community law but the primacy of the German constitutional and legal order with regard to fundamental rights, and above all attributed to the German order the status of last instance in cases of fundamental rights involving the ECJ and the Court itself.

In *Solange II* (dated 22 October 1986), despite intense criticism from jurists favourable to European integration, the Second Senate of the German Federal Constitutional Court maintained conditions for the application of integration law against national law, in the following terms:

> As long as the European Communities, in particular European Court case law, generally ensure effective protection of fundamental rights as against the sovereign powers of the Communities which is to be regarded as substantially similar to the protection of fundamental rights required unconditionally by the Basic Law, and in so far as they generally safeguard the essential content of fundamental rights, the Federal Constitutional Court will no longer exercise its jurisdiction to decide on the applicability of secondary

[112] Walter (2000, 7 *ff*) refers to a 'loss of unity' in European constitutional law due to globalisation.

[113] BVerfGE, 37, 271 (1974) (http://www.utexas.edu/law/academics/centers/transnational/work_new/german/case.php?id=588 – last visited on 2 December 2010).

> Community legislation cited as the legal basis for any acts of German courts or authorities within the sovereign jurisdiction of the Federal Republic of Germany, and it will no longer review such legislation by the standard of the fundamental rights contained in the Basic Law.[114]

This ruling, unlike the first, acknowledged that the ECJ at that time was acting in harmony with the fundamental rights regime enshrined in Germany's Basic Law, yet also included a reservation: if the ECJ ceased to act in accordance with that regime, the Federal Constitutional Court could once again institute constitutional review of its decisions if and when they were supposed to be internalised. Thus, the German Court did not exclude the possibility of its acting as last instance in deciding on the legitimacy of internalising ECJ decisions into German law. In other words, the German Court still affirmed itself as controller of the controller.[115] In doing so, however, it gave the constitutional courts of other EU Member States leeway to impose the same reservation, in a model of 'contrapunctual' reaction.

Another decision that is highly relevant to the debate on development is *Maastricht* (dated 12 October 1993) motivated especially by the Treaty on the European Union, which was signed at Maastricht on 7 February 1992, and entered into force on 1 November 1993. In this ruling, the Second Senate of the German Federal Constitutional Court, invoking the democratic principle, set limits to Germany's obligations in the context of developing European supranational integration.[116] Among other things, the decision established that:

> The principle of democracy therefore does not prevent the Federal Republic of Germany from being a member of a supranationally organised community of states. But it is a precondition of membership that within the union of states [*Staatenverbund*] there should also be a guarantee of legitimacy and influence emanating from the people.

Moreover, after stressing that 'the Federal Constitutional Court checks if legal acts of the European institutions and organs remain within, or break out of, the limits of the sovereign rights transferred to them (BVerfGE 75, 223)', it added:

[114] BVerfGE 73, 339 (1986), 340 (http://www.utexas.edu/law/academics/centers/transnational/work_new/german/case.php?id=572 – last visited on 2 December 2010).

[115] Here it is worth recalling the debate between Kelsen (1931) and Schmitt (1931) on the 'Guardian of the Constitution', in which, at least in the field of constitutionalism, the former's liberal thesis prevailed in practice. The problem is that in accordance with the idea of 'tangled hierarchies' all control entails counter-control and in the last analysis there is no ultimate and definitive control (Luhmann, 1987c, 63 [Engl trans 1995, 36]), although there may be 'hegemony' or predominance.

[116] BVerfGE 89, 155 (1993).This orientation was reaffirmed and strengthened by the German Constitutional Court in its judgment on the Lisbon Treaty emphasising the constitutional limits to the transfer of sovereign rights to the European Union and its competence to control the constitutionality of Union law, based on the assumption that 'national constitutional identity in the European space' is guaranteed jointly by constitutional law (in Member States) and Union law (BVerfG 2 BvE 2/08 of 30 June 2009; on this judgment, *see* Fischer-Lescano, Joerges and Wonka (eds), 2010).

> In interpreting the norms of competence through institutions and organs of the Communities, it is necessary to note that the Treaty of the Union makes a fundamental distinction between exercising a functional competence granted on limited terms and altering the Treaty, so that the outcome of its interpretation cannot be considered equivalent to an extension of the Treaty. Such an interpretation of the norms of competence would not produce any binding effect on Germany.[117]

These decisions triggered critical reactions by jurists who strongly support European integration. For Professor Joseph Weiler, for example,

> the solution offered by the German Federal Constitutional Court . . . is no conversation . . . Although the German Court mentions that these decisions have to be taken in cooperation with the ECJ, it reserves the last word to itself. A European *diktat* is simply replaced by a national one. And the national *diktat* is far more destructive to the Community, if one contemplates the possibility of 15 different interpretations.[118]

However, it is precisely in this plurality of interpretative possibilities that resides the question of transconstitutionalism between the European supranational order and the state orders linked to it.

The problem is not the assertion that this or that order has primacy or supremacy. Even when a constitutional court admits the generally dominant thesis that the EU legal order has primacy over the legal orders of Member States, this does not definitively resolve the issue of tangled hierarchies, which persists when an actual case is relevant to both the ECJ and one or more state courts with constitutional functions. First, legal qualification of the facts requires definition of the qualifying legal norm, and hence a choice of the normative text or texts to be interpreted. The ECJ may invoke different normative texts from those invoked by national courts. However, even if the texts invoked are the same, their interpretation for the purposes of a given case may lead to a different outcome with regard to the normative content applied, that is, to different legal norms. In addition, even where the norms applied are the same, the description of the facts may lead to different legal constructs, which will entail different legal definitions of the case to be resolved. The problem could be settled in an absolute and definitive manner only if all constitutional courts acknowledged without reservations that the ECJ's understanding would prevail in every case. However, this solution would undermine the idea of a constitutional 'dialogue' between courts in the context of transconstitutionalism between legal orders. A disposition to cooperate on the part of the ECJ and constitutional courts would be more adequate.

There have been developments in this direction by virtue of the strong reaction from constitutional courts to the absolute supremacy of the European Court of Justice, given the peculiarities of the constitutional orders of nation-states and the different positions taken by the respective constitutional courts. As argued by Anne-Marie Slaughter:

[117] *Ibid*, 156.
[118] Weiler, 1999, 322.

> The legal system of the European Community, now the European Union, was built through the decisions of lower national courts to send cases up to the European Court of Justice (ECJ). The ECJ was regarded not as a Supreme Court, but as a supranational court, often against the wishes of higher national courts and the Executive . . .
>
> Higher national courts, particularly constitutional courts, ultimately realized that their power was being eroded and fought back; the result is what the German Constitutional Court has called a 'cooperative relationship' between the ECJ and national high courts. This is a relationship defined court-to-court and based explicitly on respective competencies of both entities in domestic and European law. It is the basis for a European 'Community of Law.'[119]

With this view of the relations between courts, Slaughter offers a different understanding of the ECJ's position from that of Weiler, insofar as she does not see the 'Maastricht decision' as constituting a claim by the German Federal Constitutional Court to primacy over the ECJ on constitutional matters. On this subject, she notes that the:

> German Federal Constitutional Court (*Bundesverfassungsgericht*, or *BvG*), in particular has a long history of engaging and challenging the ECJ as a co-equal rather than a superior court . . . The *BvG* has been the most outspoken and perhaps the most assertive in its relations with the ECJ, but it is not alone, garnering support from the Italian, French, and Belgian high courts in more subtle guises.[120]

Evidently, there are contexts in which national high courts show greater willingness to submit more strictly to the ECJ's orientation. Examples include the UK Supreme Court's decision to suspend the enforcement of a domestic law pending judicial review by the ECJ, and the Cour de cassation, France's supreme court, which followed the dictates of the ECJ 'even in the face of threats from the French legislative to strip its jurisdiction amid age-old charges of "gouvernement par juges"'.[121] Even in these cases, however, the possibility that a court will claim co-equal status at any moment is not entirely eliminated, since the ECJ's relationship to national courts is not analogous to that of a supreme court in a federal state. The conflicts will continue, even as relations between the ECJ and state courts, both high and low, and their respective jurisprudences 'become increasingly intertwined'.[122] This entails the need for permanent processing of both 'cooperative relations' and 'conflictual relations' among legal orders and among their respective courts, even though a perfect balance cannot be reached.

The idea put forward by Weiler of setting up a Constitutional Council for the Community, in emulation of the French Constitutional Council, to ensure that laws are subject to preventive review of their validity and also to decide cases

[119] Slaughter, 2000, 1104 *f*; *cf* 2004, 82 *f*, with almost identical phrasing.

[120] Slaughter, 2004, 84; *cf* 2000, 1107 *f*, with almost identical phrasing.

[121] Slaughter, 2000, 1106; 2004, 83.

[122] Slaughter, 2000, 1108; 2004, 84. More broadly, Delmas-Marty (2006, 46 *ff*) refers to 'cross-referenced interpretation games' between courts in different orders.

involving conflicts of competence[123] would not be a serious contribution to solving the problem because it would merely introduce a new layer of constitutional bureaucracy in Europe, and one which would be subject to the same issues relating to the need to harmonise national law as are currently faced by the ECJ. Indeed, in this case the collision could be even more pronounced in light of the French Constitutional Council's claim to be the sole instance for preventive review of the constitutional validity of French laws.

It should be noted that unlike the Cour de cassation, France's Constitutional Council takes a defensive position towards EU law in constitutional issues, especially with regard to human rights. This is clearly exemplified by Decision no 92-308 DC (dated 9 April 1992), in which the Council admitted the supralegal validity of treaties ratified by the National Assembly, yet required prior revision of the Constitution as a condition for ratification and internal validity of the Treaty on European Union, based on the following rationale:

> 14. However, should an international agreement entered into to this end [transfer of powers to a permanent international organisation] involve a clause conflicting with the Constitution or jeopardising the essential condition for the exercise of national sovereignty, authorisation to ratify would require prior revision of the Constitution.
> 15. The Constitutional Council should undertake its review of the Treaty on European Union in the light of these principles.[124]

Thus, in accordance with French constitutional tradition the supreme norms of the European Union (the founding treaty and its amendments) can be submitted to review for the purposes of validating their constitutionality; this makes room for conflicts of interpretation not only with the ECJ, but also with a future European Constitutional Council with analogous competences.

Community directives may also be subject to review by the French Constitutional Council, at least indirectly via review of their transposition into domestic law. On the internalisation of directives via French law, it is worth mentioning some decisions of the Constitutional Council that are relevant to the discussion of transconstitutionalism between state and supranational orders. Given the development of Community law, Article 88-1 of the French Constitution was amended to state that the Republic 'shall participate in the European Communities and in the European Union' (after the entry into force of the Treaty of Lisbon, this provision was amended to refer only to the 'European Union'). This provision was ignored by French constitutional jurisprudence for a long time. It apparently did not contain a norm.

With Decision no 2004-496 DC (dated 10 June 2004), the Constitutional Council changed its jurisprudence by interpreting Article 88-1 as an obligation on French lawmakers to transpose Community directives.[125] By virtue of this new interpretation, limits were acknowledged on the constitutional review of

[123] Weiler, 1999, 322 *f* and 354.
[124] Constitutional Council, Decision 92-308 DC, 9 April 1992.
[125] Constitutional Council, Decision 2004-496 DC of 10 June 2004.

laws governing the transposition of Community directives. From then on, the Constitutional Council would declare a law of transposition unconstitutional only if the transposed directive conflicted with an 'explicit' provision of the Constitution. Otherwise the law would not be censured and it would be up to the 'ordinary' judge to refer the question for a preliminary ruling to the European Court of Justice, which would be expected to decide on the directive's compliance with fundamental rights. In light of this jurisprudence, the Constitutional Council ceased verifying whether laws designed to transpose Community directives were lawful under provisions of the French Constitution that protect freedom of expression, the principle of equality, and so on. In the understanding of the Constitutional Council, the laws in question did not conflict with an 'explicit provision' of the Constitution and therefore did not require constitutional review.

The next change in the Council's jurisprudence elucidated its understanding of the term 'explicit provision'. Initially it used the phrase, 'explicit and specific'. Then in Decision no 2006-540 DC (dated 26 July 2006), it asserted that the transposition of a directive must not 'run counter to' the 'constitutional identity of France'.[126] In practice this set a constitutional limit to Community integration. The lawmakers cannot transpose directives that conflict with constitutional provisions regarded as 'inherent in' France's 'constitutional identity'. Although no directives have so declared to date, and the semantic content of the expression has never been clearly and precisely defined, implementation of this jurisprudence would lead to a strong limitation and to a certain extent would constitute a hindrance to the legal integration of France into the European Union.

Also in connection with Community directives, not only the Constitutional Council no longer considers itself competent to control their constitutionality (except in cases of a 'threat to constitutional identity'), but Article 88-1 of the Constitution has served as a reference or basis for using the rules included in Community directives to control the constitutionality of transposition statutes. The argument is as follows: because Article 88-1 obliges lawmakers to transpose directives, any statute that partially or incorrectly transposes a directive shall be considered unconstitutional, at least as far as its 'clear' and 'unconditional' provisions are concerned. Incompatibility between the transposition statute and the clear and unconditional text of the directive makes the statute unconstitutional. For this reason, in Decision no 2006-543 DC (dated 30 November 2006), the Constitutional Council invalidated part of the law submitted to it.[127] Thus this is a case in which a rule of non-national origin was 'incorporated' via a constitutional provision (Article 88-1) into the rule for controlling French constitutionality.

[126] Constitutional Council, Decision 2006-540 DC of 27 July 2006.
[127] Constitutional Council, Decision 2006-543 DC of 30 November 2006.

It is worth noting that the Treaty on European Union displays a favourable position toward 'cooperative relations' between the Union and the constitutional orders of the states, especially in Article 6, paragraph 2, which states that fundamental rights are part of European Union law 'as general principles' and 'as they result from constitutional traditions common to the Member States'.[128] This 'cooperative' propensity, however, leaves open the diversity of constitutional traditions in the reading of fundamental rights. Nothing prevents a constitutional order from giving primacy to freedom of the press over privacy, whereas another may prefer the opposite. This impasse cannot be resolved with textualisations and the creation of new bureaucracies. What is required is the construction of shared methods to address these issues in every concrete case that is relevant to more than one order.

In principle, the main problem is finding models to 'compatibilise dissensus'[129] both between the legal order of the European Union and national orders, and between the national orders involved in litigation, especially between the respective courts. How can the transconstitutional 'conversation' enable a minimum of balance to be found between *legal* (internal) consistency and *legal* (external) adequacy in the decisions of a court as part of the chain of validation proper to each of the respective orders? How to reduce the negative impact caused by the externalisation of unbearable effects of an interpretation for other courts involved? These questions require a new methodology for transconstitutionalism: one which is not positively oriented by the illusory notion of optimisation based on arguments, but by an alterity that seeks to minimise the damage discourses tend to do to others with which they collide. The legal discourse of ECJ jurisprudence must be ready for permanent flexibility towards national orders, especially to tolerate different constitutional conceptions of fundamental rights when internalising supranational law. But this is a two-way street: a transconstitutional 'conversation' requires that constitutional councils and courts, as well as other courts with constitutional functions, renounce narcissism. The transconstitutional 'dialogue' requires an ability to put oneself in another's shoes.[130] This is vital to the maintenance and development of European transconstitutionalism between the supranational legal order and state legal orders.

[128] In this case, supranational expansion of these rights is manifest at the regional level, analogously to the 'transnational expansion of state fundamental rights' at the global level (Ladeur and Viellechner, 2008).

[129] Ladeur, 1986, 273.

[130] This presupposes a commitment to double contingency – ie 'being also otherwise possible' and mutual assumption of 'degrees of freedom' (Luhmann, 1987c, 184 and 186 [Engl trans 1995, 132 *f*) – in relations between courts. On double contingency as a condition for reciprocal recognition, *see* Neves, 2008, 502 *ff*. I return to this topic in Section III of the next Chapter.

IV. TRANSCONSTITUTIONALISM BETWEEN STATE LEGAL ORDERS

A constitutional 'conversation' is developing more frequently among courts in various nation-states via reciprocal references to decisions of courts in other states. Besides the fact that constitutional ideas migrate via legislation and doctrine from one legal order to another,[131] there is an intersection of problems that require a constitutional 'dialogue' at the jurisdictional level, especially via the development of constitutional or supreme courts. It is not simply a matter of observing that the decisions taken in one state order influence other state orders and have effects on the citizens of other states.[132] Nor does the question refer simply to 'transjudicialism',[133] as a form of reciprocal reference to decisions by courts in different states. In addition, transconstitutionalism between legal orders entails the invocation of decisions of constitutional courts in other states in typically constitutional cases by the constitutional court of a given state not just as *obiter dicta*, but also as building blocks for the *ratio decidendi*.[134] In this instance, 'transjudicialism' entails a re-reading of the constitutional self-founding elements of the order that takes itself as starting point and thus becomes transconstitutionalism. There follow some examples to illustrate this tendency towards constitutional entanglement among state legal orders.

While it can be said of constitutionalism in the US that 'American practice and theory have moved in the direction of emphatic provincialism',[135] and

[131] For a discussion of the migration of constitutional ideas, *see* Choudhry (ed), 2006. Addressing the subject in the context of the debate about 'imposed constitutionalism', Schauer (2005) reduces the significance of the issue of imposition and points to the inevitability of external influences (pp 918 *f*), adding: 'indeed, even the word 'migration' may suggest a more linear process than exists, and the interrelationship between national and global legal influence may be much more complex' (p 918, note 51). For a discussion of 'imposed constitutionalism' from a typically American perspective, *see also* the contributions of Feldman (2005), Sunder (2005), Levinson (2005), Choudhry (2005), Chesterman (2005) and Janis (2005). As a counterpoint, the debate on 'constitutional borrowing' can be followed via contributions to the first symposium organised by the *International Journal of Constitutional Law* (Friedman and Saunders, 2003, 177) from Davis (2003), Epstein and Knight (2003), Hasebe (2003), Osiatynski (2003), Rosenkrantz (2003) and Scheppele (2003).

[132] *See* Walter, 1999, 969; 2000, 8 *f*.

[133] Advocated in the US by former Supreme Court Justice Sandra Day O'Connor.*Cf* Slaughter, 2004, 75 *f*.

[134] The distinction between *ratio decidendi* and *obiter dictum* is more traditional in common law, but it is also sometimes relevant in civil law. On this topic, Ragazzi (1997, 5 *f*) asserts with precision: 'One of the rules of the doctrine of precedent (*stare decisis*) is that the only part of a decision that is binding for future cases is the *ratio decidendi*. Essentially, the *ratio decidendi* includes what is necessary to decide the issues before the court, while all propositions of law that are not part of the *ratio decidendi* are *obiter dicta*.' This distinction is clear in theory but imprecise in practice, as acknowledged by Ragazzi (p 6). Raz (1979, 184, note 9), albeit linked to the common law tradition, sidelines this distinction as follows: 'It is sometimes assumed that only the direct and least general reasons of the court's judgment constitute its *ratio*, while more general reasons used to defend and justify the direct ones are mere *obiter* . . . I assume that all the court's reasons of whatever generality are part of the *ratio*.' My own view is that, although the distinction should not be entirely discarded, it should be considered a gradual difference or scale between stronger, more direct reasons and weaker, more indirect reasons, to be assessed in each concrete case.

[135] Ackerman, 1997, 773.

asserted that the Supreme Court has been 'parochial' in refusing to take foreign laws into account,[136] for some years a debate has developed on the timeliness of invoking foreign jurisprudence in Supreme Court rulings.[137] In addition to the already mentioned decision in *Lawrence v Texas*, which gave rise to a debate about the invocation of foreign law by the Supreme Court (*see* p 91 above), previous cases involved significant discussions of the issue in the Supreme Court. In *Printz v United States* (decided 27 June 1997),[138] Justice Stephen Breyer filed a dissenting opinion invoking 'The Federalist', nos 42 and 43 (Madison),[139] and arguing that the experience of foreign courts and legal systems 'may nonetheless cast an empirical light on the consequences of different solutions to a common legal problem'.[140] In *Knight v Florida* (decided 8 November 1999), the Court denied certiorari for two prisoners who had been on death row for over 20 years. On this occasion Justice Breyer's dissenting opinion alluded to decisions by several courts in other countries and, while noting that 'foreign authority does not bind us', stressed that '[w]illingness to consider foreign judicial views in comparable cases is not surprising in a Nation that from its birth has given a "decent respect to the opinions of mankind"'.[141]

In a lecture on affirmative action, Justice Ruth Bader Ginsburg took note of this tendency to regard the rulings of foreign courts as elements of persuasion in the construction of a *ratio decidendi*: 'in the areas of human rights, experience in one nation or region may inspire or inform other nations or regions.' Nevertheless, in her view the US Supreme Court is not particularly willing to engage in this kind of constitutional 'conversation': whereas India's Supreme Court had taken US precedents into account, she wrote, 'the same readiness to look beyond one's own shores has not marked the decisions of the court on which I serve'.[142] A little later, however, discussing the same topic, Justice Ginsburg found evidence of change,[143] and reviewed the efforts of Justice Sandra O'Connor, according to whom: 'Although international law and the law of other nations are rarely binding upon our decisions in US courts, conclusions reached by other countries and by the international community should at times constitute persuasive authority in American courts.'[144]

It was this prior debate that led to the decision in *Lawrence v Texas*, which should be seen as the moment of transition to the development of trans-constitutionalism in the experience of the US Supreme Court and the American

[136] Slaughter, 2000, 1117 *f*.

[137] *See* Slaughter, 2000, 1117 *ff*; 2003, 197 *ff*; 2004, 75 *ff*; Baudenbacher, 2003, 513 *ff*.

[138] *Printz, Sheriff/Coroner, Ravalli County, Montanav United States*, 521 US 898 (1997).

[139] Madison, Hamilton and Jay, 1987 [1788], 276 and 279.

[140] *Printz v United States*, 521 US 898 (1997), 977. *Cf* Slaughter, 2000, 1118; 2004, 76.

[141] *Knight, aka Muhamadv Florida*, 528 US 990 (1999), 997 (the phrase in quotation marks ['decent respect . . .'] is from the Declaration of Independence). *Cf* Slaughter, 2000, 1118; 2003, 197; 2004, 77.

[142] Ginsburg, 1999. *Cf* Slaughter, 2004, 76 *f*.

[143] Slaughter, 2004, 77. *See* Ginsburg, 2005b.

[144] Cited by Slaughter, 2004, 75.

constitutional order. In the US this decision sparked a broad doctrinal discussion on 'constitutional borrowings'. The fact that a majority of Supreme Court justices now take a favourable view of such 'borrowings' leads to a constructive circularity in the relationship between legal theory and judicial practice. Academics and judges have participated actively in this debate (see above, note 131 to this Chapter).

This reticence in the US contrasts with a clear receptiveness to foreign constitutional law on the part of the Supreme Court of Canada and the Constitutional Court of South Africa. Case law for these courts shows that the jurisprudence of foreign constitutional courts or supreme courts may not only constitute *obiter dicta* but also have persuasive authority for the formation of a *ratio decidendi*. The highlight for the former is *Harvard College v Canada*,[145] where the Canadian Supreme Court reviewed a decision by the Federal Court of Appeal that had refused Harvard College a patent on the 'oncomouse', a breed of laboratory mouse genetically engineered to increase its susceptibility to cancer and thus make it suitable for cancer research. The Federal Court's Trial Division held that Harvard could patent the oncogene and the process of isolating the gene and implanting it in the mouse, but could not patent the oncomouse, arguing that the Harvard researchers had invented a process but not a mouse. By two votes to one, the Federal Court of Appeal reversed the decision and allowed Harvard's right to patent the animal. One of the majority judges based his opinion on the US Supreme Court judgment in *Diamond v Chakrabarty*, which ruled that biotechnological inventions are patentable,[146] declaring that this judgment had persuasive authority. Although the Canadian Supreme Court reversed this decision by five votes to four, ruling that higher life forms cannot be patented within the meaning of the Canadian Patent Act, both the majority and the minority referred to the ruling of the US Supreme Court.[147] The crux of the discussion was whether this sentence was applicable.

This case shows that transconstitutionalism between state legal orders cannot be constructed by means of an immediate transplant of foreign law, because it is associated with internal processes of self-validation. In this sense, Canadian Supreme Court Justice Claire L'Heureux-Dubé had rightly stressed in the late 1990s that 'the process of international influence has changed from *reception* to *dialogue*', adding:

> Judges no longer simply *receive* the cases of other jurisdictions and then apply them or modify them for their own jurisdiction. Rather, cross-pollination and dialogue between jurisdictions is increasingly occurring. As judgments in different countries increasingly build on each other, mutual respect and dialogue are fostered among appellate courts. Judges around the world look to each other for persuasive authority,

[145] *Harvard College v Canada (Commissioner of Patents)*, no 28155, judgment of 5 December 2002, [2002] 4 SCR 45.

[146] *Diamond, Commissioner of Patents and Trademarks v Chakrabarty*, 447 US 303 (1980).

[147] *See* Baudenbacher, 2003, 522 *f*, from which I have taken the above summary of the case.

> rather than some judges being 'givers' of law while others are 'receivers'. Reception is turning to dialogue.[148]

In other words, the courts in question are capable of acting reflexively both to maintain constitutional self-consistency and to pursue openness towards opportunities for learning from the experience of other courts. This would appear to be precisely the path followed successfully by the Canadian Supreme Court, despite all the obstacles inherent in a transconstitutional 'conversation'.

The South African Constitutional Court may be the clearest example of transconstitutional 'dialogue' with courts in other states.[149] The highlight here is *State v Makwanyane*, in which the Court ruled the death penalty unconstitutional.[150] In its judgment, besides referring to decisions of the European Court of Human Rights, the Constitutional Court of South Africa cited decisions of the US Supreme Court, the Canadian Supreme Court, the German Federal Constitutional Court, the Supreme Court of India, the Hungarian Constitutional Court, and the Tanzanian Court of Appeal, as well as taking into consideration judgments from the courts of two US States, California and Massachusetts.[151] This orientation is explicitly grounded in Article 39, paragraph 1, of the South African Constitution, which establishes that when interpreting the Bill of Rights (Article 7-39) any court, tribunal or forum not only 'must consider international law' (b), but also 'may consider foreign law' (c). In the above-mentioned case, both foreign constitutional law and the reasoning and conclusions of courts in other states were key elements in the South African Constitutional Court's arguments and decision, contributing to the judges' persuasive authority. This normative openness towards other legal orders and constitutional courts has made the South African Constitutional Court a benchmark for the 'constitutional conversation' model.

Other countries also offer relevant experience. In India, for example, 3,629 judgments by the Supreme Court were based on foreign law between 1950 and 2004: this corresponded to 24.6 per cent of all its decisions in the period.[152] The proportion has since declined, but remains very high, given that in 2004 alone almost 20 per cent of the Court's rulings took foreign law into account.[153] The supreme courts of other countries, such as Zimbabwe, Israel, New Zealand and Ireland, have also developed jurisprudence in which not only foreign law but also precedents from courts in other countries have been regularly cited as persuasive authority.[154] As can be seen, these are states with a wide range of different characteristics. Thus, while it may be acknowledged that in 'multinational states, with histories of colonialism, occupation and/or influence by others, and

[148] L'Heureux-Dubé, 1998, 17. *Cf* Slaughter, 2004, 74; Baudenbacher, 2003, 523.
[149] On this subject *see* Davis, 2003.
[150] *S v Makwanyane and Another*, Case no CCT/3/94, judged on 6 June 1995, 1995 (3) SALR 391.
[151] Slaughter, 2000, 1110 and 1116; 2004, 70 *f* and 73 *f*.
[152] Smith, 2006, 239 *f*.
[153] *Cf* Smith, 2006, 240 *f*.
[154] *Cf* Slaughter, 2004, 71.

increasing legal inter-connectedness with other countries, the line between "foreign" and "domestic" for concepts as intangible as "legal principles" has always been imprecise and is becoming more so',[155] transconstitutionalism should not be confused with mere 'transplants' of legal institutions[156] or linked to weaker states in the international constellation. Thus, for example, constitutional or supreme courts in West European countries with a solid legal tradition and influence on world society have not refrained from citing precedents from other states in their decisions.

The Federal Supreme Court of Switzerland has been considered a model of openness as far as the constitutional 'conversation' is concerned, with some 10 per cent of its judgments referring to foreign law.[157] While it tends to invoke the law of neighbouring countries, examples can also be found in which it cites foreign law from a global perspective, with some cases dating as far back as 1930.[158] More recently, in the sphere of copyright and patent law, that is, the constitutional law of intellectual property, the Swiss Supreme Court has been building up a significant amount of case law in the use of foreign law to ground the reasoning for its judgments.

An interesting example is the decision of 20 July 1998, in which the Swiss Supreme Court found for the exhaustion of copyright in a case involving parallel importing of a videogame, given the existence of a contract whereby the copyright holder allowed dissemination of the product abroad.[159] This decision referred indirectly to *King v L'Anza*, in which the US Supreme Court ruled similarly in a case involving copyrighted shampoo labels.[160] In that case, the US manufacturer's UK distributor, who held copyright under US law, sold products with copyrighted labels to a distributor in Malta which resold the goods to another distributor. The latter imported the goods back into the US without permission and resold them again at discounted prices to unauthorised retailers.[161] The Swiss Supreme Court, in deciding that copyright to the videogame was exhausted, acknowledged this international exhaustion precedent from the US Supreme Court.

In another case, this time concerning patent exhaustion and involving parallel-imported Kodak film,[162] the First Civil Law Division of the Federal Supreme Court of Switzerland decided by three votes to two in its judgment of 7 December 1999 to overturn a four-to-one ruling of the Zurich Commercial Court upholding international patent exhaustion.[163] In its judgment, the Swiss

[155] Smith, 2006, 225.

[156] Watson, 1977; Delmas-Marty, 2006, 103 *ff*, distinguishing the 'unilateral transplantation from hybridisation, which entails the reciprocity of exchange' (p 108).

[157] Baudenbacher, 2003, 520.

[158] *Ibid*.

[159] BGE 124 III 121.

[160] *Quality King Distributors, Inc v L'Anza Research International, Inc*, 523 US 135 (1998).

[161] *Cf* Baudenbacher, 2003, 520 *f*.

[162] BGE 126 III 129.

[163] Baudenbacher, 2003, 521.

Supreme Court discussed precedents from the European Court of Justice and other foreign courts in considerable detail.[164] It is worth noting its recognition of the existence of a 'real gap' ['*echte Lücke*'], in the following terms:

> The principle of patent exhaustion.Parallel imports of products protected by patent rights. The issue of the admissibility of parallel imports in patent law is not regulated either by national law or by international law valid in Switzerland; it is therefore necessary to start from a real gap.[165]

Given this lack of sufficient support in international and domestic law, it grounds its reasoning in a constructive 'dialogue' with foreign law, above all by citing the constitutional and supreme courts of other states, in addition to its reference to the ECJ, a foreign supranational court for Switzerland, which is not a member of the European Union. Besides this recognition of a gap in national and international law, the Swiss Supreme Court stressed its view of comparative law as one of the cornerstones for grounding its decision. In sum, the Court demonstrated a clear disposition to conduct a transconstitutional 'conversation' when faced by juridico-constitutional issues involving entanglements of different legal orders.

German experience is especially important with regard to transconstitutionalism between state legal orders, precisely because its courts frequently refer to the laws of other states even though Germany has a deeply rooted legal tradition of its own. The outstanding example in this respect is the practice of the German Federal Court of Justice, the highest appellate court for non-constitutional issues, although it has broad competencies for issues with constitutional impact. In several cases involving economic law, this court has invoked the decisions of foreign courts. For instance, in the '*Gelb/Schwarz*' case, concerning trademark protection for product colours,[166] the Federal Court, ruling in favour of protection on the grounds that the trademark was capable of distinguishing the goods or services of one producer from those of others, argued that consistent colour trademarks had been protected by decisions in other jurisdictions, in particular *Qualitex Co v Jacobson Products Co*, decided by the US Supreme Court on 28 March 1995.[167] Another example is the judgment of 23 November 2000, in a case which also discussed whether certain trademarks relating to a product's shape could be registered.[168] In rejecting the right to trademark protection in this particular case, the German Federal Court of Justice cited the decision of the US Supreme Court in *Wal-Mart Stores, Inc v Samara Brothers, Inc* (judgment of 22 March 2000), which held that 'design, like colour, is not inherently distinctive'.[169] In another decision (14 December 1999),

[164] *Ibid*.

[165] BGE 126, III 129, 129.

[166] BGH, Case I ZB 20/96, judgment of 10 December 1998, 140 BGHZ 193 (2000).

[167] *Qualitex Co v Jacobson Products Co, Inc*, 514 US 159 (1995).*Cf* Baudenbacher, 2003, 521.

[168] BGH, Case I ZB 15/98, judgment of 23 November 2000, cited by Baudenbacher, 2003, 521.

[169] *Wal-Mart Stores, Inc v Samara Brothers, Inc*, 529 US 205, 212 (2000).*Cf* Baudenbacher, 2003, 521.

when the Court confirmed that international exhaustion does not apply to patents, it cited the jurisprudence of other countries, referring specifically to decisions of the Tokyo Court of Appeal and the Supreme Court of Japan, as well as the judgment of the Zurich Commercial Court in the Kodak case that gave rise to the above-mentioned reversal by the Federal Supreme Court of Switzerland.[170] German judicial references to supreme courts or constitutional courts in other states are not limited to issues of economic law or decisions of the Federal Court of Justice. In *Caroline de Monaco II* (see Section II of this Chapter), where the issue was the protection of privacy for celebrities, for example, not only did the Federal Court of Justice[171] analyse the right to be alone as a specification of the right to privacy discussed by the US Supreme Court in *Katz v United States*,[172] but the Federal Constitutional Court, by partially upholding the decision of the *a quo* court, implicitly involved itself in the transconstitutional debate.[173]

The position of the United Kingdom, which has a very different legal system from that of Germany, also points in the direction of transconstitutional 'dialogue'. A noteworthy case occurred in 1993, when the House of Lords confirmed a ruling by the Court of Appeal to dismiss a libel suit on the grounds that local government cannot bring this type of action. The Court held, dismissing the appeal, that since it was of the highest public importance that a democratically elected governmental body should be open to uninhibited public criticism, and since the threat of civil actions for defamation would place an undesirable fetter on the freedom to express such criticism, it would be contrary to the public interest for institutions of central or local government to have any right at common law to maintain an action for damages for defamation; and that, accordingly, the plaintiff was not entitled to bring an action for libel against the defendants, and its statement of claim would be struck out.[174] The law lords acknowledged that the Court of Appeal had based its decision on US jurisprudence and said that although the issue was directly related to provisions in the US Constitution, freedom of speech was no less valid in the UK, especially in light of underlying public policy considerations.[175] This points to a growing willingness by senior members of the UK judiciary 'to accord persuasive authority to the constitutional values of other democratic nations when dealing with ambiguous statutory or common law provisions that impact upon civil liberties issues'.[176] The tendency for a judiciary rooted in a strong common law tradition in a country without a written

[170] BGH, Case X ZH 61/98, judgment of 14 December 1999, 143 BGHZ 268 (2001). *Cf* Baudenbacher, 2003, 521 *f*.

[171] BGH, Case VI ZR 15/95, judgment of 19 December 1995, 131 BGHZ 332 (1997).

[172] 389 US 347 (1967). *Cf* Baudenbacher, 2003, 522.

[173] BVerfGE 101, 361 (1999) (*see* p 88 *f* above).

[174] CA, *Derbyshire County Council v Times Newspapers Ltd and others*, judgment of 19 January 1992, [1992] 3 All ER 65; HL, *Derbyshire County Council v Times Newspapers Ltd and others*, judgment of 18 February 1993, [1993] 1 All ER 1011. *Cf* Slaughter, 2000, 1117.

[175] Slaughter, 2000, 1117.

[176] Ian Loveland, cited by Slaughter, 2000, 1117.

constitution to invoke another country's constitutional provisions and jurisprudence as a basis for its decisions when faced with juridico-constitutional problems, especially related to freedom of speech and of the press, is a strong indication of the development of transconstitutionalism. In this context, although the UK legal order opted not to adopt a constitutional document, the country's higher courts refer to the constitutional texts of other orders and even to foreign jurisprudence where the exegesis of these normative texts is concerned.

Cross-referencing of judicial decisions has been frequent among courts in European countries. In particular, triangular 'conversations' on precedents have developed among Swiss, German, and Austrian courts, but the courts of Hungary, Norway, Denmark, Sweden, Finland, Italy, France, and the UK, among others, also engage in transconstitutional 'dialogue'.[177] This posture is undoubtedly facilitated by geographical proximity and by a degree of conceptual commonality in legal semantics, both of which enable the entanglement of relevant cases for more than one legal order. However, as noted above, European constitutional and supreme courts have cited both constitutional provisions and the corresponding jurisprudence of state legal orders on other continents, with a particular openness towards the US constitutional experience.

In Latin America there is a long-standing tradition of reference to foreign constitutional provisions, jurisprudence and doctrine. Although the influence of the US has long prevailed, especially by virtue of the strong influence of its constitutional model on the origins of Latin American constitutionalism, European constitutional law and jurisprudence are increasingly invoked. German constitutionalism, in particular, has exerted significant influence more recently. It is true that, historically speaking, references to foreign constitutional texts, doctrine, and jurisprudence have largely been an expression of '*bacharelismo*',[178] figuring in 'rhetorical' judges' opinions as proof of erudition, without relevant links to the merits of the case in question. Recent jurisprudence, however, displays a tendency to include references to foreign constitutional texts and precedents as both *obiter dicta* and part of the *ratio decidendi*.

In more recent Brazilian experience, transconstitutionalism with other legal orders has developed conspicuously in the Federal Supreme Court. In important decisions relating to fundamental rights, foreign constitutional jurisprudence is cited not only in the opinions of individual justices, but also in case dockets as part of the *ratio decidendi*. In upholding an appellant's conviction on charges of

[177] Baudenbacher, 2003, 507–9.

[178] *Bacharelismo* refers to a predominance of *bachareis* (university-educated professionals, especially lawyers), in political and cultural life. It is also used to refer to a preference for rhetoric over research not only among lawyers, but also among doctors, engineers, economists and other members of the liberal professions (Chacon, 1969, 21). According to Birman and Lehmann, '*bacharelismo* is a rhetorical style associated with useless knowledge of little practical value'; 'a type of rhetoric, a style of writing, oracular and archaic, which was prevalent in politics and high culture' (Birman and Lehmann, 1999, 163, notes 13 and 14). For a critique of the generalised and simplistic use of the term with regard to Brazilian jurists, *see* Saldanha, 1978. On the various conceptions of *bacharelismo*, *see* Venancio Filho, 1977, 271 *ff*.

racism for publishing a book with antisemitic content (Holocaust denial) in the historic *Ellwanger* case (Habeas Corpus 82.424/RS, 17 November 2003), for example, references to foreign constitutional jurisprudence in the reasoning used by the Plenary of the Supreme Court played a fundamental role. This situation is reflected by the judgment docket, which contains the following paragraph:

> 9. Comparative law. The laws in modern democratic constitutional states such as Brazil call for the punishment of offences that encourage and promote racial segregation. Manifestations of the United States Supreme Court, the United Kingdom House of Lords and the California Courts of Appeal in the US have established the understanding that those who infringe the rules of peaceful social coexistence among human groups by practising racism should be punished.

In their written opinions, the justices conducted a detailed discussion of jurisprudential precedents, constitutional provisions and legislation in foreign states, with relatively little reference to domestic and international law jurisprudence.[179]

This orientation is also expressed in the Supreme Court judgment of ADI 3.112 (2 May 2007), an application for judicial review which was dismissed almost in its entirety: the Court declared Law 10826 (Estatuto do Desarmamento, enacted 22 December 2003) constitutional except for the sole paragraphs of Articles 14 and 15, as well as Article 21. The judgment highlights precedents from the jurisprudence of the German Federal Constitutional Court.[180] Similarly, in ADI 3510/DF (29 May 2008) the Court ruled in favour of the legality of using foetal stem cells for research and therapy by declaring constitutional Article 5 of Law 11105 (Lei da Biossegurança, enacted 24 March 2005).[181] Several justices discussed foreign law in their opinions on this case. A great many other examples could be given of Supreme Court judgments that cite foreign cases, although they do not always do so as part of the *ratio decidendi*, but as a contribution to the underlying reasoning.[182] This new orientation is not mere rhetoric or '*bacharelismo*',[183] but part of a significant debate in the context of a transconstitutional 'conversation'.

[179] This is evident from the large number of references to the jurisprudence of foreign states, as can be noticed from the section entitled 'Observação' of the full judgment transcript (HC 82.424/RS, judgment of 17 November 2003, TP, DJ 19 March 2004).

[180] 'BVerfGE 88, 203, 1993; BVerfGE 50, 290; BVerfGE 77, 170; BVerfGE 39, 210; BVerfGE 90, 145, 1994 (Cannabis case); BVerfGE 7, 377, 1958' (ADI 3.112, judgment of 2 May 2007, TP, DJ 26 October 2007).

[181] ADI 3.510/DF, judgment of 29 May 2008, TP, DJ 5 June 2008.

[182] *See*, eg, HC 93.050/RJ, judgment of 10 June 2008, 2nd T, DJe 1 August 2008; HC 85.779/RJ, judgment of 28 February 2007, TP, DJ 29 June 2007; ACO 633 AgR/SP, judgment of 11 April 2007, TP, DJ 22 June 2007; RE 390.840/MG, judgment of 9 November 2005, TP, DJ 15 August 2006; ADPF 54 QO/DF, judgment of 27 April 2005, TP, DJ 31 August 2007; HC 40.910/PE, judgment of 24 August 1964, TP, DJ 19 November 1964.

[183] Although many judges' written opinions still evidence a wish to demonstrate erudition that is irrelevant to resolving the case, making judgments excessively long, it should be noted that the problem is not predominantly one of the citation of foreign jurisprudential precedents but of doctrines and theories imported without proper filtering for application to the Brazilian context. This in turn relates to the limitations of doctrinal and legal thinking in Brazil (*see* Neves, 1992, 205 *ff*).

This new approach, involving the citation and use of foreign jurisprudential precedents, has more recently had repercussions for legal doctrine in Brazil. For example, in an overview of fundamental rights theory Dimitri Dimoulis and Leonardo Martins, before analysing three cases from the jurisprudence of the German Federal Constitutional Court (and to some extent justifying the analysis), state:

> The Brazilian legal community aims to give the Federal Constitution a genuinely normative status, especially after so many frustrated attempts. In this context, comparative law plays the key role of presenting models applicable to Brazilian constitutional law, provided the requisite adaptations are made.[184]

Although they focus on virtually one single experience of foreign constitutional jurisprudence, that is, Germany's, these authors already reflect to some extent the strong tendency of the Brazilian Supreme Court to engage in a 'dialogue' with foreign legal orders via the constitutional or supreme courts of other states.

Constitutional doctrine has also joined this Brazilian-style transconstitutional 'conversation'. For example, in addressing the problems of discrimination against homosexuals and same-sex civil union, Daniel Sarmento reflects the new Brazilian jurisprudential transconstitutionalism by citing the decisions of foreign courts, especially US precedents.[185] It can be said that while transconstitutionalism in the Supreme Court leans towards a 'dialogue' with German constitutionalism, recent developments in constitutional doctrine display a balance between a 'conversation' with American constitutionalism and its German counterpart, both of which have had a predominant influence on the Brazilian experience.

However, care must be taken to ensure that frequent invocation of jurisprudence from the US, German and other legal orders does not constitute just one more episode in the history of 'colonialism' in Brazil's legal culture.[186] Failure to avoid this would mean passing from the uncritical 'importation' of legal and doctrinal models to the inadequate incorporation of jurisprudential precedents. The only change would be easier access to foreign jurisprudence. Thus, it is fundamental that 'the requisite adaptations are made', so that we avoid relapsing into the old problem of 'misplaced ideas',[187] in this case involving jurisprudence and constitutional doctrine dislocated from their legal and social context, and giving rise to the paradox of a 'dialogue' with an 'alter' but no 'ego' as the other pole of communication's double contingency.[188] And this

[184] Dimoulis and Martins, 2007, 262.However, the STF continues to refer rhetorically and inconsistently to foreign case law, as can be seen in the judgment on the constitutionality of the policy of university quotas (ADPF 186, judgment of 26 April 2012, TP): US Supreme Court decisions were cited as grounds for this judgment but contradicted it on the key point (*see* Costa Neto, 2013).

[185] Sarmento, 2008, 627 *ff*. Accompanying him on this point, Barroso, 2008, especially 666 *ff*.

[186] Montoro, 1973; Neves, 1992, 206.

[187] Schwarz, 2008 [1977] [Engl trans 1992].

[188] *See* above, note 130.

could, therefore, produce a symbolic type of jurisprudence and doctrine whose normative significance would be very limited.[189]

In the plane of transconstitutionalism there are not only references to or citations of juridico-constitutional precedents from other legal orders, but also appraisals of the practice of judges and courts in other countries. For example:

> US courts have found that a Chilean court was an inadequate forum due to lack of judicial independence under the military junta; that an Iranian court was an inadequate forum due to presumed bias against Americans; and that a Romanian judgment was unenforceable because it was not achieved 'under a system of jurisprudence likely to secure an impartial administration of justice'.[190]

On the other hand, they have 'quickly rejected assertions that the Israeli or French judicial systems were inadequate, holding that it would be completely inappropriate for a US judge to speculate "that his Israeli colleagues would violate their oaths of office"', or characterise the French judicial system as less fair than the American. Similarly, they have expressed views on the standards of neutrality of English courts.[191] This posture by US courts can be interpreted as an expression of asymmetry between legal orders, given that courts in globally powerful countries tend not to be censured by US courts whereas courts in underdeveloped or developing countries are not taken seriously by judges in the US. However, Slaughter distinguishes between the situation in judiciaries that are less efficient than America's, with relevant procedural differences, and contexts in which minimal standards of impartiality are lacking. Only in the latter case, that is, where there is overt bias, systemic corruption or denial of basic due process, 'will a US Court allow a litigant to escape the bonds of contract or place and choose a US Court instead'.[192]

The question does not seem so simple to me. Whenever a country is indisposed towards transconstitutionalism, precisely because it does not adopt constitutional institutions in the modern sense, but on the contrary rejects them radically, it is almost insuperably difficult for a transconstitutional 'conversation' to take place. Merely censuring a country's courts or criticising them in comparison with those of other countries does nothing to change this state of affairs. Instead it would be fruitful if courts in countries averse to constitutionalism could be encouraged to connect, even as passive agents initially. In this regard, face-to-face meetings among judges[193] are crucial to any effort to foster positive developments.

[189] Blankenburg (1977, 42), commenting on decisions regarding abortion by the German Federal Constitutional Court, argues that they involve 'symbolic confirmation of normative claims' rather than their 'effective imposition' (*cf* Neves, 2007a, 34). Hence the appropriateness of mentioning 'symbolic jurisprudence'. STF Justice Marco Aurélio Mello used the phrase in HC 82.424/RS, discussed above. In my view, however, not just the symbolic but also the normative strength of the decision was relevant.

[190] Slaughter, 2004, 93.

[191] *Ibid.*

[192] Slaughter, 2004, 93 *f.*

[193] Slaughter, 2004, 96 *ff*; 2000, 1120 *ff.*

Nevertheless, it would be mistaken to deny a basic presupposition for the success of any model of transconstitutionalism: the difference between constitutional orders, with all their peculiarities in terms of both normative content and procedures. Slaughter is right to say in this regard that procedural variations 'such as differences in discovery, the presence or absence of contingency fees, or differences in the role of the judge, are part of the normal variation in legal systems that litigants must expect when they venture across borders'.[194] This also applies to judges when they meet face to face with judges from other state orders: they should be ready to be surprised by diversity and, where relevant, open to learning and exchange. Otherwise what prevails is a 'presumption of difference, an abstract insistence on "separate but equal" embedded in formal notions of sovereignty', resulting in the illusion that 'only big differences matter'.[195] This attitude leads to mutual distrust and the inability to conduct a transconstitutional 'dialogue'. Constitutional autism points to negation of the other, and rejection of double contingency in relations among courts as organisationally structured institutional poles. Conversely, 'where courts begin from a presumption of identity, then they scrutinise each other according to the same criteria that they would apply to other domestic tribunals in the same circumstances',[196] leading them to overlook double contingency in the illusory belief in a community of perspectives on normative interpretation and case law that masks the diversity of positions from which conflict is observed by the different legal orders and their respective courts.

It is obvious that the development of a transconstitutional 'dialogue' among state legal orders also depends on the emergence of 'judicial comity' and judicial negotiation.[197] The former, as noted above, may provide 'the framework and the ground-rules for a global dialogue among judges in the context of specific cases'.[198] There is evidently a certain difficulty with the functioning of 'judicial comity', given the competition and misunderstandings among judges, among other factors. However, in a reference to US judges, Slaughter says, 'the willingness to weather conflict reflects the certainty of ongoing interaction'.[199] Judicial negotiation is more limited and hitherto has occurred mainly in global bankruptcy cases. In these situations, court-to-court agreements are the rule, without the intermediation of international treaties.[200] It seems to me, however, that transjudicial negotiation may be significant for other areas of law when cases cross borders. For example, where cases involve environmental disasters, cross-border crime, and so on, it would be fitting to open up a space for transjudicial negotiation in pursuit of a satisfactory solution. Moreover, the possibility of future transconstitutional negotiations among supreme courts in several

194 Slaughter, 2004, 94.
195 *Ibid.*
196 *Ibid.*
197 Slaughter, 2004, 86 *ff* and 94 *ff*; 2003, 205 and 213 *ff*; 2000, 1112 *ff*.
198 Slaughter, 2004, 87; 2003, 206. *See* pp 76 *f* above.
199 Slaughter, 2004, 90; 2003, 208.
200 Slaughter, 2004, 94–6; 2003, 213–5.

countries should not be ruled out, given the entanglement and simultaneous relevance of cases that transcend state borders.

Lastly, it should be stressed that transconstitutionalism among state legal orders is the clearest symptom that transconstitutionalism should not be confused with an overarching and supra-ordained global legal order. Once again Slaughter's remarks are pertinent here. Referring to an assertion by Judge Guido Calabresi of the US Court of Appeals for the Second Circuit, she says a

> 'dialogue between the adjudicative bodies of the world community' would not be composed of US, French, German, Japanese courts and international tribunals but simply of adjudicative entities engaging in resolving disputes, interpreting and applying the law as best they can. It is a vision of a global legal system, established not by the World Court in The Hague, but by national courts working together around the world.[201]

To put this more precisely, it can be said that without the starting point in question – that is, without a transconstitutional 'conversation' among state legal orders via their respective supreme courts – a more comprehensive transconstitutionalism among legal orders of different types, in a tangled 'multilevel' world legal system, will face real difficulties to develop adequately in the context of today's heterogeneous and complex global society. It would also be unlikely to legitimate itself, given the plurality and indeed the fragmentation of this society in the plane of normative structures. The starting point for transconstitutionalism is not the negation but the opening up of state constitutionalisms to other legal orders, be they of the same or different types.

V. TRANSCONSTITUTIONALISM BETWEEN STATE AND TRANSNATIONAL LEGAL ORDERS

One of the most intriguing dimensions of transconstitutionalism is the relationship between state legal orders and legal orders that are transnational in the strict sense, that is, normative orders constructed primarily not by or from states but by private or quasi-public actors or organisations. Denying they are legal orders with a claim to autonomy no longer appears sustainable. In this regard, it is not necessary to be associated with a postmodern or deconstructionist model, as proposed emphatically by Gunther Teubner and Andréas Fischer-Lescano, who stress the growing significance of legal transnationalism in the strict sense.[202] Furthermore, Dieter Grimm, a leading jurist linked to the tradition of state constitutionalism, does not miss the importance of this development to today's world society:

> Alongside these institutions created by states [WTO, World Bank and IMF], meanwhile, are global actors like multinational firms and non-government organisations,

[201] Slaughter, 2003, 204. *Cf* Slaughter, 2004, 85; 2000, 1114, for almost identical formulations.

[202] *See*, above all, Fischer-Lescano and Teubner, 2006. *Cf* Ladeur and Viellechner, 2008.

> which, by virtue of the range of their activities, can largely follow their own systemic logic without having to respect standards and obligations that prevail within states. All the same, they too cannot live without legal regulation. The globalised sector of the economy depends on a transnational law no national legislator can provide.[203]

These orders, which are not limited to the economic dimension (although this appears to be the most relevant dimension of legal transnationalism), do not remain isolated but collide or cooperate with other legal orders, including state legal orders. In this context, the problem of transconstitutionalism also arises when constitutional issues, especially cases relating to fundamental rights or basic organisation of power, lead to the entanglement of orders and their respective supreme courts. Although it is difficult for transnational legal orders to construct themselves autonomously in the face of global functional systems and the organisations to which they are structurally linked (the economy, sports, the internet, NGOs, and so on), they do make a claim to autonomy from state law, precisely on the basis of the strength of the respective functional systems and organisations, and this, in turn, leads to problems of entanglement at the reflexive level of self-foundation between transnational orders and state orders. A few examples will serve as an empirical reference to the transconstitutional problems between these two orders.

A typical case is the new *lex mercatoria*, about which there is a great deal of discussion in the literature.[204] This is a world legal-economic order in the sphere of transnational trade, whose construction and reproduction occur primarily through contracts and arbitration deriving from communication and normatively stabilised reciprocal expectations among private actors and organisations. Neither an analysis of the structure of this order in isolation nor only a general consideration of its entanglement with the state order is relevant here. What is pertinent to the present context is to ask how constitutional problems can arise in the transversal relationship between these orders. In this regard, it is not enough simply to assert there is a relationship between the heterarchy of the *lex mercatoria* and the hierarchy of the state order. Both contain hierarchical and heterarchical dimensions. Instead, it is appropriate to focus on the complex

[203] Grimm, 2004a, 12.

[204] The ongoing debate about the new *lex mercatoria* started with Goldman (1964), who while acknowledging that it constitutes 'an incomplete legal system' argued that the 'norms it comprises – all of them except typical contracts issued by isolated firms – are certainly general legal rules (and not mere individual norms 'hung on' a state rule that recognises the obligatory force of contracts)' (1964, 192). On this discussion about the nature of the *lex mercatoria* and its autonomy from state law, see among many Lagarde, 1982; Mustill, 1987; Fouchard, Gaillard and Goldman, 1996, 813 *ff* (no 1143 *ff*); Mertens, 1997; Gaillard, 2001; Booysen, 2003, 9 *ff*; Loquin, 2006, 165 *ff*. From a systemic perspective, characterising the *lex mercatoria* as a discursive sphere or autonomous communication system (and not primarily as the expression of group or organisational interests), *see* Teubner, 1996b or 1997b. Linked to this systemic model, see the substantial work by Mendes, R, 2010. For a critical position, *see* Dezalay and Garth, 1996, who not only call transnational arbitrators 'merchants of law as moral entrepreneurs' (pp 33 *ff*), but also insinuate that their 'community' constitutes a 'mafia': 'Members of the inner circle and outsiders often referred to this group as a "mafia" or a "club"' (p 10).

entanglement of two orders characterised by tangled hierarchies and tangled heterarchies in the sphere of transconstitutionalism. Nor does it seem to me to be correct to say that it is a relationship between the centre and periphery of the legal system.

First of all, given that what is at issue is a multicentric world legal system, the centre is located in the order from which the observer is looking. Thus, the institutions that are at the centre of a given legal order, the courts, constitute part of the periphery of the legal system for another legal order. So while from the vantage point of an observer of the national legal order and state courts the *lex mercatoria* and its tribunals are on the periphery of the legal system, for the *lex mercatoria* itself and the respective arbitration tribunals, state orders and their respective courts are part of the periphery of the legal system.

Finally, I reject the thesis that both the *lex mercatoria* and transnational orders in general are linked to the spontaneous sectors of world society whereas state law is linked to its organised sectors.[205] Of course, if the high degree of organisation of the businesses and law firms that operate in the *lex mercatoria* sphere[206] is compared with the very low level of organisation of certain states in Africa and other regions of the world, it becomes clear how illusory is this approach to the problem of the relations between the *lex mercatoria* and state orders. It is vitally important to bear in mind that claims to autonomy and self-foundation, for the *lex mercatoria*, as much as for state orders, require a readiness to learn and exchange, given the flow of relevant cases for both orders. The greatest threat is mutual contempt, justified either by predominantly ideological statism to the detriment of economic development or privatism primarily based on the concrete interests of economic agents with high strategic capacity and destructive consequences for socially and economically weaker third parties. In this regard, state orders react differently to the development of the *lex mercatoria*'s institutions and organisations, while the latter tend to emphasise their autonomy and growth, with scant disposition to engage in a transconstitutional 'dialogue' with the respective entangled states in cases of concomitant interest, especially when such cases relate to fundamental rights.

On this subject, attention has been drawn to the more reticent posture of US courts towards transnational arbitration, while the French judiciary is seen as more open toward arbitration tribunals.[207] The positive disposition of French state courts towards arbitration in disputes involving transnational economic law was displayed with particular clarity in *Putrabali*, judged by the Cour de cassation, France's highest court, on 29 June 2007.[208] This was a benchmark in a development that began with *Gosset*, judged on 7 May 1967 by the Cour de

[205] From a different perspective, *see* Teubner, 2000 [Engl trans 2004a], 2003a, 25 *f* [Engl trans 2004b, 27 *f*].

[206] *Cf* Dezalay and Garth, 1996, stressing that 'international commercial arbitration has become *moreformal* and expensive, more like US litigation' (my emphasis, 60).

[207] *Cf* Slaughter, 2004, 92.

[208] *See* Pinsolle, 2008.

cassation, which 'admitted for the first time the principle of the separability of the arbitration agreement'.[209] The importance of the decision in *Putrabali* can be attributed, at first glance, to the fact that it was the first time the Cour de cassation had been called upon to rule on the enforcement of an arbitral award that had been set aside in the seat of arbitration since *Hilmarton* (June 1997).[210] In fact, however, its importance was even more fundamental, as stressed by Philippe Pinsolle: besides endorsing solutions adopted by the Paris Court of Appeal and the Cour de cassation itself in *Hilmarton* and subsequent cases, the Cour de cassation offered firmer and broader theoretical foundations for adopting this solution.[211]

The *Putrabali* case involved a maritime law dispute between an Indonesian company, PT Putrabali Adyamulia (the seller) and a French company, Société Est Epices, which later became Rena Holding (the buyer), over a contract to sell white pepper. The cargo was shipped on 27 January 2000, but the barge sank off Bangka Island in Indonesia on 1 February 2000 and the goods were lost. Pursuant to the contract, Putrabali claimed for payment in arbitration at the International General Produce Association (IGPA) in London. The two arbitrators appointed by the parties failed to reach an agreement, but an umpire found against the buyer for breach of contract. In accordance with IGPA rules, the buyer appealed to the arbitral Board of Appeal, which overturned the first award and found in favour of the buyer, ruling that there had been no breach of contract. The seller appealed against the second award to the English High Court. On 19 May 2003, the High Court partially set aside the award, finding that breach of contract had indeed occurred for lack of payment, and remitted the case back to the IGPA Board of Appeal. In a new ruling (remitted award) on 19 August 2003, the buyer was ordered to pay £163,086.04. Despite having lost the remitted award, the buyer applied to the French courts for an *exequatur* order, that is, recognition and enforcement of the second award, dated 10 April 2001, and won. The seller then appealed to the Paris Court of Appeal, which on 31 March 2005 upheld the *exequatur* order issued by the French court of first instance. Putrabali argued that the award of 10 April 2001 had been set aside and that the attempt to have it executed in France was a fraud. The Paris Court of Appeal rejected this argument on the grounds that execution of an arbitral award set aside in the country of origin could not be refused, since French procedural law did not provide for such refusal. There was nothing new about this decision in light of a series of previous rulings by French courts, including *Hilmarton* (1997). Only in response to the last-resort appeal by Putrabali did the Cour de cassation offer the innovative element with regard to transnational arbitration.[212] The decision was based on the following twofold rationale: (1) a

[209] Pinsolle, 2008, 277.
[210] On this case, *see* Gaillard, 1999, 21 *ff*.
[211] Pinsolle, 2008, 277.
[212] *Arrêt* [Judgment] no 1021 of 29 July 2007 – Court of Cassation – First Civil Chamber (Engl trans as Appendix in Pinsolle, 2008, 293–5).

transnational (the term 'international' is imprecisely used) arbitral award is not anchored in any national legal order; (2) a transnational ['international'] arbitral award is a transnational ['international'] judicial decision.[213]

The most relevant aspect of this case is the explicit acknowledgment by the highest court in France that the *lex mercatoria* is autonomous with regard to any state legal order, in accordance with a tradition already present in French jurisprudence and doctrine. It is a 'delocalised' legal order.[214] What was asserted in this case is not simply that arbitration is not anchored in the legal order of the country of origin or seat of arbitration, but in a step forward, that it is not anchored in any state order at all. This has consequences in the context of our discussion, because cases concomitantly involving the *lex mercatoria* and the state legal order in the sphere of constitutionally relevant issues require treatment in terms of transconstitutionalism, given that each of the orders concerned claims self-foundation. Thus, in some cases, in addition to a transjudicial 'dialogue' there must be a transconstitutional 'conversation' between legal orders of different kinds, above all via constructive relations between their courts.

This understanding becomes even more plausible in light of the thesis contained in the other element in the rationale for the Cour de cassation's ruling: a transnational arbitral award is a transnational judicial decision. This entails recognition that an arbitral award under the *lex mercatoria* is a judicial decision which does not require approval by any national court to be enforced. Although a court in the seat of arbitration may reject enforcement of an award within the respective state jurisdiction, this does not prevent enforcement in the territory of another state. On this subject, Pinsolle analyses as follows the reasoning of the Cour de cassation in the judgment in question (using 'international' instead of 'transnational'):

> The theoretical justification for this reasoning is found in the existence of an arbitral legal order distinct from the national legal orders. It is because the international arbitral award is grounded in the arbitral legal order, and not in the legal order of the place of arbitration, that the existence of this award is out of the reach of the courts of the place of arbitration. All that the courts of the place of arbitration can decide is that this award will be denied existence in their legal order.[215]

Pinsolle then argues that the proposition according to which, in the name of consistency, the contracting states should respect the decision of the local arbitration tribunal appears unsustainable, since it would be valid only for annulment of an arbitral award: 'When the award has not been annulled there is no such consistency and any contracting party maintains its rights to enforce or

[213] This summarised outline of the case is based on Pinsolle, 2008, who provides a detailed exposition and analysis.

[214] Pinsolle, 2008, 281 *f.*

[215] Pinsolle, 2008, 291.

not to enforce the award provided that it stays within the limits provided by the Convention.'[216]

Moreover, those who suggest this solution based on the assumption of consistency focus on the courts of the seat of arbitration, forgetting that in the first place there was an arbitral award.[217] It should be added that this proposition would entail linking the decision of the courts in the country of enforcement to the courts in the country of arbitration, regardless of consistency for the legal order in which enforcement is to take place. The problem is analogous to the enforcement of a foreign sentence by any state order with the force of *res judicata* in the terms of classical international private law. However, albeit functionally equivalent to a foreign sentence, the link to a deterritorialised legal order makes entanglement problems far more complex, especially owing to the versatility and mobility of *lex mercatoria* contracts and arbitrations. In this sense, the probability of conflicts of a constitutional nature between this legal order and state legal orders may have even more serious effects than those between two territorially delimited orders.

Of course, there are serious risks in the development of a transconstitutional 'conversation' with the new *lex mercatoria*. Although this transnational legal order firmly and successfully sustains its claim to autonomy from constitutional state orders, it is nevertheless strongly dependent on the economic system and, hence, also on its agents. Given that *lex mercatoria* serves to improve economic efficiency in the sphere of commerce, its link to the legal and constitutional principle of equality is secondary and weak. Characterised as 'a corrupt law' by one of its most important theoreticians,[218] its 'constitutional capacity' is limited, especially the capacity to engage satisfactorily with fundamental rights issues. Thus, when evaluating transconstitutionalism between the state legal order and the *lex mercatoria*, it is essential to note its limited nature, since in principle one of the orders is not primarily oriented to addressing and resolving constitutional problems. The fact that the *lex mercatoria* has little disposition for transconstitutionalism should not necessarily lead to constitutionalist antagonism against this transnational order, which would have disastrous effects for both parties. On the contrary, the transconstitutional involvement of the constitutional state with the new *lex mercatoria* could both limit its tendency to expand and also strengthen its reflexive capacity to develop with operative autonomy with regard to the concrete and particularistic interests of highly strategic economic actors.

[216] Pinsolle, 2008, 291. Pinsolle refers to the Convention on the Recognition and Enforcement of Foreign Arbitral Awards, adopted by the United Nations Conference on International Commercial Arbitration in New York on 10 June 1958, especially Art VII, para 1: '1. The provisions of the present Convention shall not affect the validity of multilateral or bilateral agreements concerning the recognition and enforcement of arbitral awards entered into by the Contracting States nor deprive any interested party of any right he may have to avail himself of an arbitral award in the manner and to the extent allowed by the law or the treaties of the country where such award is sought to be relied upon.'

[217] Pinsolle, 2008, 291 *f*.

[218] Teubner, 1996b, 279 or 1997b, 19.

One argument to refute the transnational nature of the *lex mercatoria* in the strict sense as far as arbitration is concerned may be found in the New York Convention on the Recognition and Enforcement of Foreign Arbitral Awards.[219] Indeed, in the case outlined above, the French company Rena Holding invoked Article VII of this international convention in its appeal to the French courts.[220] However, this argument remains on the surface of a complex legal phenomenon. More to the point, it can be inferred from the decision of the Cour de cassation that the legal order of transnational arbitration is not anchored in any state order. This means that in itself it is already a 'foreign' order with regard to the order of any state. What the New York Convention regulates is recognition and enforcement of foreign arbitral awards by states. This applies as much to arbitration subordinated to the procedural order of other states as to transnational arbitration, which is linked to an order that has progressively asserted its autonomy from state legal orders in general, including the order of the state in which arbitration has taken or may take place, geographically speaking. What can be seen when the New York Convention is taken into account is an entanglement of legal orders that is not restricted to bilaterality (state order/transnational order of commercial arbitration), but includes, in a 'multilevel' or multicentric world legal system, the international order and the orders of other states: in this sense, the possibilities of transconstitutional 'conversation' among legal orders are increased.

It is not only with regard to the *lex mercatoria* that the problem of entanglement between transnational and state legal orders is highlighted, with the possibility of transconstitutional collisions. The *lex sportiva*, a legal order constructed in connection with sport as a functional system of world society via transnational sporting associations, has asserted a high degree of autonomy from state law, affecting individual rights issues of a constitutional nature, especially in the field of freedom of contract and professional freedom.[221] By prohibiting athletes from defending their rights before state courts, for example, transnational sporting associations claim autonomy for their respective legal orders in matters pertaining to sports law. The problem resides precisely in the fact that sports law, as already noted, involves rights such as freedom of contract and professional freedom, from which derives the question of transconstitutionalism. This claim to exclusivity of jurisdiction is not something that remains in the plane of general and abstract norms, without practical repercussions in the plane of procedural concretisation of *lex sportiva*. Sports arbitration instances have successfully affirmed their autonomy from state courts in the praxis of dispute settlement, leading to collisions and hence to the need for a transconstitutional 'conversation'.

[219] *See* Booysen, 2003, 785 *ff*.

[220] *Cf* Pinsolle, 2008, 281, 293 and 295. See above, note 216.

[221] On the 'general principles' of the *lex sportiva*, *see* Loquin, 2007. For an analysis of the theoretical foundations of the *lex sportiva*, *see* Panagiotopoulos, 2004. A comprehensive study is offered by Latty, 2007.

The decisions of the highest transnational sports court, the Court of Arbitration for Sport (CAS), headquartered in Lausanne, Switzerland, display a clear distinction between its material jurisdiction and that of state courts. This has occurred not only in the plane of normative interpretation, but also in that of the production of evidence, as can be seen from Eric Loquin's digest of CAS awards between late 2006 and end-2007.[222] In an arbitral award issued on 19 December 2006, CAS referred with approval to a decision of the International Cycling Union (UCI) that suspended a cyclist for doping in a race held on 5–12 June 2005.[223] Two tests returned positive results (the second being a B sample requested by the cyclist) from a laboratory accredited by the World Anti-Doping Agency (WADA), identifying and confirming the presence of doping substances in the sample collected. Based on these findings, on 27 October 2006, UCI sent the laboratory's reports to the Spanish cycling federation (Real Federación Española de Ciclismo or RFEC), ordering disciplinary procedure to be followed in accordance with Article 187 of the UCI's Anti-Doping Rules. On 5 May 2006, RFEC's disciplinary committee decided that the conditions under which the analysis had been performed showed the existence 'of an incomplete process due to failure to comply with all the applicable legal requirements, thus being unable totally to guarantee the result'. The committee ruled that 'the legal maxim "in *dubio pro reo*" [is] fully applicable to this case' and acquitted the cyclist. UCI appealed to CAS on 26 June 2006, and the hearing took place on 11 October 2006.[224]

In its judgment, CAS categorically asserted the autonomy of transnational sports law from state orders. The principle of equality, an eminently constitutional concept, was fundamental to its reasoning, as can be seen from the following extract:

> The practice of a sport at the international level cannot be expected to comply with a multiplicity of potentially contradictory national rules. Endowing only national laws with the care of governing the conditions under which international competitions are to be conducted would end up in an incoherent and anti-egalitarian system, with the additional risk that the authorities would sooner or later become involved in a rush to the least repressive legislation. To avoid these undesirable outcomes, it suffices to ensure that the same sporting discipline be submitted to the same rules for all competitors, provided it takes place in an international context. The legal situation in Spain does not determine a different solution.
>
> National sovereignty, as expressed in a sports disciplinary measure decided by a national authority, is in principle and by its nature limited to national territorial application. A national decision may, however, be replaced by a decision of the international authority – CAS – in order to ensure the required uniform application of law. True, it is theoretically conceivable that a state would impose its national decisions with respect to international events taking place on its territory even in disregard of

[222] Loquin, 2008.
[223] Award no 2006/A/1119, extract and commentary by Loquin, 2008, 234–58.
[224] Loquin, 2008, 234.

> the international authority. Such an attitude would, however, contradict the effort to fight doping on the international level, and *could lead to the exclusion of the concerned state from the organisation of international competitions*. It would be surprising for a state to wish to adopt such a posture, and nothing in the texts invoked in this case suggests that such is the position taken by Spain.[225]

In accordance with this decision, the athlete would also be expelled from the association if he did not comply with the procedures of transnational sports law, as implemented by the sports association concerned (in this case UCI).[226] In the event, CAS dismissed the argument presented by the cyclist[227] that Article 24 of the Spanish Constitution guarantees the inalienable right of access to justice and the courts. Based on the norms of cycling sports established by UCI and precedents from its own jurisprudence in cases referring to France and Colombia,[228] CAS declared itself competent, asserting that the transnational sports authority is not in competition with state instances but complementary to them, and that whereas state authorities limit themselves to controlling the conduct of those who come under their jurisdiction, the international federation has authority over the sporting events governed by its own competence. In this context, according to CAS:

> A given conduct may be penalised in a given location without this necessarily entailing punishment at the international level. Similarly, a given conduct that is not penalised may nevertheless produce a ban from sporting events because it affects the fairness of the contest.[229]

The most fundamental point for the purposes of an analysis of transconstitutionalism between state orders and the transnational sports order seems to me to reside in recourse to the principle of equality. In this respect, CAS's award clearly relates to the legitimacy of the transnational order of sports law: 'It tends to submit all athletes to *equal treatment*, urging certain national federations not to be passive towards the offences committed by the athletes of their respective countries.'[230] This persuasive invocation of the norm of equality does not mean, however, that there are only relations of complementarity (the term used by CAS) between the transnational order for sports law and state orders. While CAS dismissed UCI's appeal on its merits, confirming the Spanish federation's decision, and thereby reconciled Spanish law with transnational sports law, the potential conflict between the former and the latter remains undeniable.[231] Given that the cyclist acquitted by the Spanish federation did not recognise CAS's competence to review that acquittal, based on his reading of the article in the Spanish Constitution that refers to the right to legal remedy, in

225 In Loquin, 2008, 233 *f*, compiling extracts from *Award* no 2006/A/1119 (my emphasis).
226 *Cf* Loquin, 2008, 234.
227 *Cf* Loquin, 2008, 236.
228 *See* Loquin, 2008, 239–42.
229 In Loquin, 2008, 242.
230 In Loquin, 2008, 241 (my emphasis); *cf* commentary on 254.
231 *Cf* Loquin, 2008, 253–6.

principle the situation created a clash or collision between this constitutional right to justice and the principle of equality invoked by CAS. Thus, in this case the complementarity and tension between transnational and state legal orders manifested themselves simultaneously in connection with constitutional problems, without either having *a priori* primacy, that is, possessing the *ultima ratio*. Instead, this situation points to the need for transconstitutional learning and exchange between both legal orders, especially when different interpretations of norms on competence lead to a collision as to which is the legitimate body to decide.

This situation can be seen more clearly in another CAS ruling (17 May 2007), which, based on the merits, overturned a decision taken by a national court.[232] In this case, the World Anti-Doping Agency (WADA) appealed two rulings, one by the Disciplinary Committee of the Mexican Football Federation (FMF) and the other by CAAD (Comisión de Apelación y Arbitrage del Deporte), a governmental sports regulation and arbitration body in Mexico. Both had failed to act on a positive doping test from a WADA-accredited lab (UCLA Olympic Analytical Laboratory). The player's A sample tested positive for an anabolic agent prohibited by FIFA. The result was sent to the FMF for the player to be notified and request testing of the B sample within 48 hours, failing which he would be deemed to have accepted the A sample result by default. The player's club claimed that it had not been told by the lab to notify him and argued that anyway it was up to the FMF to do so directly. The FMF had sent the lab findings to the club, expecting the club to notify the player. The FMF's Disciplinary Committee did not sanction the player because the club had failed to notify him and the committee was under the mistaken impression that the B sample had been destroyed since no confirmatory analysis had been requested. The lab later confirmed in writing to CAS that the B sample had all this time remained properly preserved (by deep-freezing) and available for analysis. The FMF appealed to CAAD, the governmental arbitration body, which confirmed the ruling of the FMF's Disciplinary Committee. CAS both dismissed the latter and declared that CAAD's decision 'has no effect on the system of sanctions established under the FIFA Statutes and Regulations'.[233] Thus, in light of the fact that the player had twice been convicted of using the same prohibited substance (the first time he had been suspended for a year), CAS declared him 'ineligible with immediate and lifetime effect' from taking part in any competition governed by FIFA.[234]

In judging the case and ruling against a state arbitration tribunal, CAS invoked analogous grounds to those used in the decision analysed above: equality of treatment for athletes involved in transnational sports. CAS categorically dismissed the argument that 'the most favourable laboratory' should be considered, proposed by the player on the grounds that he had obtained a negative test

[232] Award no 2006/A/1149 and no 2007/A/1211, extract and commentary by Loquin, 2008, 259–72.
[233] In Loquin, 2008, 270.
[234] *Ibid*.

result from a lab not accredited by WADA. While this decision by CAS overruled the ruling by CAAD, a state body, regarding the need to ensure the 'equal and consistent treatment of all participants in a sport',[235] it is important to note that this is also the root of the potential collision between the constitutional principle of equality asserted by the transnational sports legal order and the right to legal remedy with full defence based on the internal order of the constitutional state and implicitly invoked by the player. Thus, this is an issue that falls entirely within the sphere of transconstitutionalism, requiring constructive 'conversations' between transnational and state legal orders.

The imposition of decisions by CAS giving primacy to transnational sports law over the state legal orders invoked by the parties does not occur only in cases of disciplinary sanctions, however. On 19 January 2007, CAS judged a case between the famous Spanish football club Real Valladolid and a player of Paraguayan and Italian nationality, involving an alleged breach of contract. The contract between the player and Real Valladolid was signed on 17 July 2004, came into force on 1 January 2005, and was due to expire on 30 June 2010.[236] The athlete's current contract at that time was with the Paraguayan club Cerro Porteño; this expired on 31 December 2004, when it was renewed. In addition, in January 2005 the player began playing for another Spanish club, Almeria, having been transferred to this club during the same year. Real Valladolid, alleging breach of contract, applied to FIFA to have the player penalised for breach of contract without just cause. FIFA's Dispute Resolution Chamber partially accepted the suit, sentencing the player to pay Real Valladolid a sum in euros in reimbursement of an advance as well as a fine. Both the player and the club appealed to CAS, which dismissed the player's appeal but partially accepted the club's appeal, sentencing the player to pay a larger sum than that determined by FIFA's Dispute Resolution Chamber, mainly because it included interest.

The relevant point in this case is the solution to an employment contract dispute potentially involving constitutional problems of contractual autonomy, concurrently with social rights, by a transnational court of arbitration based primarily on FIFA's rules and considering only secondarily the state legal order involved. The player had invoked Paraguayan law and Spanish jurisprudence, while the club argued that FIFA's rules should be applied primarily and Swiss law secondarily (CAS is headquartered in Switzerland), as well as Spanish law for the purposes of determining the damages to be paid for breach of contract. Although CAS invoked Switzerland's federal Private International Law Act (LDIP), its ruling was grounded mainly in Article 62 (then 59), paragraph 2, of FIFA's statutes: 'CAS shall primarily apply the various regulations of FIFA and, additionally, Swiss law.' Only with regard to rescission of the contract was Spanish law applied, as mutually agreed by the parties: 'The court of arbitration drew the conclusion that the contract in dispute is governed in general by

[235] In Loquin, 2008, 262.

[236] Award no 2006/A/1082&1104, extract and commentary by Loquin, 2008, 287–304.

the legal rules, i.e. the Statutes of FIFA, and secondarily by Swiss law, whereas the right of rescission is governed by Spanish law.'[237]

The express affirmation of the primacy of transnational sports law over state law in this case does not exclude a collision between legal orders in the sphere of transconstitutionalism. There are decisions of state courts that quash or set aside the enforcement of arbitral awards in the countries concerned when they infringe fundamental principles of the respective state order or are deemed to undermine public order in the competent legal system. For example, the French National Assembly and Council of State have both found that state law prevails over sports law, and the Paris Administrative Tribunal has judged unconstitutional a provision in the bylaws of the French Football Federation (FFF).[238] Thus a transconstitutional 'conversation' between legal orders is indispensable in matters of sports law. Loquin's commentary on this subject is highly pertinent: 'Coexistence between the international [transnational] order of sports law and state law requires a compromise between the specificity of sports activities and the protection of public and private interests.'[239] It is precisely to pursue such a compromise that transconstitutionalism between the transnational and state legal orders is developing in the sphere of sports law, with collisions between fundamental rights addressed from different perspectives.

One of the arguments against the autonomy of the transnational order of sports law and for its subordination to state law could be that a final decision by CAS is appealable to the Swiss Federal Supreme Court or another state court. This derives from Article R59 of the Statutes of the Bodies Working for the Settlement of Sports-Related Disputes (CAS Code):

> The award, notified by the CAS Court Office, shall be final and binding upon the parties. It may not be challenged by way of an action for setting aside to the extent that the parties have no domicile, habitual residence, or business establishment in Switzerland and that they have expressly excluded all setting aside proceedings in the arbitration agreement or in an agreement entered into subsequently, in particular at the outset of the arbitration.[240]

However, the fact is that the exceptions were created by transnational sports law and can be modified at any time by the International Council of Arbitration for Sport (ICAS), in accordance with Articles S6, S8 and R69 of the CAS Code. Even in cases where the Federal Supreme Court of Switzerland insists on assuming competence to review or set aside the decisions of other courts, contrary to the rules of CAS,[241] this can be circumvented by the institutions of transnational sports law if they transfer their headquarters (that is, their official domicile) to

[237] Loquin, 2008, 304.
[238] *Cf* Loquin, 2008, 305–6.
[239] Loquin, 2008, 308.
[240] Available on the CAS website: http://www.tas-cas.org/code (last visited 15 November 2008).
[241] Eg a decision of 22 March 2007, in which the Federal Supreme Court of Switzerland overturned a CAS ruling on the grounds that it allegedly infringed an athlete's right of defence in court (BGE 133 III 235).

a country that is willing to recognise the autonomy of the transnational legal order of sports. The potential mobility of 'delocalised' sports law entities, alongside their competence to exclude certain states from international competitions or tournaments, means that the respective transnational legal order is 'sovereign' with regard to states and hence in competition with state legal orders, leading to the emergence of transconstitutional problems.

Another field in which state legal orders and transnational legal orders in the strict sense, made up primarily of private and quasi-public actors, are conspicuously entangled in the world society of today, involving transconstitutional problems, is internet law. Transversality between a transnational *lex digitalis*[242] and state law involves both cooperation and disputes that are hard to settle. In this regard it is important to note the regulatory powers of the Internet Corporation of Assigned Names and Numbers (ICANN), whose main remit is to manage the assignment of domain names and IP addresses.[243] ICANN's original mandate came from the US government. In 1998, President Bill Clinton directed the National Telecommunications and Information Administration (NTIA) to take steps to privatise the internet domain name system. In the same year, the NTIA called upon the 'internet community' to found a 'self-regulatory' body, to which would be transferred (not merely delegated) the power to control the internet domain name system, hitherto held by a government body. ICANN was recognised by the NTIA when it was founded by a small group of stakeholders in private entities linked to the internet.

It is true that ICANN was eventually incorporated as a non-profit organisation under the laws of the State of California, but it claims to represent the public interest of the global internet 'community'. Indeed, it defines its role as follows in its Articles of Incorporation (Article 3):

> in recognition of the fact that the Internet is an international network of networks owned by no single nation, individual or organisation, the corporation shall . . . pursue the charitable and public purposes of lessening the burdens of government and promoting the global public interest in the operational stability of the Internet.[244]

Thus, although its roots link the organisation to US law and in principle it is subordinated to the laws of California, as far as its competence and regulatory powers are concerned ICANN has decoupled from its 'creator' and can even refuse to grant a US government body the right to use a domain name. This relationship of autonomy with regard to US law is undoubtedly precarious, since in principle the NTIA has the competence to revoke the power of control transferred to ICANN, and given the technical resources it needs to have at its disposal, ICANN may not enjoy the same geographical mobility as the entities of the *lex sportiva* and *lex mercatoria* enjoy in cases where the states in which

242 *See* Teubner, 2003a, 16 *ff* [Engl trans 2004b, 18 *ff*].

243 *See* von Bernstorff, 2004; 2003; Carotti, 2007. Detailed information about ICANN can be found on the organisation's website: http://www.icann.org.

244 Available on the ICANN website: http://www.icann.org/en/general/articles.htm (last visited 5 December 2010). Quotation based on von Bernstorff, 2004, 263; 2003, 514.

they are headquartered take measures contrary to their norms and decisions. For states in general, however, ICANN wields significant legal powers of regulation concerning the domain name system, and state judiciaries are dependent on its orientations and decisions.

In this regard, it is important to note that transconstitutional entanglement occurs because ICANN's power to regulate the global distribution of domain names and assure adequate transmission of internet communications via 'root servers' and related software has 'implications not only for e-commerce and the protection of intellectual property rights, but also for consumer choice, competition, the prohibition of illicit content and the ease of political discourse'.[245] The transconstitutional problem resides in the fact that if state judiciaries understand that use of the internet by the owner of a domain name infringes a state order's constitutional principles or rules they must apply to ICANN for a fully autonomous decision. State judiciaries have neither the authority nor the technical means to issue a binding decision revoking the grant of a domain name to a user or granting the domain name to a different user. In such cases, ICANN has the power to decide whether to recognise or set aside a decision by a state judiciary according to ICANN's own legal norms. The enormous power to disconnect any internet address entails the possibility of disconnecting the websites of state judicial bodies themselves.

To question the content of a dispute settlement decision by ICANN, the parties can opt for the judicial route or arbitration, provided they respect the norms of this private entity. As stated by the document entitled *ICANN Accountability and Transparency Framework and Principles*:

> Parties may be in dispute with ICANN because they disagree not with the process but with the outcome of an ICANN decision process. The current method for dealing with disputes such as this is through the court system or via arbitration *if provided for under the terms of ICANN's agreements*.[246]

This situation entails serious problems of relationships between information rights, freedom of expression, intellectual property, image rights and even name rights, creating constitutional problems that can be understood quite differently by the state judiciary involved in settling a dispute and by ICANN. Considering the wide range of different interpretations of constitutional norms and issues by the various states, it is highly unlikely that ICANN would be able to impose a uniform solution compatible with the constitutional perspectives of all the states involved. Thus it would seem advisable for ICANN to adopt a flexible posture in line with the transconstitutionalist approach, considering the juridico-constitutional peculiarities of the respective states involved in disputes regarding the *lex digitalis*.

[245] Von Bernstorff, 2004, 262; 2003, 514.

[246] *ICANN Accountability and Transparency Framework and Principles*, available at: http://www.icann.org/en/transparency/acct-trans-frameworks-principles-10jan08.pdf (last visited 16 November 2008). My emphasis.

As noted above, ICANN is subordinated to the state laws of California and the federal laws of the US, as explicitly stated in its Articles of Incorporation (Article 3) and in the *ICANN Accountability and Transparency Framework and Principles*. In accordance with the latter document, California's Attorney General has the competence to oversee ICANN as a non-profit organisation. Moreover, as mentioned earlier, there is nothing to stop the US Department of Commerce or the NTIA from revoking or restricting ICANN's powers. This leads to an asymmetrical situation: whereas in respect of other states ICANN has the autonomy to impose its decisions regarding domain names, ultimately it does not enjoy such autonomy with regard to the US. Thus, in the case of ICANN it appears that transconstitutionalism between the state order and the transnational order of the *lex digitalis* is only apparent transconstitutionalism. At the very least, it must be said in this context that ICANN's subordination to US laws excludes comprehensive and unrestricted transconstitutionalism between the transnational and state orders. Strictly speaking, transconstitutionalism might be said to exist in the underlying plane between the US state legal order and the legal orders of other states in the sphere of the *lex digitalis*. However, this transconstitutionalism would be asymmetrical, since ultimately the US holds the power to control the internet domain name system globally, prevailing over any other state. Not even the creation of the Internet Governance Forum (IGF), a multi-stakeholder forum for policy 'dialogue' on issues of internet governance set up by the World Summit on the Information Society, which was held at Tunis on 16–18 November 2005, has affected ICANN's power, although symptomatically the US responded negatively to creation of the IGF while European countries welcomed it.[247]

It is relevant that the *lex digitalis* is strongly linked to an organisation whose origin and corporate personality are intimately bound up with the US legal order yet whose activities encompass a wide array of transnational affairs involving transconstitutional entanglements with various state orders. The distinctly private status of ICANN has led to criticism and questioning of its legitimacy, based on the argument that contrary to its own claims it is not in fact grounded in the 'internet community' but represents the interests and perspectives of a small number of internet stakeholders. Hence, the argument runs, it is not transparent but elitist and narrowly private, with no allegiance to the public interest. Given that the 'internet community' is represented in ICANN by stakeholder groups, defined as primary constituents, a question arises as to who can participate in this 'governance network'. This situation produces a problem of exclusion related to the decision-making privilege of the actors who founded ICANN. As Bernstoff notes:

> The question of who is allowed to participate in a governance network leads us to the central problem of exclusion . . . In the ICANN case, the foundational decision was taken by a handful of computer scientists from IANA [Internet Assigned Numbers

[247] For more information about the IGF, see its website: http://www.intgovforum.org/cms.

> Authority], the IEFT [Internet Engineering Task Force] and the US Department of Commerce.[248]

This gave rise to a wave of attacks on or criticisms of ICANN from NGOs and academic groups such as ICANNWatch.org, the NGO & Academic ICANN Study Group and the Boston Working Group.[249] It also led to the creation of the Internet Governance Forum. This is how von Bernstorff concludes one of his critical essays on ICANN, in defence of international public law:

> The creation of fragmented global governance structures such as the ones emerging in the field of global internet regulation is an attempt to circumvent the formalised framework for policy-making provided by international law. What we are hereby leaving behind is the allegedly discredited ideal of a global rule of law, in which procedural equality between the weak and the rich helps to channel and arbitrate diverging substantive claims. Given the structural limitations of network governance arrangements, we may eventually find out that we have given up too early.[250]

Although von Bernstorff's comments about limitations to the principle of equality and the rule of law within ICANN are correct, the reservation must be noted that several areas of international law have come under fire on the same grounds, that is, that it privileges the global powers to the detriment of weaker states in the international constellation. For present purposes, the most pertinent point about ICANN is that while it is a private entity subordinated to the US legal order, it has decoupled from its origins to become the most important institution for transnational legal regulation of the internet and the centrepiece of the *lex digitalis*, leading to transconstitutional involvements with state legal orders. ICANN's scant legitimacy actually requires changes to the *lex digitalis* to involve multiple private and public actors capable of controlling the development of internet law in a transparent manner, in accordance with a 'power sharing' model with checks and balances. While this would apparently not eliminate the transnational nature of the *lex digitalis*, it would help to engage the internet more broadly and intensely with a 'multilevel' world system, resulting in even more complex transconstitutional entanglements.

Many other transnational legal orders that have a transconstitutional relationship with state legal orders could be mentioned and analysed, including those in the vast universe of transnational NGOs.[251] The list is endless. For the sake of brevity, I will confine myself to two. First, it is worth mentioning the Basel Committee on Banking. Although this was set up in 1974 by central bank governors of the G10, and currently comprises representatives of central banks

[248] Von Bernstorff, 2004, 274 *f*; 2003, 517.

[249] Von Bernstorff, 2004, 276 *f*; 2003, 519.

[250] Von Bernstorff, 2004, 281. He concludes another article even more categorically: 'Considering the hegemonic dynamics of global governance networks, it might be concluded that our emancipatory aspirations have been used to legitimate a sophisticated strategy of economic exploitation' (2003, 526).

[251] *See* Berman, PS, 2005, 546 *ff*.

in 13 developed countries,[252] the Basel Committee has a mixed structure made up of public and private actors and is not linked to international treaties or conventions. It establishes rules on banking transactions that are directly incorporated by central banks all over the world with binding force for private-sector banks in the respective countries (and for their customers), without formal ratification of any kind.[253] This transnational condition of the Basel Committee constitutes a focus for transconstitutional entanglements, since its regulatory activities affect free enterprise and property rights usually guaranteed by state constitutions. In other words, it is a transnational legal order which responds to the self-regulatory requirements of the centre of the world economic system. Its impact on the fundamental rights of citizens deserves more careful study, especially because it lacks a minimum of support from a comprehensive public sphere and is in fact a highly opaque organisation.[254]

A very different case comes from a completely different social sphere, that of recent state policies to combat 'terrorism', especially those of the US. The case that stands out here is that of the transnational organisation Al Qaeda, constructed and developed on the basis of a complex communications network. This network has been treated by the US not as a mere criminal organisation, but as an enemy analogous to a sovereign state. As Paul Berman puts it:

> In contrast to the growth of global civil society, the development of transnational terrorist networks such as Al Qaeda is a much darker example of non-governmental networks. (The networks surrounding human trafficking and the global narcotics trade are other examples.) Such organisations can mobilise personnel and deploy money around the world, functioning as quasi-state entities. Indeed, it is significant that the United States has been willing to treat Al Qaeda almost as if it were a sovereign state to be fought in a 'war'.[255]

This situation involves transconstitutional relations between the US legal order and the transnational order of Al Qaeda. The latter has a claim to self-regulation, although this is the negative side of transconstitutionalism. Dissemination of so-called 'enemy criminal law'[256] relates precisely to the notion that this 'delocalised' order is analogous to an enemy state at war. In this case, not only is politics

[252] *Cf* Slaughter, 2004, 42 *f*; Möllers, 2005b, 257. Information on the Basel Committee on Banking can be found at: http://www.bis.org/bcbs/ (last visited 25 December 2008).

[253] *See* Möllers, 2005b, 257 *f*, highlighting the German case.

[254] Möllers (2005b, 257) says: 'There are no legal foundations for the Basel Committee. Its creation was announced in a press release at the end of 1974.'

[255] Berman, PS, 2005, 506.

[256] The idea of 'enemy criminal law' was first put forward by Jakobs (2001), based on a dubious link between his normative notion of the 'enemy' (not protected by the penal guarantees enjoyed by citizens) and the Luhmannian concept of exclusion (the negative side of the difference 'inclusion/exclusion') (Jakobs, 2001, 447 *ff*), which in fact refers to an empirical problem of today's world society, whose expansion endangers functional differentiation itself (*See* Luhmann, 1993a, 582 *ff* [Engl trans 2004, 488 *ff*]; 1995a, 146 *ff*; 1995b; 1997, v 1, 169 *f*; v 2, 618–34; 2000a, 427 *f*; 2000b, 233 *ff*, 242 *f* and 301 *ff*). It has nothing to do with organised 'terrorism', which in systems theory belongs strictly speaking to the inclusion sector of contemporary society.

transcended in the name of 'war', but constitutionalism and the rule of law are suspended internally in the name of war on 'enemy combatants'.[257] However, this reverse side of transconstitutionalism, which has implications for the asymmetry between legal forms in world society (as discussed in Chapter 5, Section I), makes possible the emergence of key problems regarding fundamental rights and the limits of state power in combating 'terrorist' organisations. The case of Guantanamo Bay detention camp, for example, triggered a worldwide debate but also had to be addressed by the US Supreme Court, which eventually ruled that prisoners detained at Guantanamo on suspicion of participating in or contributing to the terrorist activities of Al Qaeda are entitled to seek the remedy of habeas corpus from US courts, thus setting aside (albeit reticently) the Bush Administration's claim to hold prisoners there without the protection of such rights.[258] This is an indication that transconstitutionalism can also emerge positively, even in cases that refute the constitutional claims on both sides of the entanglement between a state legal order and a 'quasi-legal' or 'anti-legal' transnational order, as Al Qaeda tends to be characterised.

Finally, it is worth noting that transconstitutional entanglements between transnational and state orders do not usually present themselves in isolation. Given the wide range of different types of transnational orders, many of which are, moreover, informal, they are typically involved in transconstitutional problems with multiple types of orders at the same time (state, international, supranational and local). In addition, because they interface with various different kinds of legal order, transnational orders in the strict sense are intrinsically involved in a more direct way with transconstitutionalism in a tangled 'multilevel' world legal system.

[257] Expression used by the US Government, especially the Department of Defense, which, after *Hamdi et al v Rumsfeld* (542 US 507 [2004]), 'established Combatant Status Review Tribunals (CSRTs) to determine whether individuals detained at the US Naval Station at Guantanamo Bay, Cuba, were "enemy combatants"' (US Supreme Court, *Boumediene et al v Bush*, no 06-1195). The expression has also been used by the Supreme Court itself (see references in the next note). On 'numerous aspects in common' in the concepts of enemy criminal law and enemy combatants, *see* Díez, 2008, 529.

[258] See especially the judgments in: *Rasul et al v Bush et al*, 542 US 466 (2004); *Hamdi et al v Rumsfeld et al*, 542 US 507 (2004); *Hamdan v Rumsfeld et al*, 548 US 557 (2006); *Boumediene et al v Bush et al*, no 06-1195 (12 July 2008). *Cf* Golove, 2005; Frank, 2007; Fiss, 2007. On 22 January 2009, President Barack Obama signed an executive order requiring that the Guantanamo detention facility be closed within a year, beginning the process of reversing the Bush administration's national security policy (*cf* http://www.nytimes.com/2009/01/23/us/politics/23obama.html – last visited 5 December 2010). On 20 May 2009, however, the US Senate denied the funds requested by President Obama to close the facility (*cf* http://www.nytimes.com/2009/05/21/us/politics/21detain.html – last visited 5 December 2010). On Obama's frustrated attempt to close the Guantanamo detention centre, *see* Corcoran, 2011. *See also* p 175 below.

VI. TRANSCONSTITUTIONALISM BETWEEN STATE LEGAL ORDERS AND EXTRA-STATE LOCAL ORDERS

Another side of transconstitutionalism points to the problematic relationship between state legal orders and extra-state orders of native collectivities, whose anthropological and cultural assumptions are not compatible with the model of state constitutionalism. In this case, it is evidently a matter of archaic orders that do not have principles or secondary rules of organisation and therefore do not fit into the reflexive model of constitutionalism. Strictly speaking, they do not admit juridico-constitutional problems of human rights and legal constraints on power. As underscored above (p 83), when normative orders of this kind collide with institutions of a state's constitutional legal order, a 'unilateral transconstitutionalism' of tolerance and, to some extent, learning is required. This form of transconstitutionalism is indispensable because, although the legal orders in question are very far from complying (in many of their norms and practices) with the model of human rights and legal constraints on power that prevails in the legal system of world society, the mere unilateral granting of 'human rights' to their members runs counter to transconstitutionalism. Measures in this direction tend to have destructive effects on bodies and minds, and are contrary to the very concept of human rights (*see* p 160 below). In this context there is a paradoxical aspect to transconstitutionalism, insofar as it is involved in constitutional 'conversations' with normative orders that lie outside constitutionalism itself. This situation, however, results from the necessity, intrinsic to transconstitutionalism, of not excluding the development of alternative institutes that make possible a constructive 'dialogue' with these orders of people who are anthropologically and culturally 'different' and have lived for millennia in the territory of the respective state. Thus, transconstitutionalism, albeit limited, does not lose its significance for the development of the normative dimension of contemporary world society.

Latin American experience is rich in juridico-constitutional problems deriving from entanglements between native normative orders and state constitutional orders, especially with regard to fundamental rights. In many cases, an attempt is made to address the problem via the model of constitutional integration of the plurality resulting from the normative particularities of indigenous communities. In this perspective, the outstanding examples are the Constitutions of Colombia and Bolivia,[259] which contain criteria for building links between state law and the normative laws of indigenous communities. The most pronounced

[259] On the relations between the state and the legal regimes of indigenous communities in these countries, *see* respectively Botero, 2005 and Rivero, 2005 (dealing more broadly with 'interculturalisation' in the context of the Bolivian constitutional reform process). On the problematic situation in Guatemala, *see* Sieder, 2007, comparing it with the '(possibly exceptional) case of Colombia' (pp 236 *ff*). For an overview of indigenous rights in Latin America, *see* Carbonell, 2004; Iturralde G, 2005; Grote, 1999.

claim to constitutional integration of these communities is found in the recent Bolivian Constitution, which establishes that Bolivia is a 'Unitary Social State of Plurinational, Community-Based Law' (Article 1), including the indigenous communities as political units with power, the right to autonomy and self-government, and the right to participate in the 'formation' of the state (Articles 2; 30–32; 146, paragraph VII; 147, paragraph III; 269, paragraph I; and 289–96). The Peruvian Constitution also affords an interesting example, stating that 'Native Communities are legally recognised and enjoy legal status', that 'they are autonomous in terms of their organisation' (Article 89), and that they 'may exercise jurisdictional functions within their territory in accordance with customary law, provided they do not violate fundamental rights of the individual' (Article 149). Albeit more narrowly, the Brazilian Constitution displays elements of this claim to integrate indigenous communities within the sphere of state constitutionalism (in Articles 231 and 232). However, the Brazilian model for constitutional integration of indigenous peoples basically focuses on the recognition and protection of 'their original rights to the lands they traditionally occupy', determining the competence of the Union to demarcate them. It does not establish a regime of institutional autonomy or determine community jurisdictions or forms of self-organisation. As Rita Laura Segato remarks:

> However, because these territories do not behave as true jurisdictions, devolution of land has not been accompanied by an equivalent process of reflection and reconstruction of their own instances for dispute settlement, increasing levels of institutional autonomy in exercising their own justice, and gradual retrieval of legal practices. The figure of tutelage still in force today under the Indian Statute [*Estatuto do Índio*], even though this was partially repealed by the new Constitution, contributes to reducing each indigenous person in her individuality to the ambivalent regime of subordination-protection by the national state.[260]

This limited definition of integration and institutional autonomy for indigenous communities in the Brazilian Constitution increases the probability of collisions between the Brazilian state legal order and the normative orders of indigenous communities.[261] But the possibility of emergence of these collisions, by virtue of the entanglement of differing perspectives on the treatment of crucial problems of constitutional law, is also present in those countries where the claim to constitutional integration of the institutional autonomy of indigenous communities has been more pronounced and more broadly implemented in juridico-constitutional practice.

In some cases, what is at stake is the constitutionally guaranteed rights of minors in the sphere of sexual freedom, a legal good protected by classifying sexual intercourse with a person under 14 as the criminal offence of statutory

[260] Segato, 2011, 359.

[261] The case involving the rights of indigenous communities and private enterprise in the Raposa Serra do Sol Indigenous Reservation (Petition 3.388/RR, judgment of 19 March 2009, TP, DJ 31 March 2009) is an expression of the persistence of these collisions, despite the decision in favour of the native communities.

rape. Because sexual intercourse between adults and minors under 14 is common and considered morally and legally licit in Latin American indigenous communities, this situation gives rise to collisions between normative orders with constitutional implications. Peruvian jurisprudence has applied the concept of 'culturally conditioned misunderstanding', in accordance with Article 15 of Peru's Penal Code, to resolve in concrete cases this conflict between two perspectives on fundamental rights, one oriented to the protection of the child's sexual freedom and the other to the protection of the cultural autonomy of indigenous people. The article in question reads as follows:

> Whoever commits a punishable act by virtue of culture or custom without being able to understand the criminal nature of the act or assume his or her responsibility based on such understanding shall be exempted from responsibility. When the said ability is diminished for the same reason, the punishment shall be attenuated.

In decisions relating to sexual violence against minors in indigenous communities, this provision has been combined with Article 2, paragraph 19, of the Peruvian Constitution, which establishes the right of all individuals to 'ethnic and cultural identity'.[262] In cases where 'culturally conditioned misunderstanding' or limited ability to understand is the key argument for attenuation of punishment, or in cases where such incapacity serves as a basis for excluding the criminal liability of a member of an indigenous community, it bears repeating that what is at stake is a way of reconciling two perspectives on fundamental rights based on interpretations of legal and constitutional texts, one linked to cultural identity and the other associated with sexual freedom and protection of minors. This solution does not entirely exclude an outcome that dissatisfies both sides, especially when what is involved is statutory rape against a minor of 14 who is not a member of an indigenous community. In this case, an absolute solution for one side can lead to serious conflicts between the indigenous community and non-indigenous people living nearby. This requires a judicial posture of careful prudence between different normative orders, which will depend on a concrete analysis of the fundamental rights involved.

Another interesting example of the entanglement of constitutionally relevant problems in the sphere of the relations between state legal orders and the normative orders of indigenous communities in Latin America comes from constitutional regulation of the matrimonial regime. In Brazil, the monogamous model of marriage is inferrable from the Constitution (Article 226), and bigamy is a crime (Article 235 of the Penal Code). The indigenous communities that live in Brazil tend to adopt polygynous institutional relations. In principle, these should not present major problems, as they can be equated to stable extraconjugal relations. Doubts arise, however, when it is recalled that while polygyny is legitimate under indigenous law, it leads to social rights problems when issues arise with regard to the right of indigenous women who are concubines or

[262] Some cases are presented on the website *Alertanet en Derecho y Sociedad*: http://www.alertanet.org/F2b-Sentencias-pe.htm (last visited 19 November 2008).

'wives' of the same man to a widow's pension, in accordance with Article 201.V of the Brazilian Constitution. In such cases the courts have tended to grant the equivalent of a single pension to be shared among the women who submit claims, so as to uphold the principle of equality among all citizens covered by the national insurance system.[263] However, this transconstitutional solution compromises the guarantee in Article 201.2 of the Constitution that no benefit may be less than the minimum wage. This is unquestionably a precarious way of circumventing a collision between normative orders and irreconcilable principles, but it is nonetheless an example of the search for a constitutional 'dialogue' in accordance with a model of transconstitutional tolerance.

One of the most delicate recent cases involved relations between the Brazilian state legal order and the normative order of the Suruwaha people who live in Tapauá, a municipality located in Amazonas State, and remained voluntarily isolated until the end of the 1970s.[264] Under Suruwaha customary law, children born unhealthy or disabled must be killed. Another case involved the Yawanawa living in Acre on the border between Brazil and Peru, among whom a customary normative order required the killing of one newborn twin. In this context, it also became public that practices of this kind were common among the Yanomami and other indigenous groups. This situation led to controversy, since it involved a practically irresolvable conflict between the right to cultural autonomy and the right to life. The problem had already come to light in 2002 when a Yawanawa woman attending a human rights workshop at FUNAI, the National Indian Foundation, described her community's practice of killing one sibling when twins were born and said she was a victim of this customary law, being a mother of twins.[265] In this context, the problem was also presented as a conflict between the right to cultural autonomy and women's rights.[266]

However, it became a subject for widespread public debate in connection with the child's right to life, above all via ample diffusion in the mass media, thanks to coverage of a case involving a Suruwaha infant with severe growth hormone deficiency condemned to death by the tribe but removed by a missionary couple.[267] The impact of this case on public opinion led Congressman Henrique Afonso, representing the state of Acre, to draft a bill that would have

[263] A typical example is the case of Public Civil Action 2004.31.00.700374-6, brought before the Federal District Court of First Instance of the District of Amapá (Juizado Federal da Seção Judiciária do Amapá), which ruled that Masaupe Waiãpi, Ana Waiãpi and Sororo Waiãpi, widows of Parara Waiãpi, must share the survivor's pension and the balance withdrawn from the deceased's FGTS severance fund account. The terms of the settlement accepted by the court reserved the right of the Federal Attorney-General's Office to go to court at any future time for a review of the right of the deceased's wives to receive the full amount of the state benefits concerned. I am grateful to Federal Judge Márcio Barbosa for kindly providing permission to use this information, which he originally presented in a paper submitted for the Master's Degree programme at Instituto Brasiliense de Direito Público in 2007.

[264] Segato, 2011, 363.

[265] Segato, 2011, 357 *f*.

[266] *See* Segato, 2003, especially 31, also referring to globally notorious cases of female circumcision or clitoridectomy in African countries.

[267] *Cf* Segato, 2011, 363.

criminalised this practice in indigenous communities (Projeto de Lei 1057/2007). The initial statement of the bill's purpose (ementa) reads as follows: 'Act establishing ways to combat harmful traditional practices and protect the fundamental rights of indigenous children and children belonging to other societies said to be non-traditional.'[268] As a basis for specific measures to combat such practices, including the criminalisation of any people who know of them through contact with the indigenous community but fail to notify the competent authorities and of authorities who fail to take appropriate action (Articles 3, 4 and 5), Article 2.I-VIII itemises the following reasons given for 'neonatal homicide': 'cases where one of the parents is absent'; 'cases of multiple gestation'; 'newborns with physical and/or mental illnesses'; 'when there is gender preference'; 'when there is a short interval between a previous pregnancy and the birth in question'; 'cases where the number of children appropriate for the group is exceeded'; 'newborns with some blemish or birthmark that distinguishes them from the rest'; 'when they are considered unlucky for the family or group'. The bill also proposes to define types of 'child homicide in cases when the group believes a child is undernourished because of a curse or involving any other belief that leads to intentional death from malnutrition' (Article 2.IX). These hypotheses specified in the bill as well as others referring to sexual abuse, ill-treatment and other physical and mental aggression against children based on traditional customs (Article 2.X-XII), correspond to practices observed to take place among the indigenous communities located in the territory of the Brazilian state. The Human Rights Committee held a public hearing to discuss the bill in the Chamber of Deputies, Brazil's lower house.[269] While the measure was not taken further, the context in which it was drafted and the discussion to which it led constituted a unique instance of transconstitutional 'dialogue' between the state legal order and the local normative orders of indigenous communities.

The bill's drafters and advocates took as their basic starting point the idea of the absolute primacy of the individual's fundamental right to life in accordance with Western, Christian morality. Secondarily, the mother's fundamental right

[268] Available at http://www2.camara.gov.br/proposicoes (last visited on 24 December 2008).

[269] Convened by the Human Rights Committee of the Chamber of Deputies in August 2007, the hearing took place on 5 September 2007 (*cf* Segato, 2011, 357 and 369). Major alterations to this bill later reduced it to generic declarations and promises of support for the respective communities, in the following terms:

> Art 54-A. Respect and support for traditional indigenous practices are reaffirmed whenever such practices are in conformity with the fundamental rights established in the Federal Constitution and with the international treaties and conventions on human rights to which the Federative Republic of Brazil is a party.
>
> Sole paragraph. The agencies responsible for indigenous peoples policy shall offer suitable opportunities for indigenous peoples to acquire knowledge about society as a whole when the following practices are identified by anthropological studies:
>
> I – infanticide
> II – indecent assault or rape
> III – abuse
> IV – physical and mental violence against children and their parents.

to motherhood also contributed to the proposition behind the bill. This unilateral advocacy of individual rights to the detriment of the cultural autonomy of indigenous communities did not seem adequate to those who took part in the debate from a broader anthropological perspective. Straightforward criminalisation of indigenous practices in the name of protecting the right to life, moreover, can be seen as tantamount to cultural genocide and destruction of the community via the destruction of its most deeply held beliefs.

Rita Laura Segato is one of the anthropologists who participated intensely in the debate, including the public hearing held on 5 September 2007 in the Chamber of Deputies.[270] Her remarks were a great help in clarifying the implications of this collision and pointed to the need for a transversal communication between normative orders in terms that can be considered appropriate to a constructive model of transconstitutionalism. In the context of the debate, Segato acknowledged that she was faced with 'the ungrateful task of arguing against this bill, but at the same time I would wager strongly on a change in customs'.[271] Her contribution included a report on empirical research showing that there were 16 births, 23 suicides, two homicides of newborns (referred to as 'infanticide' by the anthropologists but not in the same technical sense as the legal definition used in the Penal Code), and one death from disease among 143 Suruwaha between 2003 and 2005. Thus while 7.6 per cent of all Suruwaha deaths in the period were due to 'infanticide', 57.6 per cent were due to suicide.

This situation points to an understanding of life that differs starkly from the Christian one predominant in the West. The view traditionally held by indigenous peoples is that a good life is a life without excessive suffering for both the individual and the community. In other words, it makes sense to live only if life is placid and enjoyable. Thus, infant homicide is justified in certain cases.[272] According to this view, the meaning of life and death for the Suruwaha deserves as much respect as the meaning attributed by Christianity: 'We also found a complex, sophisticated vision of great philosophical dignity that owes nothing to Christianity.'[273] The argument is fortified by reference to Yanomami practice giving women absolute autonomy to decide whether their children should live. The mother withdraws into the forest to give birth, so that delivery occurs outside the context of social life, leaving the choice to the mother:

> If she does not touch the newborn child or welcome it into her arms, but leaves it on the ground where it fell, that means it has not been accepted into the world of culture and social relations. It is therefore not human. Thus it is cannot be said that a homicide has occurred from the viewpoint of this indigenous group, since one who remains on the ground is not a human life.[274]

[270] *See* Segato, 2011, 370 *ff*.
[271] Segato, 2011, 358.
[272] Segado, 2011, 364 *f*.
[273] Segato, 2011, 364.
[274] Segato, 2011, 365.

This very different idea of human life genuinely entails a delicate problem, which I also consider incompatible with the mere imposition of external conceptions of life and death by means of what in another context I have paradoxically called 'human rights imperialism'.[275] This is valid not only from an anthropological-cultural or anthropological-legal standpoint, but also from the specific constitutional law perspective that is sensitive to transconstitutionalism.

In this context, it is fundamental to consider the collision between two distinct perspectives on rights while endeavouring to avoid 'injustice' by imposing one, the order of the strongest, on the other, the order of the weakest. On one side is the right to collective autonomy, on the other the right to individual autonomy. Simply submitting the former, considered the expression of an ethical way of life, to the latter, considered the expression of universal morality as the basis for human rights,[276] does not seem to be the most appropriate solution in a model of transconstitutionalism. On the contrary, in this context of radical collision between the state legal order and indigenous normative orders, it is necessary to consider and weigh the relative importance of 'the individual subject's right to life and the collective subject's right to life', as Segato argues.[277] The 'ultracriminalisation' of homicide practised against newborn children within indigenous communities proposed by the above-mentioned bill (Projeto de Lei 1057/2007) could lead to 'ethnocide by eliminating cultural values indispensable to the biological and cultural life of a people'.[278] A legal solution, moreover, would have implications that it would be hard to make compatible with the constitutional order of the Brazilian state.[279] Under such circumstances, a search for a different route would appear necessary.

The proposal that appears best suited to transconstitutionalism resides in guaranteeing 'ethnic jurisdiction or an ethnic forum', so that each indigenous community can 'settle its disputes and work out a solution to internal dissent in its own way'.[280] This does not simply mean tolerance by the most powerful, or

[275] Neves, 2005, 23 and 27 [Engl trans 2007, 432 and 436].

[276] Klaus Günther, while arguing that '[t]he appropriate application of legitimate norms may not harm forms of life *without reason*' (my emphasis), actually appears to be in favour of this approach insofar as he claims that 'conflicts between principles of justice and orientations of the good life at the postconventional level can only be resolved universalistically, that is, in favour of justice' (1988, 196 [Engl trans 1993, 153]). It should be noted, however, that in the terms of Habermas's theory of communicative action and discourse, which Günther espouses, the collision in this case would be between post-conventional and pre-conventional morality. On the levels of development of moral consciousness in Habermas's theory of social evolution, *see* Neves, 2006a, 25 *ff*.

[277] Segato, 2011, 367. At the above-mentioned public hearing, Segato explained what she understood by 'the expression "right to life"' in this context: 'This expression can indicate two different types of right to life: the individual's right to life, ie protection for the individual subject of rights; and the right of life of collective subjects, ie to protection for the life of peoples in their condition as peoples' (Segato, 2011, 372).

[278] Botero, 2006, 156, also cited by Segato, 2011, 367.

[279] Specifically Art 231 of the Federal Constitution: 'Recognition is hereby granted to the social organisation of the Indians, their customs, languages, beliefs and traditions, and their originary rights to the lands which they have traditionally occupied. The federal government shall demarcate those lands, and shall protect and ensure respect for all of their possessions.'

[280] Segato, 2011, 375 and 377.

even tolerating the intolerant,[281] but rather the ability to acknowledge the autonomy of others, that is, of the sphere of communication, of the different language game or the different life form of indigenous people, without submitting them to the models of state constitutionalism. It is even less appropriate to speak of 'decent' and 'indecent' societies, or societies that are worthy or unworthy of 'dialogue' with the 'liberal' societies of the constitutional democratic state,[282] as if we were not all in the same world society with collisions and conflicts between domains of communication and language games. Nevertheless, it is necessary to bear in mind that, not just from an anthropological standpoint but also from that of transconstitutionalism, faced with dissent and disputes within indigenous communities, not least with regard to the practice of killing infants,

> the role of the state, in the person of its agents, must be to be available to supervise, mediate or intervene with the sole aim of ensuring that the internal process of deliberation can take place freely, without abuse by the most powerful individuals in that society.[283]

In this regard the transconstitutional stance aims to place a legal limit on abusive power inside the community. This is because if there is manipulation of community decisions by the most powerful, without legitimacy in the respective normative order, the result is the disappearance of the ethnic autonomy that is the starting point for a constitutional 'dialogue'. Hence, it can be seen that no form of presentation of autonomy for social spheres, including those constructed by indigenous communities that are not functionally differentiated, is absolute: all are relative in the context of today's world society.

This delicate problem is not confined to the dilemma between ethical relativism (oriented to particular cultures) and moral universalism (oriented to human rights). It also points to the possibility of coexistence between legal orders based on distinct historical experiences,[284] requiring moderation, especially on the part of the constitutional state, with regard to their claim to concretise their specific norms when these collide with the norms of indigenous communities with essentially different cultural foundations. Discretion and self-restraint seem in this case to be the right way to go about engaging in constructive 'conversations' capable of stimulating internal self-transformation by indigenous

[281] Rawls, 1990 [1972], 216–21.

[282] Rawls, 1999, 4 *f* and 59 *ff*.

[283] Segato, 2011, 375. On this point, Segato adds: 'Nor it is appropriate to demand the withdrawal of the state, because as evidenced by the many demands for public policy in this matter raised by indigenous peoples on the basis of the 1988 Constitution, after the intense and pernicious disorder created by contact, the state can no longer simply abstain. It must remain permanently available to offer guarantees and protection when called upon to do so by members of the communities, provided that such intervention involves a dialogue between representatives of the state and representatives of the community in question. Its role in this case can be none other than to promote and facilitate dialogue between the powers of the village and its weakest members' (2011, 375 *f*).

[284] *See* Segato, 2011, 375–7; *see also* 2006 for a broader treatment. On the intrinsic relationship between universalism and difference, *see* Neves, 2002.

communities so that they have less conflictual relationships with the state order. An attempt to pursue internal models of optimisation in accordance with the theory of principles could be disastrous under these circumstances. Instead, when dealing with the 'other', with the different order of indigenous peoples, it is advisable to adopt a transconstitutional stance of self-containment with regard to the fundamental rights whose optimisation could lead to disintegration of life forms, with destructive consequences for the minds and bodies of the members of the communities involved.

The local normative orders of indigenous communities do not enter into transconstitutional relationships only with state orders. As evidenced by International Labour Organization (ILO) Convention no 169, for example, indigenous local orders are involved in transconstitutional entanglements with various types of normative orders in the 'multilevel' world legal system. The next Chapter discusses this topic.[285]

VII. TRANSCONSTITUTIONALISM BETWEEN SUPRANATIONAL LAW AND INTERNATIONAL LAW

Emerging by virtue of the growing openness of state constitutions to legal spheres beyond the state, transconstitutionalism is also developing between supranational and international law. In this case, although the formation and structural development of entangled legal orders in connection with legal problems are grounded in states as primary subjects, the process in question does not involve state orders. At this level, transconstitutionalism develops as originally state constitutional competences are taken over by suprastate and interstate bodies or entities. At the interface between internationally protected human rights and supranationally guaranteed fundamental rights, in particular, there arise legal problems that lead to an entanglement of orders and therefore require a constitutional 'conversation'. Here, one of the highlights is the relationship between the ECtHR and the normative order of the EU, including the ECJ. It is also worth mentioning the entanglement of legal problems between the WTO and the EU. Some cases are significant with regard to these two aspects.

Although the EU does not formally belong to the European Convention on Human Rights system, which allows only states to join, the jurisprudence of the ECtHR has affirmed its competence to control EU acts and norms. *Matthews v United Kingdom*, judged by the ECtHR on 18 February 1999, concerned the exclusion of voters in Gibraltar by European Parliament election rules under the 'Act concerning the election of the representatives of the European Parliament by direct universal suffrage' (20 September 1976).[286] In this case, this EU normative act was reviewed in light of Article 3 of Protocol no 1 to the European Convention on Human Rights, which establishes that members of the Convention system are

[285] *See* pp 166 *f* below.

[286] *Matthews v United Kingdom* (Application no 24833/94).

obliged to hold free elections by secret ballot to choose the legislature. The Court interpreted Article 3 extensively, determining that its scope was not restricted to national parliaments but was extensive to the European Parliament, which belonged to the EU. Thus, the Court ruled that the UK Government's decision not to allow the applicant to take part in the election violated her right to choose the legislature in free elections by secret ballot. In analysing this case, it is relevant to note that the 1976 Direct Elections Act was not properly speaking an internal act of the EU, since it derived from a treaty among the Member States and thus constituted a normative law additional to the treaty that founded the Union. Bearing this detail duly in mind, it is important to note the tendency to extend the competence of the ECtHR in the protection of human rights in Europe, opening up European supranational 'constitutionalism' to a 'dialogue' with international legal spheres.[287]

The ECtHR has developed an intense transconstitutional relationship with the ECJ. When cases have come before the ECJ that are regulated in parallel by EU norms, the ECtHR has examined them, attempting to reconcile the perspectives and avoid conflicts. On one hand, the ECtHR has sometimes relinquished its own line of argument to follow the ECJ's orientation; on the other, the ECtHR has on occasion opted not to follow a precedent established by the ECJ.[288] Thus, a transconstitutional 'dialogue' is in progress between an international order and a supranational order via the respective courts of law, precisely because there is a reciprocal willingness to learn and exchange, rather than a disposition to impose unilaterally the positions consolidated by each of the courts concerned. It is true that the ECtHR has acted more as a 'giver' than as a 'receiver' of legal orders, and has not regularly displayed a concern to play an active part in the global 'conversation' between supreme courts or constitutional courts.[289] However, the fact that certain participants in the constitutional 'dialogue' have greater powers of persuasion and influence does not necessarily entail the negation or deformation of transconstitutionalism between legal orders. The same could be said, and with far greater reason, of the US Supreme Court, which is more a 'giver' than a 'receiver' of legal models for resolving constitutional problems. The constitutional 'dialogue' breaks down only when it is not a simple matter of the overbearing influence of a 'giver of law', but rather one of the 'imposition' of constitutional models to the detriment of the adequate development of other legal orders.

The relationship between the EU and the WTO is also relevant. Because the EU has a seat on the WTO alongside each of its Member States, the entanglement between the international legal and economic order based on the WTO

[287] My synthesis of this case is based on Walter, 1999, 978 *f*.

[288] Baudenbacher, 2003, 512, referring to the following cases as examples: *Pellegrin v France* (Application no 28541/95), judgment of 8 December 1999; *Frydlender v France* (Application no 30979/96), judgment of 27 June 2000 (both following the ECJ line); *Funke v France* (Application no 10828/84), judgment of 25 February 1993 (against the ECJ line).

[289] Baudenbacher, 2003, 512, using terminology from Slaughter, 2003, 201 *f*, who says: 'The international tribunal most frequently cited is the European Court of Human Rights' (2004, 80).

and the supranational order of the EU tends to be frequent and intense. More major disputes have been taken before the WTO's Dispute Settlement Body between the EU and the US than between France and Germany or the UK and the US.[290] Many of these involve pluridimensional entanglements between the WTO, EU and non-Member States, especially the US, that is, transconstitutionalism in the sphere of a 'multilevel' or multicentric world legal system (*see* below, Chapter 4), as in disputes revolving around regulation of the market for bananas or the EU ban on imports of US beef produced with the aid of growth hormones.[291] Even in these cases, however, bilateral entanglements can be seen in the positions taken by the ECJ on the WTO rules and those of the WTO's Dispute Settlement Body with regard to EU directives. In the case of the beef hormone ban, the Appellate Body of the WTO affirmed its incompatibility with the treaty that set up the WTO. Only when the EU upheld the ban was the 'multilevel' model adopted for treatment of the case (*see* pp 150 *f* below).

Thus an analysis of the relationship between the international legal order of the WTO and the supranational legal order of the EU shows that the ECJ has indirectly adopted the orientation of not recognising immediate legal effects for WTO normative provisions. In its judgment of 23 November 1999, relating to the decision on regulation of the banana market[292] and invoking the goal of leaving open a space for negotiation on trade policy, the ECJ responded negatively to the question whether in implementing the normative control procedure provided for in the first paragraph of Article 230 of the Treaty establishing the European Community (as it was then called) a Member State could require a review of the legality of EU secondary law in the light of WTO rules.[293] Based on this decision, Nettesheim argues for addressing an individual's claim to resort to WTO rules by starting from the assumption that the ECJ will not set aside its own jurisprudence on the legal order deriving from the General Agreement on Tariffs and Trade (GATT), formed in 1947, to which it did not attribute immediate effect.[294] Given the link between this orientation of the ECJ and the involvement of various states in the plane of the two orders, transconstitutionalism between the supranational legal order of the EU and the international legal order of the WTO becomes particularly problematic and develops in the direction of a plurilateral transconstitutionalism on multiple 'levels'. This is discussed in Chapter 4.

Complementarily, it is worth noting that relations between the Court of Justice of the European Free Trade Association (EFTA) and the ECJ also involvestransconstitutionalism between legal orders, the EFTA Court being international and the ECJ supranational. There is more harmony here, in con-

[290] Uerpmann, 2001, 567.

[291] Uerpmann, 2001, 567 and 569.

[292] ECJ, C-280/93, judgment of 5 October 1994, *Federal Republic of Germany v Council of the European Union*.

[293] ECJ, C-149/96, judgment of 23 November 1999, *Portuguese Republic v Council of the European Union*. *Cf* Nettesheim, 2001, 397 *f*.

[294] Nettesheim, 2001, 398.

trast with the conflictual relationship between the EU and the WTO, but this derives mainly from more openness on the part of the EFTA Court towards ECJ jurisprudence, and there is practically no reciprocity by the latter. It is most unusual for a judgment by the EFTA Court not to cite ECJ decisions. Moreover, because the EFTA Court operates without advocates-general, it frequently cites the opinions of the ECJ's Advocates-General.[295] A model of 'conversation' between the EU and EFTA has therefore been constructed in which the 'giver' of ideas is practically speaking the supranational entity via its Court of Justice, while EFTA features basically as the 'receiver'.

Lastly, it is also worth noting that the EU, as practically the only comprehensive experience of supranationalism in the proper sense of the term, has been a focus for transconstitutionalism in several directions. The fact that it binds states through treaties but in addition directly obliges citizens and the respective state bodies through EU secondary law makes it more versatile and sensitive to transconstitutional entanglements of various kinds. Hence, it has been the most important instance for multilateral transconstitutionalism to emerge and develop, acting as a key conveyor belt in a 'multilevel' or multicentric world legal system and serving as an example for experiences in other parts of the world.

[295] Baudenbacher, 2003, 512, referring to several cases.

4

Transconstitutionalism in a 'Multilevel' or Multicentric World Legal System

I. MULTIANGLE TRANSCONSTITUTIONALISM BETWEEN ORDERS OF THE SAME KIND AND ORDERS OF DIFFERENT KINDS

TRANSCONSTITUTIONALISM BETWEEN TWO legal orders, be they of the same or of different kinds, may not only occur in the forms discussed in the previous Chapter. Besides these, it is possible to envisage the entanglement of constitutional problems between two international orders, between two transnational orders, between an international order and a transnational order, between an international order and a local order, between a transnational order and a local order, between transnational orders and supranational orders, between local orders, between a supranational order and a local order, and prospectively between supranational orders in the strict sense. As a rule, however, transconstitutionalism tends to involve more than two legal orders, which may be of the same or different kinds. These complex situations point to a 'multilevel' world legal system in which pluridimensional transconstitutionalism occurs as a result of the simultaneous relevance of one and the same juridico-constitutional problem to a range of legal orders.[1]

This reference to a 'multilevel world legal system', an expression that has become a commonplace and originates in the concept of a 'multilevel policy system',[2] calls for prior clarification regarding the term 'levels' in order to avoid any suspicion that what is being expounded here entails a pyramidal or hierarchical model of the legal orders of world society. Nor is this expression as used here intended to affirm a division of labour between these orders, which would imply a plane of supraordination, making unnecessary a discussion of the delicate problems of transconstitutionalism. Much less is it a matter of linking the notion of a 'multilevel' system with the inflationary concept of a relation

[1] In this sense, the situation is more complex than that presented in the 'glocalisation of law' model (Randeria, 2003; *cf* Robertson, 1995).

[2] Specifically in connection with Europe, *see* Scharpf, 1994, especially 17 *f*; 2002. In this context, another expression found in the literature is 'multilayered global governance' (Held and McGrew, 2002, especially 9). For reception in the legal sphere, *see* among many others Pernice, 1999; 2002; Joerges and Petersmann (eds), 2006; Petersmann, 2008; Joerges, 2003. On interjudicial conflicts, *see* Sauer, 2008.

between plural (and complete) constitutions. Nevertheless, the expression 'multilevel system' appears to have been used predominantly in this sense of a hierarchy and division of labour, especially when constitutional issues are involved. The following assertion by Pernice is a good example:

> The outcome is a *tiered connecting of complementary constitutions*, a system with multiple levels of public power in which the respective material spheres have limited competence to perform the public tasks with which they are entrusted, in accordance with the division of labour.[3]

Moreover, as evidenced by this passage the emphasis has been placed on the 'public' and the political ('power'), rather than the relations between legal orders in the entanglement of public and private.

The use made here of the expression 'multilevel world legal system' is intended to stress a plurality of orders whose structural types, forms of differentiation, models of self-comprehension and modes of concretisation are sharply distinct and peculiar, a multiplicity from which result entanglements in which none of the orders can present itself legitimately as the holder of the discursive *ultima ratio*. Thus, the phenomenon in question is a *multicentric* system in which heterarchical relations prevail between orders, although there is hierarchy within each order. The circular nexus between orders admits only the notion of 'tangled hierarchies', which is incompatible with a 'tiered connecting' of them.[4] In this context, there is entanglement among various legal orders, each of which claims self-grounding to a greater or lesser extent and which are confronted by juridico-constitutional problems that are equally relevant to all. Thus, issues of fundamental rights or relating to the legal limitation and control of power, as well as legally regulated participation in political procedures, constituting central problems of constitutionalism in the modern sense, reappear tangled in a web of case settlement claims from different orders. Under these circumstances, it would be a mistake to deny the cognitive openness of the orders concerned towards the social systems with which they find themselves faced, as it would prevent the emergence of constitutional transversality. But what is specifically alarming in the plane of the connection between legal orders is the always-present risk of normative closure of one order towards another, to the detriment of an adequate solution to common constitutional problems. In this case, what tends to happen instead is destructive fragmentation or hindrance of the construction of 'bridges of transition' between different legal orders.

Transconstitutionalism in the multicentric world legal system presents itself as a fundamental model for enabling this risk to be treated satisfactorily. In this context, not only do constitutional problems emerge for a plurality of orders, but there is also a 'development of constitutional elements at different levels'.[5]

[3] Pernice, 2006, 511 *f*.

[4] In this sense, Hofstadter also uses the term 'level', especially in his discussion of 'tangled hierarchies'. *See* 1979, 684 *ff*.

[5] Walter, 2000, 8, who also refers to the 'emergence of a network of constitutional elements' (p 7).

In some cases, one of the orders involved may not positively contain constitutional elements. Nevertheless, when faced with constitutional problems in the context of a complex world society and with claims from other legal orders, an order initially averse to constitutionalism tends to develop constitutional elements in its discourse that may help to resolve the problems. Mere contempt for collisions tends to have negative effects in every direction, not least for the order itself if it insists on ignoring the transconstitutional links posited by common problems. Thus, transconstitutionalism presents itself as a functional requirement and normative claim in a multicentric world legal system.

In light of the above, transconstitutional entanglements may present themselves simultaneously between state, supranational, international, transnational and local orders whenever a juridico-constitutional problem arises that is relevant to them in a particular case. As a rule, all types of order are not concurrently faced by the same constitutional problem, but it is usual for more than two legal orders, which may or may not be of different types, to establish a transconstitutional connection via legal cases that are relevant to them all simultaneously. A number of examples of such multiangle entanglements among legal orders are discussed below.

One of the evident manifestations of the entanglement of different orders that face legal problems with constitutional implications, as already mentioned in passing (*see* p 146 above), is the European Union's ban on imports from the United States of meat and meat products from animals treated with growth hormones. The validity of this ban, based on *supranational* norms protecting the fundamental right to health, was challenged by the United States, a *state* unit, at the World Trade Organization (WTO), an *international* entity, with the argument that the ban was a violation of free-trade principles. In its report dated 16 January 1998, the Appellate Body of the WTO ruled that the EU ban on imports of hormone-treated beef was incompatible with WTO norms.[6] The EU ban remained in force, however, and 15 months later (on 17 May 1999) the US applied to the Dispute Settlement Body (DSB) of the WTO for the right to retaliate against US$ 220 million per year.[7] The EU requested arbitration on 2 June 1999.[8] In a report circulated on 12 July 1999, the arbitrators decided partially in favour of the US, establishing reprisals equal to US$ 116.8 million.[9] Thus, the possibility of 'trade wars' was not eliminated, but 'they are judicially regulated in a broad manner'.[10] What the case in question shows is the impossibility of defining in advance an ultimate centre of dispute settlement, let alone the simplistic affirmation of optimisation models. Advocacy of the right to health was relegated in the name of international free trade. The decision might be considered irrational from the standpoint of a model more radically based

[6] WT/DS26/AB/R, WT/DS48/AB/R.
[7] WT/DS26/ARB, § 1.
[8] *Ibid.*
[9] *Ibid*, §§ 83 and 84.
[10] Uerpmann, 2001, 569.

on the right to health, but simply affirming such a right is insufficient. The crux is involvement in the multiangle network of arguments among legal orders in which risk, uncertainty and the possibility of disillusion are inherent in the complexity of the multicentric world system.

A European case with major public repercussions in the global plane led to a discussion of French constitutional law in relation to the European Convention on Human Rights and the Charter of Fundamental Rights of the European Union, which was part of the 'Treaty establishing a Constitution for Europe'. Although this constitutional treaty was rejected by the French in a referendum held on 29 May 2005, and did not enter into force (while the Charter of Fundamental Rights came into effect only with the entry into force of the Treaty of Lisbon on 1 December 2009 – *see* p 69 above), its compatibility with the French Constitution was submitted to the French Constitutional Council, leading to Decision 2004-505 DC, dated 19 November 2004 (*see* p 90 above). In one part of this decision (items 14–22), where it undertook a preventive analysis of the draft Charter of Fundamental Rights of the European Union, the Constitutional Council considered Article 9 of the European Convention on Human Rights to be in harmony with the principle that France is a secular republic (Article 1 of the French Constitution), invoking Decision 4774/98 of the European Court of Human Rights (*Leyla Sahin v Turkey*). Thus, supranational law was interpreted in accordance with a norm of international law by the constitutional review body of a state to affirm the peculiarity of a principle of state constitutional law. That is, Article II-70 of the proposed Treaty establishing a Constitution for Europe (supranational law), which recognised the right of everyone, whether individually or in community with others, to manifest religion or belief in public, was to be interpreted in accordance with Article 9 of the European Convention on Human Rights as interpreted by the ECtHR to safeguard the uniqueness of France's constitutional tradition with regard to the principle of secularism. Here, it is worth noting an example from the educational field to stress the uniqueness of the principle of secularism to France in the EU context: whereas in other states this principle serves only to forestall any attempt to make religious education obligatory but does not prohibit religious education itself, France's public schools are not allowed to teach religion at all, in accordance with the French juridico-constitutional order.

Based on this principle, in its preventive review of the Charter of Fundamental Rights of the European Union the French Constitutional Council could have chosen to declare the Charter unconstitutional or resorted to the exegetical figure of 'congruence conditioned by interpretation' (*conformité sous réserve d'interpretation*), entailing interpretation of the supranational treaty in accordance with the national constitution. It did not opt for either route, however. Instead, it invoked precedent, citing a decision of the ECtHR in which this international court ruled that Article 9 of the European Convention on Human Rights leaves signatory states 'considerable leeway' enabling each one to regulate religious freedom within public schools with a certain margin of discretion.

As formulated in the decision of the French Constitutional Council, the matter was defined on the basis of the following premises:

> In particular, if the first paragraph of Article II-70 recognises the right of everyone, whether individually or in community with others, to manifest religion or belief in public, the explanations of the Praesidium specify that the right guaranteed by this article has the same meaning and same scope as the right guaranteed by Article 9 of the European Convention for the Protection of Human Rights and Fundamental Freedoms . . . Article 9 of the Convention has been constantly applied by the European Court of Human Rights, on the latest occasion in the decision referred to hereinabove [Application 44774/98], in harmony with the constitutional traditions of each Member State; the Court has thus given official recognition to the principle of secularism recognised by various national constitutional traditions and leaves States considerable leeway to define the most appropriate measures, taking into account their national traditions, to reconcile the principle of freedom of religion and that of secularism; the provisions of Article 1 of the Constitution whereby 'France is a secular republic' which forbid persons to profess religious beliefs for the purpose of non-compliance with the common rules governing the relations between public communities and private individuals are thus respected.[11]

Based on this decision, it became clear that as far as religious freedom and the principle of secularism were concerned there would be no incompatibility between the (supranational) Constitutional Treaty of the European Union, then still subject to referendum and later rejected, and French constitutional law, albeit in light of an international convention and its interpretation by a national body with powers of judicial review with regard to constitutionality. This appears to be one of the most evident examples of the implausibility and inappropriateness of insisting on provincial constitutionalism, despite the strong legal tradition and claim to 'constitutional identity' of the state in question. The case involved links among legal orders of three types – state, supranational and international – so a satisfactory and opportune decision could be made. This situation suggests that the solution of the most relevant legal problems in a 'multilevel' world system requires transconstitutional entanglements involving different legal orders.

Another recent case of significance, this time to the question of federalism, relates to the autonomy of the Basque Country. This case involves 'multilevel' relations among an international, state, and local or regional order linked to a state. In a unanimous ruling issued on 11 September 2008, the Constitutional Court of Spain ruled unconstitutional a referendum scheduled for 25 October 2008 on Basque self-determination.[12] According to the Constitutional Court, the referendum was unconstitutional because only the central government in

[11] Paragraph 18 of Constitutional Council Decision 2004–505 DC.

[12] JCC 103/2008, 11 September 2008, judgment of Unconstitutionality Appeal no 5707-2008, proposed by the President of the Government of Spain against Basque Parliament Law 9/2008 of 27 June 2008, 'convening and regulating a popular consultation for the purpose of ascertaining public opinion in the Autonomous Community of the Basque Country on commencing negotiations for achieving peace and political normalisation'.

Madrid could hold such a 'popular consultation'. The Basque Country, through the head of the regional executive, was dissatisfied with the decision and stated immediately after its announcement that an appeal would be lodged against the Constitutional Court's ruling with the European Court of Human Rights.[13] Although the Basque government has not yet taken this initiative, the situation points to the entanglement of relevant constitutional problems among legal orders in the sphere of transconstitutionalism, with implications for the maintenance of unity of the state or the form of the state, which in some measure is subordinated to the decisions of an international court.

In the sphere of sports law, besides the collisions between state law and transnational sports law already mentioned in Section V of Chapter 3, it is important to note that other legal instances are also involved in the web of transconstitutional problems relating to sports law. Intercession by the European Court of Justice between state law and the transnational legal order of sports law has been considerable. Examples include the ECJ's rulings in *Bosman* and *Kolpak*, handed down on 15 December 1995 and 8 May 2003 respectively.[14]

In these judgments the ECJ ruled that nationality clauses restricting the number of foreign players in clubs belonging to national football federations were illegal. The rationale was based on the principle of freedom of movement, and in particular the decisions rejected the argument that discrimination in granting access to employment could be justified on purely sports-related grounds, especially the need to encourage young nationals to train and the need to strengthen national teams. In response to the line taken by the ECJ, the European Commission wrote to FIFA to complain that certain provisions in the rules governing application of the FIFA statutes to the activities of players' agents were in conflict with EU competition law. This led FIFA to adopt new rules on 1 March 2001. This was considered acceptable by the EC and judged not to conflict with competition law by the Court of First Instance of the European Communities (known as the General Court of the European Union since 1 December 2009).[15] In this context, it can be observed both in the sphere of the Court of Justice of the European Union (known as the Court of Justice of the European Communities until 30 November 2009) and in that of sports law doctrine, many rules enforced by the transnational order of sports law may conflict with European competition law, which deems sports federations to be 'associations of companies' with the capacity to 'abuse their dominant positions'.[16]

A comparison of the force of EU law with that of transnational sports law shows that the EU adopts a posture of greater autonomy toward transnational sports federations than states, since there are no European federations whose

[13] *Cf Euronews* of 12 September 2008, available at: http://www.euronews.net/pt/article/12/09/2008/basques-take-referendum-case-to-strasbourg/ (last accessed 23 November 2008).

[14] ECJ, C-438/00, judgment of 8 May 2003, *Deutscher Handballbund v Maros Kolpak*; ECJ, C-415/93, judgment of 15 December 1995, *Union royale belge des sociétés de football association and others v Bosman and others*.

[15] Loquin, 2008, 306 *f*.

[16] Loquin, 2008, 307.

development and maintenance are relevant factors in legitimation of the Union. On the contrary, national sports federations are linked primarily to transnational federations, on which states are dependent for the domestic development of sports, one of the factors in their legitimation. Hence the important role played by EU law in terms of transconstitutional intermediation between the legal orders of its Member States and the transnational legal order of sports.

This does not mean, however, that European law has acted only restrictively with regard to the rules of transnational sports law. Both ECJ decisions and statements issued by the European Commission have expressed the position that the interest of the sports legal order enjoys primacy over European competition law. For example, an EC press release dated 18 April 2002 stated that 'FIFA's aims of extending good practice, raising professional standards and protecting its members from unqualified or unscrupulous agents prevail over competition considerations', serving legitimate objectives inherent in sports.[17] Elsewhere it justifies anti-doping rules, although they limit the economic interests of competition, as a contribution to 'assuring the fair and regular development of athletic contests'.[18] In all these cases of intercession by the EU and its organisations in the respective state orders and the transnational order of sports law, it is possible to see the confluence of complex transconstitutional problems which often entail the containment of state bodies with competence in constitutional matters, and the expansion of the competence and activity of supranational and transnational bodies in respect of directly or indirectly constitutional matters.

In the case of Al Qaeda, which is a transnational network but is treated by the US almost as a sovereign state (*see* pp 134 *f* above), 'multilevel' transconstitutional entanglement can be seen particularly in connection with the involvement of NATO, which considered the attacks of 11 September 2001 a military action rather than a criminal one.[19] In this case, the multiangle relationships among state legal orders, international orders and transnational orders treated specially as 'paralegal' or 'anti-legal' display elements of asymmetry, given the force of the US order to the detriment of the international order. Nevertheless, under such circumstances the significant fact is that the Al Qaeda transnational network cannot be seen merely as a criminal organisation subordinated to the prosecutory action of international law and state orders in collaboration, but should instead be dealt with as a normative order opposed to the requirements of the international order and the orders of constitutional states, and often as an ally of state orders that act outside constitutionalism.[20] Furthermore, it displays an effective claim to autonomy from the dominant orders in the inter-

[17] *Ibid. See also* http://europa.eu/rapid/pressReleasesAction.do?reference=IP/02/585&format=HTML&aged=0&language=EN&guiLanguage=en – last visited on 17 December 2010.

[18] Loquin, 2008, 307 *f*.

[19] Berman, PS, 2005, 506.

[20] The problem of the link between 'terrorism' and certain states was stressed long ago by Cassese, A, 1989, 597 *ff*.

national and state spheres, offering an alternative proposal for the creation of a different world 'order'. For all these reasons, it is involved in constitutional problems in various planes of the 'multilevel' world system, in the form of a transnational normative order with significant implications for issues of fundamental rights, limitation of power, and limits to the territorial sovereignty of states and the jurisdiction of international organisations and courts.

Finally, an interesting example involving the Brazilian legal order is the case of imports of retreaded tyres by Brazil. This dispute touches on Brazilian constitutional law, the legal orders of Uruguay and Paraguay, the laws of Mercosur, and the legal order of the WTO. On 17 December 2007, the WTO Dispute Settlement Body (DSB), in adopting the WTO Appellate Body Report of 3 December 2007, which modified the Panel Report of 12 July 2007, upheld an appeal by Brazil to ban imports of retreaded tyres from the EU based on arguments relating to protection of the environment. However, this decision established that the Brazilian policy of continuing to import retreaded tyres from Paraguay and Uruguay entailed discrimination and should therefore be abolished, and the DSB did not accept the Brazilian claim that the number of retreaded tyres imported from Paraguay and Uruguay was insignificant.[21] Later the European Communities requested binding arbitration. An arbitration award by a WTO-appointed arbitrator determined that the reasonable period for Brazil to implement the recommendations and rulings of the DSB was 12 months from the adoption of the Panel Report and Appellate Body Report on 17 December 2007, that is by 17 December 2008.[22]

The problem posed by the DSB's decision was that the Mercosur Permanent Review Court had previously ruled against a petition from Argentina requesting a ban on imports of retreaded tyres from Uruguay, reaffirming earlier decisions, based on the understanding that such a ban would infringe Mercosur legal principles.[23] Brazil initially attempted to circumvent both decisions by proposing to cap the number of retreaded tyres imported from Paraguay and Uruguay, leading to simultaneous conflict with the norms of Mercosur and the WTO in diametrically opposite directions. However, conflict between the administrative bodies that established norms banning imports of retreaded tyres and judicial bodies that declared the norms in question to be unconstitutional led to dissension and strife concerning the issue within the Brazilian state apparatus.

The situation became more complicated when a claim of non-compliance with a fundamental precept deriving from the Constitution (as provided for by Article 102, § 2) was put before the Supreme Court by the Office of the Presidency on 29 September 2006 (ADPF 101/2006). The court was asked to declare unconstitutional and illegal judicial decisions that had admitted the importation of retreaded tyres based on the argument that the infraconstitutional norms that prohibit this

[21] WT/DS332/AB/R; WT/DS332/R.

[22] WT/DS332/16, of 29 August 2008. For more on this case, *see* Perotti, 2009.

[23] Award 1/2005 of 20 December 2005; Award 1/2007, of 8 July 2007; Award 1/2008 of 25 April 2008.

practice were unconstitutional. The core reasoning underlying this motion was the claim that these decisions infringed Article 225 of the Constitution, which states: 'Everyone has the right to an ecologically balanced environment, which is a public good for the people's use and is essential to a healthy life. The Government and the community have a duty to defend and preserve it for present and future generations.' Given the significance of this issue, a public hearing was held on 27 June 2008.[24]

Finally, the Supreme Court ruled partially in favour of the motion, prohibiting imports of retreaded tyres in general but allowing for some exceptions when such imports were based on Mercosur laws and guaranteeing *res judicata*.[25] This settled the dispute from the standpoint of domestic law. Nevertheless, the situation points to the pressing problems of combating provincial constitutionalism in the Brazilian case. At the same time, it evidences the great difficulty of achieving a satisfactory solution for all the orders involved. Above all, there is a fundamental need for decisions to attain a minimum of internal consistency unless the solutions proposed are to lose all credibility. The positions taken by Brazil, with authorities in different sectors opposing or supporting imports of retreaded tyres, and banning imports of such tyres from the EU on the basis of environmental and health arguments but simultaneously admitting imports of the same products when the country of origin is Uruguay or Paraguay, were inconsistent from both the domestic and international standpoints: this confusion was not satisfactory either for the WTO or for Mercosur, let alone for a consistent perspective on state constitutional law governing environmental protection. Until the Supreme Court's judgment of ADPF 101/2006 (a decision that is open to criticism, but at least put the house in order), this inconsistency and opportunism showed that the road travelled by Brazil in the case of retreaded tyre imports ran in the opposite direction to a model open to the requirements of transconstitutionalism among legal orders, instead approaching a blend of simplistic 'pragmatism' in foreign policy and juridico-constitutional provincialism. In this regard, it is increasingly important to review the constitutional paradigms so as to make possible a more solid 'transconstitutional conversation' with entangled normative orders around problems in the 'multilevel' world legal system, especially by the Brazilian Supreme Court. However, this should entail not outbursts of rhetorical eloquence and bragging, whether of an internationalist, transnationalist, or supranationalist nature, at the expense of the Brazilian constitutional order but affirmation of that order as a partner in the construction of a multiangle transconstitutionalism.

[24] See the official site of the Supreme Court (STF): http://www.stf.jus.br/portal/cms/verTexto.asp?servico=processoAudienciaPublicaAdpf101 (last visited on 24 November 2008).

[25] ADPF 101/DF, judgment of 24 June 2009, TP, DJe 4 June 2012. This was a majority decision, with only Justice Marco Aurélio dissenting.

II. PLURIDIMENSIONAL TRANSCONSTITUTIONALISM OF HUMAN RIGHTS

From the cases analysed in the previous section, it can be inferred that transconstitutionalism in a 'multilevel' or multicentric world legal system relates directly or indirectly to problems of 'fundamental rights' or 'human rights'. These expressions carry a degree of ambiguity that requires a certain preliminary delimitation so that the question can be treated in the sphere of transconstitutionalism.

When the idea of the rights of man or human rights arose in the age of liberal revolutions,[26] it was distinguished from the concept of citizenship. While the former referred to the rights of every human being, the latter referred to the rights of the members of a particular political collectivity, and more precisely of a state.[27] However, the idea of human rights also entailed the right of every single person to citizenship ('a right to have rights').[28] This situation has recently acquired a certain relevance to the semantics of human rights, according to which these rights entail civil rights ('negative freedoms'), political rights ('positive freedoms')[29] and social rights ('entitlements in the narrow sense'[30] or '*droits-créances*'[31]).

Later, especially owing to the influence of Germany's relatively late experience of constitutionalism, the expression 'fundamental rights' came into use to refer to positivated rights guaranteed by state constitutions.[32] However, their content included both the private rights of citizenship in the classical sense and human rights.[33] A distinction was therefore proposed between fundamental rights constitutionally guaranteed by states and internationally protected

[26] Discussing the French case, Gauchet (1989) refers to the 'revolution of the rights of man'. Brunkhorst alludes to the 'ideas of 1789' with the formula 'patriotism of human rights', but argues that they are heirs to two traditions: 'Judaeo-Christian brotherly solidarity and Graeco-Roman civic solidarity' (2002, 79 [Engl trans 2005, 55]).

[27] *See* Neves, 2006a, 175 *f*, referring to Marx, 1988a [1844], 356 *f* and 361 *ff*.

[28] A frequently cited formulation by Arendt (1973, 296 *f*), used however not primarily in the sense of human rights but rather of citizenship. From a different perspective, and with a foundational claim, there is a discussion of the 'right to human rights' (Brunkhorst, Köhler and Lutz-Bachmann (eds), 1999), and human rights are associated with 'the fundamental right to justification' (Forst, 2007, 291 *ff*).

[29] This distinction between negative and positive freedoms, which has become a commonplace, was first made by Berlin, 1975 [1958]. On this subject, *see* Passerin d'Entrèves, 1962, 279–310; Macpherson, 1990, 95 *ff*; Taylor, 1979; Habermas, 1992, 325 *ff* [Engl trans 1996, 268 *ff*]; Ladeur, 2000, especially 81 *ff*.

[30] In the terminology employed by Alexy, 1986, 454 *ff* [Engl trans 2002, 334 *ff*]. *Cf* Arango, 2005, 37 *ff*. Schmitt (1993 [1928], 169 *f*) uses the expression 'the individual's essentially socialistic (diluted social) rights to positive services from the state'.

[31] In contradistinction to '*droits-libertés*', in the language of Ferry and Renaut, 1992, 26–32.

[32] The title of the Second Part of Germany's 1919 Weimar Constitution (Arts 109–165) read as follows: 'Fundamental rights and fundamental duties of the Germans'. Part I (Arts 1–19) of the 'Basic Law' (Germany's 1949 Constitution) employs only the expression 'fundamental rights'.

[33] *Cf* Schmitt, 1993 [1928], 157 *ff*.

human rights, which may even have to be affirmed against states.[34] Nevertheless, in both cases there is an intersection between the category of civil, political and social rights, and new rights (collective rights and those referring to 'affirmative action').[35]

Efforts to make distinctions at the theoretical level continue, however. For Luhmann, for example, fundamental (constitutionally positivated) rights serve 'to maintain a differentiated communication order' or, conversely, react to 'the danger of dedifferentiation'.[36] While in his early work Luhmann called human rights 'eternal'[37] and hence did not take them seriously, he later emphasised that 'among the most important indicators of a global legal system is the increasing attention paid to the violation of human rights'.[38] Human rights relate to the problem of exclusion, he argued, and are therefore oriented to the inclusion of the human being as a person in society's functional systems, especially law.[39] However, Luhmann advocated a restrictive semantics of human rights, so as to include only those situations involving outrageous, 'extremely severe' violations of human dignity in the ambit of world society, 'such as officially condoned disappearances, deportations and expulsion by force, illegal killings, arrests and tortures with the knowledge of or under the protection of state bodies'.[40] This restriction is not justified in my view.

Just as the reaction to scandalous and flagrant violations of human rights such as torture and genocide is one of 'the most important indicators of a global legal system', it cannot be denied that the lack of minimum conditions for survival on the part of a large proportion of the world's population today, equivalent to the absolute social exclusion of the human groups involved, has also been considered an outrageous and scandalous violation of 'human dignity' and hence of human rights taken as a synonym for generalised legal inclusion. In both cases, what is at stake is the paradox of affirming normative (counterfactual) expectations against the very practices that systematically flout them. The difference resides in the fact that human rights in the strict sense, referring basically to the prohibition of violence (political, police, or military) against individuals or groups, can be institutionalised and, above all, can be positivated and implemented procedurally worldwide, especially in the wake of

[34] *See*, under the influence of German juridico-constitutional doctrine, Dimoulis and Martins, 2007, 40 *ff*.

[35] This very broad view of human rights, including so-called 'third-generation' and even 'fourth-generation' rights, has given rise to criticism of the vagueness and even the innocuousness of this concept. Thus, Norberto Bobbio (1996, xi) refers to the 'third generation of rights' arguing that it 'is still too vague and heterogeneous for an exact definition'; drawing on this critique, Danilo Zolo (1993, 259) objects to the 'normative inflation of the concept of citizenship', noting 'the risk of diluting its historical and functional significance'. *Cf* Neves, 2005, 12 *f* [Engl trans 2007, 421 *f*], albeit with objections to a strict conception of human rights according to the classical liberal model.

[36] Luhmann, 1965, 24 *f*. *Cf* Ladeur and Augsberg, 2008, 5 *ff*.

[37] Luhmann, 1965, 23.

[38] Luhmann, 1993a, 574 [Engl trans 2004, 482].

[39] Luhmann, 1993a, 582 *ff* [Engl trans 2004, 488 *ff*].

[40] Luhmann, 1993a, 579–81 [Engl trans 2004, 485–7].

transformations in international law, whereas the institutionalisation of social rights and many so-called third-generation human rights is weak and the prospects of their positivation and procedural implementation on a global scale are negative. The latter have been institutionalised and positivated on a wide scale only in a very restricted ambit of a few social and democratic constitutional states. Given the precariousness of their institutionalisation and the difficulty of their procedural implementation, these can be called *weak* human rights, as distinguished from *strong* human rights, whose positivation and even procedural implementation lie within the reach of the multicentric world legal system, especially in the sphere of *ius cogens*.[41]

Based on this theoretical context, I propose to define human rights primarily as normative expectations of legal inclusion for every single person in world society, and hence of universal access to law as a social subsystem.[42] This definition does not preclude arguing that human rights also react to the 'the danger of dedifferentiation' or serve 'to maintain a differentiated communication order', as mentioned above with regard to the fundamental rights constitutionally positivated by states. This is because the orientation to or structural preference for inclusion in functional systems, especially law, is closely related to the maintenance of a differentiated communication order in world society and hence to the differentiation of law. The greater the exclusion in certain spheres of world society, the more limited the realisation of functional differentiation in the respective social contexts.[43] Hence the fragility of human rights affirmation in the corresponding territories or weakly differentiated functional spheres.

Thus, both human rights and fundamental rights concern the inclusion of people and the differentiation of society. Their contents practically coincide. The difference resides in their claims to validity. Fundamental rights are valid within a specific state constitutional order. Human rights claim validity for the 'multilevel' or multicentric world legal system, that is, for any existing legal order in world society (not merely the international legal order). Of course, in practice these expressions can be used in the opposite sense: 'fundamental rights (or freedoms)' used in supranational or international treaties or conventions; 'human rights' used for the catalogue of rights positivated in state constitutions.[44] From the

[41] Brunkhorst, 2002, 191 *ff* [Engl trans 2005, 142 *ff*]; Neves, 2005, 13 [Engl trans 2007, 422 *f*].

[42] Neves, 2005, 8 *ff* [Engl trans 2007, 417 *ff*].

[43] Luhmann (1993a, 582 [Engl trans 2004, 488]), formulating a paradox, says 'there is a stark difference between inclusion and exclusion that, while it is produced by functional differentiation, is incompatible with it and ultimately undermines it'. More peremptorily, he adds: 'If, however, the inclusion of some depends on the exclusion of others, this difference undermines the normal functioning of functioning systems. This affects law, specially' (1993a, 584 *f* [Engl trans 2004, 490]). On this problem and more overarchingly, based on Brazilian experience, *see* Neves, 1992; *see also* 1994 [Engl trans 2005].

[44] Here it is worth mentioning on one hand the titles of the 'Charter of *Fundamental Rights* of the European Union' and the 'European Convention for the Protection of Human Rights and *Fundamental Freedoms*', as well as the Preamble to the Charter of the United Nations: '*fundamental* human *rights*'; and on the other hand the French Constitution, which lacks an explicit catalogue of 'fundamental rights' but whose Preamble refers to the 'Rights of Man . . . as defined by the Declaration of 1789'.

theoretical standpoint, however, the definitions and differences presented serve my argument and are supported by dominant legal practices.

Teubner proposes another theoretical distinction between fundamental and human rights, attempting to distinguish between them qualitatively in terms of content. Starting from the systemic conception that human beings are part of the environment of society,[45] Teubner considers human rights from the perspective of the *human individual's exclusion* from society, that is, as 'intended guarantees of the integrity of mind and body' with regard to society and its subsystems.[46] In this sense, he argues as follows: 'The human rights question in the strictest sense must today be seen as endangering the individual's integrity of body and mind by a multiplicity of anonymous and today globalised communication processes.'[47] Fundamental rights, on the contrary, are oriented to *inclusion of persons*. Thus he seeks to distinguish between 'personal fundamental rights and human rights'.[48]

It seems to me, however, that 'inclusion' of persons and the human individual's 'exclusion' are indissociable in the ambit of systems theory, constituting two sides of the same coin. The integrity of body and mind can be guaranteed in society, its functional systems and organisations only if inclusion of the respective persons is guaranteed: that is, if society does not treat people as mere bodies and minds but as worthy of personality,[49] that is, worthy of being 'addresses for the communication process'.[50] In other words, inclusion as a person is what makes respect for the integrity of body and mind possible. As a two-sided form, the person constitutes a structural coupling between human being and society,[51] serving to face the danger both that the integrity of the person's biopsychic substrate will be violated or destroyed by the expansion of society and that, on the contrary, the latter will be destroyed and disintegrated by lack of limits on human desires and drives.

Having made these reservations, I now want to note that the conditions for the ascent of human rights in modern society relate to the emergence of structural dissension regarding not only the plurality of communication spheres with a claim to autonomy (systemic complexity), but also the heterogeneity of expectations, interests, and values held by individuals and groups.[52] Thus it is necessary to delimit the concept of human rights, defining them as normative expectations of generalised legal inclusion under the conditions of structural dissension in world society. Understood thus, human rights are located at the

[45] *Cf*, eg, Luhmann, 1987a, 133 *f*; 1987c, 286 *ff* [Engl trans 1995, 210 *ff*]; 1997, vol 1, 30.

[46] Teubner, 2006, 175 [Engl trans 2006, 338].

[47] Teubner, 2006, 180 [Engl trans 2006, 341].

[48] Teubner, 2006, 175 [Engl trans 2006, 337 *f*].

[49] In Luhmann's formulation, this derives from the fact that in the 'area of inclusion', 'human beings count as persons', whereas in the 'area of exclusion', they 'are no longer perceived as persons but as bodies' (1997, vol 2, 632 *f*; 1995b, 262 *f*; 1993a, 584 *f* [Engl trans 2004, 490).

[50] Luhmann, 1989, 367, note 11.

[51] In a more precise formulation, this means: 'Persons serve as a structural coupling between mental and social systems' (Luhmann, 1995c, 153).

[52] Neves, 2005, 8 *ff* [Engl trans 2007, 418 *ff*].

frontier of the legal system, linking it with a morality of inclusion and dissension, which circulates with relevance in the ambit of today's world society in competition with other moral models. It can be said that certain forms of their expression ('weak' human rights) have not yet crossed the frontier of the legal system, as it were, in the broader sphere of world society, since they lack a minimum of legal institutionalisation, positivation and conditions for procedural implementation, while other forms ('strong' human rights) have indeed crossed the frontier and are struggling to be concretised and implemented.[53]

The question of human rights, which arose as a juridico-constitutional problem in the state sphere, now pervades all types of legal orders in the multicentric world legal system: state, international, supranational, transnational, and local. It is a central issue in transconstitutionalism. Controversy about human rights derives from the possibility of different interpretations of the concept, the conflict-ridden plurality of interpretations/concretisations of related norms, and the practical incongruence of different types of human rights. A liberal reading, for example, may come into conflict with a social democratic understanding of human rights. Interpretations of a normative text may lead to different case solutions. Invoking one type of human rights may clash with the validity claim of another type.

The situation worsens when it is recalled that the various orders of the multicentric world legal system have significantly different understandings of human rights questions. Indeed, many are averse to the idea of human rights as rights that claim to be valid for every single person. It is in this context that the pluridimensional transconstitutionalism of human rights takes on special significance, by cross-cutting legal orders of every kind and stimulating both cooperation and collisions. In what follows I discuss a number of examples in which human rights issues entangle simultaneously with various legal orders, leading to collisions that are hard to resolve and for this very reason requiring a transconstitutional 'conversation' via 'bridges of transition' that allow for reciprocal learning by the orders involved.

First, it is relevant to note the existing transconstitutional 'dialogue' among supreme courts or constitutional courts, which invoke jurisprudential precedents not only from other foreign courts but also from international courts or tribunals, especially the European Court of Human Rights (ECtHR). As mentioned earlier, this 'dialogue' includes the US debate on the invocation of foreign law, involving allusions to both the laws of other countries and international law with regard to human rights (see above, pp 91 and 107 *f*). This debate, which intensified with the decision in *Lawrence v Texas* (2003) protecting the right of homosexuals to engage in intimate conduct, was further fortified by the judgment of 1 March 2005 in *Roper v Simmons*,[54] in which the US Supreme Court ruled five to four that it is unconstitutional to impose capital punishment

[53] Neves, 2005, 13 [Engl trans 2007, 422 *f*].

[54] *Roper, Superintendent, Potosi Correctional Center v Simmons*, 543 US 551 (2005).

for crimes committed while under the age of 18, in light of the Eighth Amendment's prohibition of 'Cruel and Unusual Punishment'.[55] Christopher Simmons murdered Shirley Crook when he was 17. A few days before committing the murder he persuaded a friend to take part in the crime, arguing that they would 'get away with it' 'because they were minors'.[56] They carried out the murder in a shocking and cruel manner. The jury found Simmons guilty of 'first-degree murder' and recommended a death sentence.[57] Writing for the majority that overturned the death sentence, Justice Anthony Kennedy stressed that 'the United States now stands alone in a world that has turned its face against the juvenile death penalty'.[58] Dissenting, Justice Antonin Scalia complained that: 'Though the views of our own citizens are essentially irrelevant to Court's decisions today, the views of other countries and the so-called international community take centre stage.'[59] This position in favour of provincial constitutionalism having been defeated once again by a preference for openness to constitutional 'dialogue', the discussion now turns to the theoretical foundations and practical significance of the invocation of foreign and international law by the US Supreme Court.

This 'dialogic' stance in terms of admitting the pluridimensional transconstitutionalism of human rights should not be confused with mere convergence between domestic law, on one hand, and foreign and international law, on the other. In *Roper v Simmons*, Justice Scalia accused the court of desiring convergence with the laws of other countries, proposing resistance by national constitutions to foreign influence.[60] But neither the 'Resistance Model' nor the 'Convergence Model' is appropriate for transconstitutionalism. As stressed by Vicki C Jackson, '[t]he Convergence Model sees national constitutions as sites for implementation of international law or for the development of transnational norms', whereas the 'Resistance Model' advocates both that state constitutions serve 'as a basis for resisting globalisation's economic pressures', especially in less developed countries, and that they act 'as an affirmative reason to resist constitutionalising human rights norms derived from transnational sources', particularly in American federalism.[61] Against these two positions oriented to include or exclude each other unrestrictedly, Jackson proposes a third, which she terms the 'Engagement Model' and defines as follows:

> Third, constitutional law can be understood as a site of engagement between domestic law and international or foreign legal sources and practices. On this view, the constitution's interpreters do not treat foreign or international material as binding, or

[55] *See* the commentary by *Harvard Law Review* [Editorial Board], 2005. For analysis of the case, *see* Jackson, 2005; Waldron, 2005; Young, 2005; Steiker, 2006.

[56] *Roper v Simmons*, 556, 600 and 621; *Harvard Law Review* [Editorial Board], 2005, 104.

[57] *Roper v Simmons*, 557 *f*; *Harvard Law Review* [Editorial Board], 2005, 104.

[58] *Roper v Simmons*, 577.

[59] *Roper v Simmons*, 622. *Cf Harvard Law Review* [Editorial Board], 2005, 103. Citing the 'dialogue of the judges on the death penalty', Delmas-Marty (2006, 53 *ff*) also refers to this case (p 61).

[60] Jackson, 2005, 112. *Cf Roper v Simmons*, especially 627 *f*.

[61] Jackson, 2005, 112–14.

as presumptively to be followed. But neither do they put on blinders that exclude foreign legal sources and experience. Transnational sources are seen as interlocutors, offering a way of testing understanding of one's own traditions and possibilities by examining them in the reflection of others.[62]

Strictly speaking, this 'Engagement Model' corresponds to a model of transversal entanglement in which the 'bridges of transition' between legal orders occur at the constitutional level. Mutual exchange and learning constitute the positive side of this entanglement. However, precisely because mere convergence is not involved, there are moments of collision which entail the affirmation of one constitutional identity at the expense of another. This 'dialectics' of transconstitutionalism entails a two-sided form, with the positive value being constructive interlocution between legal orders.

In his discussion of *Roper v Simmons*, Jeremy Waldron resorts reconstructively to the ancient Roman concept of *ius gentium*, affirming that it differs from the modern concept of international law by referring comprehensively to a repertory of knowledge that applies both to domestic law and to *ius inter gentes*.[63] He then points to a modern *ius gentium*, whereby judges and lawmakers refer reciprocally to the knowledge of their peers in other parts of the world, just as scientists refer mutually to their experiences, thus enabling an accumulation of knowledge. Thus *ius gentium* was supposed to represent 'the accumulated wisdom of the world on justice and right'.[64] This knowledge was 'accumulated not from the musings of philosophers', but 'from the decisions of judges and lawmakers grappling with real problems'.[65] And it was accumulated 'not just in the crude sense of one thing being added to another, but in the sense of overlap, duplication, mutual elaboration, and the checking and rechecking of results that is characteristic of true science'.[66] Although modern *ius gentium* is no 'guarantor of truth', there is no 'sensible alternative to paying attention to the established body of findings to which others have contributed over the years'.[67] Based on this argument, Waldron sustains that the citation of foreign and international law by the U.S. Supreme Court should not be thought of as a 'piecemeal practice',[68] but as a way of acting in a network of connections among various legal orders to solve common problems.[69]

It is true that Waldron appeals to the ancient concept of *ius gentium*, which does not seem to be adequate to the complex problems of transconstitutionalism, and to theoretical assumptions that in my view are simplistic, according to

[62] Jackson, 2005, 114, exemplifying with ancient cases of partial agreement and disagreement by the US with British law (*Marbury v Madison* [1803]) and by Canada with US law (*cf R v Keegstra* [1990]), but also including in this model the solution that prevailed in *Roper v Simmons* (pp 114 *ff*).

[63] Waldron, 2005, 133 *ff*.

[64] Waldron, 2005, 138.

[65] *Ibid*.

[66] Waldron, 2005, 138 *f*.

[67] Waldron, 2005, 139.

[68] Waldron, 2005, 144 *f*.

[69] *See* Waldron, 2005, 143 and 145.

which he distinguishes between 'law as will' and 'law as reason', corresponding respectively to the views of those who oppose and those who defend 'modern *ius gentium*'.[70] Nevertheless, he offers interesting elements for an understanding of the significance of transconstitutional 'dialogue', since by presenting law as 'a problem-solving enterprise'[71] he hints at the need for openness towards the experiences of other constitutional orders as a key condition for an adequate solution to the legal problems of today's world society, especially in the sphere of human rights. Agreement with Waldron is therefore possible in the following terms: although in *Roper v Simmons* the US Supreme Court did not articulate general ideas about a transconstitutional 'conversation', in this and other cases it has responded to the development of transconstitutionalism.[72]

Although the US experience has been developing from a 'Resistance Model' toward an 'Engagement Model' (engagement in transconstitutional 'dialogue'), some constitutional or supreme courts have adopted the 'Convergence Model' since this model emerged, mainly owing to the lack of a solid constitutional tradition. The Constitutional Court of South Africa, influenced by the traumatic experience of apartheid, may perhaps be the court that has most regularly invoked not only constitutional norms and jurisprudential precedents from courts in other countries, as already mentioned (p 109 above), but also human rights conventions and international human rights tribunals, especially the European Convention on Human Rights and the ECtHR, for the formation of its own *ratio decidendi* in making decisions. This is particularly clear in *State v Makwanyane*, which, as mentioned earlier, ruled the death penalty unconstitutional in South Africa on the basis of ECtHR jurisprudence.[73] The Supreme Court of Zimbabwe also cited ECtHR jurisprudence in ruling that corporal punishment for adults is cruel and unusual and unconstitutional when applied to minors.[74] In Israel, a ban on certain interrogation methods used by the Internal Security Agency, considered 'inhumane and degrading' by the High Court of Justice in 1999, was grounded in the ECtHR's decision in *Ireland v United Kingdom* (1978).[75] In the UK, the Judicial Committee of the Privy Council (JCPC), serving as the final appeal court for Jamaica, commuted a Jamaican's death sentence to life imprisonment on the basis of a decision by the ECtHR.[76] In numerous cases, the Inter-American Court of Human Rights and the UN Human Rights Committee have adopted methods of interpretation used by the ECtHR.[77] In all such instances, ECtHR judgments have mere persuasive force, since the ECtHR does not have formal authority over the courts or

[70] Waldron, 2005, 146 *f*.
[71] Waldron, 2005, 146.
[72] *Ibid*.
[73] Slaughter, 2004, 80. *See* Strydom, 2004, 187 *ff*.
[74] Slaughter, 2004, 80 *f*.
[75] Case of *Ireland v United Kingdom* (Application no 5310/71), judgment of 18 January 1978. *Cf* Slaughter, 2004, 81.
[76] Slaughter, 2004, 81.
[77] *Ibid*.

committee in question.[78] However, the persuasive elements grounded in the legitimacy of the ECtHR as a model for human rights protection function in large measure as a dimension of the *ratio decidendi*, and are therefore not confined to *obiter dicta* or mere rhetorical citation. In some cases, this results from constitutional self-binding by a legal order to foreign and international norms of human rights protection. This applies particularly to Article 39, paragraph 1, *b* and *c*, of the South African Constitution, as already noted (p 109 above).

In Brazil, not only is foreign law often cited in human rights cases (*see* pp 113 *ff* above) but, in terms of pluridimensional transconstitutionalism, reference to conventional norms of international law and the jurisprudence of international courts is usual. In the above-mentioned *Ellwanger* case (Habeas Corpus 82.424/RS)[79] in which the Plenary of the Supreme Court (STF) upheld an appellant's conviction on charges of racism for publishing a book with antisemitic content (Holocaust denial) and ruled against application of the statute of limitations, besides numerous references to foreign law, the justices also cited countless acts and norms of international public law and invoked *Jersild v Denmark*, judged by the ECtHR in September 1994.[80] In many other judgments, the STF has displayed evidence of its disposition to join a transconstitutional 'dialogue' in the multicentric system where various legal orders are concomitantly articulated to solve constitutional human rights problems.[81] This is not a matter of adopting a simple 'Convergence Model' based on Article 5, paragraph 2 of the Federal Constitution, and later on paragraphs 3 and 4 of the same Article, introduced by Constitutional Amendment no 45 in 2004.[82] Much less is it a retreat to a 'Resistance Model' based on a provincial interpretation of these constitutional provisions.[83] The most adequate path in human rights issues appears to be the 'Engagement Model', or rather a transversal entanglement among legal orders, whereby all orders would be capable of reconstructing themselves permanently by learning from the experience of other orders concomitantly interested in solutions to the same constitutional legal problems of fundamental or human rights. The absolute alternative 'convergence or resistance' carries respectively potential elements of self-destruction for the constitutional order or hetero-destruction of other legal orders.

[78] *Ibid.*

[79] HC 82.424/RS, judgment of 17 November 2003, TP, DJ 19/03/2004.

[80] *Jersild v Denmark* (Application no 15890/89), judgment of 23 September 1994.

[81] *Cf* HC 82.959/SP, judgment of 23 February 2006, TP, DJ 01/09/2006; and references in notes 181 and 182 to Chapter 3 above.

[82] For a 'Convergence Model', *see* Mello, 2001; Trindade, 2003; 2000; Piovesan, 2008a, 51 *ff*; Mazzuoli, 2001, 33 *ff*; 2005; 2007, 682 *ff*; Galindo, 2005. More cautiously, Sarlet (2001, 77–95 and 132–5; 2006; 2010) and Gomes (2008, especially 189) relativise the 'Convergence Model', albeit displaying a preference for this model. Uniquely, Tavares (2005, 47 *f*) argues for the reception of human rights treaties prior to Constitutional Amendment no 45/2004 as constitutional norms with the entry into force of this amendment.

[83] Dimoulis and Martins (2007) strangely opt for a 'Resistance Model' in relation to international human rights norms (pp 40–51) but enthusiastically support a 'Convergence Model' with regard to foreign law, especially the jurisprudence of Germany's Federal Constitutional Court (pp 261 *ff*). *See* p 115 above.

Besides the invocation of norms and precedents from other legal orders, especially citation of foreign and international laws and jurisprudence by national courts, it is important to note cases relating to fundamental and human rights in which courts hand down binding judgments that cut across various legal orders. In this regard, it is worth paying particular attention to the approach taken by the Inter-American Court of Human Rights (IACHR) in judging *Yakye Axa v Paraguay* and *Sawhoyamaxa v Paraguay*,[84] regarding property rights to the territories of the Yakye Axa and Sawhoyamaxa indigenous communities, located in Paraguay. In these interesting cases, the IACHR decided not in accordance with the technical and legal concept of private property defined in terms of state constitutional law, but primarily taking into account the cultural notion of 'ancestral property', which is traditional in such communities. Pushing into the background a fundamental right that is constitutionally assured in the *state* sphere, the IACHR found in favour of the right of an *extra-state local* community to its territory in order to protect human rights guaranteed in the international sphere. This multiangled entanglement around human and fundamental rights would not be possible without willingness on the part of the various orders, especially the state order, to give ground to the perspectives of other normative orders on the significance and applicability of colliding rights.

Problems of pluridimensional entanglement around human rights also arise in cases involving indigenous communities where sexual intercourse between adults and minors and the killing of newborn babies are considered legitimate, as discussed in Section VI of Chapter 3, especially in connection with transconstitutionalism between state orders and extra-state local orders. In this context it is relevant to note ILO Convention 169 concerning Indigenous and Tribal Peoples in Independent Countries,[85] which states in Article 8, paragraph 2: 'These peoples shall have the right to retain their own customs and institutions, where these are not incompatible with fundamental rights defined by the national legal system and with internationally recognised human rights.' This provision further complicates the collision between native local orders and the order of state fundamental rights and international human rights. A literal reading of the provision, applied to absolute protection of sexual freedom for minors and of the lives of newborns, would tend to lead to ethnocide against the respective indigenous communities. In my view the arguments presented above in Chapter 3, Section VI (especially pp 139 *ff*), do not lose their significance by virtue of this reference to international law. In such cases, it is necessary but not sufficient to engage in a complexly adequate re-reading of both state fundamental rights norms and international human rights norms. A superficial universalism of human rights, based in linear fashion on a certain Western ontological conception of such rights, is incompatible with a constitutional

[84] *Comunidad Indígena Yakye Axa v Paraguay*, judgment of 17 June 2005 Series C no 125 (for an analysis of this case, *see* Ramírez, 2005); *Comunidad Indígena Sawhoyamaxa v Paraguay*, judgment of 29 March 2006, Series C no 146 (for summaries of both cases, *see* Piovesan, 2008b, 71–3).

[85] On this Convention, *see* the brief exposition by Wolfrum, 1999.

'dialogue' with indigenous orders that do not correspond to this model. On the contrary, a refusal to engage in a constructive 'dialogue' with indigenous orders on these issues is itself a violation of human rights, since it would entail the 'ultracriminalisation' of the entire community of perpetrators of the acts concerned, indiscriminately affecting their bodies and minds by means of destructive interference. In such cases, what is required in the name of positive transconstitutionalism is the willingness of state and international orders to experience the surprise of reciprocal learning from the experience of the other, the indigenous community in its self-understanding.

It should also be noted that the transconstitutional articulation of human rights often involves the state, international, and transnational dimensions. In the case of intellectual property protection, which involves elements of national and international law as well as transnational law proper,[86] an outstanding example is *Hazel Tau v Glaxo and Boehringer*, brilliantly analysed from the standpoint of systems theory by Teubner.[87] This case argued before the Competition Commission of South Africa pitted AIDS activists against transnational corporations and discussed the right of HIV-positive South Africans to antiretroviral drugs.[88] It involved the following questions: Do the pricing policies pursued by multinational pharmaceutical companies violate human rights? Can people with HIV/AIDS be complainants in litigation brought directly against multinational pharmaceutical companies based on the fundamental right to life? Is there a human right of access to medication in the private sector? And in general, do human rights oblige only states or are they also an obligation directly for transnational private actors?[89] The CCSA found for the complainants in a decision partly grounded in domestic law (Section 8(a) of the Competition Act 89 of 1998), ruling that the 'excessive pricing of ARVs [antiretrovirals] is directly responsible for premature, predictable and avoidable deaths of people living with HIV/AIDS, including both children and adults'.[90] Besides leading to a discussion of the problem of the horizontal effects of fundamental rights in the transnational sphere (with 'much more dramatic dimensions' than in the 'national' sphere[91]) and thus transcending the national sphere, this case points to problems of entanglement between orders of regulation. Simple internationalist recourse to a generous interpretation of TRIPS (Trade-Related

[86] *See* Fischer-Lescano and Teubner, 2006, 67 *ff*.

[87] Teubner, 2006 [Engl trans 2006], with vast references to the literature and allusions to analogous cases; Fischer-Lescano and Teubner, 2006, 73 *ff*.

[88] Competition Commission of South Africa, *Hazel Tau et al v GlaxoSmithKline, Boehringer Ingelheim et al*, judgment of 16 December 2003. Previously, in *Minister of Health v Treatment Action Campaign*, judgment of 5 July 2002 [2002 (5) SALR 721], the South African Constitutional Court had found in favour of the rights of HIV-positive people to the appropriate medicine. *Cf* Bilchitz, 2003.

[89] Teubner, 2006, 161 [Engl trans 2006, 327].

[90] *Hazel Tau v Glaxo and Boehringer*, § 17. *Cf* Teubner, 2006, 162 [Engl trans 2006, 328]; Fischer-Lescano and Teubner, 2006, 76.

[91] Teubner, 2006, 162 [Engl trans 2006, 328].

Aspects of Intellectual Property Rights),[92] exclusively invoking the transnational model of self-regulation or arguing for a definitive state solution based on national sovereignty, are not sufficiently complex responses in these cases. Nor do the limits to legitimacy for the respective orders serve as an ultimate argument for their exclusion from the process of seeking a legally consistent and socially adequate solution. Without the *ultima ratio* present in any of the orders, the transconstitutional solution referring to human rights in the case in point demonstrates that what matters most is to restrict the tendency for certain legal orders to expand at the expense of others (avoiding the danger of dedifferentiation), and to limit the expansion of orders of regulation and the respective organisations that tend to increase exclusion, thus destroying people's bio-psychic substrate.[93] Instead of optimisation, the key is to avoid the maximising tendency of legal orders linked to money and power, communication media whose capacity for imperial expansion has proved strongest in today's world society.[94] However, transconstitutional decisions cannot lead to the paralysis of an order, whether linked to money or to power, since in a supercomplex society this will lead to a process of dedifferentiation that is harmful to all social spheres.

Another issue that stands out in the field of patent law is the problem of so-called 'biopiracy'. This serious question transcends the transnational forms of global economic self-regulation, the international order and state instances of the so-called developing countries to encompass the local anthropological and legal forms adopted by traditional, even archaic, peoples, especially indigenous communities.[95] Starting from a supposed universality of patent law, traditional forms of knowledge and technology acquisition tend to be considered lacking in legal significance and to be suppressed. This solution is evidently not the most suitable from a transconstitutional perspective on human and fundamental rights. To the extent that native local communities' life forms and forms of normative regulation are usurped or destroyed by biopiracy, patent law presents itself as 'anti-law'. Thus any model of internationalism or transnationalism, or even statism, also proves inadequate in this context: it is fundamental that 'ancestral' common-law rights be respected with regard to the 'intellectual property' of local extra-state communities, which moreover are entitled to compensation for the damage that can be caused to such communities by 'modern' exploitation of the respective raw materials.[96] In this case, too, the collision

[92] Piovesan, 2008c, 149. On the problematic implications of the TRIPS Agreement for developing countries, *see* Bass, 2002–2003. Koskenniemi (2004, 206) has this to say: 'The domination of Western interests was nowhere more visible than in the conclusion of the Agreement on Trade-Related Aspects of Intellectual Properties (TRIPS), designed to protect copyrights, patents and trademarks overwhelmingly owned by Western companies.'

[93] *See* Ladeur and Augsberg, 2008, especially 105, linking the danger of dedifferentiation with the issue of the individual's inclusion/exclusion from world society.

[94] *Cf* Fischer-Lescano and Teubner, 2006, 7 and 25 *ff*.

[95] *See* Teubner and Fischer-Lescano, 2008.

[96] *Cf* Teubner and Fischer-Lescano, 2008, 45.

between the fundamental rights of 'modern' intellectual property and human rights relating to 'ancestral' intellectual property can be solved only through a transconstitutionalism capable of halting the expansion of the legal forms coupled to the monetary mechanism.

The examples presented here regarding the pluridimensional transconstitutionalism of human rights seem to me to corroborate the idea that, while it is not possible to relinquish classical constitutional state law, generally linked to a constitutional text, constitutionalism is opening up to spheres beyond the state not exactly owing to the emergence of other (non-state) constitutions but rather because eminently constitutional problems, especially those relating to human rights, intersect simultaneously with several legal orders that entangle with each other in their search for solutions. Thus, transconstitutionalism can be said to be the constitutional law of the future, requiring a higher degree of interdisciplinarity. In this sense, it is vitally important to construct a specific methodology for transconstitutionalism.

III. OUTLINES OF A METHODOLOGY OF TRANSCONSTITUTIONALISM

The method of transconstitutionalism cannot be reduced to the identity model of a given legal order. The starting point is 'double contingency'.[97] In principle, the problem of double contingency is present in the reciprocal observation relations between ego and alter in interaction. However, the question of double contingency is not confined to interaction, where the poles 'ego' and 'alter' refer to (but cannot be confused with) persons, since alter and ego may also refer to social systems.[98] In this sense, ego and alter may be not only law as an overarching functional system but also its organisations and legal orders (the latter being strictly speaking partial systems in the internal differentiation of the legal system, which is segmentary in territories or functional, according to the system or social problem to which the order is related). Thus, transconstitutionalism entails the permanent question of double contingency between different legal orders, and particularly between their courts of law.

Double contingency means that ego takes into account that the actions of *alter* can be different from what he expects and vice versa. Although there can be no such thing as 'pure double contingency' – because of the conditioning of interaction[99] and the 'absorption of uncertainty' by means of 'stabilising expectations'[100] – '[a]ny attempt to calculate the other will inevitably fail'.[101] This

[97] Luhmann, 1987c, 148 *ff* [Engl trans 1995, 103 *ff*]; 1987a, 32 *ff*; 2002b, 315 *ff*. The concept of double contingency derives, according to Luhmann (1987c, 148 [Engl trans 1995, 103 and 522 *f*]; 2002b, 317), from Talcott Parsons and a group of researchers associated with him. *Cf* Parsons *et al*, 1951, 16; Parsons, 1968, 436.

[98] Luhmann, 1987c, 152 and 155 [Engl trans 1995, 106 and 108].

[99] *Cf* Luhmann, 1987c, 168 and 185 *f* [Engl trans 1995, 118 and 133].

[100] Luhmann, 1987c, 158 [Engl trans 1995, 110].

[101] Luhmann, 1987c, 156 [Engl trans 1995, 109].

entails the mutual assumption of 'degrees of freedom'[102] (an alter's actions may be entirely different from those expected by ego and vice versa), which converts behaviour into action: 'Behaviour becomes action if it is found free to be determined differently.'[103] And double contingency itself as a 'catalytic agent' of the 'autocatalysis of social systems'[104] assumes reciprocal freedom in the form of 'a self-conditioning indeterminacy', bringing about a self-referential circle: 'I do not allow myself to be determined by you, if you do not allow yourself to be determined by me.'[105] Hence double contingency involves a combination of non-identity and identity: 'ego experiences alter as alter ego. But along with the *nonidentity of perspectives*, ego also experiences the *identity of this experience* on *both* sides.'[106]

Double contingency always involves the question of recognition.[107] Here I want to take a step beyond the argument I developed in a recent study[108] and consider recognition between legal orders or courts as a problem of double contingency. The problem (of the negation) of recognition arises precisely when one of the poles in the relationship of reciprocal observation between ego and alter is not willing to tolerate the other's 'freedom', because he does not think of his own behaviour as action (since it could not be different from the behaviour projected by ego) and/or because he does not take the non-identity of his own perspective seriously. When 'being also otherwise possible'[109] for alter's behaviour is not part of ego's experience, the former's perspective is overlooked. Lastly, if we bear in mind that '[o]ne of the most important consequences of double contingency is the emergence of *trust* or *distrust*',[110] we can say that negating recognition of the other leads to such an expansion of distrust that it prevents the construction of interactions grounded in double contingency.

Transconstitutionalism depends on a method that does not focus on a blind identity. Isolated legal orders are evidently led, especially through their supreme or constitutional courts, to consider their own identity first and foremost, since otherwise they dilute themselves as orders without differentiation from their

[102] Luhmann, 1987c, 186 [Engl trans 1995, 133].
[103] Luhmann, 1987c, 169 [Engl trans 1995, 120].
[104] Luhmann, 1987c, 170 *ff* [Engl trans 1995, 120 *ff*].
[105] Luhmann, 1987c, 167 [Engl trans 1995, 117].
[106] Luhmann, 1987c, 172 [Engl trans 1995, 121 *f*].
[107] A warning: double contingency in interaction assumes reciprocal observation by persons as social constructions or communication addresses and is not an interpsychic relationship between human beings. As 'black boxes', ego and alter refer to interacting people whose actions and experiences remain indeterminate. *See* from a different perspective indebted to Mead (1962 [1934]), Honneth, 1994, 114 *ff*, whose theory of intersubjective recognition derives from the Hegelian concept of the 'struggle for recognition' (1994, especially 54 *ff*; *cf* Hegel, 1967 [1805–06], especially 200 *ff*). According to Honneth (1994, 12), the model of a 'struggle for recognition' lost its theoretical significance in the *Phenomenology of the Spirit* (*cf* Hegel, 1988 [1807], 127 *ff*; Honneth, 1994, 104 *f*). For an insight into the dominant debate on recognition, *see* Taylor, 1992a, 43 *ff*; 1992b; Fraser, 2004; Fraser and Honneth, 2003.
[108] Neves, 2008, 502 *ff*.
[109] Luhmann, 1987c, 184 [Engl trans 1995, 132].
[110] Luhmann, 1987c, 179 [Engl trans 1995, 127].

environment. If, however, they are confronted by common problems, especially when these are constitutional in nature, alterity simply has to be taken into consideration on pain of becoming reciprocally blocked. Thus it is vitally important for the construction of a methodology of transconstitutionalism to see as indispensable the permanent reconstruction of 'constitutional identity' by virtue of a permanent consideration of alterity.[111] This does not mean negating identity as if in an innocent model of pure convergence. It means being ready to open up not just cognitively but also normatively to other entangled orders in concrete cases. The results will remain uncertain, of course, but only if this readiness exists will it be possible to absorb the originary dissensus. The alternative leads to reciprocal blockage and the impossibility of resolving significant constitutional problems in fundamental and human rights, and in respect of the organisation (control and limitation) of power.

Application of the 'balancing' model oriented by the criterion of optimisation, in accordance with the theory of principles, especially as formulated by Alexy,[112] appears far more controversial in the case of transconstitutionalism than within any given constitutional order.[113] Besides being a paradigm which on one hand is strongly linked to the positions of groups and therefore 'focuses attention both cognitively and normatively on short-term effects, neglecting the long term',[114] and on the other hand does not adequately take into account the problem of the incommensurability of perspectives,[115] it is a model grounded in a very radical notion of identity. First, it assumes the identity of principles as unlimited prima facie rights that can be restricted only by the process of balancing with other principles.[116] Even prima facie, however, *ego*'s right founded on a principle entails limitation of *alter*'s right founded on the same principle and vice versa (typically, for example, the fundamental right of freedom). This means there is not only collision between principles but also collision within principles in the basic alterity of law. Moreover, it is assumed that these identities are transcended in a balancing higher identity, that is, a common denominator that optimises colliding principles. In fact, if one principle is weighted more than another when a collision occurs, this can only be done via 'injustice' to the

[111] From an entirely different perspective grounded in psychoanalytical assumptions, Rosenfeld (1998, 144 *ff*) associates the 'identity of the constitutional subject' with the viewpoint of 'the other'.

[112] Alexy, 1986, especially 71 *ff* [Engl trans 2002, 44 *ff*], who developed his sophisticated model out of Dworkin, 1991 [1977], especially 16–80. For the reception of Alexy's theory of the principles in Brazil, *see* da Silva, VA, 2009, 43 *ff*. On the discussion about principles theory, *see* among many Ávila, 2008; Steinmetz, 2001; Barroso and Barcelos, 2005; Martins, 2008.

[113] For criticisms of the balancing model, *see* among many Ladeur, 2007b, 343 *ff* (referring here to a 'devaluation of fundamental rights via unlimited balancing'); 2004b; Ladeur and Augsberg, 2005, 158 *ff*; Christensen and Fischer-Lescano, 2007, 148 *ff*; Schlink, 1976, 127 *ff*; 2001, 455 *ff*; Jestaedt, 1999; Müller, 1995, 62 *ff*; Habermas, 1992, 310 *ff* [Engl trans 2004, 254 *ff*].

[114] Ladeur, 2007b, 367, who, however, is wrong in my view to link the model of 'unlimited balancing' intrinsically to the welfare state and focuses too narrowly on the liberal paradigm of society (*cf* especially 371).

[115] Christensen and Fischer-Lescano, 2007, 199 *ff*, with arguments derived from Kuhn, 1996, 198 *ff*.

[116] *See*, eg, Alexy, 1986, especially 273 and 342 *f* [Engl trans 2002, 196 and 248], on the 'general right to liberty'.

other, at least initially. Only through an alterity model constructed precisely in the search for a permanent possibility of alteration of identity in the face of the other can the paradox of colliding fundamental rights be processed. If this paradox is repressed or sublimated by an instance of optimisation, it tends to return later in a blocking or destructive form.[117]

As already noted, if application of the 'optimising balancing' model is problematic within a given constitutional order, it is especially debatable when applied to relations between legal orders regarding fundamental rights in the sphere of transconstitutionalism. The tendency to 'optimise' in relations between radically different 'constitutional identities' may lead not just to illusions but also to reciprocal 'narcissistic' paralysis. The key in this case is to construct mechanisms that serve to rearticulate identity via observation of the solution offered by the other order to a given problem. Rather than affirming optimisation, it is appropriate to speak of containment as the first step in the transconstitutional method.[118] But this containment is not an end in itself. It relates to double contingency, to the ability to be surprised by others, to acknowledge the possibility of an open future, which cannot be predetermined by any of the orders entangled in the case. A willingness to seek out the normative 'findings' of others is crucial,[119] in order to fortify one's own capacity to offer solutions to common problems.

Thus, the starting point for the method of transconstitutionalism cannot be a given legal order, let alone the orders of the most powerful, but must instead be the constitutional problems with which the various orders are entangled.[120] From the initial disconnection between orders imprisoned in their respective identities, transconstitutionalism enables rules and principles to articulate reciprocally in seeking a solution to the case. In this perspective, the development of a method of transconstitutionalism opens up the possibility of constructing a transversal rationality in the relations between the principles and rules of different legal orders. This entails considering three levels of relations between the principles and rules of different legal orders. Each of these levels is entangled with the others in circular fashion: principle–principle, rule–rule, principle–rule (if more than two orders are involved, the situation becomes still richer in possibilities for entanglement). An understanding of the multiple

[117] Discussing the 'paradoxes of interpretation', Ladeur and Augsberg (2005) warn that instead of denying or merely noticing such paradoxes it is necessary to 'deparadoxify' by permanently processing paradoxes (pp 150 *f*), in order to avoid destructive effects for the legal system. Acknowledging this in the sphere of transconstitutionalism means precisely acknowledging the limits of one's own interpretation in light of the perspectives of the other orders involved, and thereby reducing the momentum of the violence that is intrinsic in every decision. On paradox in law, *see* Teubner, 2003b.

[118] It is relevant to note here the tendency for the various social spheres or discourses to maximise their own rationalities to the detriment of other's rationalities, as stressed by Fischer-Lescano and Teubner (2006, 25 *ff*). *Cf* Teubner, 2008, 32 *f* [Engl trans 2009, 33].

[119] To recall the contribution of Waldron (2005, 132, 139 and 145), discussed in the preceding item (pp 163 *f* above).

[120] *Cf* Baudenbacher, 2003, 523.

interfaces can offer new insights, not least into the theory of the relations between principles and rules.[121]

A model that emphasises alterity and entails a constant search for ways to rearticulate identity vis-à-vis the other evidently has its limits in the 'multilevel' or multicentric world legal system. As already mentioned, there are legal orders that are not disposed to engage in a transconstitutional 'dialogue'. This does not mean they should be methodologically excluded from transconstitutionalism. Above all with regard to such orders, transconstitutionalism faces a delicate challenge: how to offer methods that lead to internal transformation through reciprocal inducements? If straightforward 'imposed constitutionalism' (*see* note 131 to Chapter 3 above) is excluded, this entails a certain capacity for finding in the other's order the elements that can serve its self-transformation as a first step in the transconstitutional 'dialogue'. This initial limitation is problematic and at times it will not even be possible to begin a transconstitutional rapprochement.

Nevertheless, in a world of common constitutional problems for a plurality of legal orders, the transconstitutional method seems more adequate to the passage from a simple situation of unstructured fragmentation to one of constructive differentiation among legal orders in the plane of their respective self-groundings than definitive linear hierarchical methods, be they international, state, supranational, transnational, or even local juridico-anthropological. Thus, based on a methodology of transconstitutionalism it is necessary to reject both a hierarchical methodological model and the mere affirmation of the fragmentation of law without any methodological horizon at all. Faced with fragmentation, the transconstitutional method must develop in search of the construction of 'bridges of transition' that enable more constructive (or less destructive) relations to be fostered among legal orders, via the pluridimensional articulation of their principles and rules to address common juridico-constitutional problems that require solutions acceptable to all the orders involved, without an ultimate decision-making instance. Instead of authority, transconstitutionalism requires method.

[121] Thus what is being proposed here is not a retreat to the classical rules model. Principles such as norms of norms are reflexive instances that are indispensable to the legal system, serving to demarcate and construct rules in the process of concretisation (on reflexive mechanisms or reflexivity, *see* Luhmann, 1984a; 1987c, 601 and 610–16 [Engl trans 1995, 443 and 450–5]). But this should not be confused with a linear hierarchical relationship of grounding. What is affirmed here is circularity (or 'tangled hierarchies'): while principles serve to demarcate and construct rules, rules are fundamental to the application of principles in the process of concretisation. There is a relationship of reflexivity in the static plane of the legal system, just as there is reflexivity in the dynamic dimension between constitution and law, and between both of the latter and the decisions of law courts in applying the law. On the static and dynamic aspects of law, *see* Kelsen, 1960, 72 *ff*, 114 *ff*. and 196 *ff*.

5

Excursus: Limits and Possibilities of Transconstitutionalism in Terms of Empirical Conditions, Functional Requirement and Normative Claim

I. EMPIRICAL CONDITIONS: TRANSCONSTITUTIONALISM VERSUS ASYMMETRY OF THE FORMS OF LAW

THERE ARE RELEVANT negative empirical conditions for the realisation of transconstitutionalism in today's world society. It can also be said that transconstitutionalism bears within itself a positive dimension, the development of transversal rationality among legal orders, and a negative dimension, the blocking and destructive relations among them. Thus, its limits are not only determined from outside the legal system via the superimposition or 'colonisation' of legal orders by social systems that instrumentalise the law.[1] Also, from the legal order's internal standpoint, transconstitutionalism is self-blocked by the asymmetries of the forms of law, although these asymmetries are conditioned by the above-mentioned external factors.[2]

First, however, I should clarify my use of the expression 'forms of law' (in the plural). The 'form of law' ('*Rechtsform*') is a term used in the Marxist tradition, analogously to the concept of commodity form,[3] but it is used in the singular by Marxists.[4] In both cases, the term refers to a distance between structural forms of society (in law and the economy) and concrete subjects, that is, to forms of 'alienation' ('*Entfremdung*'). My intent in referring to 'legal forms' in the plural is to disconnect my arguments from this tradition to a certain extent. Thus, I consider the various ways in which the primary code difference of law (legal/illegal) relates in the temporal, social, material, and territorial dimensions to the legal programmes and criteria for judging and resolving conflicts

[1] On this subject *see* Neves, 2009b; *cf* Chapter 2 above, especially pp 53 *ff*, 64 and 73 *f*.

[2] *See* Neves, 2009c, 850 *ff*.

[3] 'The commodity as the elementary form of bourgeois wealth' or the 'general elementary form of wealth' (Marx, 1988b [1863–1867], 24 and 27). In clarifying his concept, Marx refers to the existence of commodities in precapitalist social formations: 'Only on the basis of capital, of capitalist production, does the commodity in fact become the *general elementary form of wealth*' (p 28).

[4] *See* Buckel, 2008.

(particularly constitutional, statutory and customary norms, judicial and administrative rulings, private juristic acts, doctrinal models, and judicial precedents). Speaking of multiple manifestations of the 'form of law' would be appropriate if it were a matter of adhering to the Marxist tradition. However, using the expression 'forms of law' is more adequate in order to emphasise plurality.

The asymmetries of legal forms create obstacles or impairments to transconstitutionalism by virtue of the fact that in certain contexts one is stronger than another and ignores the other's claims and demands. This superimposition of one legal form over another does not imply the formation of a hierarchical order or organisation in the traditional sense of a stepped structure, but instead leads to diffuse mechanisms of oppression or negation of the autonomy of some legal forms by others.

In international relations, expansion of the power code to the detriment of the legal code is associated with the immunisation and untouchability of the legal orders of the 'great powers'[5] in the sphere of public international law. A significant aspect is the impotence of international organisations to control US legal practices and impose appropriate sanctions on the US. For example, international arms control by law is rejected by the US (as well as China and Russia) as unacceptable, as if it constituted an illegitimate interference in the country's internal affairs. Yet arms control is demanded, especially by the US, when it is a matter of the weakest countries in the international constellation, and is indeed imposed by the competent international bodies. Moreover, as far as jurisdictional competence is concerned, US courts are unwilling to acknowledge the competence of international courts to judge cases in which public international law claims are brought against the US and, in exceptional cases, against US official bodies, organisations or citizens. The Guantanamo Bay Detention Camp is exemplary in this regard. The US judiciary has categorically refused to admit any possibility of a decision by an international court, even though the characteristics of the litigation show that the case involves not only an internal matter relating to violations of the US Constitution or the rule of law, but also an important question relating to violations of public international law.[6] Thus, anti-constitutional practices develop in the interior of constitutional states and their 'migration'[7] undermines the realisation of transconstitutionalism.

[5] I refer to 'great powers' advisedly. My intent in using this expression is to refer to states – understood here as organisations that constitute the centre of each '(territorial) political system' (Luhmann, 2000a, 244) – which by virtue of the intensity of their power enjoy the greatest capacity to act, thereby causing dedifferentiating effects on world society (*see*, eg, Luhmann, 1993a, 579 *f* [Engl trans 2004, 486]; Koskenniemi, 2002, 480 *ff*; 2004, 202 *ff*).

[6] *See* Wolfrum, 2003, especially 52–62 and 77 *f*; Hillgenberg, 2005; Amann, 2004; Jinks and Sloss, 2004. *See also* Siehr, 2004, who discusses the international law implications of the so-called 'war against international terrorism' in the UK and US. *See* pp 134 *f* above.

[7] In this regard, Scheppele (2006) refers to the 'migration of anti-constitutional ideas' in connection with the measures taken to combat terrorism in the wake of 9/11; Roach (2006) discusses the post-9/11 migration of Britain's Terrorism Act 2000; and Gross (2006) writes of the 'migration of anomalies'.

This situation is closely linked to the problem of the asymmetries of the forms of law among state legal orders. In this regard, it is necessary to take a step beyond noting that the operative autonomy of law in face of its social environment has been realised only in a few consolidated constitutional states.[8] This means facing the question of determining to what extent the legal orders and legal cultures of strong states in the context of world society have destructive effects on the development of legal forms by other states. The most evident problem here is that of 'post-colonial' or 'neo-colonial' oppression of positive experiences with law in peripheral countries. When deviant forms of legal relations emerge with regard to the market, the distribution of power, cultural identity, education and so on, intervention is frequently proposed and executed, so that the legal understanding of the dominant state again prevails. This implies a markedly asymmetrical conception of 'sovereignty': while sovereignty is almost absolute for the bearer of certain legal forms, it is highly relativised or entirely ignored in the case of legal forms that deviate from the dominant forms in their experiences with power, money, and knowledge.

Analogously, the relations of private regimes with forms of law in peripheral countries are distant from the transconstitutional model in most cases. Systematic corruption of the forms of law in fragile states via private self-regulation in the transnational plane, benefiting large, multinational corporations, is not something to be considered only from the perspective of a left-wing critique of capitalism. This problem should also be taken seriously with a view to recognising or strengthening the discursive autonomy of the plural spheres of world society. Transnational private legal orders, in which the law is a 'medium' for the economy,[9] develop a type of instrumental rationality in the legal sphere according to which all emergent normative claims of the forms of law in weaker countries tend to be judged as disruptions of their expansionary dynamics. This is why such orders tend to ignore the claims in question, with destructive effects for the respective forms of law. In the field of patent protection, this problem is evidenced by the example of biopiracy, discussed earlier (p 168 *f* above). In this case, the developmentalist argument may be merely a cover for forms of misappropriation of material and immaterial assets by transnational groups, to the detriment of the citizens of the respective states and also of members of the corresponding native communities.

In connection with this problem, it is also important to stress that the central instances of the state are often unwilling to support or collaborate with local forms of law. This results in oppression of local legal claims in the name of state unity. The opposite is not unusual: blind separatism on the part of local communities that are unwilling to coexist with the heterogeneity of a people and the

[8] Neves, 2006b; 2007b; 2009b.

[9] I use here an expression coined by Habermas (1982a, vol 1, 536 *f* [Engl trans 1987, vol 1, 365 *f*]), although I disagree with the theoretical assumptions underlying his distinction between 'law as medium' and 'law as institution', a dichotomy which he himself abandoned later on (1992, 502, note 47 [Engl trans 1996, 416 and 562, note 48]). On this subject, *see* Neves, 2006a, 108 *f*.

plurality of the public sphere in a constitutional state. Destructive reciprocal effects often derive from conflicts between the claim to unity of a federal, regional, or unitary state and the claims to autonomy of their respective Member States, regions, provinces, or departments. However, unofficial forms of law are also making increasingly strong claims to legal autonomy, often associated with oppressive measures by the state, as well as non-negotiable conflicts originating in local demands for autonomy.[10] In this case, it is rather a question of negative entanglements, because no room is left for reciprocal learning in terms of transconstitutionalism. On the contrary, the situation is dominated by conflicts of intolerance, which ultimately cannot be treated or resolved by means of legal forms and in the last instance may lead to armed violence and a refusal of the rule of law.

It is also important to highlight the asymmetries of legal forms with regard to the various functional spheres of the legal system. Certain forms of law become dominant through tightly consolidated structural couplings with other partial spheres of society. Thus, for example, contracts and property serve as structural couplings between law and the economy (*see* pp 26 *f* above) and constitute strong, if not the strongest, forms of law in world society. In other areas, couplings remain in the operative plane or, when they extend to the structural level, are very weak. Examples include environmental law, which concerns the relations between human beings and nature, and social law, oriented to inclusion of the person. The legal forms of contract and property affirm themselves expansively against the legal forms of environment and inclusion. In the context of new developments in world society, the functionally determined forms of economic law are increasingly stronger than the territorially conditioned forms of political law in the constitutional state. Environmental law and social law, directed to inclusion, constituted secondary forms of law in world society compared with both the legal forms relating to the economy and those relating to state politics. Associated with this is the fact that the legal forms of human rights also remain very fragile compared with the legal forms of political power and the economy: to the extent that their coupling with the moral discourses of the inclusion of persons or the exclusion of human beings (*see* p 160 above) is blocked by the discourses of the market and power in a regular and systematic manner, they continue to belong to one of the predominantly symbolic forms of law in the plane of world society.[11]

From what has been expounded above, it can be inferred that transconstitutionalism is a scarce resource of world society. Stable transconstitutional

[10] Discussing these conflicts in a different context, Luhmann (2000a, 218 *f*) offered the following warning: 'It may come about in the foreseeable future that we find ourselves facing conflicts of an entirely different kind: ethnic conflicts, religious conflicts, conflicts of identity, conflicts about values, norms and convictions that cannot be negotiated. Countless fundamentalist movements, like those that have unexpectedly been reborn in recent decades, offer proof that these non-trivial conflicts still exist just as they were before and that the idea that all conflicts could be reduced politically to conflicts of interest was an illusion.' *Cf* Neves, 2006a, 222–24.

[11] Neves, 2005 [Engl trans 2007]. *See* p 61 *f* above.

entanglements among legal orders have so far occurred only in very limited portions of the 'multilevel' world system in territorial or functional terms. The outlook remains unfavourable to positive developments. Nothing could be more illusory than the idea that experiences of transversal rationality in transconstitutionalism among legal orders are generalised or in a position to become so in the short or medium term. These experiences are part of the privileges of some legal spheres in an acutely asymmetrical world society.

In sum, it can be seen that strong forms of law superimpose themselves oppressively on fragile forms of law in the 'multilevel' world system. Thus the state forms of law of the 'great powers' remain untouchable by public international law and immunised against it. These legal forms also behave oppressively towards the legal forms of the weaker countries in the international constellation. This is evident, above all, when the latter take steps that deviate from the dominant pattern in introducing social changes. Similarly, the transnational legal orders instrumentalised by the major business corporations have a destructive effect on the legal forms of the so-called developing countries, as well as non-state local communities. In the sphere of conflict between the state unit and local autonomies, there is frequent repression of local forms of law by central forms on one hand, as well as blind reactions by local legal forms against the central forms of the respective state on the other. Last, the asymmetries of legal forms lead to repression of the fragile legal forms of environmental law, social law, and human rights, permanently suppressed by the strong forms of contract law, property law, market law, and power-related law. The same rule applies to all these cases: there can be no transconstitutionalism without relative symmetry of the forms of law.

Transconstitutionalism is part of the functional requirements and hence of the normative claims of world society, as discussed below. Nevertheless, from an empirical standpoint the persistent *exploitations* of legal discourses in the context of asymmetrical forms of law impose themselves very solidly against such requirements and claims. These *exploitations* of law drive growth of the exclusion sectors of world society in a manner incompatible with the development of transconstitutionalism.

II. FUNCTIONAL REQUIREMENT: BEYOND CONSTITUTIONAL UTOPIA AND FRAGMENTATION – PROMOTING A 'DIFFERENTIATED COMMUNICATION ORDER' (SYSTEM INTEGRATION)

In the plane of research into public international law and transnational legal orders, use of the term 'fragmentation' has become a commonplace to designate the lack of unity of law in today's world society.[12] In this theoretical context, when

[12] *See* Fischer-Lescano and Teubner, 2006; 2007; Teubner, 2006,175 *ff* [Engl trans 2006,338 *ff*]; Fischer-Lescano, 2005,187 *ff*; Koskenniemi and Päivi, 2002; Koskenniemi, 2004, 205 *f*; 2006a; 2006b; 2008,70 *ff*. Ladeur and Viellechner (2008,60) rightly point out, however, that tendencies towards fragmentation already exist within national states themselves.

fragmentation is not recognised the alternative presented is 'constitutional utopia'.[13] From the standpoint of a systemic functional approach, mere affirmation of teleological utopias or simple recognition of fragmentation does not constitute an alternative but rather indicates respectively excess of normativism or realism in addressing the legal problems of world society.

Fragmentation in itself means nothing from the standpoint of system integration. Fragments may remain entirely disconnected, in which case they will have paralysing or destructive effects on other fragments. The problem is how to integrate these fragments into a 'differentiated communication order'.[14] How can relations of interdependency among the fragments be constructed? This is the question of system integration.

Luhmann defines integration (or system integration) as a 'reduction in the degree of freedom for subsystems' or as a 'limitation of degrees of freedom for selections',[15] thus suggesting, negatively as *dependency*, that this notion points both to interdependency among systems and to dependency for persons on functional systems.[16] With regard to the dependency of persons on social systems, Luhmann says world society is over-integrated and thus requires de-integration.[17] However, it should be noted that the interdependency of social systems points to strong negative tendencies toward disintegration (fragmentation), which also entails a danger of dedifferentiation. It is possible to argue in this case that a certain degree of intersystemic disintegration contributes to excessive integration (dependency) of persons with regard to social systems. However, this question of the excessive integration of persons intersects with the problem of 'social integration' (inclusion/exclusion),[18] so the primary aspect of the concept of integration is systemic interdependency, especially among functional systems. Thus, what world society needs is more system integration, so that mere fragmentation does not lead to splinters or debris without functional meaning.

In this respect, from the standpoint of the legal system transconstitutionalism serves as *one* structural model of functional connection among the fragmented functional spheres of world society. This is because what is lacking in mere fragmentation is structure.[19] First, by offering 'bridges of transition' between legal orders that in principle are fragmented, transconstitutionalism helps structure the legal system without leading to an ultimate hierarchical

[13] *See* Koskenniemi, 2006a.

[14] Luhmann, 1965, 25. *See* p 158 above.

[15] Luhmann, 1997, vol 2, 603 and 631.

[16] Luhmann, 1997, vol 2, 618 *ff*.

[17] Luhmann, 1997, vol 2, 618 and 631 *f*; *cf* 1993a, 584 [Engl trans 2004, 489]; 1995b, 259 *f*.

[18] 'We want to replace the theme of social integration with the inclusion/exclusion difference' (Luhmann, 1997, vol 2,619).

[19] Luhmann has this to say on the concept of structure: 'Structures anchor a fragment of the possible as expectable' (Luhmann, 1987a, 41). Later he adds: 'Structures are indeed necessary since they restrict the space for adequate connections among operations so broadly that the development of one operation after another is feasible. It might also be said that they are a necessary reduction of complexity' (Luhmann, 1997, vol 1, 437).

unity.[20] It may present itself as the reflexive structure of the 'multilevel' or multicentric world legal system (consistency). In addition, it can contribute to the legal system's capacity to respond to the complex problems of world society by offering normative models for the treatment of conflictual relations among the various social systems (adequate complexity).[21] Mere fragments internal and external to the legal system find in transconstitutionalism, from the partial standpoint of law, the constitutional elements that can contribute to its structural connection and hence help promote a differentiated communication order.

Unlike Luhmann, I do not refer to the 'maintenance' of a differentiated communication order (*see* p 158 above), since this formulation is valid only to specific social dimensions of the planet.[22] The significant complexity of world society makes functional differentiation essential, but such differentiation has come about only to a limited extent and this is one of the paradoxes of today's world society. Its basic functional requirement is only very sparsely realised. This problem relates as much to systemic corruption as to fragmentation and indeed these two phenomena are connected to some extent. The question, therefore, is the need to 'promote' the stable structures of a differentiated communication order by transversely connecting the fragments. This will be achieved neither by teleological 'constitutional utopias' nor by ultimate normative orders, but by models that offer conditions for an 'interweaving' of the fragments. By promoting 'dialogue' among legal orders on constitutional issues and linking identity to alterity in their relations, transconstitutionalism fosters differentiated communication both between the legal system and the outside world, and within the legal system itself.

III. NORMATIVE CLAIM: BEYOND HEGEMONY AND COMMUNITY – PROMOTING INCLUSION ('SOCIAL INTEGRATION')

Although the normative dimension is not totally disconnected from the functional dimension, it is necessary to distinguish between the plane of functional requirements (relations between problems and solutions) and that of normative claims, which has to do with expectations that are counterfactually stabilised in the sphere of world society.[23] From this derive elementary normative structures related to the highly complex multicentric society.[24] Transconstitutionalism

[20] Thus it is not a matter of seeking the unity (supposedly lost or to be maintained) of public international law, as a strategy against the 'danger of fragmentation' (Dupuy, 1999).

[21] The assumption here is that 'socially adequate legal concepts' (Luhmann, 1974, 49 *ff*) depend upon legally adequate concepts (Neves, 1992, 208; *cf* Luhmann, 1990e, 10).

[22] *Cf* Neves, 2006b, especially 266 *ff*.

[23] On the distinction between normative expectations (resistant to the reality that disappoints them) and cognitive expectations (willing to learn and change in response to the disappointments of reality), *see* Luhmann, 1987a, 40–53; 1987c, 436–43 [Engl trans 1995, 319–25].

[24] On the distance he takes from normative theories of society, Luhmann explains: 'This sceptical abstinence vis-à-vis norm-centred theory does not, of course, imply that one can imagine a possible societal life without norms. Binding oneself to norms or values is a pervasive aspect of social life' (1987c, 444 [Engl trans 1995, 325 *f*]).

presents itself as a basic normative counterpoint to both the expansionary primacy of the cognitive *structures* of world society (linked to the economy, technology, and science) and the *semantics* of the control of information (and knowledge) by the mass media.

A tendency in critical studies of legal internationality or transnationality is the affirmation of the hegemonic nature of law.[25] Thus Koskenniemi argues that public international law is a 'hegemonic technique'[26] and points to the professional capacity to distinguish between 'hegemonic and counter-hegemonic narratives'.[27] In this context, 'community' is presented as the alternative in the following terms: 'Unlike claims of privilege or interest, claims of law constitute the claimants as members of a legal, and thus also a political, community.'[28] From this perspective, although international law is considered a hegemonic technique with regard to interests and privileges, the 'international world' is considered a 'political community'.[29]

The hegemony model, developed most completely in the work of Gramsci,[30] becomes vague if used without specific contours. Plural relations between hegemony and counterhegemony are inherent in any 'political community' and can be transcended only in the 'utopia' of a purely moral community. Thus it is not appropriate to posit an alternative between hegemony and community.

Beyond this, however, the concept of 'political community' applied to the 'international world' is inadequate, since the concept of community implies a type of social relationship of membership, as well as solidarity grounded in the sharing of common values.[31] The notion of political community serves to describe premodern forms of society.[32] In its turn, membership, under contemporary conditions of differentiation between society and organisation, refers to belonging to a given organisation (*see* p 9 above). The 'international world' is not an organisation. For world society, indeed, any attempt to use the rhetoric of community is rather a rhetorical expression of the hegemonic discourse. What we do have are communication systems, language games, different groups and individuals, in a heterogeneous confluence of interests, values, and expectations in general. Indubitably there are community formations within today's world society (or 'international world'), but understanding the term as 'political community' is both a theoretical and a practical disaster.

[25] On this subject, *see* Koskenniemi, 2004; Buckel and Fischer-Lescano, 2008; Buckel and Fischer-Lescano(eds), 2007.

[26] Koskenniemi, 2004, 198.

[27] Koskenniemi, 2004, 202.

[28] Koskenniemi, 2004, 214.

[29] 'Freedom and equality, however, can be realised only if the international world is understood as a political community' (Koskenniemi, 2004, 215).

[30] Gramsci, 1999, distinguishing hegemony (civil society) and domination (state) (especially 145).

[31] It can be said, with Habermas (1992, 198 *f* [Engl trans 1996, 160 *f*]), that community is an ethical unit with collective values defined as preferences regarding the 'good life' for the respective group.

[32] Hence the distinction between community (ancient, traditional) and society (modern) deriving from Tönnies (1979, especially 3–6, 34, 73 *ff*), via Weber (1985, especially 21–3). *Cf* Neves, 1992, 11 *ff*.

What is required for today's world society is the promotion of inclusion, via the reduction of the growing exclusion sector. In this regard, Luhmann warns of the danger of an 'avalanche of exclusion' as welfare states are dismantled even in the most developed parts of the world.[33] This relates to social integration in the sense used by systems theory: 'a person's chance to achieve social consideration'.[34] Strictly speaking, inclusion means access to the benefits of functional systems, and exclusion entails lack of access to such benefits. There is a paradox here: greater social integration (more inclusion) leads to less system integration (more degrees of freedom in relation to systems).[35] Thus while excluded, or rather under-included, sectors are over-integrated (hyperdependent on systems: 'deprived', without 'freedom'), over-included sectors, especially in peripheral modernity, enjoy access to the benefits of social systems but do not depend on their restrictions (lack of capacity for imputation on the part of the respective social systems) and thus tend to promote de-integration. This entails a relationship between the normative dimension of social integration and the functional dimension of system integration: systemic corruption, a moral problem of world society according to Luhmann (and requiring moralisation in pathological cases – *see* p 31 above), can develop intensely when sectors are over-included and exclusion or under-inclusion (dependent sectors without access to systemic benefits) therefore increases. Furthermore, although exclusion is paradoxically produced as a side-effect of functional systems it undermines functional differentiation (*see* note 43 to Chapter 4 above).

The promotion of inclusion linked to a confrontation with the various forms of systemic corruption in the plane of world society is more likely to take place if transconstitutionalism develops in the tangled 'multilevel' legal system rather than in isolated orders, especially if the latter have claims to constitute communities. This is because the legal identity of each order linked to transconstitutionalalterity makes possible the universalisation of rights, regardless of membership of a given community. A fundamental assertion falls into place at this point: what is required in the sphere of transconstitutionalism is not membership or community, but the promotion of generalised inclusion, or better still the reduction of increasing primary exclusion, especially with regard to law, in the context of a heterogeneous and differentiated communication structure. Hence, the importance of perceiving that not only systemic corruption is a moral problem of today's world society, but so is the associated exclusion of huge swathes of world society from the elementary benefits of functional systems. If moralisation in today's world society has meaning for functional systems only in pathological cases, then it must be concluded that the goal of transconstitutionalism's normative claim is to affirm itself counterfactually against the 'pathologies of normalcy'.

[33] Luhmann, 2000a, 427 *f*.
[34] Luhmann, 1997, vol 2, 620.*Cf* note 18 to this Chapter.
[35] Luhmann, 1997, vol 2, 631.

Final Comment: The Other Can See Your Blind Spot

THE CONSTITUTION PRESENTS itself as the basic instance of normative self-grounding for the state as a territorial politico-legal organisation. As the basic criterion for the state legal order's self-understanding, the constitution cannot be put aside by interpreters and enforcers of the constitutional order, or rather by those upon whom it is incumbent to concretise it as an order with normative force, especially constitutional judges and courts. In this sense, it constitutes an 'inviolate level' (in Hofstadter's sense) of the legal order of the constitutional state. But in the dynamic constitutional game the 'inviolate level' may be involved (tangled) with other levels, forming a 'supertangled level'.[1] In our context, this means that although the constitutions of constitutional states normatively bind their concretisers, especially constitutional courts and judges, they are permanently reconstructed via interpretation and application by those same concretisers. This is the paradox of tangled hierarchies: a constitutional ruling is normatively subordinated to the constitution and affirms what is constitutional by concretising the constitution.

In Brazil's recent experience, the transformation of the understanding of the hierarchical position of treaties on human rights ratified without the procedural requirements of Article 5, paragraph 3, of the Federal Constitution in the case law of the Supreme Court (STF) is a clear demonstration that the inviolability of a constitution is defined dynamically by normative acts subordinated to that order. Under previously dominant case law, which persisted from the time the 1988 Constitution came into force until recently, it was clear that treaties were on the same hierarchical level as ordinary law.[2] The new case law, fixed in the already cited judgment of RE 466.343/SP (together with HC87.585/TO and RE 349.703/RS) on 3 December 2008, established the supralegality of treaties on human rights, with a significant number (albeit a minority of four to five) of justices voting to place human rights treaties ratified by Brazil on the same level as constitutional norms, although none of them wanted to maintain previous case law.[3] The Constitution as an 'inviolate level' was reconstructed by 'lower' normative levels. Whereas in principle the Constitution is a normative 'metalanguage' with regard to the acts of constitutional jurisdiction, constituting the

[1] *See* Hofstadter, 1979, 686 *ff*.

[2] *Cf* Mendes, Coelho and Branco, 2007, 659 *ff*, citing a huge volume of case law.

[3] RE 466.343/SP, RE 349.703/RS, HC 87585/TO, judgment of 3 December 2008, TP, DJe 05/06/2009 and 26/06/2009 (*see* pp 92 *f* above).

respective 'object language', it became the 'object language' for those acts, which from a different angle were transformed into a 'metalanguage'.[4] This case is a clear indication that the constitutionally self-grounded state legal order entails tangled hierarchies or 'strange loops' involving even the (in principle) inviolate level, that is, the constitution itself.

However, the example cited presents nothing special with regard to any act of constitutional jurisdiction. What it evidences above all is the profound change that has taken place under the conditions prevailing in today's world society, whereby transconstitutionalism is transcending provincial or parochial constitutionalism. This change, which I have tried to show in this book through a discussion of various cases, should be taken seriously. The state has ceased to be a privileged locus for solving constitutional problems. Albeit fundamental and indispensable, it is only one of several loci for cooperation and competition in pursuit of solutions to such problems. The increasing system integration of world society has led to the de-territorialisation of juridico-constitutional problem cases, which, as it were, have emancipated themselves from the state. This situation, however, should not lead to new illusions, such as a search for definitive 'inviolate levels': internationalism as *ultima ratio*, in a new absolute hierarchisation; supranationalism as a legal panacea; transnationalism as fragmentation to cast off the shackles of the state; localism as the expression of a definitively inviolate ethicality.

Against these tendencies, transconstitutionalism entails the recognition that the various legal orders entangled in the search for a solution to a constitutional problem case that is concomitantly relevant to all of them – involving fundamental or human rights and the legitimate organisation of power – must pursue transversal forms of articulation in order to develop such a solution, each observing the others in an effort to understand its own limits and possibilities for contributing to the solution. Its identity is thereby reconstructed as long as it takes alterity seriously, always observing the other. In my view this is productive and enriching for identity itself, since every observer has a 'blind spot' and hence limited vision due to being in a certain position or observing from a certain vantage point.[5] However, while it is true, considering the diversity of vantage points from which alter and ego observe, that 'I see something you don't see',[6] it should be added that what is unseen by one observer owing to this 'blind spot' can be seen by another. In this sense, it can be affirmed that transconstitutionalism entails the recognition of the limits to observation of any given order and acknowledges the alternative: *the other can see your blind spot*.

[4] This is why the hierarchisation of metalanguage and object language, to use the terms of Bertrand Russell's theory of types, (1994 [1908], 75–80), is unsustainable, at least (to me) outside pure formal logic or mathematics. Hofstadter (1979, 21 *ff*) goes further, including these fields in his critique of Russell.

[5] Von Foerster, 1981, 288 *f*.

[6] Luhmann, 1990g [Engl trans 2002].

Bibliography

Ackerman, B (1991) *We the People 1: Foundations* (Cambridge, MA/London: Harvard University Press).
—— (1997) 'The Rise of World Constitutionalism' 83 *Virginia Law Review*, 771–97.
—— (1998) *We the People 2: Transformations* (Cambridge, MA/London: Harvard University Press).
Albert, M (2005) 'Politik der Weltgesellschaft und Politik der Globalisierung: Überlegungen zur Emergenz von Weltstaatlichkeit' in B Heintz, R Münch, and H Tyrell (eds), *Weltgesellschaft: Theoretische Zugänge und empirische Problemlagen* (*Sonderheft der Zeitschrift für Soziologie*, Stuttgart: Lucius & Lucius) 223–38.
—— (2007) 'Einleitung: Weltstaat und Weltstaatlichkeit: Neubestimmungen des Politischen in der Weltgesellschaft' in M Albert and R Stichweh (eds), *Weltstaat und Weltstaatlichkeit: Beobachtungen globaler politischer Strukturbildung* (Wiesbaden: VS Verlag) 9–23.
Albert, M and Schmalz-Bruns, R (2009) 'Antinomien der Global Governance: Mehr Weltstaatlichkeit, weniger Demokratie?' in H Brunkhorst (ed), *Demokratie in der Weltgesellschaft* (*Soziale Welt, Sonderband* 18, Baden-Baden: Nomos) 57–74.
Alexy, R (1986) *Theorie der Grundrechte* (Frankfurt am Main: Suhrkamp) [Engl trans: *A Theory of Constitutional Rights* (Oxford: Oxford University Press, 2002)].
—— (1999) 'Die Institutionalisierung der Menschenrechte im demokratischen Rechtsstaat' in S Gosepath and G Lohmann (eds), *Philosophie der Menschenrechte* (Frankfurt am Main: Suhrkamp) 244–64.
Almer, J (2008) 'Inter-Institutional Bargaining in the EU: Comitology and Financial Services' *Swedish Studies in European Law 2* (Oxford/Portland: Hart) 105–27.
Alt, H (2002) 'Konzeptuelle Metaphern und gesellschaftliche Prozesse' 13 *TRANS. Internet-Zeitschrift für Kulturwissenschaften*, September 2002.
Amann, DM (2004) 'Guantánamo' 42 (2) *Columbia Journal of Transnational Law*, 263–348.
Arango, R (2005) *El concepto de derechos sociales fundamentales* (Bogotá: Universidad Nacional de Bogotá/Legis).
Arendt, H (1973) *The Origins of Totalitarianism*. New edition with added preface (New York: A Harvest Book).
—— (1989) *The Human Condition* (Chicago/London: The University of Chicago Press) [1st edn 1958].
Aristotle (1944) *Politics*. With an English translation by H Rackham (Cambridge, MA/London: Harvard University Press).
Atlan, H (1979) *Entre le cristal et la fumée: Essai sur l'organisation du vivant* (Paris: Seuil).
Ávila, H (2008) *Teoria dos princípios: da definição à aplicação dos princípios jurídicos* 8th edn (São Paulo: Saraiva).
Bandeira de Mello, CA (1993) *Conteúdo jurídico do princípio da igualdade* 3rd edn (São Paulo: Malheiros).

Barreto, IC (2007) 'Les effets de la jurisprudence de la Cour européenne des droits de l'homme sur l'ordre juridique et judiciaire portugais' in *Liber Amicorum Luzius Wildhaber: Human Rights – Strasbourg Views / Droits de l'homme – Regards de Strasbourg* (Kehl/Strasbourg/Arlington, VA: Engel) 65–89.
Barroso, LR (2008) 'Diferentes, mas iguais: O reconhecimento jurídico das relações homoafetivas no Brasil' in D Sarmento, D Ikawa and F Piovesan (eds), *Igualdade, diferença e direitos humanos* (Rio de Janeiro: Lumen Juris) 661–93.
Barroso, LR and de Barcelos, AP (2005) 'O começo da história: a nova interpretação constitucional e o papel dos princípios no direito brasileiro' in VA da Silva (ed), *Interpretação constitucional* (São Paulo: Malheiros) 271–316.
Bass, NA (2002–2003) 'The Implications of the TRIPS Agreement for Developing Countries: Pharmaceutical Patent Laws in Brazil and South Africa in the 21st Century' *George Washington International Law Review* 34 (Washington: George Washington University) 191–222.
Baudenbacher, C (2003) 'Judicial Globalization: New Development or Old Wine in New Bottles' in *Texas International Law Journal*, vol 38 (Austin: University of Texas at Austin School of Law Publications) 505–26.
Beck, U (1997) *Was ist Globalisierung? Irrtümer des Globalismus – Antworten auf Globalisierung* (Frankfurt am Main: Suhrkamp).
——1999) *Schöne neue Arbeitswelt – Vision: Weltbürgergesellschaft* (Frankfurt am Main/New York: Campus).
Bergström, CF (2005) *Comitology: Delegation of Powers in the European Union and the Committee System* (Oxford: Oxford University Press).
Berlin, I (1975) 'Two Concepts of Liberty' (1958) in I Berlin, *Four Essays on Liberty* (London/Oxford/New York: Oxford University Press)118–72 [reprint of the 1st edn 1969].
Berman, HJ (1983) *Law and Revolution: The Formation of the Western Legal Tradition* (Cambridge, MA/London: Harvard University Press).
Berman, PS (2005) 'From International Law to Law and Globalization' 43 (2) *Columbia Journal of Transnational Law* 485–556.
Biaggini, G (2000) 'Die Idee der Verfassung – Neuausrichtung im Zeitalter der Globalisierung?' in 141 (119 in the new series) *Zeitschrift für Schweizerisches Recht* 445–76.
Bickel, AM (1978) *The Supreme Court and the Idea of Progress* (New Haven/London: Yale University Press).
Bilchitz, D (2003) 'South Africa: Right to Health and Access to HIV/AIDS Drug Treatment' 1 (3) *International Journal of Constitutional Law* 524–34.
Birman, Pand Lehmann, D (1999) 'Religion and the Media in a Battle for Ideological Hegemony: the Universal Church of the Kingdom of God and *TV Globo* in Brazil' 18 (2) *Bulletin of Latin American Research* 145–64.
Blankenburg, E (1977) 'Über die Unwirksamkeit von Gesetzen' 63 *Archiv für Rechts- und Sozialphilosophie* 31–58.
Blumenberg, H (1998) *Paradigmen zu einer Methaphorologie* (Frankfurt am Main: Suhrkamp).
Bobbio, N (1984) *Il futuro della democrazia: Una difesa delle regole del gioco* (Turin: Einaudi).
——(1989) 'Il terzo assente' in N Bobbio, *Il terzo assente: Saggi e discorsi sulla pace e la guerra* (Turin: Sonda) 215–17.

——(1996) *The Age of Rights*, Engl trans by A Cameron (Cambridge: Polity Press).

Böckenförde, E-W (1983) 'Geschichtliche Entwicklung und Bedeutungswandel der Verfassung' in *Festschrift für Rudolf Gmür* (Bielefeld: Gieseking) 7–19.

Bodin, J (1986) *Les six Livres de la République. Livre premier*. Paris: Fayard [1st edn, Paris, 1576].

Booysen, H (2003) *Principles of International Trade Law as a Monistic System* (Pretoria: Interlegal).

Bordes, J (1967) *Politeia dans la pensée grecque jusqu'à Aristote* (Paris: 'Les Belles Lettres').

Botero, ES (2005) 'Reflexiones en torno de la jurisdicción especial indígena en Colombia' 41 *RevistaII DH/Instituto Interamericano de Derechos Humanos* 225–51.

——(2006) *Entre el Juez Salomón y el Dios Sira. Decisiones interculturales e interés superior del niño* (Bogotá, Universidad de Amsterdam y Unicef).

Bradley, K St C (1997) 'The European Parliament and Comitology: On the Road to Nowhere' 3 *European Law Journal* 230–54.

Brooks, RE (2005) 'Failed States, or the State as Failures' 72 (4) *University of Chicago Law Review* 1159–96.

Brunkhorst H (1999) 'Heterarchie und Demokratie' in H Brunkhorst and P Niesen (eds), *Das Recht der Republik* (Frankfurt am Main: Suhrkamp) 373–85.

——(2002) *Solidarität: Von der Bürgerfreundschaft zur globalen Rechtsgenossenschaft* (Frankfurt am Main: Suhrkamp) [Engl trans: *Solidarity: From Civic Friendship to a Global Legal Community* (Cambridge, MA: MIT Press, 2005)].

——(2007) 'Zwischen transnationaler Klassenherrschaft und egalitärer Konstitutionalisierung. Europas zweite Chance' in P Niesen and B Herborth (eds), *Anarchie der kommunikativen Freiheit: Jürgen Habermas und die Theorie der internationalen der Politik* (Frankfurt am Main: Suhrkamp) 321–49.

——(2008a)'Kritik am Dualismus des internationalen Rechts– Hans Kelsen und die Völkerrechtsrevolution des 20. Jahrhunderts' in R Kreide and A Niederberger (eds), *Transnationale Verrechtlichung. Nationale Demokratien im Kontext globaler Politik* (Frankfurt am Main/New York: Campus) 30–62.

——(2008b) 'Taking Democracy Seriously: Europe after the Failure of its Constitution' in EO Eriksen, C Joerges and F Rödl (eds), *Law, Democracy and Solidarity in a Post-national Union: The Unsettled Political Order of Europe* (London/New York: Routledge) 213–29.

Brunkhorst, H, Köhler, WR and Lutz-Bachmann, M (eds) (1999) *Recht auf Menschenrechte: Menschenrechte, Demokratie und internationale Politik* (Frankfurt am Main: Suhrkamp).

Buckel, S (2007) *Subjektivierung und Kohäsion: Zur Rekonstruktion einer materialistischen Theorie des Rechts* (Frankfurt am Main: Velbrück).

——(2008) '"Judge without a legislator" – Transnationalisierung der Rechtsform' in H Brunkhorst and R Voigt (eds), *Rechts-Staat: Staat, internationale Gemeinschaft und Völkerrecht bei Hans Kelsen* (Baden-Baden: Nomos) 269–81.

Buckel, S and Fischer-Lescano, A (eds) (2007) '*Hegemonie gepanzert mit Zwang: Zivilgesellschaft und Politik im Staatsverständnis Antonio Gramscis*' (Baden-Baden: Nomos).

Buckel, S and Fischer-Lescano, A (2008) 'Emanzipatorische Gegenhegemonie im Weltrecht' in R Kreide and A Niederberger (eds), *Transnationale Verrechtlichung. Nationale Demokratien im Kontext globaler Politik* (Frankfurt am Main/New York: Campus) 114–33.

Burdeau, G (1949) *Traité de Science Politique* 2nd edn (Paris: Librairie Générale de Droit et de Jurisprudence) vol I.
Burgorgue-Larsen, L (2009) 'El Sistema Interamericano de Protección de los Derechos Humanos: Entre clasicismo y creatividad' in A von Bogdandy, CL Arroyo and MM Antoniazzi (eds), *¿Integración suramericana a través del derecho? Un análisis multidiciplinario y multifocal* (Heidelberg: Max Planck Institute for Comparative Public Law and International Law/Madrid: Centro de Estudios Constitucionales) 287–338.
Calliess, G-P (2002) 'Reflexive Transnational Law: The Privatisation of Civil Law and the Civilisation of Private Law' *Zeitschrift für Rechtssoziologie* 23 (Stuttgart: Lucius & Lucius) 185–216.
Canotilho, JJG (1991) *Direito constitucional* 5th edn (Coimbra: Almedina).
——(2006) *'Brancosos' e interconstitucionalidade: Itinerários dos discursos sobre a historicidade constitucional* (Coimbra: Almedina).
Carbonell, M (2004) 'Constitución, minorías culturales y derechos indígenas en América Latina' in FS Migallón (ed), *Estudios jurídicos en homenaje a Antonio Martínez Báez* (Mexico: Porrúa/Universidad Nacional Autónoma de México) 61–78.
Carotti, B (2007) 'L'Icann e la governance di Internet' 57 *Rivista Trimestrale de Diritto Pubblico* 681–721.
Cassese, A (1985) 'Modern Constitutions and International Law' 192 (3) *Recueil des Cours: Collected Courses of the Hague Academy of International Law* 331–475.
——(1989) 'The International Community's 'Legal' Response to Terrorism' 38 *International Law and Comparative Law Quarterly* 589–608.
——(2005a) *International Law* 2nd edn (Oxford/New York: Oxford University Press).
——(2005b) *I diritti umani oggi* (Rome/Bari: Laterza).
Cassese, S (2007) 'La funzione costituzionale dei giudici non statali. Dallo spazio giuridico globale all'ordine giuridico globale' 57 *Rivista Trimestrale de Diritto Pubblico* 609–26.
Chacon, V (1969) *Da Escola do Recife ao Código Civil (Artur Orlando e sua geração)* (Rio de Janeiro: Simões).
Chesterman, S (2005) 'Imposed Constitutions, Imposed Constitutionalism, and Ownership' 37 (4) *Connecticut Law Review* 947–54.
Choudhry, S (2005) 'Old Imperial Dilemma and the New Nation Building: Constitutive Constitutional Politics in Multinational Polities' 37 (4) *Connecticut Law Review* 933–45.
——(ed) (2006) *The Migration of Constitutional Ideas* (Cambridge: Cambridge University Press).
Christensen, R and Fischer-Lescano, A (2007) *Das Ganze des Rechts. Vom hierarchischen zum reflexiven Verständnis deutscher und europäischer Grundrechte* (Berlin: Duncker & Humblot).
Comparato, FK (1999) *A afirmação histórica dos direitos humanos* (São Paulo: Saraiva).
Copi, IM (1961) *Introduction to Logic* 2nd edn (New York: Macmillan).
Corcoran, EB (2011). 'Obama's Failed Attempt to Close Gitmo: WhyExecutive Orders Can't Bring About Systemic Change' 9 (2) *University of New Hampshire Law Review* 207–35.
Costa Neto, J (2013) 'A citação meramente retórica de precedentes judiciais estrangeiros no julgamento da ADPF 186 (cotas raciais na UnB)' 7 *Observatório da Jurisdição Constitucional* (forthcoming).

Dahl, RA (1972) *Polyarchy: Participation and Opposition* 2nd impression (New Haven/London: Yale University Press).

Dallari, D (1991) *Elementos de teoria geral do Estado* 16th edn (São Paulo: Saraiva).

Da Silva, JA (2000) *Poder constituinte e poder popular (Estudos sobre a sobre a Constituição)* (São Paulo: Malheiros).

Da Silva, VA (2009) *Direitos fundamentais: O conteúdo essencial, restrições e eficácia* (São Paulo: Malheiros).

——(2010) 'Colisões de direitos fundamentais entre ordem nacional e ordem transnacional' in M Neves (ed), *Transnacionalidade do direito: novas perspectivas dos conflitos entre ordens jurídicas* (São Paulo: Quartier Latin) 101–12.

Davis, DM (2003) 'Constitutional Borrowing: The Influence of Legal Culture and Local History in the Reconstitution of Comparative Influence: The South African Experience' 1 (2) *International Journal of Constitutional Law* 181–95.

De Barros Carvalho, P (2008) *Direito tributário: linguagem e método* (São Paulo: Noeses).

De Búrca, G (2003) 'Sovereignty and the Supremacy Doctrine of the European Court of Justice' in N Walker (ed), *Sovereignty in Transition* (Oxford/Portland, OR: Hart) 449–60.

De Keyser, P (2001) 'Exploring WTO Dispute Settlement in US Anti-Dumping Act 1916: An Easy Case?' *Jean Monnet Working Paper* 11/01 (Cambridge, MA: Harvard Law School/Jean Monnet Program) 33 pp.

Deleuze, G and Guattari, F (1976) *Rhizome: Introduction* (Paris: Minuit).

Della Cananea, G (2003) *L'Unione europea: Un ordinamento composito* (Roma/Bari: Laterza).

Delmas-Marty, M (2006) *Les forces imaginantes du droit (II): Le pluralisme ordonné* (Paris: Seuil).

——(2007) *Les forces imaginantes du droit (III): La refondation des pouvoirs* (Paris: Seuil).

De Oliveira, ML (ed) (2007) *O sistema interamericano de proteção dos direitos humanos – interface com o direito constitucional* (Belo Horizonte: Del Rey).

Derrida, J (1967) *De la Grammatologie* (Paris: Minuit).

——(1994) *Force de loi – Le 'Fondement mystique de l'autorité'* (Paris: Galilée) [Engl trans: 'Force of Law: The "Mystical Foundation of Authority"' (1990) 11 *Cardozo Law Review* July/Aug 919–1045].

De Ulhoa Cintra, G (1963) *De status civitatis: Alguns aspectos da cidadania romana* (São Paulo: livre-docência thesis presented at the University of São Paulo).

De Witte, B (1998) 'Sovereignty and European Integration: the Weight of Legal Tradition' in A-M Slaughter, A Stone Sweet and JHH Weiler (eds), *The European Court and National Courts – Doctrine and Jurisprudence: Legal Change in Its Social Context* (Oxford: Hart) 277–304.

Dezalay, Y and Garth, B (1996) *Dealing in Virtue: International Commercial Arbitration and the Construction of a Transnational Legal Order* (Chicago: University of Chicago Press).

Díez, CG-J (2008) 'Enemy Combatants versus Enemy Criminal: An Introduction to the European Debate Regarding Enemy Criminal Law and Its Relevance to the Anglo-American Discussion on the Legal Status of Unlawful Enemy Combatants' 11 *New Criminal Law Review* 529–62.

Dimoulis, D and Martins, L (2007) *Teoria geral dos direitos fundamentais* (São Paulo: Revista dos Tribunais).

Dorsen, N (moderator) (2005) 'A Conversation Between US Supreme Court Justices – The Relevance of Foreign Legal Material in US Constitutional Cases: A Conversation Between Justice Antonin Scalia and Justice Stephen Breyer' 3 *International Journal of Constitutional Law* 519–41.

Ducrot, O and Schaeffer, J-M (1995) *Nouveau dictionnaire encyclopédique des sciences du langage* (Paris: Éditions du Seuil).

Dudena, RA (2008) *Constitucionalismo europeu: auto-reprodução e hierarquias entrelaçadas no sistema constitucional europeu* (Lisbon: Master's Thesis presented at the Universidade Clássica de Lisboa and at the University of Hanover).

Dupuy, P-M (1997) 'The Constitutional Dimension of the Charter of the United Nations Revisited' in *Max Planck Yearbook of United Nations Law* 1 (Heidelberg: Max Planck Institute for Comparative Public Law and International Law) 1–33.

——(1999) 'The Danger of Fragmentation or Unification of the International Legal System and The International Court of Justice' 31 *New York University Journal of International Law and Politics* 791–807.

Dworkin, R (1991) *Taking Rights Seriously* 6th impression (London: Duckworth) [first published 1977].

Eisenstadt, SN (2000a) *Die Vielfalt der Moderne* (Weilerswist: Velbrück Wissenschaft).

——(2000b) 'Multiple Modernities' 129 (1) *Daedalus* 1–29.

Engels, F (1988) 'Die Lage Englands. II. Die englische Konstitution' in K Marx and F Engels. *Werke*15th edn (Berlin: Dietz Verlag) vol I, 569–92 [first published in: *Vorwärts!*, no 75, 18 September 1844].

Epstein, L and Knight, J (2003) 'Constitutional Borrowing and Nonborrowing' 2 (3) *International Journal of Constitutional Law* 196–223.

Eskridge, WN (2004) 'United States: *Lawrence v Texas* and the Imperative of Comparative Constitutionalism' 1 (2) *International Journal of Constitutional Law* 555–60.

Esmein, A (1913) 'La maxime *Princeps legibus solutus est* dans l'ancien droit public français' in P Vinogradoff (ed), *Essays in Legal History* (London: Oxford University Press) 201–14.

Fassbender, B (1998) 'The United Nations Charter as Constitution of the International Community' 36 (3) *Columbia Journal of Transnational Law* 529–619.

——(2007) ''We the Peoples of the United Nations': Constituent Power and Constitutional Form in International Law' in M Loughlin and N Walker (eds), *The Paradox of Constitutionalism: Constituent Power and Constitutional Form* (Oxford: Oxford University Press) 269–90.

——(2008) 'Friede und Recht. Hans Kelsen und die Vereinten Nationen' in H Brunkhorst and R Voigt (eds), *Rechts-Staat: Staat, internationale Gemeinschaft und Völkerrecht bei Hans Kelsen* (Baden-Baden: Nomos) 127–47.

Feldman, N (2005) 'Imposed Constitutionalism' 37 (4) *Connecticut Law Review* 857–89.

Ferrajoli, L (1997) *La sovranità nel mondo moderno. Nascita e crisi dello Stato nazionale* (Rome-Bari: Editori Laterza).

Ferry, L and Renaut, A (1992) *Philosophie politique 3 – Des droits de l'homme à l'idée républicaine* 3rd edn (Paris: Presses Universitaires de France) [1st edn 1985].

Fischer-Lescano, A (2003) 'Die Emergenz der Globalverfassung'63 (3) *Zeitschrift für ausländisches öffentliches Recht und Völkerrecht* 717–60.

——(2005) *Globalverfassung: Die Geltungsbegründung der Menschenrechte* (Weilerswist: Velbrück).

Fischer-Lescano, A, Joerges, C and Wonka, A (eds) (2010) *The German Constitutional Court's Lisbon Ruling: Legal and Political Science Perspectives – ZERP Diskussionsbeiträge* 1/2010 (Bremen: University of Bremen).
Fischer-Lescano, A and Teubner, G (2006). *Regime-Kollisionen: Zur Fragmentierung des globalen Rechts* (Frankfurt am Main: Suhrkamp).
—— (2007) 'Fragmentierung des Weltrechts: Vernetzung globaler Regimes statt etatischer Rechtseinheit' in M Albert and R Stichweh (eds), *Weltstaat und Weltstaatlichkeit: Beobachtungen globaler politischer Strukturbildung* (Wiesbaden: VS Verlag) 37–61.
Fiss, O (2007) 'The War Against Terrorism and the Rule of Law' in *Liber Amicorum Luzius Wildhaber: Human Rights – Strasbourg Views/Droits de l'homme – Regards de Strasbourg* (Kehl/Strasbourg/Arlington, VA: Engel) 1239–63.
Forst, R (2007) *Das Recht auf Rechtfertigung: Elemente einer konstruktivistischen Theorie der Gerechtigkeit* (Frankfurt am Main: Suhrkamp).
Fouchard, P, Gaillard, E and Goldman, B (1996) *Traité de l'arbitrage international* (Paris: Litec).
Frank, TM (2007) 'United States – *Hamdan v Rumsfeld*: President Power in Wartime' 5 (2) *International Journal of Constitutional Law* 380–8.
Fraser, N (1992) 'Rethinking the Public Sphere: A Contribution to the Critique of Actually Existing Democracy' in C Calhoun (ed), *Habermas and Public Sphere* (Cambridge, MA: The MIT Press) 109–42.
—— (2004) 'Institutionalizing Democratic Justice: Redistribution, Recognition, and Participation' in S Benhabib and N Fraser (eds), *Pragmatism, Critique, Judgment: Essays for Richard J Bernstein* (Cambridge, MA: The MIT Press) 125–47.
Fraser, N and Honneth, A (2003) *Umverteilung oder Anerkennung? Eine politisch-philosophische Kontroverse* (Frankfurt am Main: Suhrkamp).
Friedman, B and Saunders, C (2003) 'Symposium: Constitutional Borrowing – Editor's Introduction' 1 (2) *International Journal of Constitutional Law* 177–80.
Friedman, LM (2004) 'Frontiers: National and Transnational Order' in K-H Ladeur (ed), *Public Governance in the Age of Globalization* (Aldershot: Ashgate) 25–50.
Fromm, E (1956) *The Sane Society* (London: Routledge & Kegan Paul).
Frowein, JA (1983) 'Die Verpflichtungen erga omnes im Völkerrecht und ihre Durchsetzung' in R Bernhardt *et al* (eds), *Völkerrecht als Rechtsordnung – Internationale Gerichtsbarkeit – Menschenrechte: Festschrift für Hermann Mosler* (Berlin/Heidelberg/New York: Springer-Verlag) 241–62.
—— (1994) 'Reactions by Not Directly Affected States to Breaches of Public International Law' in *Recueil des Cours: Collected Courses of the Hague Academy of International Law* 248 (1994) IV (Hague: Académie de Droit International de La Haye/Dordrecht: Nijhoff, 1995) 345–437.
—— (2000) 'Konstitutionalisierung des Völkerrechts' in *Völkerrecht und Internationales Recht in einem sich globalisierenden internationalen System – Auswirkung der Entstaatlichung transnationaler Rechtsbeziehungen* (*Berichte der Deutschen Gesellschaft für Völkerrecht*, vol 39) (Heidelberg: Müller) 427–45.
—— (2003) 'The Incorporation of the European Convention on Human Rights into the Legal Order of Germany' in MD Đilas and V Đeri ,*The International and the National: Essays in Honour of Vojin Dimitrijevi* (Belgrade: Belgrade Centre for Human Rights)207–14.
Fustel de Coulanges, ND (1908) *La Cité antique – Étude sur le culte, le droit, les institutions de la Grèce et de Rome* 20th edn (Paris: Hachette) [1st edn 1864] [Engl trans: *The*

Ancient City: A Study on the Religion, Laws, and Institutions of Greece and Rome (Kitchener, Ontario: Batoche Books, 2001)].

Gabriel, RH (1940) *The Course of American Democratic Thought. An Intellectual History since 1815* (New York: The Ronald Press Company).

Gaillard, E (1999) 'The Enforcement of Awards Set Aside in the Country of Origin' 14 (1) *ICSID Review – Foreign Investment Law Journal* 16–45.

——(2001) 'Transnational Law: a Legal System or a Method of Decision Making?' 17 (1) *Arbitration International* 39–72.

Galindo, GRB (2005) 'A reforma do judiciário como retrocesso para a proteção internacional dos direitos humanos: um estudo sobre o novo § 3º do artigo 5º da Constituição Federal' 7 (1)*Cena Internacional* 83–102.

Gauchet, M (1989) *La Révolution des droits de l'homme* (Paris: Gallimard).

Geiss, R (2004) 'Failed States – Legal Aspects and Security Implications' 47 *German Yearbook of International Law* 457–501.

——(2005) *'Failed States': Die normative Erfassung gescheiterter Staaten* (Berlin: Duncker & Humblot).

Giddens, A (1991) *The Consequences of Modernity* (Cambridge: Polity Press).

Giegerich, T (2003) 'Einführung: Transnationale Konstitutionalisierung als Antwort auf die Globalisierung' in Thomas Giegerich. *Europäische Verfassung und deutsche Verfassung im transnationalen Konstitutionalisierungsprozess: Wechselseitige Rezeption, konstitutionelle Evolution und föderale Verflechtung* (Berlin: Springer) 1–13.

Ginsburg, RB (1999) 'Affirmative Action as an International Human Rights Dialogue'. Lecture delivered at Cardozo Law School on 17 February 1999. Available at the American Bar Associationwebsite [first published (2000) 18 (1) *Brookings Law Review*].

——(2005a) '*Brown v Board of Education* in International Context' 36 (3) *Columbia Human Rights Law Review* 493–511.

——(2005b) '"A Decent Respect to the Opinions of [Human]kind": The Value of a Comparative Perspective in Constitutional Adjudication' 64 (3) *Cambridge Law Journal* 575–92.

Göbel, A (1995) 'Paradigmatische Erschöpfung. Wissenssoziologische Bemerkungen zum Fall Carl Schmitts' in A Göbel, D van Laak and I Villinger (eds), *Metamorphosen des Politischen. Grundfragen politischer Einheitsbildung seit den 20er Jahren* (Berlin: Akademie) 267–86.

Goldman, B (1964) 'Frontières du droit et 'lex mercatoria' 9 *Archives de Philosophie du Droit* 177–92.

Golove, D (2005) 'United States: The Bush Administration's 'War on Terrorism' in the Supreme Court' 3 (1) *International Journal of Constitutional Law* 128–46.

Gomes, LF (2008) 'Direito internacional dos direitos humanos: vigência, validade e operacionalidade do princípio *pro homine* in Z Fachin (ed), *20 anos de Constituição Cidadã* (Rio de Janeiro: Forense/São Paulo: Método) 179–90.

Gordon, R (1997) 'Saving Failed States: Sometimes a Neocolonialist Notion' 12 *American University Journal of International Law & Policy* 903–74.

Gramsci, A (1999) *Selections from the Prison Notebooks*. Edited and translated by Q Hoare and GN Smith (London: ElecBook).

Grau, ER (2002) *Ensaio e discurso sobre a interpretação do direito* (São Paulo: Malheiros).

Greven, MT (1999) *Die politische Gesellschaft. Kontingenz und Dezision als Probleme des Regierens und der Demokratie* (Opladen: Leske & Budrich).

Grimm, D (1987) 'Entstehungs- und Wirkungsbedingungen des modernen Konstitutionalismus' in Dieter Simon (ed), *Akten des 26. Deutschen Rechtshistorikertages: Frankfurt am Main, 22. bis 26. September 1986* (Frankfurt am Main: Klostermann) 45–76.

——(1989) 'Verfassung'in Görres-Gesellschaft (ed), *Staatslexikon: Recht • Wirtschaft • Gesellschaft* 7th edn (Freiburg/Basle/Vienna: Herder) vol V, cols 633–43.

——(1995a) 'Konstitution, Grundgesetz(e) von der Aufklärung bis zur Gegenwart' in H Mohnhaupt and D Grimm, *Verfassung: Zur Geschichte des Begriffs von der Antike bis zur Gegenwart; zwei Studien* (Berlin: Duncker & Humblot) 100–41.

—— (1995b)*Braucht Europa eine Verfassung?* (Munich: Carl Siemens Stiftung, series 'Themen', vol 62).

——(2004a) 'Can the 'Post-National Constellation' be Re-Constitutionalized?' *TranState Working Papers*no 2 (Bremen: University of Bremen).

——(2004b) 'Integration durch Verfassung: Absichten und Aussichten im europäischen Konstitutionalisierungsprozess' 32 (4) *Leviathan: Zeitschrift für Sozialwissenschaft* 448–63.

Gross, O (2006) '"Control Systems" and the Migration of Anomalies' in S Choudhry (ed), *The Migration of Constitutional Ideas* (Cambridge: Cambridge University Press) 403–30.

Grote, R (1999) 'The Status and Rights of Indigenous Peoples in Latin America' 59 *Zeitschrift für ausländisches öffentliches Recht und Völkerrecht* 497–528.

Grotius, H (1950) *Drei Bücher vom Recht des Krieges und des Frieden.* German version edited by Walter Schätzel (Tübingen: Mohr) [original: *De jure belli ac pacis – libri tres*, Paris, 1625].

Günther, K (1988) *Der Sinn für Angemessenheit: Anwendungsdiskurse in Moral und Recht* (Frankfurt am Main: Suhrkamp) [Engl trans: *The Sense of Appropriateness: Application Discourses in Morality and Law* (Albany: State University of New York Press, 1993)].

——(2001) 'Rechtspluralismus und universaler Code der Legalität: Globalisierung als rechtstheoretisches Problem' in L Wingert and K Günther (eds), *Die Öffentlichkeit der Vernunft und die Vernunft der Öffentlichkeit: Festschrift für Jürgen Habermas* (Frankfurt am Main: Suhrkamp) 539–67.

Günther, K and Randeria, S (2001) *Recht, Kultur und Gesellschaft im Prozeß der Globalisierung.* Série *Suchprozesse für Innovative Fragestellungen in der Wissenschaft*no 4 (Bad Homburg: Werner Reimers Stiftung).

Habermas, J (1982a) *Theorie des Kommunikativen Handelns* 2nd edn (Frankfurt am Main: Suhrkamp) 2 vols [1st edn 1981] [Engl trans: *The Theory of Communicative Action* (Boston: Beacon Press) vol 1, 1984; vol 2, 1987].

——(1982b) *Zur Rekonstruktion des Historischen Materialismus* 3rd edn (Frankfurt am Main: Suhrkamp) [1st edn 1976].

——(1988) 'Law and Morality' (The Tanner Lectures on Human Values, delivered at Harvard University, 1 and 2 October 1986), trans by Kenneth Baynes, in Sterling M McMurrin (ed), *The Tanner Lectures on Human Values*vol 8 (Salt Lake City: University of Utah Press) 217–79.

——(1992) *Faktizität und Geltung: Beiträge zur Diskurstheorie des Rechts und des demokratischen Rechtsstaats* (Frankfurt am Main: Suhrkamp) [Engl trans: *Between Facts and Norms: Contribution to a Discourse Theory of Law and Democracy* (Cambridge: Polity Press/Oxford: Blackwell, 1996)].

Habermas, J (1996) 'Kants Idee des ewigen Friedens – aus dem historischen Abstand von 200 Jahren' in J Habermas, *Die Einbeziehung des Anderen: Studien zur politischen Theorie* (Frankfurt am Main: Suhrkamp) 192–236.

——(1998a) *Die postnationale Konstellation: Politische Essays* (Frankfurt am Main: Suhrkamp) [Engl trans: *Post-National Constellation Political Essays* (Cambridge: Polity Press/Oxford: Blackwell, 2001)].

——(1998b) 'Jenseits des Nationalstaats? Bemerkungen zu Folgeproblemen der wirtschaftlichen Globalisierung' in Ulrich Beck (ed), *Politik der Globalisierung* (Frankfurt am Main: Suhrkamp) 67–84.

——(2000) 'Bestialität und Humanität: Ein Krieg an der Grenze zwischen Recht und Moral' in Reinhard Merkel (ed), *Der Kosovo-Krieg und das Völkerrecht* (Frankfurt am Main: Suhrkamp) 51–65.

——(2001) 'Braucht Europa eine Verfassung?' in J Habermas, *Zeit der Übergänge: Kleine Politische Schriften IX* (Frankfurt am Main: Suhrkamp) 104–29.

——(2004) 'Hat die Konstitutionalisierung des Völkerrechts noch eine Chance?' in J Habermas, *Der gespaltene Westen: Kleine Politische Schriften X* (Frankfurt am Main: Suhrkamp) 113–93.

——(2005) 'Eine politische Verfassung für die pluralistische Weltgesellschaft?' in J Habermas, *Zwischen Naturismus und Religion: Philosophische Aufsätze* (Frankfurt am Main: Suhrkamp) 324–65.

——(2007) 'Kommunikative Rationalität und grenzüberschreitende Politik: eine Replik' in P Niesen and B Herborth (eds), *Anarchie der kommunikativen Freiheit: Jürgen Habermas und die Theorie der internationalen Politik* (Frankfurt am Main: Suhrkamp) 406–59.

——(2008) 'Europapolitik in der Sachkasse: Plädoyer für eine Politik der abgestuften Integration' in J Habermas, *Ach, Europa: Kleine Politische Schriften XI* (Frankfurt am Main: Suhrkamp) 96–127.

——(2011) *Essay zur Verfassung Europas* (Berlin: Suhrkamp).

Hannikainen, L (1988) *Peremptory Norms (Jus Cogens) in International Law: Historical Development, Criteria, Present Status* (Helsinki: Finnish Lawyers' Publishing Company).

Hart, HLA (1994) *The Concept of Law* 2nd edn (Oxford: Clarendon Press) [1st edn 1961].

Harvard Law Review [Editorial Board] (2005) 'Comment: The Debate over Foreign Law in *Roper v Simmons*' 119 (1) *Harvard Law Review* 103–8.

Hartwig, M (2005) 'Much Ado About Human Rights: The Federal Constitutional Court Confronts the European Court of Human Rights' 6 (5) *German Law Journal* 869–94.

Hasebe, Y (2003) 'Constitutional Borrowing and Political Theory' 1 (2) *International Journal of Constitutional Law* 224–43.

Hedigan, J (2007) 'The Princess, the Press and Privacy: Observations on *Caroline von Hannover v Germany*' in *Liber Amicorum Luzius Wildhaber: Human Rights – Strasbourg Views/Droits de l'homme – Regards de Strasbourg* (Kehl/Strasbourg/Arlington, VA: Engel) 193–205.

Hegel, GWF (1967) *Jenaer Realphilosophie: Vorlesungsmanuskripte zur Philosophie der Natur und des Geistes von 1805–1806*, J Hoffmeister (ed) (Hamburg: Meiner) [reprint of the 1st edn 1931, originally entitled *Jenenser Realphilosophie II*].

——(1988) *Phänomenologie des Geistes* (Hamburg: Meiner) [1st edn, Bamberg/Würzburg, 1807].

Heintz, B, Münch, R and Tyrell, H (eds) (2005) *Weltgesellschaft: Theoretische Zugänge und empirische Problemlagen* (*Sonderheft der Zeitschrift für Soziologie*, Stuttgart: Lucius & Lucius).

Heintz, P (1982) *Die Weltgesellschaft im Spiegel von Ereignissen* (Diessenhofen: Rüegger).

Held, D and McGrew, A (2002) 'Introduction' in D Held and A McGrew (eds), *Governing Globalization: Power, Authority and Global Governance* (Cambridge: Polity Press) 1–21.

Heller, H (1934) *Staatslehre*. G Niemeyer (ed) (Leiden: AW Sijthoff).

Herdegen, M (1996) 'Der Wegfall effektiver Staatsgewalt im Völkerrecht: "The Failed State"' in *Berichte der Deutschen Gesellschaft für Völkerrecht* 34 (Heidelberg: CF Müller) 49–85.

Hespanha, AM (2007) *O caleidoscópio do direito: O direito e a justiça nos dias e no mundo de hoje* (Coimbra: Almedina).

Hesse, K (1980) *Grundzüge des Verfassungsrechts der Bundesrepublik Deutschland* 12th edn (Heidelberg/Karlsruhe: Müller).

Hillgenberg, H (2005) 'Incommunicado in Guantanamo' in *Internationale Gemeinschaft und Menschenrechte: Festschrift für Georg Ress zum 70. Geburtstag am 21. Januar 2005* (Cologne/Berlin/Munich: Heymanns) 133–40.

Hobbes, T (1992) *Leviathan*, R Tuck (ed) (Cambridge: Cambridge University Press) [1st edn, London, 1651].

Höffe, O (2002a) *Demokratie im Zeitalter der Globalisierung* (Munich: Beck).

—— (2002b) 'Globalität statt Globalismus. Über eine subsidiäre und föderale Weltrepublik' in M Lutz-Bachmann and D Bohman (eds), *Weltstaat oder Staatenwelt? Für und wider die Idee einer Weltrepublik* (Frankfurt am Main: Suhrkamp) 8–31.

—— (2008) 'Vision Weltrepublik. Eine philosophische Antwort auf die Globalisierung' in U Neumann and S Kirste (eds), *Rechtsphilosophie im 21. Jahrhundert* (Frankfurt am Main: Suhrkamp) 380–96.

Hoffmeister, F (2006) 'Germany: Status of European Convention on Human Rights in Domestic Law' 4 (4) *International Journal of Constitutional Law* 722–31.

Hofmann, R (2004) 'The German Federal Constitutional Court and Public International Law: New Decisions, New Approaches?' 47 *German Yearbook of International Law* 9–38.

Hofstadter, DR (1979) *Gödel, Escher, Bach: an Eternal Golden Braid* (Hassocks: The Harvester Press).

Hollerbach, A (1969) 'Ideologie und Verfassung' in W Maihofer (ed), *Ideologie und Recht* (Frankfurt am Main: Klostermann) 37–61.

Honneth, A (1994) *Kampf um Anerkennung: Zur moralischen Grammatik sozialer Konflikte* (Frankfurt am Main: Suhrkamp).

Hopkins, T and Wallerstein, I (1979) 'Grundzüge der Entwicklung des modernen Weltsystems' in D Senghaas (ed), *Kapitalistische Weltökonomie: Kontroverse über ihren Ursprung und ihre Entwicklungsdynamik* (Frankfurt am Main: Suhrkamp) 151–200.

Iturralde G, DA (2005) 'Reclamo y reconocimiento del derecho indígena en América Latina' 41 *RevistaIIDH/Instituto Interamericano de Derechos Humanos* 7–47.

Jackson, VC (2005) 'Constitutional Comparisons: Convergence, Resistance, Engagement' 119 *Harvard Law Review* 109–28.

Jakobs, G (2001). 'Personalität und Exklusion im Strafrecht' in N Courakis (ed), *Criminal Sciences in the 21st Century: Essays in Honour of Professor Dr Dionysios Spinellis* (Athens-Komotini: Ant N Sakkoulas Publishers) vol I, 447–67.

Janis, MW (2005) 'Human Rights and Imposed Constitutions' 37 (4) *Connecticut Law Review* 955–61.

Jellinek, G (1966) *Allgemeine Staatslehre* (Bad Homburg v. d. Höhe/Berlin/Zurich: Verlag Dr Max Gehlen) [reprint of the 3rd edn].

Jestaedt, M (1999) *Grundrechtsentfaltung im Gesetz* (Tübingen: Mohr).

—— (2008) 'Konkurrenz von Rechtsdeutungen statt Koexistenz von Rechtsordnungen' in H Brunkhorst and R Voigt (eds), *Rechts-Staat: Staat, internationale Gemeinschaft und Völkerrecht bei Hans Kelsen* (Baden-Baden: Nomos) 233–48.

Jessup, PC (1956) *Transnational Law* (New Haven: Yale University Press).

Jinks, D and Sloss, D (2004) 'Is the President Bound by the Geneva Conventions' 90 (1) *Cornell Law Review* 97–202.

Joerges, C (2003) *On the Legitimacy of Europeanising Europe's Private Law: Considerations on a Law of Justi(ce)-fication (Justun Facere) for the EU Multi-Level System* (*EUI Working Paper: Law*, 2003, 3, San Domenico, Florence: European University Institute) 48 pp.

—— (2007) 'Integration through De-Legalisation: An Irritated Heckler'. *European Governance Paper* (EUROGOV) no N-07-3, 28 (available at: http://www.connex-network.org/eurogov/pdf/egp-newgov-N-07-03.pdf).

Joerges, C and Neyer, J (1997) 'From Intergovernmental Bargaining to Deliberative Political Processes: The Constitutionalisation of Comitology' 3 *European Law Journal* 273–99.

Joerges, C and Petersmann, E-U (eds) (2006) *Constitutionalism, Multilevel Trade Governance and Social Regulation* (Oxford/Portland, OR: Hart).

Kadelbach, S (1992) *Zwingendes Völkerrecht* (Berlin: Duncker & Humblot).

Kadelbach, S and Kleinlein, T (2008) 'International Law – a Constitution for Mankind? An Attempt at a Re-appraisal with an Analysis of Constitutional Principles' 50 *German Yearbook of International Law* 303–47.

Kant, I (1993) 'Zum ewigen Frieden: Ein Philosophischen Entwurf'in Immanuel Kant, *Werkausgabe*, vol XI: *Schriften zur Anthropologie, Geschichtsphilosophie, Politik und Pädagogik 1*. W Weischedel (ed) 10th edn (Frankfurt am Main: Suhrkamp)191–251 [1st edn, Königsberg, 1795].

Kaufmann, RFM (2007) *Ações afirmativas à brasileira: Necessidade ou mito? Uma análise histórico-jurídico-comparativa do negro nos Estados Unidos da América e no Brasil* (Porto Alegre: Livraria do Advogado).

Kelsen, H (1925) *Allgemeine Staatslehre* (Bad Hamburg v. d. Höhe/Berlin/Zurich: Gehlen) [reprinted 1966].

—— (1931) *Wer soll der Hüter der Verfassung sein?* (Berlin: Rotschild).

—— (1946) *General Theory of Law and State*, Engl trans by A Wedberg (Cambridge, MA: Harvard University Press).

—— (1960) *Reine Rechtslehre* 2nd edn (Vienna: Franz Deuticke) [reprinted 1983].

Kempen, B (2005) 'Artikel 59' in H von Mangoldt, F Klein, C Starck (eds), *Kommentar zum Grundgesetz* (Munich: Franz Vahlen) vol 2, 1473–1519.

Koselleck, R (1989) 'Zur historisch-politischen Semantik asymmetrischer Gegenbegriffe' in R Koselleck, *Vergangene Zukunft: Zur Semantik geschichtlicher Zeiten* (Frankfurt am Main: Suhrkamp) 211–59 [Engl trans: 'The Historical-Political Semantics of Asymmetric counterconcepts' in Reinhart Koselleck, *Futures Past: On the Semantics of Historical Time* (New York: Columbia University Press, 2004) 155–91].

——(2006) 'Begriffsgeschichtliche Probleme der Verfassungsgeschichtsbeschreibung' in R Koselleck *Begriffsgeschichten* (Frankfurt am Main: Suhrkamp) 365–401.

Koskenniemi, M (1995) 'The Police in the Temple – Order, Justice and the UN: A Dialectical View' 6 *European Journal of International Law* 325–48.

——(2002) *The Gentle Civilizer of Nations: The Rise and Fall of International Law 1870–1960* (Cambridge: Cambridge University Press).

——(2004) 'International Law and Hegemony: A Reconfiguration' 17 *Cambridge Review of International Affairs* 197–218.

——(2006a) 'The Fate of Public International Law: Constitutional Utopia or Fragmentation?' *Chorley Lecture*. London: London School of Economics and Political Science, 7 June 2006, 46 pp.

——(2006b) 'International Law: Between Fragmentation and Constitutionalism'. Lecture, Canberra, 27 November 2006, 18 pp.

——(2008) 'Formalismus, Fragmentierung, Freiheit – Kantische Themen im heutigen Völkerrecht' in R Kreide and A Niederberger (eds), *Transnationale Verrechtlichung. Nationale Demokratien im Kontext globaler Politik* (Frankfurt am Main/New York: Campus) 65–89.

Koskenniemi, M and Päivi, L (2002) 'Fragmentation of International Law? Postmodern Anxieties' 15 *Leiden Journal of International Law* 553–79.

Krajewski, M (2001) *Verfassungsperspektiven und Legitimation des Rechts der Welthandelsorganisation (WTO)* (Berlin: Duncker & Humblot).

Kuhn, TS (1996) *The Structure of Scientific Revolutions* 3rd edn (Chicago/London: The University of Chicago Press).

Laclau, E (1994) 'Why do Empty Signifiers Matter to Politics?' in J Weeks (ed), *The Lesser Evil and the Greater Good. The Theory and Politics of Social Diversity* (London: Rivers Oram Press) 167–78.

Ladeur, K-H (1986) '"Prozedurale Rationalität" – Steigerung der Legitimationsfähigkeit oder der Leistungsfähigkeit des Rechtssystems?' 7 *Zeitschrift für Rechtssoziologie* 265–74.

——(1992) *Postmoderne Rechtstheorie: Selbstreferenz – Selbstorganisation – Prozeduralisierung* (Berlin: Duncker & Humblot).

——(1997) 'Towards a Legal Theory of Supranationality – The Viability of The Network Concept' 3 (1) *European Law Journal* 33–54.

——(2000) *Negative Freiheitsrechte und gesellschaftliche Selbstorganisation: Die Erzeugung von Sozialkapital durch Institutionen* (Tübingen: Mohr).

——(2004a) 'Globalization and Conversion of Democracy to Polycentric Networks – Can Democracy Survive the End of Nation State?' in K-H Ladeur (ed), *Public Governance in the Age of Globalization* (Aldershot: Ashgate) 89–118.

——(2004b) *Kritik der Abwägung in der Grundrechtsdogmatik* (Tübingen: Mohr).

——(2007a) 'Schutz von Prominenz als Eigentum – Zur Kritik der *Caroline*-Rechtsprechung des Bundesverfassungsgerichts' in K-H Ladeur, *Das Medienrecht und die Ökonomie der Aufmerksamkeit* (Cologne: Halem) 113–46.

——(2007b) *Der Staat gegen die Gesellschaft: Zur Verteidigung der Rationalität der 'Privatrechtsgesellschaft'* (Tübingen: Mohr).

Ladeur, K-H and Augsberg, I (2005) 'Auslegungsparadoxien: Zur Theorie und Praxis juristischer Interpretation' 36 *Rechtstheorie* 143–84.

——(2008) *Die Funktion der Menschenwürde im Verfassungsstaat: Humangenetik – Neurowissenschaft – Medien* (Tübingen: Siebeck).

Ladeur, K-H and Viellechner, L (2008) 'Die transnationale Expansion staatlicher Grundrechte: Zur Konstitutionalisierung globaler Privatregimes' 46 *Archiv des Völkerrechts* 42–73.

Lagarde, P (1982) 'Approche critique de la lex mercatoria' in *Le droit des relations économiques internationales: études offertes à Berthold Goldman* (Paris: Librairies Techniques) 125–50.

Langer, S (1995) *Grundlagen einer internationalen Wirtschaftsverfassung – Strukturprinzipien, Typik und Perspektiven anhand von Europäischer Union und Welthandelsorganisation* (Munich: Beck).

Lassalle, F (1987) 'Über Verfassungswesen' (1862) in Friederici, HJ (ed), *Reden und Schriften* (Cologne: Röderberg) 120–47.

Latour, B (1997) *Nous n'avons jamais été modernes: Essai d'anthropologie symétrique* (Paris: La Découverte).

Latty, F (2007) *La lex sportiva: recherche sur le droit transnational* (Leiden: Nijhoff).

Lauterpacht, H (1950) *International Law and Human Rights* (London: Stevens and Sons).

Law, DS (2008) 'Globalization and the Future of Constitutional Rights' 102 (3) *Northwestern University Law Review* 1277–1349.

Lefort, C (1981) 'Droit de l'homme et politique' in C Lefort*, L'invention Démocratique: Les limites de la domination totalitaire* (Paris: Fayard) 45–83.

Levinson, S (2005) '"Imposed Constitutionalism": Some Reflections' 37 (4) *Connecticut Law Review* 921–32.

Lévi-Strauss, C (1973) 'Introduction a l'œuvre de Marcel Mauss' in M Mauss, *Sociologie et Anthropologie* 5th edn (Paris: Presses Universitaires de France)vol I, IX–LII [1st edn 1950].

Lewandowski, ER (2004) *Globalização, regionalização e soberania* (São Paulo: Juarez de Oliveira).

L'Heureux-Dubé, C (1998) 'The Importance of Dialogue: Globalization and the International Impact of the Rehnquist Court' 34 (1) *Tulsa Law Journal* 15–40.

Locke, J (1980) *Second Treatise of Government*, CB Macpherson (ed) (Indianapolis/ Cambridge: Hackett Publishing Company) [1st edn, 1690].

Loewenstein, K (1965) *Political Power and the Governmental Process* 2nd edn (Chicago: The University of Chicago Press).

Loquin, E (2006) 'Les règles matérielles internationales' in *Recueil des Cours: Collected Courses of the Hague Academy of International Law* 322 (2006) (The Hague: Académie de Droit International de La Haye/Leiden: Nijhoff, 2007) 9–241.

——(2007) 'L'utilisation par les arbitres du TAS des principes généraux du droit et le développement d'une *lex sportiva*' in A Rigozzi and M Bernasconi (eds), *The Proceedings before the Court Arbitration for Sport* (Bern: Weblaw/Zurich: Schulthess) 85–108.

——(2008) 'Tribunal Arbitral du Sport: 2 Chronique des sentences arbitrales' 1 *Journal du Droit International Clunet* 233–309.

Lucas Pires, F (1997) *Introdução ao direito constitucional europeu (seu sentido, problemas e limites)* (Coimbra: Almedina).

Luhmann, N (1965) *Grundrechte als Institution: Ein Beitrag zur politischen Soziologie* (Berlin: Duncker & Humblot).

——(1973a) 'Politische Verfassungen im Kontext des Gesellschaftssystems' 12 *Der Staat* 1–22 and 165–82.

——(1973b) *Zweckbegriff und Systemrationalität: Über die Funktion von Zwecken in sozialen Systemen* (Frankfurt am Main: Suhrkamp).
——(1974) *Rechtssystem und Rechtsdogmatik* (Stuttgart: Kohlhammer).
——(1975) 'Die Weltgesellschaft' in N Luhmann, *Soziologische Aufklärung 2: Aufsätze zur Theorie der Gesellschaft* (Opladen: Westdeutscher Verlag) 51–71.
——(1980) 'Gesellschaftliche Struktur und semantische Tradition' in N Luhmann, *Gesellschaftsstruktur und Semantik: Studien zur Wissenssoziologie der modernen Gesellschaft* (Frankfurt am Main: Suhrkamp) vol 1, 9–71.
——(1981a) *Ausdifferenzierung des Rechts: Beiträge zur Rechtssoziologie und Rechtstheorie* (Frankfurt am Main: Suhrkamp).
——(1981b) *Politische Theorie im Wohlfahrtsstaat* (Munich: Olzog).
——(1981c) 'Machtkreislauf und Recht in Demokratien' 2 *Zeitschrift für Rechtssoziologie* 158–67.
——(1983a) *Legitimation durch Verfahren* (Frankfurt am Main: Suhrkamp) [1st edn Neuwied/Berlin: Luchterhand, 1969].
——(1983b) 'Die Einheit des Rechtssystems' 14 *Rechtstheorie* 129–54.
——(1984a) 'Reflexive Mechanismen' in N Luhmann, *Soziologische Aufklärung 1: Aufsätze zur Theorie sozialer Systeme* 5th edn (Opladen: Westdeutscher Verlag) 92–112 [first published (1966) 17 *Soziale Welt* 1–23].
——(1984b) 'The Self-Reproduction of the Law and its Limits' in FA de Miranda Rosa (ed), *Direito e mudança social* (Rio de Janeiro: OAB/RJ) 107–28.
——(1986a) 'Die Codierung des Rechtssystems' 17 *Rechtstheorie* 171–203.
——(1986b) 'Interaktion, Organisation, Gesellschaft: Anwendungen der Systemtheorie' in N Luhmann, *Soziologische Aufklärung 2: Aufsätze zur Theorie der Gesellschaft* 3rd edn (Opladen: Westdeutscher Verlag) 9–20.
——(1986c) *Ökologische Kommunikation: Kann die moderne Gesellschaft sich auf ökologische Gefährdungen einstellen?* (Opladen: Westdeutscher Verlag).
——(1987a) *Rechtssoziologie* 3rd edn (Opladen: Westdeutscher Verlag) [1st edn, Reinbek bei Hamburg: Rowohlt, 1972, 2 vols].
——(1987b) 'Die Zukunft der Demokratie' in N Luhmann, *Soziologische Aufklärung 4: Beiträge zur funktionalen Differenzierung der Gesellschaft* (Opladen: Westdeutscher Verlag) 126–32.
—— (1987c)*Soziale Systeme: Grundriß einer allgemeinen Theorie* (Frankfurt am Main: Suhrkamp) [Engl trans: *Social Systems* (Stanford: Stanford University Press, 1995)].
——(1988a) *Die Wirtschaft der Gesellschaft* (Frankfurt am Main: Suhrkamp).
——(1988b) *Macht* 2nd edn (Stuttgart: Enke) [1st edn, 1975].
——(1988c) 'Positivität als Selbstbestimmtheit des Rechts' 19 *Rechtstheorie* 11–27.
——(1989) *Gesellschaftsstruktur und Semantik: Studien zur Wissenssoziologie der modernen Gesellschaft* (Frankfurt am Main: Suhrkamp) vol 3.
——(1990a) 'Verfassung als evolutionäre Errungenschaft' 9 *Rechtshistorisches Journal* 176–220.
——(1990b) *Liebe als Passion: Zur Codierung von Intimität* 5th edn (Frankfurt am Main: Suhrkamp).
——(1990c) *Die Wissenschaft der Gesellschaft* (Frankfurt am Main: Suhrkamp).
——(1990d) *Paradigma lost: Über die ethische Reflexion der Moral – Rede anläßlich der Verleihung des Hegel-Preises 1989*, with a '*Laudatio*' by R Spaemann (Frankfurt am Main: Suhrkamp).

Luhmann, N (1990e) 'Interesse und Interessenjurisprudenz im Spannungsfeld von Gesetzgebung und Rechtsprechung' 12 *Zeitschrift für Neuere Rechtsgeschichte* 1–13.

—— (1990f) 'Die Stellung der Gerichte im Rechtssystem' 21 *Rechtstheorie* 459–73.

—— (1990g) 'Ich sehe was, was Du nicht siehst' in N Luhmann, *Soziologische Aufklärung 5: Konstruktivistische Perspektiven* (Opladen: Westdeutscher Verlag) 228–34 [Engl trans: 'I See Something You Don't See' in N Luhmann, *Theories of Distinction: Redescribing the Descriptions of Modernity* (Stanford: Stanford University Press, (2002) 187–93].

—— (1991) 'Der Gleichheitssatz als Form und als Norm' 77*Archiv für Rechts- und Sozialphilosophie* 435–45.

—— (1993a) *Das Recht der Gesellschaft* (Frankfurt am Main: Suhrkamp) [Engl trans: *Law as Social System* (Oxford: Oxford University Press, 2004)].

—— (1993b) 'The Code of the Moral' 14 (3–4) *Cardozo Law Review*January 995–1009.

—— (1993c) 'Das Paradox der Menschenrechte und drei Formen seiner Entfaltung' in *Rechtsnorm und Rechtswirklichkeit: Festschrift für Werner Krawietz zum 60. Geburtstag* (Berlin: Duncker & Humblot).

—— (1994) 'Europa als Problem der Weltgesellschaft' in 2 *Berliner Debatte INITIAL: Zeitschrift für sozialwissenschaftlichen Diskurs* 3–7.

—— (1995a) *Gesellschaftsstruktur und Semantik: Studien zur Wissenssoziologie der modernen Gesellschaft* (Frankfurt am Main: Suhrkamp) vol 4.

—— (1995b) 'Inklusion und Exklusion' in N Luhmann, *Soziologische Aufklärung 6: Die Soziologie und der Mensch* (Opladen: Westdeutscher Verlag) 237–64.

—— (1995c) 'Die Form "Person"' in N Luhmann, *Soziologische Aufklärung 6: Die Soziologie und der Mensch* (Opladen: Westdeutscher Verlag) 142–54.

—— (1996) *Die Kunst der Gesellschaft* 2nd edn (Frankfurt am Main: Suhrkamp).

—— (1997) *Die Gesellschaft der Gesellschaft* (Frankfurt am Main: Suhrkamp) 2 vols.

—— (1998) 'Der Staat des politischen Systems: Geschichte und Stellung in der Weltgesellschaft' in U Beck (ed), *Perspektiven der Weltgesellschaft* (Frankfurt am Main: Suhrkamp) 345–80.

—— (1999) 'Ethik in internationalen Beziehungen' 50 *Soziale Welt* 247–54.

—— (2000a) *Die Politik der Gesellschaft* (Frankfurt am Main: Suhrkamp).

—— (2000b) *Die Religion der Gesellschaft* (Frankfurt am Main: Suhrkamp).

—— (2000c) *Organisation und Entscheidung* (Frankfurt am Main: Suhrkamp).

—— (2000d) 'Die Rückgabe des zwölften Kamels: Zum Sinn einer soziologischen Analyse des Rechts' in G Teubner (ed), *Die Rückgabe des zwölften Kamels: Niklas Luhmanns in der Diskussion über Gerechtigkeit* (Stuttgart: Lucius & Lucius) 3–60.

—— (2002a) *Das Erziehungssystem der Gesellschaft* (Frankfurt am Main: Suhrkamp).

—— (2002b) *Einführung in die Systemtheorie*, D Baecker (ed) (Heidelberg: Carl-Auer-Systeme).

—— (2004) 'Codierung und Programmierung: Bildung und Selektion im Erziehungssystem' (1986) in N Luhmann, *Schriften zur Pädagogik*, D Lenzen (ed) (Frankfurt am Main: Suhrkamp) 23–47.

—— (2005) *Einführung in die Theorie der Gesellschaft* (Heidelberg: Carl-Auer).

Luhmann, N and De Giorgi, R (1992) *Teoria della società* (Milan: Franco Angeli).

Lutz-Bachmann, M (2002) 'Weltweiter Frieden durch eine Weltrepublik? Probleme internationaler Friedensicherung' in M Lutz-Bachmann and J Bohman (eds), *Weltstaat oder Staatenwelt? Für und wider die Idee einer Weltrepublik* (Frankfurt am Main: Suhrkamp) 32–45.

Lyotard, J-F (1979) *La condition postmoderne* (Paris: Minuit).
——(1983) *Le différend* (Paris: Minuit) [Engl trans: *The Differend: Phrases in Dispute* (Minneapolis: University of Minnesota Press, 1988)].
MacDowell, DM (1989) 'The Oikos in Athenian Law' 39 (1) *The Classical Quarterly* New Series 10–21.
Macpherson, CB (1990) 'Berlin's Divisions of Liberty' in CB Macpherson, *Democratic Theory: Essays in Retrieval*, 6th impression (Oxford: Oxford University Press/Clarendon Press) 95–119.
Maddox, G (1989) 'Constitution' in T Ball, J Farr and RL Hanson (eds), *Political Innovation and Conceptual Change* (Cambridge: Cambridge University Press) 50–67.
Madison, J, Hamilton, A and Jay, J (1987) *The Federalist Papers* (1788) (London/New York: Penguin).
Maduro, MP (2003) 'Contrapunctual Law: Europe's Constitutional Pluralism in Action' in N Walker (ed), *Sovereignty in Transition* (Oxford/Portland, OR: Hart) 501–37.
——(2006) *A Constituição plural: constitucionalismo e União Européia* (Cascais: Principia).
Maliska, MA (2006) *Estado e século XXI: A integração supranacional sob a ótica do direito constitucional* (Rio de Janeiro/São Paulo: Renovar).
Martins, L (2008) 'Da distinção entre regras e princípios e seus problemas epistemológicos, metodológicos e teórico-jurídicos' in GS Leite (ed), *Dos princípios constitucionais – Considerações em torno das normas principiológicas da Constituição* (São Paulo: Método) 327–50.
Marx, K (1988a) 'Zur Judenfrage' in K Marx and F Engels,*Werke* 15th edn (Berlin: Dietz Verlag) vol I, 347–77 [first published in: *Deutsch-Französische Jahrbücher* (Paris) 1844].
——(1988b) *Ökonomische Manuskripte: 1863–1867: Text – Teil I.* K Marx and F Engels, *Gesamtausgabe (MEGA)* (Berlin: Dietz) vol IV, part 1.
Maturana, HR (1982) *Erkennen: Die Organisation und Verkörperung von Wirklichkeit. Ausgewählte Arbeiten zur biologischen Epistemologie.* German trans by WK Köck (Braunschweig/Wiesbaden: Vieweg).
Maturana, HR and Varela, FJ (1980) *Autopoiesis and Cognition: The Realization of the Living* (Dordrecht: D Reidel Publishing Company).
——(2006) *El árbol del conocimiento: Las bases biológicas del entendimiento humano* 18th edn (Santiago: Editorial Universitaria) [1st edn 1984].
Maus, I (1989) 'Justiz als gesellschaftliches Über-Ich. Zur Funktion von Rechtsprechung in der "vaterlosen Gesellschaft"' in W Faulstich and GE Grimm (eds), *Sturz der Götter? Vaterbilder im 20. Jahrhundert* (Frankfurt am Main: Suhrkamp) 121–49.
——(1997) 'Staatssouveränität als Volkssouveränität. Überlegungen zum Friedensprojekt Immanuel Kants' in W Loth (ed), *Jahrbuch 1996 des Kulturwissenschaftlichen Instituts im Wissenschaftszentrum NRW* (Essen: Altes Rathaus) 167–94.
Mayer, H (2007) *Das österreichische Bundes-Verfassungsrecht* 4th edn (Vienna: Manz).
Mazzuoli, V de O (2001) *Direito internacional: tratados e direitos humanos fundamentais na ordem jurídica brasileira* (Rio de Janeiro: América Jurídica).
——(2005) 'O novo § 3° do art. 5° da Constituição e sua eficácia' in *Revista da AJURIS*, vol XXXII, no 98 (Porto Alegre: Associação dos Juízes do Rio Grande do Sul) 303–31.
——(2007) *Curso de direito internacional público* 2nd edn (São Paulo: Revista dos Tribunais).
McIlwain, CH (1940) *Constitutionalism Ancient and Modern* (Ithaca, New York: Cornell University Press).

Mead, GH (1962) *Mind, Self, & Society: from the Standpoint of a Social Behaviorist.* Edited and with an Introduction by CW Morris (Chicago/London: The University of Chicago Press) [1st edn 1934].
Meier, H (1994) *Die Lehre Carl Schmitts.Vier Kapitel zur Unterscheidung Politischer Theologie und Politischer Philosophie* (Stuttgart/Weimar: Metzler).
Mello, CD de A (2000) *Direito constitucional internacional – Introdução* 2nd edn (Rio de Janeiro: Renovar).
——(2001) 'O parágrafo 2° do artigo 5° da Constituição Federal' in RL Torres (ed), *Teoria dos direitos fundamentais* 2nd edn (Rio de Janeiro: Renovar) 1–33.
Mendes, G (2010) 'A justiça constitucional nos contextos supranacionais' in M Neves (ed), *Transnacionalidade do direito: novas perspectivas dos conflitos entre ordens jurídicas* (São Paulo: Quartier Latin) 243–86.
Mendes, G, Coelho, IM and Branco, PGG (2007). *Curso de direito constitucional* (São Paulo: Saraiva/Brasília: IDP).
Mendes, R (2006) 'Sentido da teoria geral do direito, globalização e harmonização do método jurídico' in PB Casella and VLV Liquidato (eds), *Direito da integração* (São Paulo: Quartier Latin) 87–104.
——(2010) *Arbitragem,* Lex Mercatoria *e Direito Estatal: Uma Análise dos Conflitos Ortogonais no Direito Transnacional* (São Paulo: Quartier Latin).
Mertens, H-J (1997) '*Lex Mercatoria*: A Self-Applying System Beyond National Law?' in G Teubner (ed), *Global Law without a State* (Aldershot: Dartmouth) 31–43.
Mohnhaupt, H (1995) 'Konstitution, Status, Leges fundamentales von der Antike bis zur Aufklärung' in H Mohnhaupt and D Grimm, *Verfassung: Zur Geschichte des Begriffs von der Antike bis zur Gegenwart; zwei Studien* (Berlin: Duncker & Humblot), 1–99.
Möllers, C (2003) 'Verfassunggebende Gewalt – Verfassung – Konstitutionalisierung: Begriff der Verfassung in Europa' in A von Bogdandy (ed), *Europäisches Verfassungsrecht: Theoretische und dogmatische Grundzüge* (Berlin: Springer) 1–57.
——(2005a) 'Netzwerk als Kategorie des Organisationsrechts – zur juristischen Beschreibung dezentraler Steuerung' in J Oebbecke (ed), *Nicht-normative Steuerung in dezentralen Systemen (Nassauer Gespräche der Freiherr-Vom-Stein-Gesellschaft*, vol 7) (Stuttgart: Franz Steiner Verlag) 285–302.
——(2005b) 'Transnationale Behördenkooperation: Verfassungs- und völkerrechtliche Probleme transnationaler administrativer Standardsetzung' *Zeitschrift für ausländisches öffentliches Recht und Völkerrecht* 351–89.
Mommsen, T (1982) *Abriss des römischen Staatsrechts.* Darmstadt: Wissenschaftliche Buchhandlung [reprint of the 2nd edn 1907].
Montoro, AF (1973) 'Filosofia do direito e colonialismo cultural: transplante de institutos jurídicos inadequados à realidade brasileira' 10 (37) *Revista de Informação Legislativa* 3–20.
Mosler, H (1976) 'Völkerrecht als Rechtsordnung' *Zeitschrift für ausländisches öffentliches Recht und Völkerrecht* 6–49.
——(1980) *The International Society as a Legal Community* (Alphen aan den Rijn: Sijthoff & Noordhoff).
Müller, F (1990) *Essais zur Theorie von Recht und Verfassung*, R Christensen (ed) (Berlin: Duncker & Humblot).
——(1994) *Strukturierende Rechtslehre* 2nd edn (Berlin: Duncker & Humblot).
——(1995) *Juristische Methodik* 6th edn (Berlin: Duncker & Humblot).

——(1997) *Wer ist das Volk? Die Grundfrage der Demokratie – Elemente einer Verfassungstheorie VI* (Berlin: Duncker & Humblot).

Münch, F (1983) 'Bemerkungen zum ius cogens' in R Bernhardt *et al*(eds), *Völkerrecht als Rechtsordnung – Internationale Gerichtsbarkeit – Menschenrechte: Festschrift für Hermann Mosler* (Berlin/Heidelberg/New York: Springer-Verlag) 617–28.

Mustill, Lord Justice [Michael J] (1987) 'The New Lex Mercatoria: The First Twenty-five Years' in M Bos and I Brownlie (eds), *Liber Amicorum for The Rt Hon Lord Wilberforce* (Oxford: Oxford University Press) 149–83.

Nassehi, A (2002) 'Politik des Staates oder Politik der Gesellschaft? Kollektivität als Problemformel des Politischen' in K-U Hellmann and R Schmalz-Bruns (eds), *Theorie der Politik: Niklas Luhmanns politische Soziologie* (Frankfurt am Main: Suhrkamp) 38–59.

Nettesheim, M (2001) 'Von der Verhandlungsdiplomatie zur internationalen Verfassungsordnung: Zur Entwicklung der Ordnungsformen des internationalen Wirtschaftsrechts' in CD Classen *et al* (eds), *'In einem vereintem Europa dem Frieden der Welt zu dienen . . .': Liber amicorum Thomas Oppermann* (Berlin: Duncker & Humblot) 381–409.

Neves, M (1992) *Verfassung und Positivität des Rechts in der peripheren Moderne: Eine theoretische Betrachtung und eine Interpretation des Falls Brasilien* (Berlin: Duncker & Humblot).

——(1994) 'Entre subintegração e sobreintegração: a cidadania inexistente' 37 (2) *DADOS – Revista de Ciências Sociais* 253–75 [Engl trans: 'Between Under-Integration and Over-Integration: Not Taking Citizenship Rights Seriously' in J Souza and V Sinder (eds), *Imagining Brazil* (Lanham, MD: Lexington Books, 2005) 61–90].

——(1995) 'Da autopoiese à alopoiese do direito' 42 *Revista Brasileira de Filosofia* 117–41.

——(2002) 'Gerechtigkeit und Differenz in einer komplexen Weltgesellschaft' 88 *Archiv für Rechts- und Sozialphilosophie* 323–48.

——(2005) 'A força simbólica dos direitos humanos' 4 *Revista Eletrônica de Direito do Estado* Oct/Dec 35 [Engl trans 'The symbolic force of human rights' 33 (4) *Philosophy & Social Criticism* 411–44].

——(2006a) *Entre Têmis e Leviatã: uma relação difícil – o Estado democrático de direito a partir e além de Luhmann e Habermas* (São Paulo: Martins Fontes).

——(2006b) 'Die Staaten im Zentrum und die Staaten an der Peripherie: Einige Probleme mit Niklas Luhmanns Auffassung von den Staaten der Weltgesellschaft' 12 *Soziale Systeme: Zeitschrift für soziologische Theorie* 247–73.

——(2007a) *A constitucionalização simbólica* 2nd edn (São Paulo: Editora WMF Martins Fontes).

——(2007b) 'Grenzen der Autonomie des Rechts in einer asymmetrischen Weltgesellschaft: Von Luhmann zu Kelsen' 93 (3) *Archiv für Rechts- und Sozialphilosophie* 363–95.

——(2008) 'Verfassung und Öffentlichkeit: zwischen Systemdifferenzierung, Inklusion und Anerkennung' 47 *Der Staat* 477–509.

——(2009a) 'La concepción de Estado de derecho y su vigencia práctica en Suramérica, con especial referencia a la fuerza normativa de un derecho supranacional' in A von Bogdandy, CL Arroyo, and MM Antoniazzi (eds), *¿Integración suramericana a través del derecho? Un análisis multidiciplinario y multifocal* (Max Planck Institute for Comparative Public Law and International Law/Madrid: Centro de Estudios Constitucionales) 51–78.

Neves, M (2009b) 'Transversale Verfassungen? Konstitutionalismus: Vom Staat zur Weltgesellschaft' in H Brunkhorst (ed), *Demokratie in der Weltgesellschaft* (*Soziale Welt, Sonderband* 18, Baden-Baden: Nomos) 75–97.

——(2009c) 'Transversale Rechtsvernetzungen und Asymmetrien der Rechtsformen in der Weltgesellschaft' in G-P Callies *et al* (eds), *Soziologische Jurisprudenz: Festschrift für Gunther Teubner zum 65. Geburtstag* (Berlin: De Gruyter) 841–56.

Oeter, Stefan (1999) 'Europäische Integration als Konstitutionalisierungsprozeß' 59 (3) *Zeitschrift für ausländisches öffentliches Recht und Völkerrecht – ZaöRV* 901–17.

——(2007) '*Ius cogens* und der Schutz der Menschenrechte' in *Human Rights, Democracy and the Rule of Law: Liber amicorum Luzius Wildhaber* (Zurich: Dike/ Baden-Baden: Nomos) 499–521.

Öhlinger, T (2008) 'Hans Kelsen – Vater der österreichischen Bundesverfassung?' in *Festschrift für Wilhelm Brauneder zum 65. Geburtstag: Rechtsgeschichte mit internationaler Perspektive* (Vienna: Manz) 407–24.

Ortiz, PC (2009) 'El Sistema Interamericano de Derechos Humanos: democracía y derechos humanos como factores integradores en Latinoamérica' in A von Bogdandy, CL Arroyo, and MM Antoniazzi (eds), *¿Integración suramericana a través del derecho? Un análisis multidiciplinario y multifocal* (Max Planck Institute for Comparative Public Law and International Law/Madrid: Centro de Estudios Constitucionales) 231–85.

Osiatynsky, W (2003) 'Paradoxes of Constitutional Borrowing' 1 (2) *International Journal of Constitutional Law* 244–68.

Paine, T (1992) *Rights of Man* [1791–1792], G Claeys (ed) (Indianapolis/Cambridge: Hackett).

Panagiotopoulos, D (2004) 'Theoretical Foundation of Sports Law' in D Panagiotopoulos (ed), *Sports Law (Lex Sportiva) in the World: Regulations and Implementation* (Athens: Sakkoulas) 17–80.

Parsons, T (1968) 'Interaction: Social Interaction' in *InternationalEncyclopedia of the Social Sciences*, vol 7 (New York: The Macmillan Company &The Free Press/London: Collier Macmillan Publishers) [reprinted 1972], 429–41.

Parsons, T *et al* (1951) 'Some Fundamental Categories of the Theory of Action: A General Statement' in T Parsons and EA Shils (eds), *Toward a General Theory of Action* (Cambridge, MA: Harvard University Press [6th impression 1967], 3–29.

Passerin d'Entrèves, A (1962) *La Dottrina dello Stato: Elementi di Analisi e di Interpretazione* (Turin: Giappichelli).

Pedler, RH and Schaefer, GF (eds) (1996) *Shaping European Law and Policy: The Role of Committees and Comitology in the Political Process* (Maastricht: European Institute of Public Administration).

Pernice, I (1995) 'Deutschland in der Europäischen Union' in J Insensee and P Kirschhof (eds), *Handbuch des Staatsrechts der Bundesrepublik Deutschland*, vol VIII (Heidelberg: Müller) 225–80.

——(1999) 'Multilevel Constitutionalism and Treaty of Amsterdam: European Constitution-Making Revisited?' 36 (4) *Common Market Law Review* 703–50.

——(2002) 'Multilevel Constitutionalism in the European Union' 27 *European Law Review* 511–29.

——(2006) 'Artikel 24 [Übertragung und Einschränkung von Hoheitsrechten]' in H Dreier (ed), *Grundgesetz-Kommentar* 2nd edn (Tübingen: Mohr) vol 2, 501–31.

Perotti, AD (1998) 'Los Tribunales comunitarios en los procesos de integración: El caso del Tribunal de Justicia de la Comunidad Andina' 43 (17) *Revista Jurídica del Perú* 282–314.

——(2002) 'Tribunales supranacionales. La Corte Centroamericana de Justicia' 3 *Revista Costarricense de Derecho Constitucional* 153–252.

——(2009) '¿Quién paga los costos del incumplimiento de las sentencias del Tribunal Permanente de Revisión (MERCOSUR)? Responsabilidad del Estado por violación del Derecho de la integración' in *El Derecho – ED*, Suplemento de Derecho Administrativo [Buenos Aires: Universidad Católica Argentina], 31 March 2009, 1–8.

Peters, A (2006) 'Compensatory Constitutionalism: The Function and Potential of Fundamental International Norms and Structures' 19 *Leiden Journal of International Law* 579–10.

Petersmann, E-U (1991) *Constitutional Functions and Constitutional Problems of International Economic Law: International and Domestic Foreign Trade Law and Foreign Trade Policy in the United States, the European Community and Switzerland* (Fribourg, Switzerland: University Press Fribourg).

——(1995) 'The Transformation of the World Trading System through the 1994 Agreement Establishing the World Trade Organization' 6 *European Journal of International Law* 161–221.

——(2008) 'Multilevel Constitutionalism and Judicial Protection of Freedom and Justice in the International Economic Law of the EC' in A Arnull, P Eeckhout, and T Tridimas (eds), *Continuity and Change in EU Law: Essays in Honour of Sir Francis Jacobs* (Oxford: Oxford University Press) 338–53.

Pinsolle, P (2008) 'The Status of Vacated Awards in France: the Cour de Cassation Decision in Putrabali' 24 (2) *Arbitration International* 277–95.

Piovesan, F (2008a) *Direitos humanos e o direito constitucional internacional* 9th edn (São Paulo: Saraiva).

——(2008b) 'Igualdade, diferença e direitos humanos: perspectivas global e regional' in D Sarmento, D Ikawa, and F Piovesan (eds), *Igualdade, diferença e direitos humanos* (Rio de Janeiro: Lumen Juris) 47–76.

——(2008c) 'Direitos humanos e propriedade intelectual: proteção internacional e constitucional' in LLG Ribeiro and LAA Berardi (eds), *Estudos de direito constitucional em homenagem à professora Maria Garcia* 2nd edn (São Paulo: IOB) 131–66.

Pontes de Miranda, FC (1960) *Comentários à Constituição de 1946* (Rio de Janeiro: Borsoi) vol I.

Posner, RA (1988) *Law and Literature: A Misunderstood Relation* (Cambridge, MA/London: Harvard University Press).

Preuss, U (1990) *Revolution, Fortschrift und Verfassung: Zu einem neuen Verfassungsverständnis* (Berlin: Wagenbach).

Radbruch, G (2003) *Rechtsphilosophie* [1932], R Dreier and SL Paulson (eds) 2nd edn (Heidelberg: Müller).

Ragazzi, M (1997) *The Concept of International Obligations Erga Omnes* (Oxford: Clarendon Press).

Ramírez, AD (2005) 'El caso de la comunidad indígena *Yakye Axa vs Paraguay*' 41 *Revista IIDH/Instituto Interamericano de Derechos Humanos* 349–64.

Ramírez, SG (2008) 'Cuestiones de la jurisdicción interamericana de derechos humanos' 8 *Anuario Mexicano de Derecho Internacional* 187–221.

Randeria, S (2003) 'Glocalization of Law: Environmental Justice, World Bank, NGOs and the Cunning State in India' 51 (3/4) *Current Sociology* 305–28.

Rawls, J (1990) *A Theory of Justice* [1972] (Oxford: Oxford University Press).

——(1999) *The Law of Peoples, with 'The Idea of Public Reason Revisited'* (Cambridge, MA/London: Harvard University Press).

Raz, J (1979) *The Authority of Law: Essays on Law and Morality* (Oxford: Clarendon Press).

Rivero, RM (2005) 'La interculturalización de la justicia: Reflexiones en torno a Estado y derechos en Bolivia' 41 *Revista IIDH/Instituto Interamericano de Derechos Humanos* 195–208.

Roach, K (2006) 'The Post-9/11 Migration of Britain's Terrorism Act 2000' in S Choudhry (ed), *The Migration of Constitutional Ideas* (Cambridge: Cambridge University Press) 373–402.

Robertson, R (1995) 'Glocalization: Time-Space and Homogeneity-Heterogeneity' in M Featherstone, S Lash, and R Robertson (eds), *Global Modernities* (London: Sage) 25–44.

Rosenfeld, M (1998) 'The Identity of the Constitutional Subject' in P Goodrich and DG Carlson (eds), *Law and the Postmodern Mind: Essays on Psychoanalysis and Jurisprudence* (Ann Arbor: The University of Michigan Press) 143–74.

Rosenkrantz, CF (2003) 'Against Borrowings and other Nonauthoritative Uses of Foreign Law' 1 (2) *International Journal of Constitutional Law* 269–95.

Ross, A (1950) *Constitution of United Nations: Analysis of Structure and Function* (Copenhagen: Ejnar Munksgaard).

Rousseau, J-J (1922) *Du contrat social ou principes du droit politique* [1762], edited and introduction by G Beaulavon 3rd edn (Paris: Rieder).

Rudolf, B (2003) 'European Court of Human Rights: Legal Status of Postoperative Transsexuals' 1 (4) *International Journal of Constitutional Law* 716–21.

——(2006) 'Council of Europe: *Von Hannover v Germany*' 4 (3) *International Journal of Constitutional Law* 533–9.

Russell, B (1994) 'Mathematical Logic as based on the Theory of Types' [1908] in *Logic and Knowledge – Essays 1901–1950* (London/New York: Routledge) 59–102 [1st edn 1956].

Sabadell, AL and Dimoulis, D (2010) 'O Tribunal Penal Internacional em face da Constituição brasileira e a questão da ineficácia social dos direitos fundamentais' in M Neves (ed), *Transnacionalidade do direito: novas perspectivas dos conflitos entre ordens jurídicas* (São Paulo: Quartier Latin) 157–86.

Saldanha, N (1978) 'O chamado "bacharelismo" brasileiro: ensaio de revisão' 17 (21) *Convivivm* 477–84.

Sarlet, IW (2001) *A eficácia dos direitos fundamentais* 2nd edn (Porto Alegre: Livraria dos Advogados).

——(2006) 'A reforma do judiciário e os tratados internacionais de direitos humanos: observações sobre o § 3.° do art. 5.° da Constituição' 8 (37) *Interesse Público* May/June 49–64.

——(2010) 'Direitos fundamentais e tratados internacionais em matéria de direitos humanos: revisitando a discussão em torno dos parágrafos 2.° e 3.° do art. 5.° da Constituição Federal de 1988' in M Neves (ed), *Transnacionalidade do direito: novas perspectivas dos conflitos entre ordens jurídicas* (São Paulo: Quartier Latin) 73–99.

Sarmento, D (2008). 'Casamento e união estável entre pessoas do mesmo sexo: perspectivas constitucionais' in D Sarmento, D Ikawa, and F Piovesan (eds), *Igualdade, diferença e direitos humanos* (Rio de Janeiro: Lumen Juris) 619–59.

Sauer, H (2008) *Jurisdiktionskonflikte in Mehrebenensystem: Die Entwicklung eines Modells zur Lösung von Konflikten zwischen Gerichten in vernetzten Rechtordnungen* (Berlin/Heidelberg: Springer).

Scharpf, FW (1994) *Community and Autonomy: Multilevel Policy-Making in the European Union* (*EUI Working Paper RSC*, no 94, 1, San Domenico, Florence: European University Institute) 32 pp.

—— (1999) *Governing in Europe: effective and democratic?* (Oxford: Oxford University Press).

—— (2002) 'Regieren im europäischen Mehrebenensystem – Ansätze zur einer Theorie' 1 *Leviathan: Berliner Zeitschrift für Sozialwissenschaft* 65–92.

Schauer, F (2005) 'On the Migration of Constitutional Ideas' 37 (4) *Connecticut Law Review* 907–19.

Scheppele, KL (2003) 'Aspirational and Aversive Constitutionalism: The Case for Studying Cross-Constitutional Influence through Negative Models' 1 (2) *International Journal of Constitutional Law* 296–324.

—— (2006) 'The Migration of Anti-constitutional Ideas: the Post-9/11 Globalization of Public Law and the International State of Emergency' in S Choudhry (ed), *The Migration of Constitutional Ideas* (Cambridge: Cambridge University Press) 347–73.

Schlink, B (1976) *Abwägung im Verfassungsrecht* (Berlin: Duncker & Humblot).

—— (2001) 'Der Grundsatz der Verhältnismäßigkeit' in P Badura and H Dreier (eds), *Festschrift 50 Jahre Bundesverfassungsgericht* (Tübingen: Mohr) vol 2, 445–65.

Schluchter, W (1979) *Die Entwicklung des Okzidentalen Rationalismus* (Tübingen: Mohr).

Schmale, W (1988) *Entchristianisierung, Revolution und Verfassung: Zur Mentalitätsgeschichte der Verfassung in Frankreich, 1715–1794* (Berlin: Duncker & Humblot).

Schmitt, C (1931) *Der Hüter der Verfassung* (Tübingen: Mohr).

—— (1993) *Verfassungslehre* 8th edn (Berlin: Duncker & Humblot) [1st edn 1928].

—— (1996) *Der Begriff des Politischen: Text von 1932 mit einem Vorwort und drei Corollarien* 6th edn [4th reprint of the 2nd edn 1963] (Berlin: Duncker & Humblot).

Schumpeter, JA (1942) *Capitalism, Socialism, and Democracy* (New York/London: Harper & Brothers).

Schwarz, R (2008) 'As idéias fora do lugar'in Roberto Schwarz, *Ao vencedor as batatas: Forma literária e processo social nos inícios do romance brasileiro* 5th edn, 4th reprint [São Paulo: Duas Cidades/Editora 34], 9–31 [1st edn 1977] [Engl trans: '*Misplaced ideas*: Literature and Society in Late-Nineteenth-Century Brazil' in R Schwarz, *Misplaced ideas: Essays on Brazilian Culture* (*London*: *Verso*, 1992) 19–32].

Segato, RL (2003) *Uma agenda de ações afirmativas para as mulheres indígenas do Brasil.* Series Antropologia 326 (new version) (Brasília: Departamento de Antropologia/UnB).

—— (2006) 'Antropologia e direitos humanos: alteridade e ética no movimento de expansão dos direitos universais'12 (1) *Mana: Estudos de antropologia social* 207–236.

—— (2011) 'Que cada pueblo teja los hilos de su historia. El pluralismo jurídico en diálogo didáctico con legisladores' in V Chenaut, M Gómez, H Ortiz, and MT Sierra (eds), *Justicia y diversidad en América Latina. Pueblos indígenas antela globalización* (México, DF: CIESAS/Quito: FLACSO) 357–81.

Serres, M (1997) *Le Parasite* [1980] (Paris: Hachette Littératures).

Sieder, R (2007) 'The Judiciary and Indigenous Rights in Guatemala' 5 (2) *International Journal of Constitutional Law* 211–41.

Siehr, A (2004) 'Derogation Measures under Article 4 ICCPR with Special Consideration of the 'war Against International Terrorism' 47 *German Yearbook of International Law* 545–93.
Skinner, Q (1989) 'Language and political change' in T Ball, J Farr, and RL Hanson (eds), *Political Innovation and conceptual Change* (Cambridge: Cambridge University Press) 6–23.
Slaughter, A-M (2000) 'Judicial Globalization' 40 *Virginia Journal of International Law* 1103–24.
——(2003) 'Global Community of Courts' *Harvard International Law Journal* 191–219.
——(2004) *A New World Order* (Princeton/Oxford: Princeton University Press).
Slaughter, A-M and Burke-White, W (2007) 'The Future of International Law is Domestic (or, The European Way of Law)' in J Nijman and A Nollkaemper (eds), *New Perspectives on the Divide between International and National Law* (Oxford: Oxford University Press) 110–33.
Smend, R (1968) 'Verfassung und Verfassungsrecht (1928)' in R Smend. *Staatsrechtliche Abhandlungen und andere Aufsätze* 2nd edn (Berlin: Duncker & Humblot) 119–276.
Smith, AM (2006) 'Making Itself at Home. Understanding Foreign Law in Domestic Jurisprudence: The Indian Case' 24 *Berkeley Journal of International Law* 218–72.
Solon, AM (1997) *Teoria da soberania como problema da norma jurídica e da decisão* (Porto Alegre: Fabris).
Spencer Brown, G (1971) *Laws of Form* (London: George Allen and Unwin) [reprint of the 1st edn 1969].
Steiker, J (2006) 'United States: *Roper v Simmons*' 4 (1) *International Journal of Constitutional Law* 163–71.
Steinmetz, WA (2001) *Colisão de direitos fundamentais e o princípio da proporcionalidade* (Porto Alegre: Livraria do Advogado).
Stichweh, R (2000) *Die Weltgesellschaft: Soziologische Analysen* (Frankfurt am Main: Suhrkamp).
——(2002) 'Die Entstehung einer Weltöffentlichkeit' in H Kaelble, M Kirsch, and A Schmidt-Gernig (eds), *Transnationale Öffentlichkeiten und Identitäten im 20. Jahrhundert* (Frankfurt am Main: Campus) 57–66.
——(2007) 'Dimensionen des Weltstaates im System der Weltpolitik' in M Albert and R Stichweh (eds), *Weltstaat und Weltstaatlichkeit: Beobachtungen globaler politischer Strukturbildung* (Wiesbaden: VS Verlag) 25–36.
Stourzh, G (1975) 'Vom aristotelischen zum liberalen Verfassungsbegriff. Zur Entwicklung in Nordamerika im 17. und 18. Jahrhundert' in F Engel-Janosi, G Klingenstein, and H Lutz (eds), *Fürst, Bürger, Mensch: Untersuchungen zu politischen und soziokulturellen Wandlungsprozessen im vorrevolutionären Europa* (Munich: R Oldenbourg, 1975) 97–122.
Strydom, H (2004) 'South Africa and International Law – From Confrontation to Cooperation' 47 *German Yearbook of International Law* 160–213.
Sunder, M (2005) 'Enlightened Constitutionalism' 37 (4) *Connecticut Law Review* 891–905.
Tavares, AR (2005) *Reforma do judiciário no Brasil pós-88: (des)estruturando a justiça. Comentários completos à Emenda Constitucional n.º 45/04* (São Paulo: Saraiva).
Taylor, C (1979) 'What's Wrong with Negative Liberty?' in Alan Ryan (ed), *The Idea of Freedom. Essays in Honour of Sir Isaiah Berlin* (Oxford: Oxford University Press) 175–93.

——(1992a) *The Ethics of Authenticity* (Cambridge, MA/London: Harvard University Press).
——(1992b) *Multiculturalism and 'The politics of recognition': an Essay.* With commentary by A Gutmann (ed), SC Rockefeller, M Walzer, and S Wolf (Princeton: Princeton University Press).
Teubner, G (1987a) 'Hyperzyklus in Recht und Organisation. Zum Verhältnis von Selbstbeobachtung, Selbstkonstitution und Autopoiese' in H Haferkamp and M Schmid (eds), *Sinn, Kommunikation und soziale Differenzierung: Beiträge zu Luhmanns Theorie sozialer Systeme* (Frankfurt am Main: Suhrkamp) 89–128.
——(1987b) 'Episodenverknüpfung. Zur Steigerung von Selbstreferenz im Recht' in D Baecker *et al* (eds), *Theorie als Passion: Niklas Luhmann zum 60. Geburtstag* (Frankfurt am Main: Suhrkamp) 423–46.
——(1988) 'Gesellschaftsordnung durch Gesetzgebungslärm? Autopoietische Geschlossenheit als Problem für die Rechtssetzung' in D Grimm and W Maihofer (eds), *Gesetzgebungstheorie und Rechtspolitik* (*Jahrbuch für Rechtssoziologie und Rechtstheorie* 13, Opladen: Westdeutscher Verlag) 45–64.
——(1989) *Recht als autopoietisches System* (Frankfurt am Main: Suhrkamp).
——(1996a) 'Altera Pars Audiatur: Das Recht in der Kollision anderer Universalitätsansprüche' 65 *Archiv für Rechts- und Sozialphilosophie*, *Beiheft* 199–220.
——(1996b) 'Globale Bukowina: Zur Emergenz eines transnationalen Rechtspluralismus' 15 *Rechtshistorisches Journal* 255–90.
——(1996c) 'Des Königs viele Leiber: Die Selbstdekonstruktion der Hierarchie des Rechts' 2 *Soziale Systeme: Zeitschrift für soziologische Theorie* 229–55.
——(ed) (1997a) *Global Law without a State* (Aldershot: Dartmouth).
——(1997b) 'Global Bukowina: Legal Pluralism in the World Society' in G Teubner (ed), *Global Law without a State* (Aldershot: Dartmouth, 1997a) 3–28.
——(1998a) 'Nach der Privatisierung? Diskurskonflikte im Privatrecht' 19 *Zeitschrift für Rechtssoziologie* 8–36.
——(1998b) 'Vertragswelten: Das Recht in der Fragmentierung von *Private Governance Regimes*' 17 *Rechtshistorisches Journal* 234–65 [Engl trans: 'Contracting Worlds: Invoking Discourse Rights in Private Governance Regimes' 9 *Social and Legal Studies* 399–417].
——(2000) 'Privatregimes: Neo-Spontanes Recht und duale Sozialverfassungen in der Weltgesellschaft' in D Simon and M Weiss (eds), *Zur Autonomie des Individuums. Liber Amicorum Spiro Simitis* (Baden-Baden: Nomos, 2000) 437–53 [Engl trans: 'Global private regimes: Neo-spontaneous Law and Dual Constitution of Autonomous Sectors in World Society?' in K-H Ladeur (ed), *Public Governance in the Age of Globalization* (Aldershot: Ashgate, 2004a) 71–87].
——(2003a) 'Globale Zivilverfassungen: Alternativen zur staatszentrierten Verfassungstheorie' 63 (1) *Zeitschrift für ausländisches öffentliches Recht und Völkerrecht* 1–28 [Engl trans: 'Societal Constitutionalism: Alternatives to State-centred Constitutional theory?' in C Joerges, I-J Sand, and G Teubner (eds), *Transnational Governance and Constitutionalism* (Oxford: Hart, 2004b) 3–28].
——(2003b) 'Der Umgang mit Rechtsparadoxien: Derrida, Luhmann, Wiethölter' in C Joerges and G Teubner (eds), *Rechtsverfassungsrecht. Recht-Fertigung zwischen Privatrechtsdogmatik und Gesellschaftstheorie* (Baden-Baden: Nomos) 25–45.
——(2006) 'Die Anonyme Matrix: Zu Menschenrechtsverletzungen durch "private" transnationale Akteure' 45 (2) *Der Staat* 161–87 [Engl trans: 'The Anonymous Matrix:

Human Rights Violations by "Private" Transnational Actors' 69 *Modern Law Review* 327–46].

Teubner, G (2008) 'Selbstsubversive Gerechtigkeit: Kontingenz- oder Transzendenzformel des Rechts' 29 (1)*Zeitschrift für Rechtssoziologie* 9–36 [Engl trans: 'Self-subversive Justice: Contingency or Transcendence Formula of Law?' 72 *Modern Law Review* 1–23].

——(2012) *Verfassungsfragmente: gesellschaftlicher Konstitutionalismus in der Globalisierung* (Berlin: Suhrkamp) [Engl trans: *Constitutional Fragments: Societal Constitutionalism and Globalisation* (Oxford: Oxford University Press, 2012)]

Teubner, G and Fischer-Lescano, A (2008) 'Cannibalizing Epistemes: Will Modern Law Protect Traditional Cultural Expressions?' in CB Graber and M Burri-Nenova (eds), *Traditional Cultural Expressions in a Digital Environment* (Cheltenham: Edward Elgar) 17–45.

Teubner, G and Willke, H (1984) 'Kontext und Autonomie: Gesellschaftliche Selbststeuerung durch reflexives Recht' 6 *Zeitschrift für Rechtssoziologie* 4–35.

Thürer, D (1996) 'Der Wegfall effektiver Staatsgewalt: "The Failed State"' 34 *Berichte der Deutschen Gesellschaft für Völkerrecht* 9–47.

Toledo, RV (2009) 'La contribución del Tribunal de Justicia Andina al proceso de integración suramericana' in A von Bogdandy, CL Arroyo, and MM Antoniazzi (eds), *¿Integración suramericana a través del derecho? Un análisis multidiciplinario y multifocal* (Heidelberg: Max Planck Institute for Comparative Public Law and International Law/Madrid: Centro de Estudios Constitucionales) 397–412.

Tomuschat, C (1995) 'Die internationale Gemeinschaft' 33 *Archiv des Völkerrechts* 1–20.

——(1997) 'International Law as the Constitution of Mankind' in United Nations (ed), *International Law on the Eve of the Twenty-first Century: Views from the International Law Commission* (New York: United Nations) 37–50.

——(2008) *The Human Rights: Between Idealism and Realism* 2nd edn (Oxford: Oxford University Press).

Tönnies, F (1979) *Gemeinschaft und Gesellschaft: Grundbegriffe der reinen Soziologie* (Darmstadt: Wissenschaftliche Buchgesellschaft) (reprint of the 8th edn, 1935).

Trindade, AAC (2000) *A proteção internacional dos direitos humanos e o Brasil (1948–1997): as primeiras cinco décadas* 2nd edn (Brasília: UnB).

——(2003) *Tratado de direito internacional dos direitos humanos* 2nd edn (Porto Alegre: Fabris) vol I.

——(2007) 'Prefácio. A Corte Interamericana de Direitos Humanos: um testemunho para a história' in ML de Oliveira (ed), *O Sistema Interamericano de Proteção dos Direitos Humanos: interface com o direito constitucional* (Belo Horizonte: Del Rey) XVII–XLIII.

Tushnet, M (2004). 'Some Legacies of *Brown v Board of Education*' 90 (6) *Virginia Law Review* 1693–1720.

——(2008) 'The Inevitable Globalization of Constitutional Law', paper presented at the seminar 'The Changing Role of Highest Courts in an Internationalizing World', sponsored by the Hague Institute for the Internationalisation of Law, on 23–24 October 2008, 22 (available at: SSRN: http://ssrn.com/abstract=1317766).

Tyrell, H (2005) 'Singular oder Plural – Einleitende Bemerkungen zu Globalisierung und Weltgesellschaft' in B Heintz, R Münch and H Tyrell (eds), *Weltgesellschaft: Theoretische Zugänge und empirische Problemlagen* (*Sonderheft der Zeitschrift für Soziologie*) (Stuttgart: Lucius & Lucius) 1–50.

Uerpmann, R (2001) 'Internationales Verfassungsrecht' 56 (11) *Juristenzeitung – JZ* 565–73.

Venancio Filho, A (1977) *Das arcadas ao bacharelismo (150 anos de ensino jurídico no Brasil)* (São Paulo: Perspectiva).

Ventura, D (2003) *As assimetrias entre o Mercosul e a União Européia: os desafios de uma associação inter-regional* (Barueri/SP: Manole).

Verdross, A (1926) *Die Verfassung der Völkerrechtsgemeinschaft* (Vienna/Berlin: Springer).

Verdross, A and Simma, B (1984) *Universelles Völkerrecht: Theorie und Praxis* 3rd edn (Berlin: Duncker & Humblot).

Volio, LG (2005) 'Los Pueblos indígenas y el ejercicio de los derechos políticos de acuerdo a la Convención Americana: El Caso Yatama contra Nicaragua' 41 *Revista IIDH/Instituto Interamericano de Derechos Humanos* 317–45.

Von Bernstorff, J (2003). 'Democratic Global Internet Regulation? Governance Networks, International Law and the Shadow of Hegemony' 9 (4) *European Law Journal* 511–26.

—— (2004) 'The Structural Limitations of Network Governance: ICANN as a Case in Point' in C Joerges, I-J Sand, and G Teubner (eds), *Transnational Governance and Constitutionalism* (Oxford/Portland, OR: Hart) 257–81.

—— (2008a) 'The Changing Fortunes of the Universal Declaration of Human Rights: Genesis and Symbolic Dimensions of the Turn to Rights in International Law' 19 (5) *European Journal of International Law* 903–24 (available at: http://ejil.oxfordjournals.org/cgi/reprint/19/5/903).

—— (2008b) 'Kelsen und das Völkerrecht: Rekonstruktion einer völkerrechtlichen Berufsethik' in H Brunkhorst and R Voigt (eds), *Rechts-Staat: Staat, internationale Gemeinschaft und Völkerrecht bei Hans Kelsen* (Baden-Baden: Nomos) 167–90.

Von Bogdandy, A (2001) 'Verfassungsrechtliche Dimensionen der Welthandelsorganisation – I. Teil: Entkoppelung von Recht und Politik' 34 *Kritische Justiz* 264–81.

—— (2003) 'Europäische und nationale Identität: Integration durch Verfassungsrecht?' 62 *Veröffentlichungen der Vereinigung der Deutschen Staatsrechtslehrer – VVDStRL* 156–93.

—— (2004a) 'Constitution in International Law: Comment on a Proposal from Germany' 47 *Harvard International Law Journal* 223–42.

—— (2004b) 'Europäische Verfassung und europäische Identität' 59 *Juristenzeitung – JZ* 53–61.

Von Foerster, H (1981) 'On Constructing Reality' in H von Foerster, *Observing Systems* (Seaside: Intersystems Publications) 288–309.

Vorländer, H (1999) *Die Verfassung: Idee und Geschichte* (Munich: Beck).

Vos, E (1997) 'The Rise of Committees' 3 *European Law Journal* 210–29.

Wagner, M (2003) 'Die wirtschaftlichen Maßnahmen des Sicherheitsrates nach dem 11. September 2001 im völkerrechtlichen Kontext – Von Wirtschaftssanktionen zur Wirtschaftsgesetzgebung?' 63 *Zeitschrift für ausländisches öffentliches Recht und Völkerrecht* 879–920.

Wahl, R (2002) 'Konstitutionalisierung – Leitbegriff oder Allerweltsbegriff?' in CE Eberle, M Ibler, and D Lorenz (eds), *Der Wandel des Staates vor den Herausforderungen der Gegenwart: Festschrift für Winfried Brohm zum 70. Geburtstag* (Munich: Beck) 191–207.

—— (2007) 'Das Verhältnis des EMRK zum nationalen Recht – Die Relevanz unterschiedlicher Entwicklungsphase' in *Human Rights, Democracy and the Rule of Law: Liber amicorum Luzius Wildhaber* (Zurich: Dike/Baden-Baden: Nomos) 865–94.

Waldron, Jeremy (2005) 'Foreign Law and the Modern *Ius Gentium*' 119 *Harvard Law Review* 129–47.

Walker, N (2002) 'The Idea of Constitutional Pluralism' 65 *Modern Law Review* 317–59.

Wallerstein, I (1979) 'Aufstieg und künftiger Niedergang des kapitalistischen Weltsystems' in D Senghaas (ed), *Kapitalistische Weltökonomie: Kontroverse über ihren Ursprung und ihre Entwicklungsdynamik* (Frankfurt am Main: Suhrkamp) 31–67.

——(2006) *World-Systems Analysis: An Introduction*, 4th impression (Durham, NC/London: Duke University Press).

Walter, C (1999) 'Die Europäische Menschenrechtskonvention als Konstitutionalisierungsprozeß' 59 (4) *Zeitschrift für ausländisches öffentliches Recht und Völkerrecht – ZaöRV* 961–83.

——(2000) 'Die Folgen der Globalisierung für die europäische Verfassungsdiskussion' 115 (1) *Deutsches Verwaltungsblatt – DVBl* 1–13.

Walzer, Michael (1983) *Spheres of Justice: A Defense of Pluralism and Equality.* New York: Basic Books.

——(1998) 'Vorwort zur deutschen Ausgabe', German trans by C Offe, in M Walzer, *Sphären der Gerechtigkeit: Ein Plädoyer für Pluralität und Gleichheit* (Frankfurt am Main: Suhrkamp) 11–14.

Watson, A (1977) 'Legal Transplants' in A Watson, *Society and Legal Change* (Edinburgh: Scottish Academic Press) 98–114.

Weber, M (1985) *Wirtschaft und Gesellschaft: Grundriß der verstehenden Soziologie* 5th edn, J Winckelmann (ed) (Tübingen: Mohr) [1st edn 1922].

Weiler, J (1999) *The Constitution of Europe: 'Do the New Clothes have an Emperor?' and Other Essays on European Integration* (Cambridge: Cambridge University Press).

Welsch, W (1991) 'Gesellschaft ohne Meta-Erzählung?' in W Zapf (ed), *Die Modernisierung moderner Gesellschaften: Verhandlungen des 25. Deutschen Soziologentages in Frankfurt am Main 1990* (Frankfurt am Main/New York: Campus) 174–84.

——(1996) *Vernunft: Die zeitgenössische Vernunftkritik und das Konzept der transversalen Vernunft* 2nd edn (Frankfurt am Main: Suhrkamp).

——(2002) *Unsere postmoderne Moderne* 6th edn (Berlin: Akademie Verlag).

Wildhaber, L (2005) 'The Role of Comparative Law in the Case-Law of the European Court of Human Rights' in *Internationale Gemeinschaft und Menschenrechte: Festschrift für Georg Ress zum 70. Geburtstag am 21. Januar 2005* (Cologne/Berlin/Munich: Heymanns) 1101–7.

Willke, H (1992) *Ironie des Staates: Grundlinien einer Staatstheorie polyzentrischer Gesellschaft* (Frankfurt am Main: Suhrkamp).

——(1997) *Supervision des Staates* (Frankfurt am Main: Suhrkamp).

——(2001) *Atopia: Studien zur atopischen Gesellschaft* (Frankfurt am Main: Suhrkamp).

——(2002) *Dystopia: Studien zur Krisis des Wissens in der modernen Gesellschaft* (Frankfurt am Main: Suhrkamp).

Wittgenstein, L (1997) 'Philosophische Untersuchungen' [1945–1949] in L Wittgenstein, *Werkausgaben* 11th edn (Frankfurt am Main: Suhrkamp) vol 1, 225–580.

Wolfrum, R (1999) 'The Protection of Indigenous Peoples in International Law' 59 *Zeitschrift für ausländisches öffentliches Recht und Völkerrecht* 369–82.

——(2003) 'The Attack of September 11, 2001, the Wars Against Taliban and Iraq: Is there a Need to Reconsider International Law on the Recourse to Force and the Rules in Armed Conflict?' 7 *Max Planck Yearbook of United Nations Law* 1–78.

Young, EA (2005) 'Foreign Law and the Denominator Problem' 119 *Harvard Law Review* 148–68.
Zolo, D (1993) 'Democratic Citizenship in a Post-communist Era' in D Held (ed), *Prospect for Democracy: North, South, East, West* (Cambridge: Polity Press) 254–68.
—— (2007) 'The Rule of Law: A Critical Reappraisal' in P Costa and D Zolo (eds), *The Rule of Law: History, Theory and Criticism* (Dordrecht: Springer) 3–71.
Zumbansen, P (2006) '*Transnational Law*' in Jan Smits (ed), *Encyclopedia of Comparative Law* (London: Edward Elgar) 738–54.

Index